No One to Tell

The Golden Glory Years of Sales

Doug Booth

No One to Tell

Copyright ©2013 R. D. Booth
All Rights Reserved

No One to Tell

For Robert and Gladys

The two classiest people I never knew

No One to Tell

Be wary of riding the tallest waves;
Behind those tallest waves the deepest troughs threaten.

Doug Booth

No One to Tell

No One to Tell

I would have preferred life in the 1500s, in Spain, by the sea, as an aristocrat of course. Nothing vulgar. A much more civilized time, a romantic time undiluted by juvenile acronyms and adulterated PC, political correctness, once women got their way rather than men having their way with women. Which apparently wasn't the greater plan, my hoped-for era of swords and taverns and wenches freely cavorting. Though I did live through and survive the 70s. The question was: Would I survive the current week? I certainly did hope so, albeit not completely convinced. Otherwise, who would I tell?

Chapter One
February 23rd, 2006

The plane was full, but for two seats. I knew that because I was the last one to board, standing in the aisle by the emergency row.

The girl was sitting by the portside window, her right leg crossed over her left, delineating her space, which was fine with me because if I was about to plummet to Earth upside down at 700 km per hour I would have something else to think about.

Of course the pilot wouldn't say as much in his pre-flight blurb, wanting to reassure us. Though, of greater importance at the moment, the seat between us was empty and would remain so. The uniformed in-flight caretaker already giving me the evil eye, commanding me to sit, counting down.

The girl's legs were bare, long, tanned and shapely. Like me, I assumed, she'd come from points south, her glow real and fresh. She was a pro, nothing at her feet but her purse. She wasn't smiling. Nor would she. She had no reason. Smiling onboard was a quasi-invitation to speak. She was in her own world, as was I. We'd get along just fine. We were going home.

*

That last week was an absolute bitch, and not entirely because of the blonde one at Corporate, the Office Manager, fired two weeks later immediately following her final meeting with the Production Manager when she was discovered atop the president's desk with her clothes strewn across the floor, her ass in the air and her eyes wide open with shock because her mouth was otherwise occupied.

Living in Montreal and working in the American Southeast was a perfect job... from anyone's perspective but mine. Particularly the last week in Florida when all I wanted to do was sleep throughout my homeward journey. Which was impossible because the thought of dying in my sleep was less appealing than consciously wondering at the outcome of my fourth flight from or to hell in as many days.

I didn't look much better than I felt. Making matters worse, my connecting flight did not depart Philly on time.

The week was a disaster, my second trip to the Sunshine State in three weeks, cut short. And I wouldn't be home for another five hours, although at the time I wasn't convinced. I was certain however that my career and brief tenure with the company would come to an end in concert with the month of February. I'd done enough. I'd done my time.

I don't believe in powers greater than those found in math, and I can't think of any particular time in my life when any higher power that might exist has ever been concerned with my whereabouts or well-being. Nor do I believe in ghosts or angels from my past. Yet that week was one for the books, the final chapter, and one I could not ignore. Somebody or something was sending me a clear message. All I had to do was get home in one piece.

Monday, February 20th, was a prolonged glimpse into hell starting with the ten-dollar-an-hour wannabes at airport security at 5:00 AM and a cancelled direct flight to Tampa at 5:30. At 7:00 I was flying to Orlando where I arrived fifteen hours later through Philly and worsening weather.

The first flight, at the time, was the worst I could

No One to Tell

remember. Until I boarded my connection, which I then believed would be the highlight of my week. Assuming I survived, not very hopeful.

Landing in Orlando the airline rep assured me that my luggage would be forwarded to my hotel the next day. No fuss. Why bother? I was conditioned. In fact I always travelled with partly completed Baggage Claim Forms to save time because that same airline had caused me twenty-two impromptu shopping sprees over the previous two years. Of greater importance was getting a car and finding a restaurant.

Car rental companies are unique, however. They urge customers to reserve in advance, then implement a first-in-line policy which allowed someone to drive away in my mid-size. I got the hearse: A black thing with tiny wheels that had the appearance of a toolbox better suited to a New Orleans funeral.

I was on the road at 10:30, wet roads, high winds prevailing from somewhere, my pulse rate as high as my blood pressure. Everything pretty much closed, parking lots empty. MacDonald's was the only restaurant open that I could see, though eating inside a Macdonald's at 11:00 PM smacks of desperation: A collection of losers and lost souls exposed under bright florescent lights

I chose the quiet of solitude, the darkness of a near-abandoned parking lot for cheeseburgers and a Coke in the back of a hearse with the tailgate raised, breathing wet air, one leg dangling over the bumper. Loss of face not an issue despite the four bros with hearing disabilities slouched in a Mustang GT with the windows down, which they were apparently using as a Rhythm and Blues festival. I was hungry. And I was tired.

Yet, somehow, even at midnight, five-stars and a couple of straight vodkas have a way of balancing a bad day.
*

No One to Tell

Tuesday began early in a perfectly pressed shirt, if not perfectly fresh, thinking I would take advantage of being in Orlando. I called a client on his cell to invite him to breakfast. He always ate his breakfast and lunch at his desk. He didn't have much of a life. He didn't answer. So I called his office, hoping to catch him before he ordered-in.

The owner of the company answered. Not the secretary. Unfortunately, my client wouldn't be coming to work, I was told. He'd died an hour earlier at home while dressing. I offered my condolences and drove to Tampa.

The I-4 is an 82-mile speedway. Normal speed: 80, 90, 95. The passing lane not intended for the timid or uninitiated. I wasn't in a hurry. I was doing eighty, a few cars ahead of me. Then only one, the one somewhere inside a cloud of dull, grey smoke, the one braking, swerving to the right. I swerved to the left with the others. The smoke mixed with a maelstrom of dust and gravel on the soft shoulder, doors flung open, orange flames flaring. I've never seen anyone run the way those guys did into a ditch, clambering onto an open field until the boom that sounded like muted thunder very soon after. They weren't looking over their shoulders.

Lucky guys.

Arriving on time for my 11:00 AM, booked for lunch and the entire afternoon with the client, I discovered I didn't have an 11:00 AM despite my confirmed appointment. The guy was British, new to the job, new to the States, and I hadn't previously been to that Port Authority. He couldn't see himself doing business with a Québec-based company, supporting the separatist movement and the possible break-up of the Empire. That would be the Empire he chose to leave.

I asked whether he was serious. He was, irrespective of the fact that I'm an Anglophone and a Liberal. He shrugged. He couldn't possibly.

No One to Tell

Neither could I. I walked out. We cannot be rude to rude people. It's impossible, although I did suggest that he…Well, the words don't matter. I spoke in French, his reaction sufficient compensation for a lost day. I ate lunch alone, spending my afternoon on the phone ten miles north of Tampa in one of those off-the-highway hotels because a convention in town had commandeered the better accommodations for the week.

As promised, my luggage had arrived.

*

Wednesday I finished early by virtue of a sick client, another who was up to his ass in alligators, and a potential client whose potential was worth more to me in his opinion than mine. I thanked him, gave him the name of a local source, left him and went to the hotel to change, thinking I would find a restaurant with a terrace, drink some wine and get back to the hotel for a swim. Until I barely missed stepping on the Black Moccasin stretched out on the black asphalt under the driver's door of my hearse. A pole-vaulter couldn't have done better. I watched the thing from afar for fifteen minutes, until finally snaking its way to the pool to ruin my afternoon. I went to the Front Desk to check out.

Newly situated by another pool, I phoned Thursday's appointments to confirm since clients increasingly consider appointments as tentative at best. Until shit hits the fan. Both accounts wanted to reschedule for Friday PM. Thursday was shot. So was Friday morning, which I normally left open for contingencies like them and the guy fighting off alligators. Not this time. They each wanted afternoon appointments and I wasn't staying a fifth night to spend Saturday in airports. I cancelled, with deepest regrets, and called the airline. No Wednesday flights were available, which was just as well. I didn't feel like a one-hour drive to Orlando when the pool was so much more inviting.

*

No One to Tell

Thursday the weather had changed. I woke early and mechanically, well before the maniacal rush-hour race along the I-4, to catch a 7:00 AM flight that departed at eleven. Another flight from Hell. Big time. Planes on the tarmac smeared by thick rain swirling chaotically against concourse windows.

Immediately after take-off the crew were instructed to take their seats, which they did quickly, where they remained throughout the flight, one of them facing us from her little pull-down seat, us being me and two teenage first-timers: Sky Virgins.

The girl by the window, the younger of the two, the one I had politely displaced from my aisle seat when boarding, was trembling on the verge of tears, clasping her hands, rubbing her arms, tapping her feet, moaning, groaning. She wasn't very happy. Poor baby. Like anyone else was thrilled.

She leaned slightly forward, looking past the other girl and straight at me. No escape. She said, "Sir, mister, can you please hold my hand?"

Say what?

Why me? But I did, under the duress of the attendant's prompt. She said, "The poor girl wants to hold your hand." A slight pause meant to intimidate me, six eyes staring. Then, "Hold her hand."

The last teenage girl I held hands with is now in her sixties and, if memory serves, she wasn't trying to squeeze mine into pulp. But the motherly attendant was telling her to squeeze as hard as she could to get her mind off the turbulence that wouldn't last much longer, when the rest of us were certain we might very well crash upside down, burst into flames and die.

The girl was a human vice.

Several minutes later, her sister, a new revelation, seated between us with very bare legs and a very bare midriff I was trying hard not to come into contact with as I was reaching across her for humanitarian purposes, timidly informed me that she needed to "barf." I believed her. Barfing in-flight is serious business. She leaned toward the attendant, held in place by her belt and my arm, and hurled.

I discovered later that the man in the aisle seat diagonally behind me who passed me the bag in quick response to my snapping fingers was their father. Not the brightest bulb. The mother was seated behind me, who, for some reason, thought I needed a rolled-up newspaper. I didn't. Even if I did, the window girl hadn't let go of my right hand and when the symphony was over my left was holding a bag of puke over the aisle while feeling that I was strapped to a pissed-off Brahma bull at a rodeo.

That lasted through to Philly, arriving at 2:00 for a three o'clock departure.

Belated kudos to the pilot.

Touching down, I regained possession of my crippled hand, transferring ownership of the bag to the father. The girls were cute in a Bambi kind of way, but whatever happened to 'thank you'?

I forgot them once in the concourse.

Five hours later we were moments away from pulling back from the gate when a 300-pound, maybe three-fifty male of the specie was still in the aisle fiddling with his carry-on, scratching himself where moss could grow on a humid day, seemingly unconcerned that his ass was in my face or that the beautiful young woman with legs to her neck couldn't believe her eyes. She was probably thinking he was on the verge of a stroke or an orgasm, appalled by the thought of either event.

Another woman, in the aisle seat adjacent to mine, was wearing an equally pained expression. He'd be sitting beside her, in the middle. I was the lucky one, despite the pilot's warning about a bumpy ride. The seat beside me was empty. Good. By the window was the knockout brunette with the to-die-for legs. She was drop-dead gorgeous in a short linen skirt I doubt she was sitting on, her breasts snugly housed in a form-fitting silk blouse and she'd already discreetly commiserated with me regarding the two-sided itchy beef burger attached to my face.

Three minutes to go. He was instructed to sit. Legs' and my heart went out to the woman.

Legs and I exchanged glances before sitting in silent prayer, the requisite pre-flight prayer: Please, do not arrive late! Please, do not sit here! She was also secretly praying that, if no one did, I would keep my mouth shut and not talk to her for the next two hours en route to Montreal. I wouldn't, though her legs were the one good thing about the entire week. She was the embodiment of every girl I hadn't slept with.

I don't remember most of the few thousand good flights, except the L-1011 from Toronto to Montreal on which I was the only passenger. That was different, but I do remember the bad ones, which invariably involved someone beside me, in front of me, or someone's demon spawn doing something gross in close proximity to me.

I certainly don't remember the last time I sat beside something worth looking at twice.

We were in the final countdown to departure, mere moments remaining, Legs and I anxious for all the signs familiar to frequent fliers, hoping the flight would be a good one despite the turbulence, one I wouldn't remember apart from her legs. I was in the emergency row. That's a good thing, since the two-metre long fellow in front of me who hadn't stopped twitching from nervous tension wasn't able to recline his seat.

He'd complained that his seat was broken, garnering a practiced smile and matter-of-fact explanation from a condescending attendant. Apparently she wasn't convincing and he hadn't stopped trying to force it back.

One of those attendants was on the intercom talking with the flight deck. Our situation was looking good. Everyone was seated, even Burger Boy with his warm and scented fingertips, though my eyes were glued to the forward cabin.

Then the worst happened. Shit! Legs had the same reaction. I heard her exasperated sigh.

There he was, from out of nowhere, Mr. Murphy Law, swaying, jiggling from side to side as though walking a tightrope. I hated him instantly. I put him at twenty-five, 1, 9 metres and a half-kilo extra for every one of his years with a face flushed enough to possibly leak toxic fluid through one of its pulsating orifices. He was in Dockers, a blue denim shirt, a blue blazer with fake brass buttons, no tie and I didn't have to look to see that he was wearing fake oxblood penny loafers.

Further prayer served no purpose as he came closer: a wasted wish disregarded like all the others. That's how I paid for all my bitching: Flying. Flying was, and is, my hair shirt: The Book of James, James T. Barrett; though not mine exclusively. Flying is something we can all do when we feel we haven't suffered sufficiently in life, particularly through Philly.

He was coming closer, clearly pleased by the row numbers that he wouldn't have to walk too much farther. Shit. I didn't look up; neither did Legs.

"I think this is my seat?" he said.

He actually said that as a question, gazing around at the overhead bins as though the numbers might change, leaving no doubt that later in the evening he might say "Mom, I *think* I'm home?" This guy definitely lived at home. Or possibly he was an expert. Experts always start a sentence with "I think."

I stood, not as though I had a choice. More as a matter

of personal protection as I wasn't sure what he'd planned for the ten-kilo knapsack hanging from his shoulder like a dead pendulum. Legs glanced our way. She wasn't certain either and as Murphy moved in, reaching to store his knapsack under the seat in front, she crossed her legs in the opposite direction, tugging at a skirt we both knew couldn't be tugged.

His complexion deepened from fire engine red to beet purple from bending over. He plopped into the seat, pulled his bunched-up Dockers from around his crotch, tugged at the edges of his blazer and expelled enough air from lungs hidden under layers of untrimmed fat to lift the sparse hairs belonging to the head in front of him. He'd made it. He was a survivor, going home to Mom.

I'd already commandeered the armrest between us, so he did the same with the one between him and Legs because he knew she wouldn't say anything. And she didn't. But she was thinking, and I knew she was definitely praying.

He scanned his new environment, his head bobbing, pleased as punch, as though he'd made a decision to buy the plane and all its occupants. He very much liked his seat. The irresistible long legs came next. Then he ogled her breasts, but not her face. Then me, then her legs and her breasts.

In your dreams, fat boy.

He hadn't yet noticed the tiered rubber plugs sticking in my ears, apparently. He began talking to me. Who does that before takeoff?

I pulled out one plug, helping him to understand I didn't want to talk, replacing the travel-aid, terminating the inquisition. The guy's seat wasn't yet warm and he wanted to know what I did, for whom and where. I wanted to know why he was spread out like he was at the frigging beach. I hate strangers touching me. Mind you, I might have made an exception had I thought to slide into the middle seat.

No One to Tell

We rolled back from the terminal, first in line for takeoff, the pilot advised us, because the rest of the world was already at home.

The next few minutes were a time when all onboard shared the commonality of vulnerability, sardines in a can with zero influence over what happens next in their lives. Prior to takeoff a monotone voice informed us that, whenever the seatbelt sign might be extinguished, we were *not* free to move around the cabin. Like that was even possible. The implication being that we should not stop thinking about our mortality, nor breathe normally once again.

We were flying into Montreal's worst snowstorm of the season.

*

I had always hated high school with a passion. Or, I liked school and hated teachers with a passion, which is a more probable assessment: an authority thing, a boss and sir thing.

I was heading in no particular direction, with no idea along what path I would travel. I simply knew I had to get out, which didn't mean dropping out, but getting out, escaping into premature adulthood, becoming part of the distinguished body of Night School alumni. I became an adult overnight, at least in my own view, forging a path toward university.

For a brief time I had contemplated a career in social work, taking an active role in the community in an attempt to gain practical experience. That trial was short-lived. Within the first year of visiting cons and ex-cons, gathering data for term papers that would very soon serve no purpose, I discovered a certain lack of empathy for crooks, murderers and druggies. Compassion wasn't developing as a strong point of mine, although somewhat requisite to the profession.

No One to Tell

Vince was a nice guy, white-collar and an embezzler. At the age of forty he'd spent half his life in jail. His upcoming parole would be his last chance to stay out. If he went back, he'd stay in. The Law was different then. The courts were tough and cops had balls.

One of his cellblock roomies was Gus, not your usual tongue-in-cheek con. He'd once tried unsuccessfully to eat a razorblade sandwich, succeeding in making future verbal communication somewhat difficult. Vince thought I should spend some time with Gus to gain more insight and boost Gus' morale. His parole had just been denied.

Then there was the guy who tried to drown himself in his stainless steel toilet and, when that failed, he tied one sleeve to a bar and the other to his neck in order to achieve a longer-lasting result the day before I was scheduled to meet with him. Others' life-long issues were decidedly not for me, yet I had no clear vision of what I really wanted to achieve. Then came university. Then came W&W in my final year and the world changed.

I continued my studies at night towards a degree in Modern Languages, thinking all the while that I wanted to teach or interpret Spanish; the latter marginally more lucrative. I had to make a choice, which I did over drinks in the faculty lounge with my Spanish professor whose then current salary was less than half what I was earning. Nor did he have a company car or an open-ended expense account.

Sort of a no-brainer, he proposed. The decision was made and I've never regretted the choice.

My career began and, with it, my real education. Sales, for me, would soon become synonymous with teaching and learning, seeing and being. I'd found the best of both worlds and was on my way to more than 3000 hotel-nights across North America, countless airports, countless flights, some 15,000 plus restaurants, well over two million kilometres in twenty-five vehicles, innumerable rental vehicles and places most people never get to see from northern mines and paper mills to US and Canadian military bases and Port Authorities, breweries, packaging plants, crematoriums and the biggest cargo ship afloat.

That's education, once the proper foundation is laid, one that continued for thirty plus years until this last trip that I'm sharing with Legs and Murphy Law, one that began at Wiley & Wiley Machine Works on May 05, 1975.

Who I am now is the net result of a life spent with strangers: the good, the bad and the ugly, Fleeting acquaintances with people who came and went with their own agendas, as I have with mine.

No One to Tell

Chapter Two
1975 - 1978

May 05, 1975. I was in sales, where I had to be, at Wiley & Wiley Machine Works, better known as W&W. We were nearing the end of the golden era of sales, though I didn't know at the time: Two-hour lunches, three on Fridays, expense accounts that didn't require receipts, cash only, no credit cards, no Blackberries or iPhones, no faxes, no laptops or tablets, and, best of all, no email or voice-mail. I'd just made it in time. Thank you, Lord, even if you don't know who I am.

I was experiencing a revelation, a new world, a new dimension and a new me. I was there. I was part of it; not really knowing why, what it meant, or where it would lead, if anywhere. Of course, at the beginning the new me had more to do with my new company car, my new expense account and the new company-paid lunches than with any sense of why I'd been selected to represent such a prominent firm that had seen the turn of the last century and whose name alone would get you in to see a customer.

My own car had failed me weeks earlier, towed by a junk dealer with a rewarding fifteen bucks in my hand. A rear panel had gone, a front panel was threatening, and the framework holding the gas tank in place had rusted through. The battery was held in place with a beer carton and wire rope and the roof caved-in whenever I opened my window.

No One to Tell

Neither was a key required because no one would ever steal the thing and ignition simply required raising the hood and inserting my 40cm screwdriver for contact.

The car sagged in half when the tow cable raised the front bumper and I thought he would demand his fifteen dollars, but he didn't, which helped pay for my taxi from the downtown train station to the offices of W&W.

I passed through the main doors at precisely 7:50 AM. Then through another set that were less impressive and led to the customer reception and pick-up area where he was standing with rolled up shirtsleeves as the door crashed into his back. He said "good morning," not looking happy, not looking sad, turning away to climb onto a forklift to move a few crates. He was built like a brick shithouse, probably from all those years of lifting crates and forklifts, introducing himself as Ian before he drove off.

I had wanted to use the mirror I knew was behind those doors, but seeing Ian I went through them instead and up the marble stairs that were virtually vertical because of the clearance required by the equipment on the main floor. When I got to the second-floor landing I stopped. I looked sharp in my new two-piece custom-made suit and accoutrements.

I was ready. The ride was about to begin. I took a deep breath.

The second floor of W&W was the Sales floor: 1000 square metres of marbled floors and high ceilings, oak-panelled private offices contrasting against more intricately panelled outer walls and yellowed windows along which austere cubicles separated by glass shields and brass-handled doors partitioned the managers from the great unwashed masses, the plebeians of the work world, us, the salesmen.

Of the ten or so different departments, I was joining the newly created and elite Industrial Refractories Division.

No One to Tell

The little glossy black desks were lined in rows, each with hard and squeaky wooden swivel chairs that gnawed and banged constantly at the side panels of the desks and, every so often, our knees. The drawers required strength to open and their tops were littered with binders and folders, pencils and pads, each one equipped with a pyramid-shaped black rotary dial phone that was either too heavy to lift or stuck in place by time.

Most importantly, on my desk, which I got to only after coffee with Paul in his cubicle, were the keys to a brand new metallic baby blue, 350, four-barrel, two-door Malibu classic with mags, 215s and air. Life was good.
*

Official papers were filled out and signed, promises made and hands shaken. We meandered our way through offices and desks for more welcoming handshakes, ending the tour with a peek into the General Sales Manager's panelled sanctum, a fast hello, a faster good-luck with permission to call him Mack. Then back to Paul's glassed-in compartment, thinking that Mack looked like a Marine.

Paul was soft-spoken, unassuming, and well-dressed in his signature taupe and tan suits which made most others appear a little unkempt. When he shook hands he looked into the person's eyes until releasing his grip. When he spoke he commanded your full attention; when you spoke to him, he listened intently. When you had a question you were expected to have the basis of an answer or a partial solution to any problem. That was Paul. He was also a millionaire.

I was responsible for eastern Ontario and western Québec with a target exceeding my budget. Paul said the target was conservative. Who knew the difference? Not me. So I agreed. I would become one of their experts in industrial wear-resistant ceramics and carbides, concentrating on pulp & paper, mining and research applications.

The word 'focus' wasn't yet in vogue. I'd be dealing with engineers, plant managers and senior buyers on big-ticket items. The job wasn't a quick learn because the learning would never stop, Paul once telling me that I would only ever be an expert relative to the knowledge held by those around me, which meant I would never learn anything by listening to myself talk.

Notes, notes and more notes, followed by questions, questions and more questions. But first I'd be given into the capable hands of Duke for initiation, guidance on corporate policy, procedural information, field support and protocol; something, I discovered, Duke was only vaguely familiar with. He was going to be busy getting me up and running, but first things first. The new car needed gas, for which I needed money, which meant expenses. So we went to see Mary on the third floor.

Mary was a crowd stopper. Her measurements go unrecorded, but she was near perfect. Pretty much like Legs. She had an authoritarian air with black horn-rimmed glasses, liquid eyes, pageboy brunette hair, sheer silk blouses most days with either matching demi-bras or camisoles that were years ahead of their time and figure-hugging A-line skirts with high back vents that caused significant daily work interruptions.

Her waistline line appeared cinched, only in contrast to her outstanding breasts, her double Ds that seemed to contain enough stored energy to light up a small town. She wore low-heeled pumps to complete her perfection, when other women wore buckled platform shoes. That was Mary.

The other women were attuned to the unfair advantage and attention. Rightly so, given they were wearing three or six-to-a-pack underpants and support garments while Mary was wearing collection lingerie. Duke was in lust and whether he needed money or not, he made at least one weekly trip up to admire Mary's double Ds.

Mary distributed expenses according to vouchers signed by management to approve funding requested by the sales rep to finance his week. Paul never questioned, though he often made adjustments in our favour. Receipts were never required as proof of an expense; simply the weekly vouchers paid out in cash and Duke cautioned that I should never pay for my own cigarettes. I never did. I was a good student.

Mary's spectacular breasts served one other purpose on the third floor. The twin marvels kept me from convulsing every time I saw one of the nearby bookkeepers in his mid-thirties who performed the daily ritual of painting the entire top of his head with black shoe polish in an effort to recapture something that was important to him: youth, vigour and image. Whatever. Thinking back, I can only imagine the inside condition of his pullover.

*

My first week was filled with novelty and excitement, much of my time spent with Duke. We were on our way out that first day to meet the others for lunch, passing Ian who was getting into his aging and broken-down wagon that reminded me of my recently towed wreck. He looked as though he'd really worked up a sweat that morning down on the floor and I commented on how unfortunate he must feel to have worked all these many years with nothing to show for it.

Duke waved to Ian and yelled "hello," sticking out his hand out for a shake the closer we got to one another. He introduced me matter-of-factly and with a simple "welcome" Ian's hands closed on mine like steel traps. Duke asked how the "shitbox" was going. Ian, cracking a smile, replied that it did the job. Duke hadn't been talking about Ian's wagon, but the spotlessly clean Mercedes parked beside it. Ian apparently had two jobs.

No One to Tell

*

The summer was one of endless parades through cavernous and thundering paper mills, personal guided tours through silver and gold mines. Back then people had time, or took time, the more formal visits with engineers and industrial designers who listened, questioned and took notes when we spoke doing more to help me than I did them at first. Such was the beginning of my information acquisition and learning curve, a time of new relationships and blueprinting my reputation.

The blueprint would be a continuous work in progress with refinements over time. I would spend countless hotel-nights memorizing product details and applications, creating solutions to my invented application problems. I practiced speaking effectively and concisely in order to convey pertinent information with influential ease; making certain I was confident with every aspect, every phase of each component and its range of applications.

I also believed the more I extruded from my time with clients the more that would translate into financial gain. I differentiated myself early on by creating a need to be in a customer's office, not making impromptu and meaningless cold calls.

*

He was old, out of date and out of shape. His wife hated him, so did his kids. He hated his boss and he hated his job as buyer for a manufacturer of ladies' hosiery. His life sucked and he blamed me when I walked through his office door.

My smile was sincere. I did really hope he'd had a good weekend and I sat to begin my presentation the moment I realized he wasn't going to stand or shake my hand. I asked pertinent questions about production performance, in response he threw me their brochure; I asked about the performance of particular specialty components we'd supplied, in response he threw me our brochure saying that if he needed something he'd call Fred.

I took a different tack at that point, believing I'd get more of his attention. What I got was his soles: Matching size-twelves that hung off the feet he plunked onto his desk before crossing his ankles directly in line with my face. When I realized what he was doing I sat waiting, watching the grotesque manoeuvre, hoping he'd land on his head or his ass where I assumed his head was. He didn't.

Instead we sat in silence and waited together. He eventually asked me to leave, with his feet on the floor. I never went back and had I thought for a moment that he was in fact an omen of events yet to come, I would have saved myself a lot of grief twenty-four years later.

They weren't cloned, but the guy wasn't alone, I would then discover. All the people of Goonieville were that way: hateful and spiteful.

*

My fourth joint call was planned a week in advance. I was the one to call and explain the need for our visit to the Plant Manager at the mill northwest of Ottawa. We wanted the plant as a Key Account and I had spent much of the previous week at the Pulp and Paper Institute studying glossaries of terms, scribbling definitions and learning as much as I could about the industry and that mill in particular.

I would do the trip with Paul and, as outlined in Procedures, when possible, all workdays would begin at the office unless otherwise approved. So we met at my place. Paul had an aversion to certain of the higher echelon who'd never served in the Forces but ran the Sales Department as though he was a Marine. He often ignored certain of Mack's conventions. Paul was independently wealthy and didn't give a shit. His mother had recently died in Holland and had left her little Dutch boy a few million.

Regimentation existed, but no formal sales education programme or sales methodology was in place at Wiley & Wiley, or anywhere else. You either sold or you didn't. Just follow the Golden Rules, when you discovered what they were, and do what the boss told you to do. We were expected to learn by watching and listening, seeing and hearing, thereby understanding the need of the customer which, of course, meant knowing and understanding the entire product range and the potential for application.

Instruction didn't exist beyond the osmotic. The single exception sales course at the time was offered by an established copier company, which very few enrolled into due to the nature of the content. They turned out identical, dark-suited androids devoid of personality, style or technique that spoke, worked and dressed alike. Their two-week training was geared to a reactive sales approach of answering objections and turning the tables as opposed to taking a proactive, positive and consultative approach. They didn't last long.

I identified the few reps I would learn from, including Paul who was easy going, not given to managerial haughtiness. He knew a lot about selling. He was in fact my primary resource and for three years I would learn by watching and taking notes.

In later years joint calls became a management tool to assess and dissect the details of one's performance in front of a client. Ostensibly to resolve unfathomable issues or assure the client of this or of that, when everyone present was very aware of the bullshit, all at the client's expense.

Such wasn't the case at Wiley & Wiley. Joint calls were relaxed, instructive and fun, a time of camaraderie and no one took notes unless on behalf of the customer.
*

Wiley & Wiley wanted the account badly and I was responsible for making things happen, which I did. Bill would be my premier client for the next six years. Having him together with Paul at the outset of my career was extremely fortunate. Paul was certainly influential, and what I learned from Bill was the importance of consistently bringing value to a customer. The methodology of logic in an era of no methodology, of seeing beyond a specific need, of determining the cause of the need, of creating long-term solutions by turning reaction into pro-action, of preparing to meet all future needs while others waited for those future needs to become current problems.

Delivering once was good, delivering consistently was reputable and during those formative stages I saw the value of dealing with upper management as opposed the more circuitous, time consuming route of going through the backdoor.

That first meeting went well, until the liquor recovery room, but that only came after lunch. Back then business was business and lunch was not business. Lunch was lunch, a time to relax and discover who you were dealing with without pulling strings or pulling a cellphone from your pocket to demonstrate that any unknown caller was immediately more important than your guest.

Bill and I would enjoy many lunches together and come to know a fragment of each other's personal side from a distance. Bill was no exception to an early rule of mine: Friends don't exist in business and anyone who suggests differently is unfamiliar with the human condition.

After lunch came the initiation, the famous Liquor Recovery Room. During our return drive to Montreal Paul kindly offered several times to pull over and I can still remember the grin, but I was able to hold off. When I arrived home late, however, I puked out my brains into a garbage can.
*

The Talisman was central to a week's agenda and in the

summer the hotel provided two outdoor pools. One particular night I'd already dipped in once, my French Horn drying on the doorknob at 1:00 AM. All was quiet and peaceful, so I decided to wrap myself in a towel and sit at the edge of the pool with my feet hanging over the edge about five metres from the patio doors of my room.

Submersed lights lined both sides, but the deck lights had been extinguished two hours earlier. The night wasn't hot, but the air was warm and the water was tempting amidst the ambiance of a Japanese garden decorated with trees, flowers and garden-size strolling bridges crossing over intricate flora and manicured shrubbery. Comfortable double benches and cushioned deck chairs were strewn about for the enjoyment of guests and the stillness was absolute.

The knot was undone, the towel came off and I slid in for a midnight dip, into the three-metre deep end to breaststroke my way to the shallows, not wanting to disturb anyone, not wanting anyone to disturb me. The width of the pool was five metres, the length twice that. I felt great with a few laps done. The setting was serene with the only lighting shining out from the water around me, which is why I didn't see them.

I'd just passed the midway point of my third or fourth lap, passing them en route to the deep end, catching a glimpse of the women on a shadowed bench. I stopped at the end, crossed my arms over the rounded edging of the deck and took a moment to think things through. This was somewhat of a quandary.

Climbing from a pool onto its edge isn't normally problematic, but when you're the only one climbing and you're naked, concentration really is the key to any hope of success. I had two options: I could bring the towel into three metres of water, flounder and flail and look like an idiot, or I could pull myself onto the edge, stand tall with renewed vitality, reach for the towel, then wrap and walk. Not like the girl at 755

*

Friday afternoon I arrived home early. I was at the outside pool patio having a couple of beers with the tenant in 1405, a German representative of an aircraft landing gear manufacturer, soaking up a few rays.

We were alone until she came out through the pool doors, laying out her blanket near the fence about ten metres from us. She paid no attention to us. But we were eyeing her because, like all males, we wanted to know whether, once stripped of her cover-up, she'd be worth further attention. We suspected maybe so. This wasn't our first encounter from a distance.

She looked a little pinkish, always at the pool working on the perfect tan, usually in something small and stringy. That day she was wearing a polo dress which, with one fluid motion, she pulled inside out over her head.

She was momentarily lost, her head cloaked in a jumbled mix of head, arms, elbows and the stretched material. What we saw up close and personal was her skin-tone bikini complete with knotted sides and ties that sometimes secured her tiny bras in place. Her tan was clearly defined against the outline of the bikinis she usually wore. Just not that day.

She was naked, the cover-up crumpled on the ground and out of reach before she realized. Worse yet, her boyfriend or husband had suddenly come up to the other side of the two-metre slatted fence as she'd begun setting her blanket. He was yelling, at us as much as her.

Stop looking! Stop looking!

Right.

We agreed her ass was very nice, not spectacular. But, hey, there. She was nicely toned, her bum, we determined, not much barer than when she was wearing a bikini. And

No One to Tell

we would have been satisfied with that. But between trying to find him between the slats, her wide eyes fixed on us, then the cover-up, then back at him because he was yelling excited commands, bending, reaching, losing time fumbling at the stretchy material to turn inside out, we got to see all of her a few different ways. Lucky guy. No flaws. No folds. No creases.

She was a true redhead, Hans and I agreeing that her usual bottoms fit perfectly with no material to spare and that her bra was marginally sufficient to conceal her nipples. So, in fact, we weren't seeing much more than on previous Fridays.

She wasn't doing well. If his-nibs hadn't been wailing, slapping the fence, she might have sat down, faced away, and taken half the time to do things right, confident that she was attractive, appealing to her audience, and possibly join us for a beer.

Hans and I clinked our glasses together. Here's to Friday afternoons!

*

Back at The Talisman, I chose my second option with no small amount of devotion to the task. Unfailing elbows and arms lifted me from the water, the other limbs and points of possible interest followed through to the position of Homo erectus. I bent at the waist for the towel, straightened with cavalier sureness, extended the towel outward, wrapped myself with a swish and a tuck and wished the ladies a silent goodnight.

Moments later, in the darkness of my room, I watched them stroll away. They were smiling, and occasionally I do wonder what if. It's not as though I didn't have booze in my room.

*

Back then, when you were home, you were home. Customers or managers didn't phone at all hours, fax machines and PCs were several years away and last minute reports weren't an issue simply because your boss forgot to ask for them earlier or wanted to stroke his boss at your expense. There was no bullshit. None of that, just a fun job, new experiences and personal time that didn't require feeling guilty or explaining to a significant other why you don't have the balls to not answer. As long as you were in by 8:00 AM, clean shaven and ready to do your thing.

Mack the Marine implemented a daily reporting system requiring that we account for virtually every minute of the day, which meant recording your arrival time, travel time to a customer, time there, time back, day's end, etc. Of course, we all detailed this critical data in minute fashion without the slightest creativity because we held the Marine in such high regard.

Though one element seriously lacking in the organization was the now much revered Time Management. The concept was unknown and, quite frankly, not required by general consensus.

They had reputation, product, and customers called us. So why be concerned with time? Logic verses tradition that would never change, though I was too gung-ho and stupid to accept that as gospel and I shut my mouth to wait for the perfect venue: The Sales Meeting, which wouldn't happen until late October.

We were in early September, Fred and I talking about vacation travel, vacation time and how much longer we both had to wait for decent time off. The firm gave one week for the first year, two weeks for the next nine and three weeks for as long as you worked for them after that. I'd only been with them four months and one week wasn't sounding very good. I needed the time in early October, which had already been approved by Paul, but two weeks is what I had booked with the travel agent because I usually preferred to tell what I had done rather than ask what I could do.

Fred was the inside guy for the Refractory Division. He was always calm and collected, never ruffled, never stressed and covered for the guys when required. Fred had been with Wiley & Wiley for not yet a full year, so he was holding out for his two weeks and would be heading to the sun. So was I, the next month. Fred and I had to do some serious talking.

*

Monk had joined the firm a few months earlier and was in deep debate with Ian and the Marine about social issues close to the Jesuit's heart: His new moustache and beard had grown appreciably, relative to their interest in his face.

Company equipment, like forklifts, were toys for Ian; toys he bought. His last name was Wiley, owner and president, and despite leaving sales activity to the Marine he often became involved when the latter was in need of reinforcements. Or he felt the need to intervene. The meeting wasn't the first 'beard' meeting, albeit the first requiring two against one. The Marine was no match for the Monk's intellect.

Though the policy was clear: No facial hair.

Monk was claiming injustice and the right to cover his face however he wished, arguing for the freedom of expression and individual rights. They argued tradition, policy and image. Neither side winning the day. Monk stood his ground. The debate would continue. Bravo! But in a white shirt he still looked like a used cue tip.

When I met the Jesuit his name was Patrice-Alexandre, though not for long, most calling him Pat, or Patty or Alex, which upset him unduly. Like many Francophones of the day he had no grasp of the Anglophone proclivity towards nicknames. I called him the Jesuit for two reasons: They had educated him and, with the budding of his facial shrubbery, he adopted the appearance of a Monk of the Order of the Balding Pate. Beyond which there was nothing characteristically outstanding about the Jesuit who stood two metres with thinning hair and a thinner humour.

He'd begun nurturing the dual growths shortly after his hire, warned repeatedly of the contravention, though he ignored most people most times with the righteousness of his own point of view, becoming indignant at the suggestion of any possible reprimand or repercussion.

I liked Monk, despite his perfection and intolerance towards the meek and the frail, meaning, of course, those who wouldn't see things his way. We got along well between eight and four and our three years together would lay the groundwork for a future association neither one envisioned at the time. Our eventual departures from W&W would seem synchronized, though each was planned well in advance.

In the meantime Monk endured one self-imposed hardship he wore as a hair shirt, one he would never surmount while in the Anglo domain, even though his command of English was superior. He was one of a few French-Canadians in the company, not yet commonly called Québécois, and one of a new breed of pacifist political activists. He carried the banner proudly, without acknowledgment.

No one was interested in his preaching at the office of the new era of freedoms and equality. We were happy with the status quo and letting things be. Work was work, not a political platform. Yet Monk continually prodded and goaded the lions, despite which, despite the opinionated blessings upon our daily bread, we all got along fine.

Monk did however have one hell of an annoying habit.
*

Friday Night on the terrace of the Edgewater along the shores of Lac-St-Louis we were heading into the final three-day weekend of sun as we tossed a few back and studied the girls in the hopes of an unexpected wind event.

No One to Tell

I was a bachelor for the weekend and Fred was a bachelor for life. He was the epitome of Mr. Cool, too popular with the ladies to ever limit himself by unique selection. He was 1, 8 or nine with permanently curled mousey blond locks, a white toothy smile, slim, in shape from working out, debonair with a sense of fashion and flair, and he drove a black Trans-Am with a quietly purring engine that belied its performance.

He was at W&W for the money, a paycheque, not a commitment. Fred was jaded, and he was happy. He was living for the moment and at that moment we were enjoying our rum and scotch while discussing our vacations. Our meal was good, the wine tolerable, but the plan was superb.

*

I arrived in Barbados on October 06, one week ahead of the officially noted date on the company roster. Fred had his assignment: protecting me. I had mine: getting tanned, drinks on the beach, girl watching, and possibly getting fired. Agreed, not a perfect plan if analyzed too closely, but certainly doable and remember the era. As for issues of guilt. None. In my defense, if I had not been where I was a very badly dressed woman from Idaho might well have drowned, would have drowned…to be more precise.

We were one hundred onboard when the famed Jolly Roger sailed into 100 separate oblivions. The setting was idyllic, the sky crystal clear and blue. The water temp was 30° C with tranquil pools of turquoise seawater, the booze was neat and four fingers deep, which meant by noon every woman onboard would become the most beautiful in the world.

I was treading some fifty metres off the starboard bow, competing against myself in a dive contest to the bottom that was some ten or twelve metres below. Surfacing for the last time with my head turned upward, my eyes closed to the salt, I torpedoed into a woman who somehow had managed to negotiate the distance from the boat to me without knowing how and without any great desire to remain where she was.

My eyes opened wide, thinking the worst, my sleek ascent abruptly turning ungainly as saltwater poured into my mouth and burned my eyes. When I broke the surface she was there, silently kicking, thrashing and gurgling: a horrible sea creature with a wet pelt of pink oily fur and eyes that ran red into green. Her nose leaked its clear viscous lining, her mouth expelling wafts of booze and bursts of seawater.

Miss Potato Head 1949 had joined in the merriment onboard and, with her well-pickled brain, she'd thrown herself into the sea heedless of clothes, heedless of shoes; her pink kerchief intact. Her untailored suit was bright pink, polyester and unfashionable, her open-toed and red plastic shoes worn to complement her ankle socks that were white. Too pissed to be scared and too bloated by expanding internal gases to sink, she explained to me in a very brief time that she couldn't swim, that she needed my help. Although I believe the gas saved her more than me. Unfortunately for me, I wasn't pissed enough.

I tore away the kerchief draping comically over her face and began towing the tubby potato lady towards the boat. Halfway, the lookout at the bowsprit dived in like a bullet and came up at arm's length to relieve me of my sputtering spud-woman. I swam alongside like a useless third arm.

With help from deckhands they grappled and hauled her out, flopping her unceremoniously onto the drop-board where she made quite a sight, sandals and all, while Josée was making a memorable scene of her own. She was hurtling my way at terminal velocity, screaming, waving and kicking at the air, plummeting from the crow's nest like a tanned and white spear to pierce the surface with hardly a ripple before treading water and happily waiting as the older lady negotiated her way out of sight.

H-E-L-L-O, Josée! Bonjour, girl! She was petite, trim and pretty with dark hair, tanned and naked, sporting excited nipples she could use to play garden darts. She'd tossed her two-piece to the deck below before jumping and I was Johnnie on the spot. Not for her bikini. I was there for saving lives, a Divine mission, not for cleaning up.

Being so small, she had trouble climbing onto the dropboard because her feet were swinging under the board instead of over and the poor thing had to hold onto me for balance and support. The assist was difficult, but I did manage to avert another tragedy at sea.

Oiled skin is slippery in salt water so the only strategy for success in such a situation is locating the centre of gravity, securing a firm hold, taking the necessary time to ascertain all is ready and gently pushing upward. She was a little too tipsy to really care she was buck-ass naked amidst a hundred partiers and adoring fans who were admiring the courage of her leap, nor by the fact she was given the smallest possible towel anyone could find.

The seventies was a unique time, a time of memories unequalled by any decade since. We didn't need Spring Break or Dares. We had the seventies.

*

At home a couple of weeks later Fred and I exchanged packages. His to me was unwrapped: two weeks of messages; mine to him was wrapped: three bottles of Barbados rum. He'd taken care of business for me during my time away. He deserved. A few weeks later he'd be in Jamaica, stocking up for himself, but first we had a meeting to survive.

All departments were invited, inside reps, Ian and the Marine. I'd done all the prep work prior to leaving on vacation, with two weeks to polish a presentation on territory alignment as well as the development of client bases within those territories.

I explained my take on how I should work in my territory to Paul who gave the go-ahead. The territory was mine, as was the budget, yet occasionally we'd review the progress together. When we discussed the subject of my presentation, he suggested I might present my views on Territory Management. Possibly Paul's idea of comedy, but I wasn't too optimistic about the outcome. Terminology like Territory Management wasn't in use. Neither was Time Management and for me the dilemma was in the wording, not the concept, but Hard Sell was in.

My tan was fading with autumnal indifference. I was at the end of my first six months in sales and not exactly an expert. Not yet. The meeting had begun the morning before and lasted through to the order-in dinner. Late Friday afternoon everyone was tired, thankful only two topics remained to discuss, one of which was mine.

Back then people spent their time; they didn't manage it. They made the best use of their time without requiring a mandated definition to help them through the week. My view was that time accountability was a concept not in line with the Marine's corporate dogma because he failed to comprehend that time was money. A cliché, but, surprisingly, even today managers are blind to that wisdom, particularly when cutting costs to impress their bosses. To the Marine, time was time, one day not very different from another. He had no appreciation of time, beyond daytime and nighttime.

My proposition was that we divide territories into workable areas according to a flexible schedule that made sense, categorizing clients according to potential: Primary, Secondary and Target. I proposed that client importance shouldn't be based on current business levels, rather short and long-term potential with an established time frame allowing for the measurement of one's progress.

No One to Tell

I was a dead man, and my mother didn't have a few million to leave me. Nor was she ready to pass on. Marine didn't have the flexibility to understand the product range of the new division required a new way of doing business, or that all the departments would benefit from new thinking. To that point they'd been a distributor of goods, an easy in and out, but the success of the Refractory Division would require engineering, attention to detail and time-consuming repeat visits.

Office days were two decades away; though I proposed that doing twenty to thirty calls a week wouldn't bring value to anyone. Apart from the fact I didn't want to do thirty calls.

He couldn't understand working smart. His brain was his Achilles heel. He was from the school of 'do what I say' because he was the boss, lacking the ability to interpret intelligence submitted by the guys in the field. If Time and Territory Management were unknown, so was Horizontal Management. The Marine liked to look down.

My motivation for devoting so much effort to laying out my territory was self-serving. I had a low tolerance level for small talk and didn't want to spend time pretending I was interested in wives, girlfriends, babies or garden projects. With rare exception, I would arrive, do what I had to do and leave. I was sincere in my greetings and my involvement, however never to the point of feigning friendship. I was in business and I was busy, despite the common consensus then and now that sales reps have a full day of free time to spend talking like peddlers, like John who shows up very briefly in twenty-five years. I never waited in a lobby beyond twenty minutes before making alternate plans, which would usually mean returning Friday morning or during the next trip. I never accepted that someone's day going awry should affect my day unless I was directly involved.

No One to Tell

Sales processes or methodologies have never required more than a logical train of thought. Profound wisdom and penetrating insight aren't fundamental or crucial to the procedure; merely a step-by-step progression towards a logical set of actions that bring a desired reaction or conclusion without bullshit. That's the realm of managers.

Profundity aside, the Marine was more inclined towards pyramidal thinking and chain of command that would be his downfall sometime too far into the future. I explained that I couldn't see the logic in arriving at 8:00 and being in the office again at four for the sole purpose of filling out daily time reports which was counterproductive.

At the meeting Ian nodded occasionally, perhaps seeing the sense in what I was saying, or agreeing with me; or maybe he was nodding because he knew I was in it up to my ass. The Marine just stared across the table with piercing blue eyes that should have given him an ice cream headache. No one took notes, not even the Marine who, in response to my presentation, asserted that a system and established rules were in place that everyone was familiar with and worked in accordance with.

Thank you for your input. Everyone will maintain the status quo.

*

Suddenly the Friday before Christmas was upon the six of us at La Tortue for a festive lunch and a few martinis. Our first was barely in our hands and Paul was ordering wine when the owner-manager arrived with the elegance and showmanship of an accomplished French chef to explain the restaurant was named in honour of the slow moving tortoise, with good reason. He went on to make clear we should plan on a good three hours, but that the three hours would be very good. He offered us a complimentary aperitif. We enjoyed, we waited, we ate succulent meals, and we left more or less according to schedule, returning to the office near four.

Paul barely made his way up the stairs. Had he fallen, Wes would have broken the impact without knowing, whereas Duke wasn't too bad, neither was Fred. I was somewhere in between and Monk was shaking his head in atonement for having exceeded his usual number of sacramental sips. He wanted to say something witty, but had no previous practice at humour. So he sat at Paul's desk looking pleased with what he might have said.

We were all huddled around Paul and Patty imitating serious discussion just as the Marine happened by on his end-of-the-day patrol. We were actually clearing Paul's desk, gathering his keys and briefcase preparatory to secreting him to our cars. I believe Duke drove him home, but I know I didn't. I went to a nearby bar for a club soda.

I wouldn't be doing much over the coming weeks. No one wanted to see you if you weren't buying lunch or giving gifts. The night was mine. I was going for a swim and a sauna while washing the car mats in the apartment building's Laundromat.

The place was dead, a cold and sterile blinding white, the sauna pre-heated. The sweat was good, though the heat was beginning to suffocate me so I left to check on the wash cycle.

All I ever wore to the sauna was a towel and knee-length robe which was hanging in the sauna area with my Hom. The air was heavy with soap and the pungent smell of cheap disinfectant used on the floors. My machine was churning with a few minutes remaining, so I interrupted the cycle, transferring the load, and jumped onto the lid of the dryer for a cheap lower body massage.

She came through the door to my side, carrying an overflowing mesh basket waist high, her arms extended under the weight. That she crossed directly in front of me meant exchanging glances. We smiled and she went to the far end of the twelve machines. I was using the first and second.

She was wearing a man's pale yellow, button-down shirt. Passing me, I saw the bordered row of buttons and the parallel row of stitched holes laying side by side, a uniform gap between them enticingly hinting at bare breasts. Not seeing was impossible, a condition of human frailty. She put her basket on the floor between her and the machine, not on the machine, her profile facing me, but I could see her shirt had come full away in the front. She studied each article, not in a hurry, reaching upward to toss the delicate items into the drum.

My machine clicked and rumbled to a stop, the girl turning slightly to see me as I was jumping down. The dryers loaded from the front. I bent at the knees, testing the mats, inserting more coins before jumping reluctantly onto my warm bleacher. My vantage from the floor was definitely more pleasing to the eye and she timed her moves well. She was beautifully naked under the open shirt that was sliding up and down her ass, displaying precisely what she wanted me to see. She wasn't washing clothes; she was conducting a heart attack.

When she finished she stood, slowly, stooping forward with both arms outstretched, bending slightly at the knees, putting the empty basket on the washer. Her shirt flared out at the tails, her half-moons showing perfectly round and white under the harsh lighting as she reached out one last time to activate the unit with one foot slightly raised and moving away from the other; choreographed to show more of what lay between very smooth curves.

Hers was the nicest and barest ass since summer, definitely deserving of attention, which I believe she realized, crossing to the door at her end, leaving her shirt untouched, ignoring me. Though as the door closed on its own, I heard another open that would lead to one of two saunas. I checked my watch, dropping onto the floor, checking my watch again, calculating when she'd return through the doors, imagining she would come through them with her shirt struggling against wet and glistening skin.

I put in more quarters and went for a sweat, to wait for the mats to dry, wondering if I'd calculated accurately.

Merry Christmas and to all a good night!

*

The 401 highway to Kingston was boring, is boring, as is the 417 to Ottawa. 1976 was well into the throes of a winter with a vile attitude and she was threatening everyone with her temper. Like most females with something on their minds, no one saw her coming. The storm was horrific, one of the worst I'd driven in at the time.

My Malibu Classic's 215s were keeping me where I had to be, though I would have preferred sitting in a hotel bar gazing out over Wolfe Island at the eastern most shore of Lake Ontario, enjoying a Johnnie Walker Red. I preferred Black at sales meetings, lunches with clients, special occasions, Christmas and restaurant dinners.

The unpredicted storm whirled off the lake with a fury that would soon bring everything to a standstill, including the 401.

I was in Kingston when the snow began falling with moderate accumulation, with one meeting left to attend at the research centre. So I didn't hurry to leave; I saw no need to cancel. That wasn't my first winter, or my last, and if things got bad I could stay over another night.

When I left the centre their day was finished. The storm had worsened. The point of no return was the last Kingston exit, leaving seventy-two kilometres in deteriorating conditions between me and Brockville. Screw it. I had a great car, Michelins, and a quad-stereo. I was set. No white knuckles either, just a bit tense. Wrong!

With no traffic I anticipated a two-hour drive with no

tracks to follow and a horizontal white curtain of blinding streaks slamming relentlessly against the windshield, assailing the glass like tracer bullets, the wipers slowly yielding under the incessant assault. My panel lights were off for better vision, as were my headlights intermittently, eliminating outside glare, reducing eye strain while shrinking the essence of all mankind.

A dim yellow glow came and went a few times, I assumed from the amber street lamps delineating the main entrance to Brockville. Just in time, as the snow was turning to pellets which was never good news. I closed the headlights once more, not wanting to miss my one chance to get off the road. Wrong again! Shit! My speed was slow at thirty km, metres per hour faster than the provincial salt spreader, the kind with the huge frigging V-shaped hopper at its rear and I was right under the thing. Holy shit!

In any bad weather I drive with my hands at eight and four, in good weather at three and nine. Ten and two gets you in trouble. My grip loosened, my foot lifted from the pedal. I stopped breathing for the longest time, gaining distance until I couldn't hear the splatter of salt pellets against the windshield and the intermittent glow faded to white, despite which my mouth stayed dry until I got onto the main road in Brockville.

The Skyline Hotel said they were sorry. The Brockville Inn said "full up" and the only other decent hotel had more people scurrying out than going in. So I kept going, this time along old highway #2 which was never a highway, but old for as long as I could remember.

My haven for the night would be the Blue Haven, a May to September waterfront motel for families on a budget, not thrilled that I would have to leave the room to eat in a cramped dining room that didn't have a license. The place certainly looked as though they'd opened to profit from the storm, and the food, I'm certain, was left over from Labour

No One to Tell

Day.

The greyish brown gravy on stale white bread and shoe-leather strips of roast beef were still gurgling in my throat when I got to the dank room at 9:00 with my suitcase that I had no intention of opening.

The voice on the radio promised the storm would abate by early morning and I was prepared for a pre-dawn escape. I slept in my clothes and my shoes, with my coat over the pillow and my arms crossed over my chest for sanitary protection. The suitcase was by my side on the bed and my overshoes were by the door.

Brockville is a scenic town on the shores of the St. Lawrence as the flow broadens into the Thousand Islands, a summer haven for boaters, beachgoers, though not necessarily sales reps.

I awoke at 5:00 AM on the shores of Lake Turd. I sat slowly, not feeling good-humoured after a fitful, cold and mummy-like sleep; not seeing clearly in the damp darkness that masked the new stink of decay and rotting waste.

I reached for the light and wanted to puke. The overflowing septic tank had exploded its contents across the entire dingy and cramped room. Orange-coloured shag reflecting light like a moss-covered lake speckled with large and small islets of human waste that likely originated in the restaurant. I could see the Inn Keeper Act on the back of the door. I couldn't make out the wording, but I'm certain no mention was made of how to escape in case of SHIT.

My mind raced. I thought to reach across to the bureau, pull out the four drawers and escape by way of a prefab causeway, suitcase in hand, to where my overshoes waited in a sea of shit. The reach would be long and precarious, much too risky to chance. Instead I positioned myself at the head of the bed in a kneeling position and, wearing my coat and gloves, with my shoulder against the wall, began bouncing up and down, each time pulling the mattress farther from the wall.

Standing in the new space, my suitcase with me, I held my breath against the soiled underside, raising the mattress and pushing towards the footboard, heaving the wobbling shape sideways as best I could, watching it stand before slumping over and falling away to make a dull splash. The rest was easy. Drawer by drawer the makeshift causeway got me to my rubbers, but only just, and I was gone.

I threw my stuff in the car and went to the restaurant, with no intention of eating. I wanted to see what was going on with several complaining men who'd congregated around the main door to the reception. They were arguing for refunds and free breakfasts elsewhere, neither of which was being offered. I walked away, halting as someone put out a hand as a Stop to ask if that was all I was going to do.

I replied "yes," until I could contact the Hotel Association and the Board of Health on Monday morning. No way could all that shit be cleaned up in so little time.

A few dozen reports were filed Monday morning, with not much satisfaction beyond the permanent closure of the motel.

*

Even mild winters seem long and arduous and this one wasn't mild, more like an ex-wife: A real bitch. Though finally an unusually warm spring was sprung, birds were chirping and I was into my second year at W&W, into my second coffee and cigarette of the day.

Saturday, May 1st was moving day for some new tenants in the high-rise at 755. I was on the twelfth floor of the solitary sixteen-floor luxury building that looked out over a huge expanse of open field. Country living in the city at its finest and I was in the habit of starting my spring and summer in-town days by taking it all in with a few peaceful moments to myself. No one then knew of condos. My apartment was a corner unit with a larger and secluded

No One to Tell

balcony enclosed by sidewalls that extended two-thirds out from the patio doors, the rest being waist-high iron rods. The other balconies were smaller, open on two sides and partitioned in the middle from adjoining neighbours.

I was standing straight against the railing, daydreaming, gazing out when the sudden movement caught my peripheral vision and I glanced downward. She was standing with her feet apart, bent at the waist and combing her cascading platinum-blonde hair, which I thought was about a metre long.

She was slim, not tanned, something under 1, 7 when straight and wearing string panties with an unclasped demi-bra. She swept her body in an upward arc that carried her hair over her head and down her back without misplacing a strand. Then she went inside.

She was nice, very nice. But she couldn't possibly be with the old fart who lived there. He wasn't rich and the hair in his nose was older than any person I knew. No way. She had to be a new arrival and I forgot about her during my week out of town.

*

May 10th was cold and wet with high winds and pelting raindrops smacking loudly at the windows. Tuesday was damp, everything soaking from the previous day's torrential rage, even the balconies were sopping wet.

Wednesday was back on seasonal track, my first coffee untouched when she tiptoed out onto the carpeted floor of her balcony. She was somewhat over to the far side, though I could see her from her shoulders to her feet. She was performing the same combing exercise as the week before, this time in panties sans bra. She was definitely European, from the North, Scandinavian. No way she wasn't. Her panties were smaller than the ones I remembered, and sheerer. Then she glanced skyward, jolting backwards with that 'I've just been caught doing something naughty' kind of reaction before retreating through her patio doors.

The next day she stood closer to the partition where I could see her from the knees down. Friday she was less timid, not by much. I could see to her waist and hated that I'd be gone for the weekend, followed by a week in the mines up north.

Then came Monday, the 24th, a well-deserved day off. I didn't like sleeping in and was outside with my coffee and cigarette. 1103 was on the same wavelength. She came out at the same time, seemingly comfortable in her panties, still not close enough for me to see her face.

They were triangular, tied at the sides and showed two good handfuls of prime ass. Her breasts were high Cs, her nipples firm with the early morning freshness. Her stomach was toned with curves and shadows, her panties crowning parted and taut legs. Her toenails were painted red. She stayed holding the comb, waiting, maybe peeking up peripherally to see me from the waist down.

Her daily ritual was becoming mine, though I almost never saw her on the weekends. I often wondered whether she stayed out as long the times I travelled out of town. Over the summer when she came out first she would wait. When I came out first she would linger with a coffee in one hand and her comb in the other. Since that first moment of shyness she hadn't worn a bra and her selection of panties was endless. Thongs then didn't have the exposure they enjoy today, but they did exist. I was witnessing the forefront of fashion evolution.

We were heading into June and much better weather. Around the time of the fall meeting I'd begun to organize my week so that as often as possible, and especially on Fridays, I'd be able to account for my time that wasn't at the office. I began travelling either Monday to Friday or Tuesday to Friday, never coming home Thursday. I also located the clients I would see at week's end on my side of

No One to Tell

town as a matter of Time Management and getting me out of travelling downtown to the office to satisfy corporate myopia.

I was familiar with how 1103 prepared for her day by mid-June. In fact I was part of the ritual many days. Although I didn't know what she did for a living, I knew Friday afternoons were hers. The first real summer month began offering some real recompense for the previous winter and Zelda from somewhere northern inched closer to where I could see her full body from head to toe, always from an angle that would conceal her face from full view.

One Friday PM, my cocktail was the paperweight for files on the various aspects of several applications when shuffling noises of chairs being opened and doors being closed broke my concentration, particularly when I heard the familiar sound of drinks being poured. One of those times when a man must rise to the occasion, by which time she was stretched out on her front, her toes extended towards me, her arms over the front edge of the lounge chair, her hands idly flipping the pages of a her magazine.

Her head was covered with a delicate straw hat, bowed at the back with a wide ribbon, her hair flowing along her arms. Her skin was white; her panties were Rio, pulled for affect with the side ties undone. Somebody, somewhere, loved me, perhaps as compensation for His previous neglect of me. Thank you.

I needed another scotch, wondering what she preferred. I wanted to know her name, but to call out would ruin the enchantment; to enquire would be worse. What did she do and how long would she stay? Suddenly I knew the summer would be too short.

When I returned sometime later she was sunning her front. Although I'd seen her all but naked so many times over the past several weeks, this was the most sensual. Her toes were pointed down, the side ribbons of her panties still untied, rising and falling with the rhythm of nervous breathing and her breasts were crowned in pink. With her hands resting on her hips, her fingers pinched the ends of the camellia ribbons, urging them upward into a tighter, smaller V, tugging, releasing, ribbons dancing, a single fingertip navigating into a barely visible runway of golden curls.

And for the first time I was seeing more of her face, equally fascinating. The rim of her hat lay just over her eyes that were covered with smoked-glass and plastic rims. Her cheekbones were high, her complexion unspoiled. Her nose was opening wide with the intake of air and the rise of her breasts; her lips pursed in a moment of enticing surrender.

I was losing my mind, very much enjoying the temporary insanity.

*

My sporadic mornings with Zelda in 1103, and the weather-related Friday afternoons, were occasions of some secrecy and I suspect the need for the new apartment-size washer and dryer had more to do with my previous Christmas celebration than with the fact that I used the Laundromat for cleaning my car mats.

The alluring interludes were kept to myself and would continue for one full year with winter's dreaded intervention.

*

At the end of a stifling week I was in Deep River for a meeting at the atomic plant in Chalk River. I stayed in Deep River that one time because I had no choice. There was nowhere else and after that one night 'nowhere' sounded pretty good. The motel walls were green, the carpet was green, the bed was green and the sheets were green. The TV was black and white and had one station. I was in the initial phase of a sales career and I was paying my dues.

I didn't have to worry about waking up. I was up all

night counting the stains on the green walls, pondering their origin; ditto for the crusty spots on the green carpet. By morning, the quandary solved, I was packed. I'd spent most of the night in the green chair with my feet on the green bed that somehow looked as though, if I had gotten into it, I wouldn't have gotten out.

ASAP I was gone with no shower. Gone. Nor had I taken a leak since arriving. There was no way I was going to touch the shower curtain. The cracked plastic was green, but only the top half, ditto for the cracked toilet that was only green on the outside.

Atomic Energy was a meeting like many new sales people experience, questions exceeding answers, promises surpassing certainty, and the first time I'd required an escort to use the men's room, though he did remain stationed outside the door, waiting to return me to the meeting. There were also colour-coded badges to identify where one was supposed to be, as much as for monthly radiation checks.

What I remember most is my departure from the company moments before my return to Montreal. The Friday was excruciatingly hot. I hadn't showered and the air conditioner hadn't worked all week. I was tired, I felt dirty because I was, and I had one more appointment in Hull which was hours away.

I hadn't seen the little lake by the side of the road on my way into the meeting because the water was much lower than road level, well beyond the first signs announcing AE… and no one was around. An already worn shirt was a good enough towel and I had time to spare. The water was sparkling, cool to desperate eyes, and I was going in. I almost made it.

The guard was pleasant enough. He seemed to understand my need, albeit not enough to let me go ahead with a refreshing dip in the lake that apparently was on company property. I just wish he'd come by before I'd managed to strip to my Jockeys, standing there with my clothes at my feet, my pride evaporating as quickly as the sweat on my back.

With that behind me, the window was fully lowered for air, my arm was partially out, resting on the doorframe so at least part of me wasn't suffocating as I headed for Hull. Not really paying attention, cruising a little faster than posted so I wouldn't miss the late-day appointment at E B Eddy, listening to tunes to drown out the wind noise.

Another car passed me like I was standing still, probably another sales guy with his own meeting to attend. We have a look, or did, like cops, just not as full of ourselves. Then too late I saw it coming at me like a bullet: A big, dark, furry bullet that wouldn't be pretty. I don't remember which came first, the splat or the heavy thud, but there it lay, wet, sticky and glued to my windshield with some of its stringier parts travelling at speed around the curve of the windshield towards my white shirt sleeve: half a marmot.

The thing wouldn't get off and the wipers made things worse, beating the thing and pulling stuff out of it. I tried panic braking, which did nothing. I had a road-kill wedgie. I had to pull over, finally evicting the thing with a long-handled window scraper and several litres of windshield wash.

By now I was really late, and I no longer had a scraper.

I pulled into the company guardhouse after four, with no great hope of seeing my customer, but these were the days when real relationships existed. People looked at you when they shook your hand; they listened when you spoke without fidgeting with iPhones and Blackberries. He was there, waiting.

"You look like shit, man!"

I did; no shit. I had thick dust on my shoes and no crease in my pants. My shirt was soaked and shapeless with sweat. I had marmot on my sleeve. I had ring around the collar, my

eyes were red, my hair was matted and wet, and I just didn't give a good fuck. Despite which, the meeting proceeded well, over at the town's favourite titty bar where I paid and got home late.
*

Those three years flew by with unprecedented speed. My client base expanded, my sales grew beyond expectation and my reputation was taking shape. Though the company began changing under what some considered the problematic leadership of the Marine following Ian's unexpected death while playing ice hockey. The changes would cast a pall over the company that would eventually be their downfall.

Whether or not I had had a sense of that, or I couldn't imagine working with the Marine as president, I decided the time had come to make a change. Mack had a stick up his ass about me and I couldn't figure out why; nor did I particularly care.

I enjoyed every part of my three years with W&W, but my time had come to an end. They could no longer provide the change or the challenge I needed. I'd worked well and was treated well, but I was at the bottom of a high seniority ladder and hadn't made any brownie points at that first October meeting. Subsequent corporate bravado get-togethers were pretty well at par. I was trying too hard to win a race in stale and stagnant waters. My timing was right to get out.

I needed a wider geographic base. I needed to see more of the country and I needed days that weren't predictable. I didn't have time to wait; I didn't have time to waste. My interpretation and application of the sales process was in need of a more progressive and strategically thinking company that was challenge-oriented and I'd already gone in search of one that would bring growth and dimension to what was a successful beginning.

No One to Tell

After that first sales meeting thirty months earlier, I maintained my sales programme as I had intended. Whenever more activity was needed on my daily reports I would use significant phone calls in place of actual visits. My number of client-visits decreased as the number and value of my major accounts increased, bringing three years of continuous double-digit growth and an income level in the high-thirties; not bad for the seventies.

You're welcome, Mr. Marine, sir.

My leaving was timely. Soon after, Mack attempted an amalgamation of departments that never succeeded, particularly the Refractories Division that always served a distinctly different client base and inevitably caused the division to fail, much to the delight of Monk Refractories.

When I told Paul of my decision to leave all he said was "we can't advance by standing still."

*

By that time, Zelda had been gone almost a year. She left July 1st, exactly fourteen months after arriving onto the eleventh floor. I waited for spring like a kid at the doors of a candy store until April showers brought her out with her comb, and with May flowers came a brand new collection of silk undies.

I never saw her in the company of a man or a woman, nor did I ever see her anywhere except the secure domain of her balcony. Probably just as well. We never spoke, never exchanging glances from behind the darkness of tinted lenses. Her skin never tanned, she simply became more pleasing with the hue of summer through to early fall, toying with the ties of her panties, playing a tormenting tug of war, pulling at them, feeling the tiny triangles strain under the mischievous stress.

Whether she was sunning on her front with her ass slightly raised, forcing my gaze to the soft embankments; or on her back, slightly arched, her breasts magnificent, allowing a wisp of blonde to tease its way each time from under countless silky shields, the new summer was filled with perfect days and every day began with eager enthusiasm. The single mystery was her scent.

June 24th was the Friday lead-in to a three-day weekend and I'd been pressed into the domestic tradition of long weekends with in-laws. Weekday mornings when I was in town had the formality of the hair grooming ritual, however Friday afternoons made the week, weather permitting, though Zelda was seldom intimidated by rain. The next week would be short as well, beginning with the three-day July 01st weekend, and I had planned to be home.

The day was the most beautiful of the year thus far with clear sunny skies from early dawn and a soft caressing breeze. I looked to see the chaise-longue gone, replaced by a formal high-back wooden dining room chair in mahogany and cushioned in a heavy woven fabric.

The morning process went as usual, except that Zelda was wearing high heels and a little green towel from her breasts to the very top of her legs, knotted at the side. She leaned against the rail, letting her hair hang over the eleven floors, the towel parting seductively to reveal what I'd seen nowhere near enough times before.

I had seen her in shoes a few times, and they were the right eye-catching accessory for the plush fleecy wrap. They also went well with hip hugger leggings the time she'd been sunning on her back with her feet planted firmly on either side of the long garden chair with her legs open wide to fingertips pressing passionate circles across near-amber tufts nestled under the white mesh fabric.

This morning, she was basking in the early morning sun, absorbing its warmth. She faced away, letting the towel fall like a cowl across the slender curvature of her buttocks, adjusting the fleece, bringing the separated ends to her centre front to tuck in the top before she sat facing outward.

No One to Tell

With her sunglasses as her only shield, she crossed her legs to cover what the open towel had exposed, squeezing and constricting with subtle pressure to invoke rapture. As she sipped her coffee, she let the towel separate, framing her hips, never looking up. She was breathtaking, breathing deeply as I stood breathless, frozen in time, wondering how the day could possibly improve. I didn't wait long. When she stood to go in, she left the towel.

I didn't see her again until much later in the day, though the chair back was draped with red, beige and white. A wine glass filled with deep yellow rested on the small plastic table that matched the chaise-longue, a familiar blue bottle of body cream standing alongside. Her shoes were summer beige. She held the green fleecy wrap against her front as she walked to the chair, curling the brim of another straw sunhat downward to conceal her face.

She sat in the chair, trapping the fleece as she leaned forward to ease off her shoes. Coming up, the towel crumpled to the balcony floor through toned thighs moving outward. One knee climbed, one delicate foot lifting, resting on the crossbar of the chair hidden from view. Then the other knee, her other delicate foot planted on the crossbar I could see, Zelda sitting as though in a jockey's saddle.

She reached for the wine, her sip deep and lingering; I gulped my scotch. She sipped once more, replacing the glass, reaching for the blue bottle, tracing white cream into an open palm, massaging them together.

Her hands were small, her fingertips sparkling bright red as they travelled from her waist to her feet, her body folding, unfolding for more cream to treat her other side to the same lustrous coating, pausing. She filled her hands once more, her eyes and mine absorbing her body, waiting, her anticipation and mine mounting, bringing a hand to each of her breasts, pressing hard, watching them swell under the upward pressure.

No One to Tell

She paused, breathing deeply, her breasts shimmering under the natural light. Her hands moved down, intently, in circles across her belly to her back. Her arms stretched out straight, palms up, palms down, palms pressed together, an exotic embrace, caressing herself longingly, held in her own arms, her glimmering breasts squirming under her tight embrace.

She reclined, studying the length of her nude torso, her parted thighs, sitting, reaching for her hat. Her glasses were gone. She was pleased. I was seeing her face for the first time, making her appear all the more naked. She began braiding her hair. Her movements were precise, her fingers threading and twisting with experienced ease. When she was done her back arched, her erect nipples betraying what I knew must be true.

Her hands came together once more, concealing the heated seam between her thighs, depriving me, her body in motion, rocking in concert to her caresses, her rhythmic spasms and sighs. Her hands came away, her legs opened wider, her body taut. She was glistening, her expression determined, her red lips pursed, her mind and her body intent on a single purpose, her hands clutching at the mahogany edges. She leaned slightly forward, her motion fluid, her hips grinding, her exotic folds working hard against the fabric cushion. Time had no meaning. She gulped air, her gasp barely audible.

I was about to drop dead, willingly, so that I might reincarnate as a cushion.

She sank into the chair depleted. Her belly was trembling, her legs unfolding, stretched out and close together as she reached for the glass that shook in her nervous or excited hand. She paused, taking a sip, remaining as she was, pensive, parting her legs, bringing a single red nail to the scintillating and sensitive wet jewel. Her body tensed anew. She was nervous and aroused, titillated, needing and wanting a flawless performance. She knew very well her audience was entirely consumed.

She reached for her glass and stood, dreamily. She was exhausted, one tiny foot in front of the other to the railing, her hip closest to the railing between us slightly out, her opposite leg slightly bent, the curves of her buttocks accentuated, splashed with the rouge of their soft weight upon the chair; one side higher and tight, the other lower and supple. She was so close, sexy and vulnerable, trusting, gazing toward the open field, her expression serene.

To see such a beautiful woman poised a whisper away, so completely naked and exposed, was inexplicably exciting and thrilling, an emotion that would go unmatched for some time.

She remained as she was until she finished her wine, occasionally caressing her breasts, her belly, occasionally shifting her weight from one foot to the other. Then, too soon, she replaced her glass. She faced away from me once more, reaching for a white laced thong that lay on the back of the chair. She leaned against the railing, slipping one foot into the panties, then the other, pulling them first to her knees, pausing, turning to face me; waiting teasingly before pulling the silky white to her hips.

She reached next for her shoes, sliding into them, reaching for the crocheted dress that was beige and short with a red ribbon that fell from the swell of her breasts to her knees. She paused once more, pulling at her hem, pivoting so slowly that I might have one drawn out view of what lay beneath. Reaching behind she did the buttons, the sunglasses went on and her wide-brimmed straw hat once again concealed her from me.

To my surprise she looked straight at me, into my eyes, her lips pursed, her mischievous smirk highlighting flushed cheeks, a small hand conveying a kiss of adieu. She was leaving.

No One to Tell

She had gone for good, but those summer days would remain with me forever.

R.I.P.

Ian died playing ice hockey with his kids, his premature demise initiating a chain of events that would lead to the closure of the company during the early '90s, after 110 years in business.

Prior to that, Paul went to work for the company in Toronto before retiring to Aruba. Duke left sales to breed blue-ribbon Goldens and Wes left to work in his cousin's pawnshop.

The Marine was eventually sent home by the family's majority shareholders. Not long after my final visit to W&W in 1991, I saw him walking into a doughnut shop with a morning newspaper and a pencil. Seeing him was tantamount to having the last word. What goes around comes around.

Ah, Mary; and the Jesuit left shortly after me in '79 to head up Monk Refractories, W&W's first competitor in Industrial Refractories.

Zelda, I discovered, was twenty-three. She was an exchange student from Belgium whose name was not Zelda. She might have been Monique or Simone, Angelique or Sylvie, though, to me, she will forever be the platinum-haired goddess from 1103. I wonder who I am to her.

Chapter Three
1978 - 1979

Legs, I recall, chose a food replacement bar once airborne. I can't imagine she had room in her body for much more. Murphy took one also, along with two bags of chips, a package of cookies and a soda. I asked for a vodka neat that didn't come until everyone had selected their goodies. Booze always comes last as an aid to airline sobriety.

He was mumbling to himself, I assume, because I didn't answer him and neither did Legs. His second mouthful went in as he spoke, churned together with the first. I gave his drop-down tray a cursory scan. He must have thought I approved because he winked and told me he was saving a "bunch of cash" for the company. Fool.

I blamed the attendant. I'd removed my earplugs as a courtesy to her. Now, because of her, I wasn't merely smelling his food, I was listening to it.

His paws were puffy and soft, each hand full. From his belt to his knees his lap was sprinkled with crumbs. I wasn't impressed. Neither was Legs. I knew without seeing her. The guy was twenty-five, tops, sitting beside killer legs, perky breasts, and he was feeding his face when he should have been calculating his chances of getting into her pants. Zero.

When he was done his crummy hand retreated into the bag of chips, not convinced, or not believing, he brought the bag to his face to confirm with one eye then the other that the bag was empty. Still not convinced he tilted his head, as though readying himself for CPR, shaking the bag into an open mouth.

He was the type to call his wife, the wife, or his girlfriend, the girlfriend. I was pretty certain Legs was thinking "Jerk."

The earplugs went in, and out, because the mini-bar girl wanted exact change. She appeared sincerely happy that Murphy had enjoyed his treats when he asked for more, her smile evaporating into airspace when she turned. Another airline candy striper had come to her from behind, not concealing that she was miffed at someone for not having change.

I had a wad of American ones, but I didn't like her, so I gave my girl a ten in return for two miniatures and a smile. Murphy ordered a beer, not thinking to cover the tab with a napkin, spraying the seat in front of him, missing me and Legs who was leaning forward asking for a Tía Maria. She had to reach around him twice, smiling at me in a way that wasn't good for Murphy when taking her drink. The second detour was to pay with ones.

I could tell he was itching to talk. My question was: Why me and not her? Or possibly I was wondering why the attendant gave me a swizzle stick when I had nothing to swizzle.

The guy sucked his teeth, I believe in a search of more food.

I thought of Ward at ICS, found lying face down on his bed a long time ago. And the man who was supposed to present at a seminar I was attending years earlier, found sitting at his hotel room desk with his face in his notebook, a real notebook, his pen still in his hand. And old Avery, who toppled over in a lobby before they zippered him into a polypropylene bag. Dying alone in a hotel room can't be

No One to Tell

good when the last thing you see is a laptop or a sales report crashing into your face. I was lucky. I'm still here to remember the highlights and low points. One cannot exist without the other, and what occurs between them is usually interesting to no one.

*

They were my first American employer. The American sales rep is different from his Canadian counterpart. They dress better, they speak with conviction, they understand teamwork from their college days, they work harder and they play harder, a point that came across loud and clear at the interview on the second to last day of June.

The day was unusually hot for the East. I was ostensibly working hard at new business development for W&W, when actually I was working hard at developing and promoting myself. I was en route to Dayton, Ohio for an interview with the president of American Durcast Inc. who would listen to me expound on my accomplishments to that point in my career, be suitably impressed and hire me. Or so I hoped.

The company had foundries and assembly plants littered across Ohio and Tennessee producing pumps and valves in various materials for various industrial applications.

We'd previously spoken at length on the phone and I was on my way to meet with him, one on one, which is the way he hired sales reps. If he liked what you were and what you could do to bring value to the company he called in managers to confirm his decision which was never reversed.

The bumpy short-haul flight I would make dozens of times over my career as a stopover to other cities began uneventfully. I was in a small window seat with my elbows tucked in, mentally reviewing points of discussion and trying to prevent my pants from creasing. I didn't need reading material because the guy sitting beside me was under the impression I should be reading the side of his newspaper that was hiding most of the seat in front of me. Nor did I have a coffee because I didn't want to risk a stain or an untimely, requisite trip to the john.

The brat in front of me was jumping, crying, taking delight in aggravating the rest of us. I caught his eye by the side of the newspaper and gave the little bugger the finger. We were about twenty minutes from landing and the mother in the row ahead, who should never have had kids, was completely unable to stop the kid's tantrum. Something was pissing him off, probably her.

Then, without warning, his eyes opened wide and he stopped crying for a brief moment. Of course I gave myself credit, believing my finger had worked. Not so. The reason was his sudden realization that internal pressure had reached its crescendo and he was on the verge of spewing out a copious, uncontrolled water-based mixture of brown chunks mixed with viscous matter that resembled uncooked mushroom soup.

I was trapped. Escape was impossible. I'd never seen a kid open his mouth as wide, a rushing torrent of gastric crap hurling its way toward me, toward the front page news and the unprotected lap of my expensive slacks. Instantly I could feel the mixture seeping through the wool blend; first hot, then cold. Not quickly enough to filter the lumpy matter, but the process had begun. Barf stink, and the chauffeur would already be at the airport waiting to deliver me to the president, carrying a little placard that I knew would read: JT Barrett reeks of barf!

The little bastard and Mom got all the attention. I got a napkin.

At least he got the guy sitting beside me as well, who had no idea what to do with his dripping tabloid.

The chauffeur was waiting, patiently with the name card held out, not particularly caring about JT Barrett. I introduced myself briefly and left him in search of a men's room while he went in search of a phone.

1978 was a cell-free zone.

I needed a men's store that wasn't in a basement or a penthouse. The chauffeur had spoken with Boss Man. We were to get there when we got there. Not a problem and the driver confessed that Boss Man had cracked up at hearing the details. He was probably pissing his pants at that very moment and, if that meant he was thinking of me, I didn't care. Then the driver cracked his own smile. We were the same age and neither one had a stick up his ass. Why pretend when you can relax? This was a first for him, and he knew a place.

I sat in the back of the limo with the privacy screen raised, the side window lowered out of consideration for the driver, thinking he might pass out if I didn't.

I bought new pants, a new jacket, a tie, the whole nine yards. Then I met Boss Man whose real name was Mr. Fredericks. He was tall and heavyset, trim and paradoxically youthfully old. Best of all: He told me to expense the clothes, irrespective of the outcome.

Paul believed that changing the position of a chair in someone's office, that he was to sit in, demonstrates a comfort zone and confidence. He was right. The mahogany desk Boss Man sat behind probably wasn't half as big from his perspective as from mine and the two high-back leather seats were immoveable. Instead, I put my briefcase on one and stood beside the other. He looked like old school, the way I look now, but when we shook hands across the desk his was like a spring-loaded vice.

He complimented my new clothes. I complimented his office and we spent the next three hours talking about my interpretation of what a good rep was or wasn't. He didn't want to know what I'd accomplished at W&W, or why I was leaving. He wanted to know how I achieved those accomplishments and how those skills were transferable to him. He wanted to know why a person wanted a particular job, not why he was leaving one. When I left his office he wished me good luck and a less eventful flight. I left feeling confident, if not completely certain.

He had an elegance that belied the appearance of a man accustomed to physical work. He wore made-to-measure grey suits with white shirts and red, yellow, or blue ties. I would come to know that when he spoke he used 'believe' and never 'think', and when he required an answer having one he liked, or at least one you believed, was generally a good thing.

The big guy in blue drove me to the airport with the windows up and the barrier down, talking mostly about Boss Man and how the old guy spent a part of each week in the plant to "stay level." He was hands-on, not pretentious like some of his managers.

I got home late Thursday, waiting all day Friday for the phone to ring. I picked up moments before five. Monday I went into Paul's office to quit. He shrugged and wished me good luck. He understood I was advancing.

*

My second trip to Dayton came not long after, July 17, consuming the first six days of my time with American Durcast. Back then companies expected the two-week notice, even from sales reps. I rented a car and got to the plant for my indoctrination. I'd previously visited dozens of foundries, but this was the first time I'd be working in one, eating in one and expected to go to the john in one.

I ate with the foundry guys, ordering-in instead of doing the brown bag thing. Anyway, I was on expenses and they ate more of my food than I did.

Foundries are places of bells, horns and whistles: arrival whistles and go-home whistles, lunch whistles and emergency whistles, even break whistles, when everyone heads for the same door with the same urgent cause.

No One to Tell

There's a first and last time for everything and that was the first and last time I went through that door into a long, narrow room with a tiled and wet floor, no windows and one fucking bad stench. Behind the door was a rack of magazines and newspapers. Some looked soggy, others had little bits of something on them, but all were crumpled and well-used. There was a coat rack no one used. Another wall was lined with sinks that were dry with an accumulation of greenish-red flecks and hairs, some straight, some not; some encrusted with drippings from the hand wash containers that were mostly full.

Then I saw the trough. The meeting place: The foundry's version of the office water cooler for a few stolen moments of putting it to the boss or bragging about putting it to the secretary. A place where all men are equal and stand shoulder to shoulder with lots of eye contact: The Male Code.

The trough wasn't very wide, or deep, and some degree of expertise and risk was involved. Caution! Slippery when wet! The real reason work boots have rubber soles. Everyone had his assigned place amidst the cacophony of coughs, farts, operatic burps and multiple jets of heavy-smelling urine splashing into a shallow river that flowed to a single drain and never ran dry. There was no vacancy, which suited me just fine.

The third wall was the one with the ceramic urns, which I couldn't see. What I saw was a row of faces, some grimacing, some red and some purple, some smiling, some intent on separating the pages of a soggy magazine. Others had cigarettes squeezed between pursed lips. The partitions were knee high, where they could lay their coats and gloves or exchange magazines with one another. Some were used for balance, but most men used their knees to avoid toppling over: An undulating row of hairy and bared knees sustaining elbows for balance and leverage; some to the left, some to the right. Others sitting, waiting with their hands clasped in prayer.

No one pointed fingers, but the noises and smells, scents not found in a bottle, were beyond my sense of community. I needed a door and went across the road to the sales department without fanfare.

*

Throughout my nine months at American Durcast I made three trips to Dayton, visiting Tennessee twice for training and conferences. The balance of my time was spent doing joint calls with Michel or avoiding them with Bartholomew, both of whom worked in the Montreal office.

Michel was easy going and talented, yet thought himself a failure because at thirty-five he was "just a salesman." He was a nice guy with no pretensions, always available when backup was needed. He was also a serious marathon runner with experience in Boston and other major events. He ran thirty km a day and knew he had a wife who knew she didn't have a husband.

Bartholomew Robertson was the Regional Sales Manager, an American Ivy Leaguer from the Northeast who had an "A" on his sweater for Asshole, or to match his personality. I had a type "F" personality and we never hit it off. He was 1,8, give or take, blond, he worked-out, loved Bart, starched his shirts and thought he was a god to be gazed upon and praised. I thought he was an asshole with a two-inch brown dick, but we hadn't been given a choice about each other when Boss Man hired me.

I can't remember meeting a more despicable person. At one point midway through my tenure we were in the wilds of New Brunswick, serious kilometres from anywhere, at a T in the road. The night was pitch black. Left or right? That's what I wondered aloud. He'd been snoozing, pissed-off at being disturbed, demanding that I do not disturb him again. Say what? I told him to go fuck himself and flipped a mental coin. The night got pretty quiet.

Not very long after, Bart had to take a leak. When I say pitch black, I mean not seeing your feet, not seeing someone or something an arm's length away and Bart didn't want to get out until we came to something resembling a closed or abandoned diner.

I was ready, though I thought he'd take more time. I suppose pissing through two inches doesn't require much time and he never realized how close he came to being stranded in complete blackness, complete sensory deprivation with only his suitcase to ward off whatever might cross his path. I slammed the trunk closed and continued driving.

When one person sees you in a particular light, there's room for error. When two people see you in that same light, there may be room for error. However, when three people see you in that particular light, that's what you are and we all knew what Bart was. But that consensus wouldn't be confirmed until my last month and would lead to the closure of the local office.

Bart was as much a cheat as he was vain. Not a good combination. He was going to literally trip on his ego and I would happily see him go down.

*

By March I'd been with the company a couple of weeks shy of those nine months, continuing to build a career and reputation. I was on course, working at being effective, studying various aspects of my career, listening to some, not listening to others.

I was landing for the second time in the State of Tennessee, at the Nashville International Airport, a trip that would end with my third and final trip to Dayton, Ohio.

*

Friday, March 16, was the day all Management, Sales & Support personnel were expected to arrive at the hotel.

Michel and I arrived last after a long day of airports, connecting flights, Michel, and delays.

Michel stood 2, 1 metres. He was a gangly tower. He gave me neck cramps and was the only person I've ever known of that particular elevation to specifically request seating at the emergency window of an aircraft. He was afraid of flying and was determined that, in the event of a situation, he would remove the panel and leap out. He went on and on about marathons, how he could be better, held back by his physique which wasn't ideal for running: He was too gawky.

Imagine my concern.

I drove to the hotel primarily because I'd rented the car and Michel didn't like driving at night. He became quiet, finally, looking intently for the dark vehicles of big-bellied State Police that were camouflaged by a starless night sky, lying in wait to nail us and make us disappear for a very long time to have sex with Darrell or his brother Darrell.

Arriving at the hotel I left Michel to himself. I needed space. I spent some politically correct time with people I'd met in Knoxville four months earlier and checked-in. I went to the bar for a Johnnie Walker Black, neat. There was also a Hospitality Suite available to company personnel, but you can get trapped in a place like that, particularly on the first night of a sixteen-day meeting. That's right. We were 150 strong in the State of Tennessee for sixteen days of learning, participating, presenting and drinking in a dry county, for which reason an 18-wheeler was parked at the rear and would remain with us for the duration.

The downside to this second Tennessee trip was sharing rooms. Something I found out about once I arrived at the reception. We came from all over the States, Canada and Mexico and Corporate was trying to economize. I didn't have a choice.

My roomie's name was Tex from Texas. He was big,

the duck under doorways kind of big, and he snored. Shit, did he ever snore. The first night I smacked him off the head with each of my pillows with no effect, losing both, despite which morning came too early.

I didn't wake to an alarm clock, or the phone. No. I awoke to "Goddamn, Jim-boy, I've got morning cock."

Say what?

Good for him. Tex from Texas had a hard-on, which would have been alright if he'd been lying on his side, or if he hadn't told me, or if he hadn't jumped out from his bed to go for leak with his Fruit of the Loom hood ornament.

That was the end of my time with Tex. I was first from the room, without prejudice. The concierge could move my bags later, though I did see Tex around and even played a game or two of backgammon with him. He was a nice guy, nothing like The Dongmeister. Nevertheless, I went in search of other arrangements and that's how I met Ihor, the DP Gypsy Gutter Slut.

*

Saturday, March 17, AM: The president's message and Valve Plant Technologies.

PM: Valve Plant tour.

Dinner: Flow Meter Calculations: Attendance and Jackets Required.

Yawn.

The day began at 8:00 AM with Boss Man greeting everyone officially from the podium, beginning his hour-long dissertation on the success and failures of the previous year, the reasons for both and the actions that would prevent failures and dismal results during the balance of the current year. Then a fifteen-minute break, a chance to pee, scratch, yawn in private and avoid commenting on anything the president had said to anyone you didn't know.

Next in line was the plant manager of the Valve Division who explained a plant tour in the afternoon that would complete the day. He brought everyone up-to-date on new equipment, changes in production and capacities, concluding by giving each of us copies of what he'd spent two hours talking about. I looked at the spiral folder, counted the pages and went for lunch.

They'd leased two huge tour buses to transport us to the plant. They didn't want anyone with rental cars getting lost or finding other reasons not to arrive at the plant on time. Then, single file, name tags, a factory coat, safety glasses, hardhat and toe caps, and ears plugs. We were in the foundry, divided into manageable groups. Everyone to a man looked impressed, nodding at this, nodding at that. The group leader pointed at this and we nodded; he pointed at that, and we nodded. Sometimes, to show the importance of something specific, he came to us individually. He put his hand on our shoulders and spoke into our foam-blocked ears. We nodded.

The tour lasted two hours, at the end of which we all applauded, looked at each other and nodded. Some of the new reps had to hit the john before heading back. They didn't know better, hurrying over to the "Toilet" door, each one rushing out muttering, "fuck this" or "fuck that."

Foundries are foundries, with certain doors best left closed.

We were on the bus, at the hotel by five-thirty for drinks, a shower, and more drinks before dinner. The second day wasn't over. We had yet to get through dinner with a guest speaker who was to expound on the virtues of Flow Meter Calculations. Shit!

*

"You're James Barrett."

This guy was standing behind me, using the vacant chair to one side as a support. Cool.

"I'm James, usually JT. You are?"

"Alexis Lenconovich, Albuquerque. Call me Ihor" His

hand came up. "You had your stuff moved into my room today. How come?"

"I didn't want to do it myself."

He threw his head back. "I was in HS when you were in cleaning up."

We shook hands. "Did I take the right bed?"

"Who cares? It's not like we'll be in them much." He smiled widely without parting his lips. "So, what's with the change of rooms?"

My brain was working to make a determination. Reading people is one of my strengths; though admittedly back then the skill was in the embryonic stage. He pulled out the chair and sat.

"Big Tex from Texas had morning cock and he snores. Do you snore?"

"No. So just the snoring bothered you?" No answer. "What do you drink?"

"J W Black."

We had two. Scotch for me, vodka for him, then Ihor, pronounced Igor, went to another table to speak with the waitress, joining me later for the dinner and a presentation given by one of many expert speakers who would present over the next two weeks.

We took to each other immediately. He was 1, 7 metres with a skin tone between tan and olive. I asked him what the influence was. He said: "People throwing shit at gypsies." I liked the guy. He was Bohemian, born to gypsy parents somewhere on the outskirts of Czechoslovakia.

He wasn't rehearsed or affected. He was Ihor and he carried it off well. He dressed in dark colours and imported European-styled shirts one half-size too small. His hair was naturally curly, stylishly long and he shaved twice a day. Whatever was in his head soon found its way to his mouth and he lived for the moment. He was gregarious, well-spoken, well-travelled and smooth. Hide the wives and daughters.

*

The son of gypsies, Ihor travelled across Europe for much of his life at his parents' side, studying as they worked at various jobs. When the time came for them to separate he continued doing what he'd been taught. He worked to play and played at work, bringing that philosophy with him to the States.

He was twenty-one when he arrived, working at a variety of short-lived, well-paying jobs until one day he found himself sitting in front of Boss Man. Then twenty-nine, he was sitting beside me. We studied her. In another time and place she might have been beautiful with a bit of help. She was stern, an all-corporate executive type, a real ball crusher, making her way across the stage with measured steps.

Ihor and I bonded quickly, spending much of our time together over the next two weeks. He was a little off-colour, a little wild and seldom serious. He loved life and he loved women more, in the very short-term.

"Tits and a brain, or just tits?" he questioned.

"Both." Giving the benefit of doubt was and is my weak point.

"Don't think so. Just tits."

"Probably nice tits, though." I try to be positive.

"They're all nice."

Ihor was an optimist.

Everyone was given note pads. We both lifted our pencils, not intending to write. What would she know about Flow Switches, Flow Meters or Flow Rates that we didn't already know?

She was at least 1, 9 in her heels, perhaps taller, with reddish hair pulled tightly into a knotted bun and creamy-white skin that might have been a porcelain mask; so I'm sure Michel was in love. Her two-piece suit was single-breasted business grey, complementing a white button-down man's shirt that opened at her neck and protruded beyond the suit collar and her wrists. Her skirt was stylish, above the knees, not too short for an executive, and her shoes were practical pumps with practical heels. She was all business.

She held a chromed telescopic pointer, thick-rimmed and oversized red glasses perched on her nose. She scanned the audience, wasting no time. She began confidently. She was no-nonsense, unsmiling, definitely on the chilly side. Ihor thought because of the icicle up her ass. We agreed she was about twenty-seven, though potentially hot without the icicle. She was very eloquent, well-versed in what she was presenting to the attentive group, not reading from the screen behind her but from the text on her lectern. She was a pro. She'd done this before, the lights dimming on cue so we could view the schematics projected from the overhead acetates. She went on for five or so minutes and we listened.

The room was warm, not stifling, which likely wasn't the case at the podium where more intense lighting was directed at the lady speaker. She removed her jacket, shrugging both shoulders and tugging at her sleeves without skipping a beat, draping it from one corner of the lectern.

She went on to explain this and that, now facing the screen, pointing for emphasis. When she turned to the attentive audience Ihor and I took a quick look at each other. She'd unbuttoned the top few buttons of her shirt. Ihor commenting that I'd been right about her breasts.

She continued talking about flow charts, explaining the data on the screen behind her while reaching to loosen the knot binding her hair as the plant manager stood to ask her to elaborate on one specific aspect of High Precision Fluid Measurement.

She responded smoothly and at length. Everyone scribbled notes. The man thanked her, the woman pausing to sip from a glass before continuing, adjusting the waistline of her skirt, hesitating. For whatever reason she seemed a little confused, a little worried, stooping slightly toward her papers, apparently trying to isolate a piece of misplaced data.

Removing her hands from her waist, she reached for the microphone, apologizing.

"Gentlemen, I'm missing something I know I came here with; if you would all bear with me for a moment."

Some guy came onto the stage, placing a stool four or five strides from where she stood.

"Thank you." She said, acknowledging him, scanning the audience from over the rim of her glasses. "That's much better. Sorry for the interruption, gents. Now," she tossed her glasses to the floor, tousling her hair, "where was I?"

She skipped away from the podium. Her skirt was gone, missing, her feet barely touching the stage as she danced toward the stool in rhythm to the music erupting from nowhere, working at the few remaining buttons of the shirt she was shrugging from her bared shoulders, tossing it into the air.

Some cheered, some looked dumb. Some jumped up and down in their seats rubbing their hands together.

I said, "Holy shit, so much for icicles."

Ihor blew air from pursed lips. "Nice tits and a brain."

She sat with both cheeks kissing the front half of the stool, her long legs extended outward, bent slightly at the knees, her toes touching the floor. She was laughing, tossing her head to and fro, her hair a burst of bright red. Her skirt lay somewhere behind the podium, long forgotten; her shirt lay on the floor nearby. We were still holding our pencils.

Her nylon-covered legs shimmered under the overhead lights, opening and closing to the rhythm of pulsating music, the silk borders tugged towards her waist by narrow pink garters leading to a narrow pink belt. Her panties were pink, sheer and laced. Her bra was push-up, pink, dotted with red rosettes, pushing to perfection. She was making eye contact with those closest to the stage, teasing them with airborne kisses, cupping her breasts. A chorus of cheers. She stopped, her lips pouty. A chorus of groans. A gentle squeeze, slender fingers tracing invisible lines to her panties, to her open and inviting bare thighs. More tender caresses, fingertips painted red sliding under silk garters. She pulled at them, letting them snap against what we could see was delicate flesh, flawless under the bright lights. Her lips oohed with pain.

Her legs came up straight spelling V for Valve, lingering, lowering them to the floor. She stood, pivoting, leaning over the stool, glancing over her shoulders demurely at the silent and awestruck audience.

We decided her panties served no purpose beyond taunting us, her hands coming from in front and under to stroke her legs, to probe mischievously at the bottom of her practically bare ass. She stood on her toes, raising her heels from her sensible pumps, kicking one shoe away. The other followed.

She braced herself, her body undulating in erotic waves, her hair flowing, stopping, her legs parting, fingertips searching, exploring. One butterfly clasp springing free, then another, silk straps dangling. She turned, one leg straight, one bent, another silk strap freed. She twirled, then another.

She was delectable, divine torture. One had to wonder who did the interview.

She faced to one side, her hands encircling one satin-finish thigh, pushing downward, the silk stocking crumpling.

Her body followed, bending from the hip. Her legs were taut, her red hair exploding. She came up straight, pulling the nylon with her, letting it break free. She twirled again, scanning the room, dropping the single stocking to the floor, waving a finger to admonish us.

She climbed the stool, hooking one foot in, raising her other leg straight up, vertical, her hands squeezing the bare and supple flesh at its base, pushing the nylon upward, smoothly, not hesitating, not stopping until reaching the tips of her painted toes when she began pulling, stretching, letting it snap away and sail to the floor. She watched its descent. She watched us, the delicate tip of her tongue peeking out to moisten her lips that were glossy and red.

Straddling the stool she arched her back, inhaling dreamily as though intoxicated by her scent, frozen in memory and time. She reached behind, seductively, teasingly, freeing her belt, waiting, launching the thin, pink band into the crowd. Zelda leaped instantly into my mind.

Squirming from the stool as she would her lover's lap, she bathed her body with moist hands, stretching her arms, stretching her legs, bending and twisting, jutting out her perfectly sculpted ass scarcely covered by hypnotic pink. Her hands travelled behind her and stayed. She was undecided. She smiled coyly, scanning us again, hearing what she wanted. She faced away, bending deeply, the silent click releasing the pressure, palms cupping her breasts, her bra falling onto the stool, her breasts free at last. She stood, teasingly, her bare back glistening with tiny beads of sweat. She turned, her arms crossed. A chorus of groans. She twisted, bending, her ass in the air, her panties askew, her hands pressed to the floor, her breasts firmly against her parted legs, her red lips smiling. Her hands glided gracefully along the length of her legs, stopping at her panties. She paused to listen, to hear, pausing, teasing.

She pulled at one side, a teasing peek. She pulled at the other side, the pink silk disappearing. She paused, listening. She wiggled, a sign that she understood, her panties reappearing, inching toward her ankles, the stage floor, teasingly, mockingly, stretched wider and wider as they came closer to her parted knees. Her ass was bare, taut and round, her slightly parted crevice compelling us to cry out for more.

She tensed one cheek, then the other. We could hear pencils breaking, mournful moans. She paused again, her lips curled into a smirk, becoming a pout. Her panties began travelling again, the wrong way. Screams of protest. Stop! Stop! The sheer material resisted, struggling against her parted thighs, begging along with all of us that she throw them to the floor. She didn't need them. Yet she persisted, one last tug hiding them instantly from our view.

She was coming back up, stopping just over the top of the stool, her breasts lingering over her bra, her hands deftly reaching behind, clasping the hooks. She stretched this way and that, pirouetting to face us, dancing, her feet parting slowly, her body sinking effortlessly into a full split where she stayed, tugging the side bands of her panties high above her waist, forcing the already sheer triangle into a pink ribbon. She eased her torso to the floor, forming a perfect Y.

She rested there, inert, our breathing stalled. We stood. We cheered. We clapped and whistled and banged on tables, yelling out our love for her. She looked up, resting on her elbows, bringing a fingertip to her lips, demanding silence. We obeyed, the entire room drunk with anticipation.

She began moving, sitting straight, her back arched. She closed her eyes, cupping her breasts, waiting, concentrating, her legs tightened at right angles to her. Silence. Suspense. Slowly, imperceptibly, her body began rising from the floor, her feet coming together in unseen increments, one towards the other, narrowing the distance between them, her legs closing, her newly fashioned ribbon ineffective, imprisoned, parting deep red curls.

There she stood, in her panties and bra as a perfect specimen, her face beaming, her hands half-cupped below her red and glossy lips to deliver our good night kiss. Then she was gone, probably to study for her Pre-Med or the Bar Exam.

Ihor and I went to the bar to swap stories, not the HS. How could I not tell him about Zelda?

In fact, he was the only one I ever told.
*

Sunday, March 18, AM: 8:00 AM – 12:00 Hands-On at the Valve Plant

Some of us went to bed early the night before; others went out for a bit of air. Most of us migrated to the HS to drink and talk about the striptease. Michel was already in the Hospitality Suite when we crowded through the door, looking at us like a marauding force invading his secret place.

We settled into poker, backgammon, conversation, billiards, TV and drinks. Michel was talking with Bart about his passion for running; he felt he had to acknowledge the guy who was his direct boss. I went to bed to avoid the bullshit.

The day began at 6:00 AM with a splintering bang at the door, scaring the crap out of Ihor and me. Twelve guys were standing at our door in outfits that were ludicrous even for the 70s, none worse than the guy wearing Adidas shorts with a singlet, mid-calf socks with braces and laced shoes.

Michel said: "We're running every day at six. Let's go."

I said: "No."

I heard: "You're running today." The voice was Bart's.

They all started talking, each trying to be heard over the other.

"Sorry, guys. No is no."

They started herding into the room and I went running,

viewed by me as an act of diplomacy. Ihor stayed. He was a gypsy with a gypsy's vocabulary and didn't give two shits about Bart.

The race started off well enough, downhill, meaning uphill on the way back. Not a good plan.

We formed a line, Michel yelled "Go!", and a bunch of guys of various waist sizes and leg strengths, who'd been up drinking all night, charged full steam along the path with shirttails flying, elbows flailing and singing some sort of Army cheerleader song that faded quickly. Bye-bye. They disappeared beyond the curved path, I went to the restaurant patio at the rear of the hotel to wait for them.

About thirty minutes later the athletes plodded to where I could witness the final leg of their endurance run to the Finish Line that was at the open veranda of the restaurant where I stood with a fresh coffee in hand wondering at the beleaguered and motley strung-out row of runners, each struggling not to come in last.

Michel and Bart shared the lead. Michel looked like a runner; Bart looked like an ad in the sports page. They were on flat ground, coming alongside the reflecting pool bordered with crushed stone and golf-course quality grass, charging, not smiling, mouths closed tight, faces strained, grimacing with effort. Michel's arms floated at his side; Bart's were stiff and ready, wanting to make contact with Michel's arm, wanting that extra edge.

Michel saw the intention, easing slightly to one side, gaining nothing but motivation. Bart moved in closer, the others far behind and more concerned about their pending heart failures. Bart came up equal to Michel, struggling with each stride before breaking away. His foot came out just enough to make contact with Michel's, robbing Michel of his balance and momentum, sending him headlong over the grass edging and palms-first into the gravel, stopping short of the water.

Bart didn't slow until he touched the designated post, keeled over, breathing heavily and sweating.

"Motherfucker" I said.

"Appropriately expressed, Mr. Barrett. I'm fully in agreement."

Boss Man was behind me, leaning with his shoulder against the trellis, drinking his coffee. I was the first, Michel was number two; Mr. Fredericks completing the opinion poll as number three. We now knew the real Bart Robertson. Michel was excused from the hands-on portion at the valve plant while the rest of us went from breakfast to the plant to assemble and disassemble components. More of a refresher for most of us.

No one wanted to be there and we took a while to get started, working under the strict supervision of the regular workers who'd come in on their day off to assist. They would each put their personal code on the work done; so we did our best at Valve Nursery School.

The afternoon was free time, or golf for those over forty.

*

I didn't see Ihor that morning until we met where everyone was spilling out from the tour buses in desperate need of their respective rooms.

When the meeting was first planned, some reps were selected at random to rent vehicles upon arrival and keep them for the duration; corporate believing the freedom would cultivate a kindred spirit amongst the guys. I was one of the few, the car was a '79 blue-green or green-blue Impala: one third green, one third blue, one third chrome and smelled new.

The hardest part was keeping the thing a secret.

The PM was free time. We didn't golf, we didn't volunteer to complete a foursome and the hour was too early to drink more than a glass of wine at lunch. So we went to the bar to plan the day over lunch, after which we drove to the State Capitol Buildings to do the tourist thing. We walked for a while, not overly wowed, leaving Andrew Jackson to maintain his vigil over the pillared façades and went to the Adelphia Coliseum along the Cumberland River where we stopped for hot dogs and to decide between Ford's Theatre and Fort Nash. The theatre won out, though as a line began forming the rain began falling and we drove to check out Vanderbilt University.

Ihor was more interested in the student body than he was in the complex and we ended up trailing behind a couple of girls. We followed blindly into a half-full and sombre auditorium that looked onto a solitary pedal harp standing by an empty chair on a deserted stage framed by tall folds of magnificent burgundy-coloured velvet curtains and oversized heavy gold braids with matching gold tassels.

The girls walked towards the front, Ihor following until I grabbed his arm.

The performer walked out with grace and poise, her feet kicking at the floor-length, long-sleeved, black velveteen gown with a gold bow at the empire waist, the sleeves extending over her hands to the loops encircling her middle fingers. She sat, tilting the towering black and gold trimmed instrument until it met with the velveteen cap-shoulder of the gown. A pause, a deep breath, the harp seeming huge against her slight frame, her agile fingers skimming effortlessly across the board of golden strings, each one responding to her precise commands.

She was performing on a concert harp: forty-seven strings and seven pedals at the base letting her change the note of individual keys, playing in any key and changing that key to another while performing. The smooth tonality produced the calming effect of a lullaby. At first Ihor was adamant that he wouldn't stay, soon sliding into his seat, closing his eyes to enjoy.

Her fingers danced and played at the strings throughout

the forty-five minute concert before she curtsied daintily, content with her performance, and I put my elbow into Ihor's shoulder to wake him.

At the hotel we joined the others at the nineteenth hole before going for supper.

*

Monday, March 19, AM: Materials Selection and Applications by Industry.
PM: Individual Presentations.

Dinner was optional for those who preferred the bar, as long as they were on the chartered buses to Cookeville by 8:00 PM. That would be nighttime, they reminded us.

Monday, 8:00 AM, felt like Friday. The day began with engineers talking down to us about material choice variables with the emphasis on Petrochemical and Chemical during the morning, Pulp & Paper and Mining in the afternoon with individual sales reps giving practical application presentations. We were divided into four groups of forty, rotating in two-hour shifts around four salons. We worked through lunch and finished at 6:00 PM.

Dinner was a function. We were leaving right after en route to Cookeville, so we went to the restaurant for a fast feed. Then to our rooms to pack, have a beer and leave. We wanted to get on the road sans hitchhikers.

Everyone was jammed in and around the tour buses, digging for their favourite beverage in the open coolers on a first-come-first served basis before rushing for the best seats. We didn't have that issue. We had the blue-green Impala and were heading east on I-40 before anyone could hitch a ride. We didn't want company too early in the game that we'd be stuck with for the duration. We were well on our way into the 140 km trip while the others were still in Nashville grabbing beers and wondering where to sit.

Ihor came prepared with a full mickey of premium

vodka, tossing it in the back with mine. We were still in Tennessee and not inclined to spend the next twenty years breaking rock and being some Bubba's bitch, not even each other's.

There's a definite advantage to leaving the herd: better living conditions. And that's what the smooth talking gypsy Gutter Slut got for us. Our quarters on the third and top floor were deluxe, relaxed with no adjoining doors and far away from everyone; especially inebriated reps who might want to come visiting, or go running.

*

Midnight came and went and we had no idea when the others arrived. We didn't care. We were into the AM and only the smart ones were in bed. A few more years would pass before I would join the fraternity of smarter, been there and done that sales reps, about the time I switched to vodka in New Orleans, or because of New Orleans.

The HS was a conference room set up away from the hotel rooms for the convenience of other guests, complete with game tables, a full bar and TV, intended to keep us out of the hotel bar which wasn't off limits. We gravitated into smaller groups pretty much by what we wanted to do: Cards, billiards, talk, sports TV, whatever. Ihor and I ended up with a guy called Jody, Jesse or Jude or some other southern-sounding J name who was bunked in with The Dongmeister and needed four for cards.

They called his roomie The Dongmeister because he never wore underwear and possessed rather large and imposing genitalia, which he didn't always care to control. He'd gone for a leak and was coming right back, but that was over an hour earlier and J was getting pissed that his roomie had probably crashed, rattling on about not saying something if you're not going to do it. So we dropped the cues and we went in search of The Dongmeister.

Naturally we went to the bar first, thinking he might be

hitting on one of the locals before closing. The place was deserted, so we headed over to their room with no real reason to find the guy except that J wanted his game of four and, having the key, he went into the room first, stopping abruptly, signalling for us to shut up and follow. We did.

The Dongmeister was on the side of the room nearest the door, dead to the world and about to wish he was dead. The magazine was unfolded at the centre, the glossy girl spread out across J's pillow for proper lighting under the swivel lamp bracketed to the corner wall.

The liquor bottle was within easy reach on the side table that separated the beds at his left, the empty glass in The Dongmeister's left hand. We moved to the far side, not breathing, careful not to make the slightest sound. The three of us had the same thought, but using the phone to call the HS would wake him. Worse; we had no camera.

He was propped up on his own pillow. His tie was undone, his shirttails rolled up and his pants were pushed past his knees. Thick-soled shoes covered his feet and pointed outward.

The dong in Dongmeister was enormous, like a huge autonomous appendage he'd tried to rip out and cast aside, purple and chafed in the struggle for supremacy. The greater portion lay exposed, poised over the top of the conquering right-hand grip, seeking to stay alive, hoping the battle was not yet lost, yet sensing defeat. Its strength and life's fluid still trickled out over the master's unyielding hold to the dark foliage of his dormant leg and onto the white linen that was their field of engagement that night; where so much spillage remained as testimony to the battle won, the battle lost.

We wanted to sit there until he woke, the opportunity was too precious, but three guys sitting in a room looking at another guy holding his big wet dick in his big wet hand wasn't what we had in mind. Besides, we had nothing to drink and we weren't touching his reserve.

We were quiet on our way to the door, destination HS. He would never have known he was the spectator event of the evening, but he chose that moment to blink awake as we passed the foot of his bed.

The expression was memorable: the gaping mouth, the gasp, the drawn out "ugh" in concert with the white eyes, the disbelief, the spastic lurch. He didn't know what to do first: look at us, the door, his magazine or his hand, his pants at his knees.

We gave him a thumbs-up. He was speechless. He was in shock. He was afraid. He knew where we were going and he couldn't get there first.

We went to the HS to dilute the memory. J went for another pillow in another room.

As for The Dongmeister, he was quiet throughout the remaining days, mellow, much like the blowhard in Chicago two decades later who thought everyone onboard should hear his opinions, who was already flying high while the jet was parked at the gate. He got mellow too. Burly cops and handcuffs seem to produce that calming effect.
*

Tuesday, March 20, AM: Individual Application Presentations.

PM: Electric and Pneumatic Actuators.

Play hard; work hard: One was optional, the other wasn't. The seminar was more like Survival 101. We performed exaggerated breathing exercises to stay awake, we rolled up little pieces of paper and threw them at someone who then threw them to someone else and at the end of the day our notebooks were filled with meaningless doodle marks.

There were twenty-five tables, each one with six settings of pads, pencils, glasses and jugs of icy tap water: aquariums of yellow particulate.

No One to Tell

Somehow we survived the morning. Now we were in Actuator 101, which proved long and hard, more so for him. He'd been out the night before like the rest of us; the difference was that most of us knew when to go home. He didn't.

His eyeballs were blood red, watery to the point of blindness and the puffiness around them was closing in more and more as the afternoon progressed beyond the midway point. His head was flopping to the front, to the back, forward, backward, then nothing. He sat motionless; his arms crossed over his chest, barely moving with the rhythm of his breathing. He was comical to watch, to most of us, not the speaker who hadn't faltered in his presentation.

The guy had placed the back of his chair against the table behind him and was facing the podium. That was the first part of his second mistake; the other was sitting so near the front. His knees were spread wide, pointing downward, his chin pressed to his tie, his eyes squeezed shut and his lower lip had fallen away from its counterpart. His first mistake was being there. Wherever he was in his dreams, he was much better off oblivious to the silent danger coming his way.

Boss Man commandeered a chair from one of the six at the table directly in line with the victim. Neither time nor noise stirred the guy from his dreamy stupor, the heaviness of silence in the room woke him.

The words were neither loud, nor harsh. They were simple and poignant. "Go home. You are no longer employed."

The guy leaned forward, dumb and unconscious, wanting to force the inexplicable from his brain to his mouth. He was waiting, unsure. But Boss Man stood and was walking away, indicating to the speaker to continue. The bleary-eyed casualty walked from the room trying hard not to appear defeated, probably too hung over to plan the next phase of his career.

The show was over. Actuators more important once again. Boring beyond imagination, but we still had to know about them…and keep our jobs.

Branes was a Product Manager and Electrical Engineer who lived in Knoxville, a real "I'm the manager" prick. He was arrogant. He spoke with a superior air to everyone who didn't sign his cheque. I raised my hand shoulder high. He pointed and I stood.

"I'd like you to explain further about transducers and how they allow for positive feedback where it's necessary to close a control loop."

"That question isn't relevant at this time."

Say what?

"I thought we were talking about actuators."

"What's your point?"

"It's not my point. It's my question, about positive feedback."

The guy actually said, "Don't waste our time. We have too much to cover and your question isn't relevant at this time."

"Thank you. Sorry for the disruption. I'll read through the tech data for the answer."

That's what I said. What I thought was "fuck you."

Ihor whispered without moving his lips. "Who bit *his* tit?"

"He's from Knoxville. Probably his dog-faced sister the night they got married."

"Watch out for him, Jamie. You're on his shitlist."

I looked over at Boss Man, twisting my mouth, raising an eyebrow and shrugging.

When Branes finished we had a fifteen-minute latrine break. A few moments later someone from across the room asked, "Can it be as simple as a visual feedback to a display or to a main electronic controller?"

Ihor looked over, this time moving his lips. "Same question you asked."

"I know. Go figure."

"Don't have to. That guy's from Knoxville too. Maybe they're kissing cousins."

"They're kissing something."

"Watch out for that guy. He's on your ass."

*

Tuesday, March 27, AM: Transportation to Knoxville.
PM: Hands-on Workshop at the Pump Division.
Dinner: Attendance required. Come as you are.

The buses were waiting once again to transport all personnel to Knoxville for an early lunch, the five or so rental cars forming a small convoy between them. No one was getting lost.

Well-fed, we were in for another delightful afternoon, this one with pumps until five. Then on to a Barbeque Dinner at the Branes'.

Like that would happen.

The end of the day couldn't come soon enough, an accurate assessment. Everyone headed to the HS. I went to the room to pour a substantial JWB, gulp it, and fall asleep. I woke in total darkness. Ihor had turned off the lights and television before leaving with the car keys. He wasn't into public transport, the way I wasn't into bullshit.

I showered and worked on a second JWB, dressing to look better than I felt before heading to the bar for dinner to see who was doing what.

I passed on dinner, picking at some hors-d'oeuvres.

People were dancing. The music was rock 'n roll, a nice break from love affairs gone wrong, dogs named Duke that died and Billie-Somebody that done did somethin' bad. I ordered my usual, at the bar, peering into the crowd through a mirror half- hidden behind an uneven façade of colours and shapes. The ceiling was pin-dotted with starlit lights, the walls were midnight blue, the ambiance casual elegance.

I felt as though I was sitting in a timeless, peaceful place.

The music was good for dancing, the right volume for talking, people doing both. I enjoyed watching them, pretending I knew a few words, humming with dums and dees and doos.

I didn't mind being alone. That's what I was, am, a loner. I was enjoying a night of freedom, smiling, minding my business, tapping my feet, getting down…alone. I was in the mood. I got up to dance, well onto the floor before I noticed two things: I had become part of a chorus line of women, line dancing. I also noticed I was a little less dark than everyone else.

The women were gorgeous, dressed to kill in little flutter sleeve dresses and short skirts with a rainbow of blouses, dancing up a storm with me at the edge of the leggy tempest doing the one, two, three, back; one, two, three, side; one, two, three, sorry. Their stocking feet didn't lose a beat, just kept on dancing, but somehow I was in the middle of the ebony floorshow doing my best to keep up with the hip thing.

I was being pulled this way, then that. Nor was I unaware that a quintet of guys was making their way to the scuffed and reverberating dance floor.

When I first saw them, not much different from linebackers who'd forgotten to remove their padding, I had a real sense that bodily pain was imminent. Not that I wanted to hurt them.

They moved in, two beside me, three in front, well-dressed in slim fitting suits of green, yellow, and burgundy with bell-bottom pants and oversized white patent leather belts. Their ties covered most of their shirtfronts between wide shimmering lapels. More importantly, they were smiling.

My dance lessons were officially underway, lasting the better part of the evening between drinks. A really good time without the BS from work. We spoke about politics back home, theirs and mine, JFK, Robert Kennedy and Doctor King. Canadians and Americans really are twins. We're alike, kinfolk differentiated by whom we chose to fear and mistrust. Either one or both manifesting as hatred. And the bartender was freaking out, which wouldn't be a term for many years.

By the time the guys got up to dance, doing their thing, the jacket was off, the tie was undone and the cuffs were folded back. Walking with them I might have appeared more like a blind man's walking stick. I was at the edge, defensively, so I could at least be seen and not crushed. I was learning the Tennessee Two-step and the floor was rockin'.

I did just fine, or so they said.

I saw another side of Tennessee. So had my dance partners, albeit with a Northern, though not Yankee, flair. Finally I said goodnight, explaining the unwritten rule about work and play, leaving them to play.

I learned new dance steps, a new handshake, met fun people I remember still, and *de-Branesed* myself. We shook hands, hugged, and I was off to bed with a smile on my face and in my step, my jacket hanging from my shoulder by a finger, my tie stuck to my shirt.

I love when heads turn.

Goodnight.

*

Wednesday, March 21, AM: Ball, Plug & Butterfly Valves.

PM: Check & Diaphragm Valves.

4:30 PM: Bus transportation to Fairfield.

Branes learned by noon that he'd just as well try to

intimidate a door and, apart from pissing him off, the day was pretty much learn, eat, learn and leave.

Ihor and I were gone by 4:30 with no freeloaders. Some of them might have looked for the green-blue Impala, but we were long gone, heading east on I-40.

More of a compound than a hotel complex, the property was impressive to drive into on the edge of the Catoosa Wildlife Management Area and once again we took advantage of an early arrival. We had a Jacuzzi, two double beds, a spacious veranda overlooking the reserve and a golf course, two white terry robes, a selection of bath soaps, shampoos, oils, skin lotions and a phone in the bathroom.

The 18-wheeler arrived earlier in the day and the HS was set up. The clerk at the desk understood we wanted to make sure everything was in place for our sales reps who'd soon be arriving and gave us the key for the inspection. Ihor took two bottles of his unpronounceable vodka, I took two JW Black and we went to our room before returning the key.

Ihor would be using the spacious spa exclusively…and frequently.

*

The club was private with a private bar in a dry Red Neck County, the fulcrum of the Bible belt for members and guests only, with free and plentiful booze. Free for us because we expensed it; free for the ladies because we expensed it.

Wednesday night was Ladies' Night, Fuckfest Night where the local ladies came to get away from coveralls, chequered shirts, cowbells and cow shit. There was a dress code in force for gentlemen in the lounge and bar area and the ladies enjoyed the attention of men in suits, white shirts, ties and shiny shoes. They wanted mannerly attention, to be treated like ladies, or at least like women.

The lounge was expansive and designer-decorated with

light-coloured textured walls, soft overhead incandescent lighting, low-profile lemon and candy-apple red sofas for two, and matching recliners that could and did fit two. The ambiance inspired romance right down to cupid-arrow swizzle sticks and spongy soft carpets. The atmosphere on one side invited quiet; on the other was a drone of constant chatter. The lounge was sedate and secluded for quiet or stolen moments; the dance bar was for meeting new acquaintances, rubbing elbows and being seen.

The place was busy throughout the evening and into the late night. The 70s at its finest: Strangers meeting, becoming friends; leaving, coming back as better friends from every floor, all night.

We were sitting in the lounge talking with Morty the Undertaker who was at the hotel complex with his wife, Morticia, attending a Funeral Director's Convention. They were partners in a funeral home in Macon, Georgia. He was the Director of Operations, she was the beautician. They were doing exactly what we were: getting some space from other morticians.

Morty was tanned, though not naturally. He'd either visited a tanning salon or had converted an old casket into a tanning table for his personal use. His demeanour was distinguished, oddly professional in a black, double-breasted suit and the open collar of his starched white shirt. His cuffs were linked together with heavy Florentine gold, looking antique against the bright and sensual fabric of the armchair that his gold-coloured tie draped over. The brushed stainless steel band of his watch was thick, the bright blue and gold behind its crystal sparkled.

He wasn't very old, fortyish, and not out of shape. He was slouched into a wide, low-profile lounge chair upholstered in new vivid velvety corduroy. His wife was perched on one of his knees. The crease in his pants was razor sharp and his black shoes were high-glossed Italian, like his hair. His fingers were manicured, his hands free of rings, save the one on his right hand that might have been from his alma mater. That hand held a crystal old-fashioned. His left was following Morticia's rhythmic rocking. She was my first Southern Belle, though not my last, dropping her Gs from suffixes when she spoke.

Ihor and I sat in a crescent sofa facing them, a low, red-lacquered table between us. We were talking bar talk: Did this, did that, been there, done that. Then, without warning, came: "Would you gentlemen like to fuck me tonight?"

Say what? We didn't have to look at each other, pretending we hadn't heard. We did hear. We looked at each other anyway. That's what she said, and she said it again.

She giggled. "Gentlemen, I asked whether ya'll would like to fuck me."

How did she know what we wanted? She meant both of us; double your pleasure.

Morticia didn't seem to me as though she should be with Morty, the Grim Reaper who wasn't grim at all. Her hair was shoulder length, blonde and cut precision-straight where it came into contact with her perfect eyebrows that sometimes would disappear behind the flaxen curtain before peeking out again. Her complexion was pure, without the slightest imperfection. She radiated an essence that was captivating, compelling. She was petite, standing 1, 6 metres, 1, 7 in stiletto cocktail sandals. But she wasn't standing. She was wearing a short silk cocktail dress, indigo blue, exposing most of her thighs, her breasts co-existing in perfect harmony with the décolleté front.

She wore no jewellery. Her skin was creamy-white in colour and texture, contrasting flawlessly against the blue of her dress. She was enjoying the caresses of her own fingertips, the softness of her bare thighs undulating under the pressure of her touch. We were transfixed. She was the quintessential woman and, yes, we both wanted to fuck her.

A popular Japanese factoid, amongst many of that country's businessmen I've met, is that North American women don't wear panties. The significance of which is solely dependent on the total package. But I do know Morticia was not on Ladies' Night. With each caress from her parted knees to the retreating blue silk, we discovered more about Morticia. I don't believe Morty could know more, or care if we did.

I declined her offer insincerely. So did Ihor with obvious reluctance. He wasn't certain about Morty's role in the invitation and didn't want to break the spell by discussing specifics, though Morty didn't seem to have a problem with loaning out his wife. He was there for a good time, and apparently he was having one. He just sat there, tapping his glossy black shoes to the music with his free hand under her dress, enjoying frequent glimpses of her bare hips as we continued the conversation, looking unashamedly up her dress.

Every so often she would get up to dance and we missed her. None of us was interested in being pushed and shoved, so we stayed seated and talked. When she came back the last time Morty had gone and I was sitting in his seat. She sat close beside Ihor, unstrapped her stilettos and tossed them onto the lacquered table. When the waitress came by we ordered another round.

I went with her and drank mine on the bar side that was as crowded as a bordello on dollar day, alive with chatter, music and dancing. Then, in a blink, everything froze with the gunshot, the music seeming too loud. I discovered later that women walking around with Derringers or .32s in their purses was a normal thing and one of them had dropped her purse.

Everyone was fine, no one killed, injured or maimed.

No one seemed overly concerned. In spite of which I

went outside for air with impeccable timing, certain I wasn't being missed by Ihor or Morticia.

He was kicking the gravelled surface with steel-toed beige work boots that stuck out from the tattered ends of his farmeralls. He was a husband. He was pissed-off, ranting, waiting outside for the reason he was pissed off: his wife. She was inside, probably getting laid and not for the first time. He wanted to take on the world, he wanted Wednesdays to stop, but he was on the outside looking in and didn't have a membership.

I empathized, explaining that I was attending an undertaker's convention. I knew nothing about his wife, but his pent up frustration wouldn't let him back down. We were evenly matched, apart from the fact I was about to ruin my suit and he didn't much care. The doorman was there, not ready to get involved beyond his jurisdiction. His job was to stop the farm boys from getting in, but he did let others know what was going on, several rushing through the door including Tex from Texas who volunteered to stand-in for me.

No one felt sorry for him. He was a kid who'd been nowhere and done nothing, beyond perhaps working hard to make a living for himself and his cheating wife. Or maybe he was a hard-ass who didn't know how to treat a lady, if she was a lady. Who knows? He was a Bubba humiliated by life. So he married the wrong woman. So what? Who didn't? He was out of his element on his own turf, standing outside an oasis of booze and babes in a dry county while his wife was inside, perhaps hitting on Bill.

He should have stayed home where he belonged, with his dog that did love him, and kick her ass out when she got home, if that's what was needed. We all turned away. We left him standing alone, waiting for the next person to exit the bar.

*

Thursday, March 22, AM: The New Technology of FRP (Fibre Reinforced Plastic).
PM: Individual Presentations.
Day six also brought about new techniques for staying awake.

By day's end notes, tech sheets and binders were piling up in uneven and unread heaps on the dresser so we decided we'd be better off storing everything in the Impala's trunk. The day was a touchy feely day for new products, suggested applications and industries.

Boss Man spoke about the incentives. He was serious. He wanted action and was going to pay premiums to get what he wanted. Big bucks, even for then.

The herd was dismissed at four, most going to our private stalls to fortify ourselves before heading to the HS

*

Thursday night the lounge/bar area was much quieter than the night before. Ihor and Morticia were sitting facing each other on a small loveseat in a secluded corner, enjoying the moment. I went over to say hi.

She was wearing a loose three-quarter sheer white chiffon top with a shallow butterfly scoop front, three-quarter sleeves and a breathtaking white-on-white satin demi-bra with embroidered edging that guaranteed the attention her breasts deserved. Her skirt was short, eggshell linen, tight and accessorized with a slim kid leather belt

She was sitting crossed-legged, her skirt hoisted for comfort, I supposed, though she was wearing panties with a narrow embroidered satin front to complete the panty-bra combo. Her legs were bare, her shoes tossed aside, and they were on their second cocktail playing touchy.

She held out a hand towards me, down-turned, waist-high. I was duty-bound to kiss its warm and fragrant softness, lingering moments longer, appreciating the embroidered satin panel, inhaling her sweet scent. When I stood, unwillingly, her hand came to the side of my leg as Ihor and I exchanged a silent communiqué, his index finger extended discreetly alongside his watch. Understood. I left them alone.

At the bar I didn't see Morty at first because the woman sitting beside him was leaning into to him, blocking my view. She was sitting side-saddle, the long sloping curve of her upper thigh exposed entirely to the knee.

The woman was the antithesis of Morticia in looks, if not in style. She wore an impossibly short, low-cut, grape-coloured, wool sheath dress that scarcely touched the barstool and Morty was leaning on one elbow capitalizing on the view.

I was trying to take my time walking over, until he saw me, signalling me around to the other side. Not openly appreciating the attraction would have been rude.

She had full, not voluptuous breasts she revealed nicely with a deep, loose fitting crossover front as she leaned forward, a delicate gold locket nestled between them acting as a beacon for lost or uncertain eyes.

Her long black hair was gathered into a loose ponytail held in place with a purple ceramic barrette. Her skin was tanned from a beach or pool, not a table or casket. She wore a single ceramic bracelet, one hand fixed to her wineglass, the other fixed to Morty's arm.

He introduced me.

She was dumb, though possibly not when she was naked with her mouth full.

"Where ya'll from?"

"Montreal."

"Where's that?" she queried, her brow slightly furrowed.

"Mexico," I answered honestly.

Morty placed his glass on the bar, not chancing the sip in progress.

"Mexico?" She was thinking, perplexed, suddenly rolling her eyes, suddenly aware. "That's right. I remember."

Morty grinned, glancing upward in prayer, away from her. "How's the conference going, JT?"

"It's a long one, and getting longer. One guy's already been canned. Even I got fried the other day. Don't know how, but for a quiet guy I get into a lot of shit."

He laughed. "Ihor told us at supper. Sorry you couldn't join us. But don't sweat it. Guys like that don't last. It's one thing to be good, something else entirely to think you're good. Branes only thinks he's good, otherwise he would have answered your question."

I shrugged. "How's yours going?"

"Good. I did my time in the spotlight this morning. Desirée's up tomorrow. Neat name you guys gave her. Morticia. Think maybe I'll put it on her business cards."

"What time's her presentation? If I can, I'll pass by. I'd like to listen in."

"She'd like that. She's up last, about 1:30. She's slated for ninety minutes."

"Nervous?"

"Not her. She wrote the book. There won't be anyone leaving early. No one ever does when she's up." He sipped his drink. "By the way. Question?"

"Sure."

"What do you think about Desirée?"

"She's gorgeous. What's to think about? You have to ask?"

He didn't answer.

"We're considering staying over tomorrow night, instead of leaving after her session and getting into Macon late, leaving round lunchtime Saturday to enjoy the ride and get home fresh."

Morty's new friend sipped her drink, easing more into

her backrest, the faintest hint of a petite nipple escaping her dress. Morty leaned in, admiring the attraction, his free hand travelling across her uncovered thigh, reaching for the nape of her neck, pulling her forward, kissing her mouth, resting his glass on the bar and reaching to cup one ready breast, then the other. Time to go. Her face disappeared, not so her breasts. Really, time to go.

He came up for air; she sipped her drink, ignoring his hand.

"She likes you."

"Who likes me?"

"Desirée, she likes you. Anyway, like I was saying, we're staying over tomorrow night. So, think about it."

"Thanks, Morty. Best offer I've had for a long time. Let's see what happens." I glanced at my watch. "Got to go. You guys enjoy. See you later. Tell Morticia I'll try for tomorrow…her presentation."

They insisted I stay, but conversation in a bar with a man fondling newfound and willing breasts was awkward. Eventually they would leave together and I'd be deserted anyway. So take the high road. I left them to do their thing, heading to the HS to join other losers who weren't getting laid that night. I'd probably be with them the next night too.

*

When I strolled through the door there was less than the usual amount of smoke in the room, which was fine with me because I'd stopped smoking one year earlier. Bill was in the corner sitting in a pensive daze, looking as though he wasn't sure whether he should drink his beer or dive into it and drown himself.

Bill was well-groomed, always picture-perfect. He was the good guy in a scripted bar brawl scene who comes out with his hat and hair intact. But that night he'd finger-combed his hair too many times into an incongruous add-on to the total image.

He was from San Francisco. He was twenty-six, the southwest rep for six or seven months and Boss Man liked him. He could do no wrong. He asked all the right questions and had all the right answers. He was the kind of guy nobody likes because anybody that good must be a suck, but everybody did like Bill.

He was the all-round nice guy, and naïve. Not that he never got out much, he did. There was always a 'girl next door' for guys like Bill. Thing is, the night before he'd taken part in Fuckfest Night, had fallen in love and what he was contemplating at that moment was plain stupid. An empty glass didn't suit the occasion. I came back with a generous few fingers in my glass and a bottle for him.

"Was she the one with the light brown hair in tight curls and the pink prom dress, the one who couldn't be more than twelve?"

"She's twenty." He swallowed half the first beer. "I'm in love with her."

"Get real. She's a one-nighter. She had a few too many free drinks, you bagged her, and she's gone."

"Didn't happen that way. We're in love, together."

"The only thing you were in were her panties. That's not love, that's party time."

He looked at me, grimacing. "No. We have something special."

His elbow was glued to the arm of a cheap armchair decorated with cigarette burns and multiple layers of stains from sources known and unknown, his head half-buried in a cupped hand.

"Don't believe you. You got lucky and laid last night. Tonight's a dry spell. Boohoo."

"I do love her, a lot"

I tried a different approach, cutting to the chase without being indelicate. "Get over it. Be pragmatic. Think into the future, next week. That's how the guy she nailed last

Wednesday feels tonight. Pull your dick out of your brain. She knows what she's doing. She wants out and you're the ticket. Besides, she's twenty with a couple of kids. How bright can she be?"

She lived in the sticks with a Bubba and her kids, Bill thinking Bubba would do better living alone. He was taking her across state lines to San Francisco with her kids, believing Bubba, the police and Boss Man would all say that's okay. They'd already planned a time and place to meet. Better said, the girl had a business plan in place, waiting, probably good enough in bed to ensure success once the right guy came along. Though she certainly didn't understand or care that, as much as Boss Man might like him, Bill would lose his job.

I suggested that, if he was truly intent on abducting her, he should let her get to San Francisco on her own with the kids. Even if he paid her travel expenses he wouldn't be charged with kidnapping, just stupidity, and he would keep his job. Going home with no job and a farm girl lover with two brats, her Bubba and the cops hot on the trail, was not a good way to conclude a conference.

I did my best to convince him with the emotional capacity of the average male in his thirties, beyond which I really didn't care. I'm not my brother's keeper. I left him at midnight with an hour to kill before Morticia might, or might not, have left the room.

I went to the bar, ignoring the barman, wondering how the French maid would look naked.

*

Morticia had gone. I missed her by minutes. Ihor was spread-eagle atop his bed in his boxers, his head centred in the pillow hugging him on both sides, his face hidden under a mask of white silk and satin that rose in tiny puffs with each breath.

Lucky bastard.

*

Friday, March 23, AM: Sales Methodology.
PM: Corporate Goals, First Quarter vs. Annual Forecast.

The morning was intended to prepare us for the afternoon.

Sales methodology: Customer Needs and Customer Wants. The methodology part is finding a balance between the two with emphasis on the need to achieve Customer Satisfaction, Loyalty and, above all, repeat business under the guise of Long-term Relationships. Not new to me, but the Durcast concept was more formal than W&W's, based on structure and reason and would play an important role throughout my career.

The day began well. I felt good. Gutter Slut felt great and Bill was smiling, which I thought was a good thing. We spent the morning nodding at each other in general agreement with the pontificating that came from the podium, blindly noting squiggly lines of important details that we would later file in the trunk.

My notes were scribbled in Pittman shorthand, fun sometimes for affect, or in French or Spanish whenever those around me were prone to reading over my shoulder.

We broke for lunch at 12:45, running into overtime. Dinner most nights was à la carte with no particular schedule to follow unless otherwise specified. Lunch wasn't that way: two weeks of sneeze board-protected offerings at the public feed trough. With 149 guys hovering like stagnant air around a single buffet island, getting your daily intake wasn't an easy task. So Ihor and I often forewent the noontime offerings. We weren't missing much. By the end of each lunch hour the remaining scraps of flotsam drifting in shallow ice water were unpleasantly reminiscent of Lake Turd.

Boss Man was up at 1:45, but Morticia was up first and

we had fifteen minutes to sit in. She was a lot better than valves, actuators and the other corporate perplexities we were halfway through. Morticia began promptly at 1:30, wasting no time reciting her performance with professional expertise. She was at the front of about seventy-five funeral directors, assistants, beauticians and other end-of-the-road specialists.

Behind her was a cloth-covered table with undulating rows of bottles, jars, atomizers, swabs, applicators and brushes. On the table in front of her was a composite cadaver, coloured to imitate a recently deceased Caucasian.

She spoke confidently, her hands working on her patient with the ease of an artist. She didn't look up. She knew everyone was intent on what she was saying and doing. She not only brought expertise and novelty to the trade, she brought vitality. She wasn't dressed in the drab black of death, but in a bright white sateen cotton two-piece suit, a brilliant red scarf tucked into the daringly buttoned tapered and collarless jacket. Her nylons glimmered, her skirt falling to a hand-width above her knees, a centre slit sharing her inner thighs with the privileged few seated closest to her as she alternated between the tables.

Her shoes were also nice, I supposed, Ihor salivating until we left unnoticed at 1:43.

*

Boss Man's main concern was ours: Corporate Goals and First Quarter vs. Annual Forecast. Annual Sales Forecasts: The Ultimate Sales Bullshit. The afternoon was all about numbers: His.

As we took our seats we knew what he was doing, what he always did at the beginning of each session and after each break: 145, 146, 147, 148 and silence. Who was missing? He spoke in a whisper to a manager, whatever he said causing the man to stand and leave.

Nobody knew at that point, some wouldn't know until

the next day, but Bill was 100 km away, heading west on the I-40 with his new family. I wondered if Bill had the good sense to at least put the car rental agreement in her name. Then he could always claim that she'd kidnapped him. The meeting continued.

Boss Man praised us all for the great job we'd done. He knew full-well we would achieve the needed year-end results because we were the greatest sales force in the business, and the regional managers would spend the needed time with each of us to re-evaluate, re-build and re-submit the forecasts we presented six months earlier for the 1979 year. The dreaded forecast: The annual apoplectic experience all sales people detest until they learn to fluff it.

*

Morticia was serious the previous Wednesday night about doing a boy-girl sandwich with Ihor and I, something Ihor and I discussed during breakfast, during the session on Methodology, during lunch and during the session on Goals. She wanted two guys at once. She was in a place where she could, with someone who would let her. The proposition was tempting. Just thinking about Desirée redirected blood flow. Nevertheless I held out and spent a lot of years kicking myself.

When I got to the room near 1:30 AM the steaming water was bubbling in the spa, both robes missing from the rack by the door, two glasses side by side on the tiled floor near the jet controls, a third at water level in Ihor's hand. Morty and Desirée had left fifteen minutes earlier, Ihor claiming with a shrug there would have been room for four.

I went for a scotch, another vodka, and boxers for the Gutter Slut. Easing into the water I asked what I'd missed. He grinned, asking which time. I asked how many. He opened one hand fully, trying to loosen a few fingers of the other that was holding his drink, still with that silly grin.

I leaned against the inside rim of the acrylic mayo jar, asking more questions. Shit!

*

Saturday, March 24, AM: Goal Achievement Development Program.
PM: New Age thinking, Advanced Agenda Preparation.

GADP was intended to leave the competition behind and would one day be called Action Business Plans, not simply a matter of choosing a company or a product to sell. We had to select a client, select an application as an objective as opposed to a sale, indicate the process by which we would achieve the objective, and the audience became the adjudicators, rating each of us on Boss Man's three questions: Why that client? Why that objective? Why would that particular process lead to success? We were brain-dead long before the end of the day.

*

The day was bright, pleasantly warm. The air was calm, with not one cloud to blemish the sky. Ihor and I were at Morty's fire engine red T-Bird shaking hands, saying goodbye. They wanted to stay over one more night, but the freezer back home was filling up faster than usual. So they were heading home. Morty looked past us, we glanced over our shoulders.

She sauntered towards us with long measured strides, her hair perfectly smooth and still, not a single errant strand; her face glowing and alive, contrasting the grey-blue death masks of her profession. Her black, patent leather stiletto sandals strapped at the ankles glistened in the sun. Her simple, deep-red linen blazer dress was form-fitting with wide lapels framing the contours of her beautiful breasts, a single over-sized black button clasping the edges together where the lapels joined.

Her hands, hidden in slanted pockets, hooked in place by red-tipped thumbs, came away. She dropped them to her sides, the rounded edges of her dress reacting naughtily to the very tops of her toned, creamy-white and bare legs, shimmering golden curls playing peekaboo with the sun, with us. Now you see me, now you don't. She had an effervescent taste for life, colour and flavour, and we saw all that and more coming our way.

She stopped abruptly, cupping my face in her hands, kissing me full and hard on the mouth, leaving a trace of something fruity. She asked that I never forget her, and I never have. When she stepped toward Ihor she put her arms high around his neck, drawing him in seductively, the tapered lines of her dress riding well-passed the top of her flawless and bare ass. Ihor pressed his hands into the smooth flesh of her naked hips. Morty rolled his eyes, shaking his head with a grin, eager for the ride home.

He reached for the toggle switch that lowered the T-Bird's white canvas top while Ihor prolonged the embrace, while I stepped back to admire natural and naked beauty.

She finished with a long, suffocating kiss, twirled and walked away, releasing the single oversized button as she slid mischievously into the convertible's luscious white leather interior. Morty would certainly enjoy the next six hours of his day and the truckers working I-75 southbound from Oak Ridge to Macon would have memorable footnotes in their logbooks for that March 24th, not to mention the unsuspecting population of downtown Atlanta.

We missed lunch and the PM portion of the meeting had begun. We were late, considered MIA and in serious crap. We didn't care. One should always walk, not run to one's execution.

We were already heading in the direction of the meeting when the T-Bird's piercing horn screamed from the widening distance. Morty was waving with one hand, speeding away with Desirée standing in the well of the passenger side, facing us. A steady current of air channelled upward against the chrome-rimmed contour of the windshield hiding her face in a frantic whirlwind of blonde hair, her arms outstretched in a final goodbye, her dress gone.

We arrived relaxed and unruffled, prepared for our respective executions, prepared for Boss Man's question about what was more important than his meeting, for which we were profusely and profoundly sorry. He graciously accepted, inviting us to join him at the podium. He thought that, since we were confident enough in our abilities to forego the beginning of his meeting, we should be the first to offer up our versions of AAP.

The concept was an elaborate version of knowing where you were going and why. Boss Man didn't want us travelling over hell's half-acre on hit-and-miss missions. He wanted our calls to have purposeful results.

GADP would ensure those results in conjunction with Advanced Agenda Preparation, later referred to as Pre-Call Planning which was as simple as having a purpose derived from knowledge already gained, or knowledge required. In either case, the concept was one of constantly bringing new information and value by creating a need. The primary need being the client's need of us.

The key to that need was knowing the client's history, bringing true value, not the perception of value, developing long-term relationships based on GADP that was consultative selling and partnering for mutual gain.

We survived.

*

Ihor was out somewhere with a girl he'd met behind the scenes that week, the same girl who'd made sandwiches for us so we could escape the daily post-trough nausea. I had a feeling Sunday's sandwiches would be very good, but Saturday night I was on my own, again.

His name was Luke. He was the Barman at the hotel and

wasn't very busy. He hadn't been since our arrival, primarily because of the HS. Saturdays were usually good tip nights, but that week we were the only game in town and many of the guys either went looking for babes or flopped in the HS or their rooms with booze from the HS.

We'd exchanged one or two words over the past few days, nothing much; polite bar banter. Luke was twenty-eight, though he seemed much younger. We got into a conversation about where he would go in the world and what he would do once he left town.

We spoke about women. Luke had known a few, but then he was in the Bible belt where sisters counted as dates. He was dressed in black slacks with a black satin stripe trimming the side of each leg, a pleated long-sleeve white shirt with a collar that pinched closed with a snap-on bow tie. If he was getting out he'd have to escape soon. I asked what he was waiting for. The reply was generic, common to underachievers. He didn't know.

His business, not mine. I was killing time, checking out the waitress who came over to fill an order. She paid no particular attention to him as she placed the glasses on a tray she was balancing on rigid and brightly painted finger tips.

She wore a to-the-bum-crease short flyaway skirt with a white crinoline lining that pushed the black satin skirt away from rows of white ruffles accenting her white undies. Her black bustier top was buttoned up the back with white ruffles trimming the push-up front. She didn't have much to push up, but bigger isn't always better. Her white apron was for show, sans pockets. Her nylons were smoky grey with seams; her high heels were black leather and stayed in her locker with her uniform after her shift. They were expensive, beyond her pay scale if she were to somehow ruin them outside the bar.

I gave her twenty-five, maybe a year more. She was

cute. Her auburn hair was tied in a severe bun to complement her French maid outfit, errant curls escaping to accentuate her…je ne sais quoi.

"That's one nice ass," I said, when she was out of slapping range, "a really nice ass."

"Suppose."

"You suppose?" I was in awe. "Let me tell you, that's a spectacular ass. Just a bit too much material." I turned towards Luke. "Somebody somewhere has something nice to play with."

He nodded and shrugged in a single gesture. She was at the other end of the bar, scribbling another order. He walked over to her. A moment later she smiled directly at me, with her eyes as much as her lips. When the order was filled she came to sit beside me.

"Thanks."

"For what?"

"You know, for what you said to Luke. Thanks for that. My name's Emma-Mae."

Of course. Aren't you all? "Mine's James or JT. Mind if I call you Mae?"

"That'll be just fine." She smiled, first at me then Luke. "And I'll call you Jamie?"

Mae shared Luke's dream of escaping, with as much chance of success. She was nice, very pretty; anywhere else with a bit of attention she might have been beautiful. Either way, some lucky guy definitely had a nice piece of candy wrapped in ruffles and black satin.

She did her rounds, but the bar and lounge were mostly empty and she was never gone long. She was very tactile, which was fine with Jamie. She began touching my knee, progressing to resting her hand midway, playing with the fabric of my pant leg against the silk lining, which, by her expression, was a new sensation for her. The motion wasn't constant, just every time I said something, or she did, or

Luke.

She also seemed to like my hand kneading her thigh, which made concentrating on what Luke was saying somewhat difficult.

Say what?

"You want to come over to the house tomorrow night. Bar closes at 11:00 on Sundays, got Monday and Tuesday off. We can sit a while and talk."

"No. Thanks." But I would have gone home with Mae. "Morning comes pretty early these days, Luke. Thanks anyway."

"Come now, Jamie." She squeezed my thigh a little harder. "We don't live but ten minutes down the road."

"We?"

My hand stopped, hers didn't.

"Me and Luke, we moved in a few years back. It's not very pretty. Still got lots of work to do."

Her eyes were chocolate brown, liquid, searching mine. I tried to read Luke. Nothing.

"Sure. Why not?"

She beamed, my pant leg creasing under a squeeze of happy approval, my hand equally delighted.

*

Sunday, March 25, AM: Properties of liquids. The Fundamentals of Viscosity, Slurries, Solids and Vapour Pressure.

PM: Chemical Processing: Corrosion and Choice.

I didn't think much about Sunday night throughout the day, preoccupied with an overflow of information about various facets of the Mining and Chemical industries.

At dinner I told Ihor about the previous evening. He thought my view on double dipping and sloppy seconds was overly altruistic, that if she wanted to get laid I should accommodate her, apart from which he was disinclined to waste time convincing me. He had another evening planned with the sandwich lady, more concerned about what time I'd be back. I had no idea, assuring him I wouldn't mind if his friend was with him whenever I did so long as her ass was in the air and not his.

I went to the bar, ordered a JW Black, neat, and spoke with Luke and Mae until we left at 11:00. Mae took a few extra moments to change before joining us at their beat-up Galaxy 500. Their trailer home was in a wooded community dotted with low-cost homes. The inside was what I expected, each room with a different motif. The common theme: Circa 60s motel. What wasn't borrowed was basic, cheap or second hand. Each piece was chipped, stained or otherwise imprinted with signs of long-term abuse.

The bathroom fixtures were shiny, inexpensive; the dollar-store shower curtain torn at several hook points. The bedroom was filled with open suitcases that probably no longer locked, the clothes inside neatly arranged. They had no dresser. A lamp sat on the floor, inside its shade not under. The rust-coloured throw covering the double bed was bowled in the middle and the pillows were wrapped into its queen-size excess. On the corner of the bed was an ensemble of white and pale blue cotton with matching panties that she'd laid out neatly sometime before Mae left for work.

I supposed they were either her only or her best baby dolls. Luke didn't seem the type to buy his woman silk, or a reason for his woman *to* wear silk.

The sofa in the living room made a noise when I sat, the weight of my body forcing dormant air through microscopic punctures along the ribbing. The other seat was the same burnt orange in 60s vinyl. The table was brown, stained with countless rings from countless glasses at the same 60s motel. A single lamp stood in the corner, dim light masking other details. The kitchen was a row of cabinets with a sink and counter framed by a fridge and stove.

Luke walked across to the veneered cabinets facing directly into the living room. She went to the bathroom, the first door down the very short hallway. The shower began running right away, the path of light coming from the private room remained bright.

Luke came with drinks when the shower stopped. Seems like Luke was a choreographer. I took the glass he offered me, watching shadows dancing in the hallway between us and the bathroom.

The shadows grew shorter, though no less defined. From his vantage in the chair Luke had a perfect view of Mae standing naked, drying herself mere steps from the corner. I had a good idea what else she was doing by Luke's mesmerized gaze. She was teasing him, taunting him. All I had to do was lean forward and put my drink on the table to see for myself that she was as pretty in the nude as I'd imagined. I didn't. They were having a bit of fun. Good for them.

She tiptoed into the bedroom in direct line with Luke's view. He was smiling. As was I, ignoring my drink, surprised when she padded into the living room shaking her hair into a carrousel of damp tresses that were dark against the fresh pink of her skin. She wasn't wearing the baby dolls. She was in a green sleep shirt, short and trimmed with ribbon, the top few buttons left open to show the swell of her breasts which were decidedly deserving of my attention. She reached for her glass, sitting beside me, crossing her legs, placing one hand in her lap, the one holding her drink, the other in my lap.

We all raised our glasses in a toast. I was looking into a glass with 3-fingers of clear liquid and Johnnie Walker wasn't clear. I knew that much.

"A home brew," he answered, "made it myself." He put his nose to the rim. "Best one yet. Go ahead. Won't bite. Might kick a bit."

No One to Tell

"You first," I insisted, half smiling, half serious.

He swallowed a substantial portion, shivered, smiled, and said, "Still see you just fine."

Mae giggled, patting my leg, squeezing. She sipped less enthusiastically. I followed suit, fairly convinced I wouldn't go blind.

We spoke about everything they wanted to do, places they wanted to see, where they wanted to work. She came from Nashville where they met a few years earlier while studying at Bartending School. After graduation they moved to Fairfield Glade, beginning their dead-end careers in the hotel lounge. They had a new house hidden in the woods that would soon become an old trailer, an old car that would get older, and I asked why. Why not an apartment in the city?

Their plan was to get out, get married, and move on. The trailer home was cheaper than renting and would generate profit when they sold sometime, whenever that might be. I wasn't convinced. To me, Emma-Mae would soon become Mamma-Mae, and Granny-Mae. Luke would stay Luke and never change. They would never leave Tennessee, never fit in to a big city. They would never recover from Small Town fever.

But that night they were having a little fun with someone they would never see again, someone who wouldn't judge or kiss and tell. I felt like an overbearing insurance agent sitting in my suit and tie, selling two kids something they couldn't afford. Luke was still in his bar outfit and when he got up for another three-fingered round I squirmed from my jacket and tie. Mae slid to where her head rested on a cushion against the squared arm of the sofa. Her ass was snugly pressed against one side of my legs, her feet on the other. One of my hands went naturally to her stomach, a centimetre from hers. The other came to rest atop her knees, midway against my chest.

No One to Tell

Luke came in smiling at Mae. She took her drink, sipping. I took mine in the knee hand. Luke sat to continue the conversation while I was moving my hand over her cotton shirt close to where the flounced hem had bunched, feeling for a waistband. Nothing. Little naughty and cute Emma- Mae smiled. I smiled. Luke drank his homemade brew.

When I stood to use the bathroom she raised her legs, pulling back her knees. Our father who art in Heaven, and while I was gone I didn't have to imagine what was going on in the living room. Luke was in the kitchen for thirds, placing them when I got back to her welcoming legs that she raised once again and strategically lowered. Her eyes were closed, dreamily, not sleepily, her lips curved in peaceful contentment: One part booze, one part contentment. Her legs swayed away from me, one slightly parted from the other. I wondered when Luke would doze off, or go to bed and leave us together on the sofa.

He was still dressed as a bartender.

I'm not sure when 3-fingers of moonshine became six or when six became nine, but 11:00 became one, then two, and Luke finally surrendered to the day. Not so Mae. She was wide awake, her knees parting, closing.

The squeezing motion of bare, warm and supple thighs against my hand felt erotic, locking my hand against the moist warmth of auburn curls. Her sigh was deep, a guttural purr. Her hair was humid, her body fluctuating between relaxed and rigid. She was indifferent to Luke sleeping so close to her, or enjoyed that he was as her hips suddenly raised, her thighs clamping more tightly against my hand.

She sank into the sofa, her drink untouched on the floor, the fourth, fifth and sixth buttons undone. Bare breasts, a naked woman, silky pubic hair, arousing scent: a rock and a hard place.

The thing about home brew is that all physical and

No One to Tell

apparent evidence is gone by morning and well-being is restored, but you have to wait until morning. I had to go. I would have stayed if Luke had gone to bed, but he was slouched in front of us which was a little too freaky.

Mae cupped her breasts, her body undulating. Our eyes locked. Not a good thing. She'd reached her point of no return. She didn't care, still trapping my hand between her thighs. I knew how she felt, what she was feeling. Both of us, lost souls searching. Searching for what?

The rock was this: I wanted to stay, to play out her fantasy, but that fantasy would one day return to haunt her. Sexual pleasure is ephemeral. She wasn't like the women who came for the Wednesday Fuckfest. She was at once innocent and lost. The hard place was this: Leaving her, extricating my hand, her scent, from between her legs, would humiliate her. She was young, naïve, living a fantasy.

I cupped one breast, lingering. Her skin was warm, moist. I cupped the other, pinching gently. She smiled; I smiled.

I rolled her onto her side, her front, kneading her buttocks, massaging her back, pushing her crumpled sleep shirt to her shoulders. So near, yet so far. She was cute, of course, appealing. She was captivating, mesmerizing. She had been throughout the entire evening and not due to Luke's brew. Her moan told me she felt good. She wanted more, likely as not unaware or not believing that she deserved more than Luke, my hands coming away smoothly, reluctantly.

She rolled onto her back, stretching, ignoring her open shirt. She wanted me to see her, to enjoy her, remember her. Ditto. She wanted to see what was in my eyes. I stood, with Mae in my arms, easing her to her feet.

She shrugged away her shirt, taking both my hands, guiding them to her breasts, pressing her hands against mine. Then she hugged me, whispering. She wanted me to kiss her. I did.

Then I whispered. I told her to leave, soon, to run somewhere far away without him and never look back. She didn't seem surprised.

We kissed again. She sprang. I'd never had legs or arms wrapped around me that tightly, or a nicer ass in my hands. I set her down, eventually, reaching for her shirt, dressing her reluctantly one through six buttons before she woke Luke, Mae and I standing in front of him.

He shrugged, rubbed his face red, and got up to find his keys before heading outside, half surprised, I believe, that his girlfriend wasn't sprawled naked on the floor. I suggested that Mae stay in where she'd be warm, cozy. But she insisted on coming outside.

The night was black as pitch, eerie. The trees were barely visible. Rustling leaves heard, not seen. The drive was a short one on a deserted country road. No problema, amigo. We were living the 70s to the fullest. Or I might have, if he'd gone to bed.

Luke got into the driver's side quietly as Mae gave me a long, crushing goodbye, the luminosity from the Galaxy's red brake lights bathing us in a sad afterglow. I felt badly for her. I could have easily tried out their droopy bed with her, but some situations are better left to the imagination than to memory and the sorrow in her eyes at that moment was perfect. She had deeper insight than Luke. Deep down, she knew. I knew. She was leaving. She kissed me and told me so. I believed her.

Luke would one day wake to see, not what he was, but what he wasn't. He'd be a Bubba on the outside, kicking gravel. Mae would be somewhere better, someday soon, just not on a Wednesday night.

I slid into the passenger side as the red glow was cancelled by the harsh white of the high beams spreading out from the obscured vehicle approaching us from behind, the gravel driveway groaning under the new weight.

"Evenin' Luke, evenin' Emma-Mae."

Luke was already out of the car. Not me, turning in my seat to see the flashing blue dome lights. Shit! Cops, booze and a broken-down Ford. Luke was going to jail. Maybe I would spend the night with Mae.

"Got the late shift, Carl?" Luke said, walking to the rear of the car where the local cop was leaning on the quarter panel.

No answer.

"Pretty late, Luke. You been havin' a party? Looks like. Don't think I need my dog to tell me there's been some drinkin'." He peered through the rear window, seeing me, speaking a little more loudly. "Good evenin'. Ya'll from down the road?"

"Sure am," I called out from the window.

"Been partyin' with Luke and Emma-Mae."

It wasn't a question, so I didn't answer. I got out. When speaking with a cop, less is more. Though Luke and Mae weren't worried or upset.

"Just driving Jamie here to the hotel, Carl. That's all."

"Don't have to bother. Goin' that way myself. Be glad to drop him off."

Luke got a slap on the back from Carl and was ordered into the house with Mae. I was ordered into the cruiser with an open hand indicating that I get in from the other side. I went to get into the back.

"Nah. Git in the front. It's not like anyone's workin'. With the missus bein' gone away for a bit, just cruisin' round when sleep don't come."

Carl was something to lay eyes on. From top to bottom, all 2, 2 metres were pure County Sheriff. He had a full head of moon-coloured hair, a barrel chest that gave the impression of being armoured under his black shirt and tie that blended eerily with the black pre-dawn sky. His belt buckle was coated in black leather and the multiple leather pouches were black. The single attraction that caught my attention was the metallic seam separating the ivory grips of his .357 emitting its own shine. The thing was imposing, to me. On him the gun looked small, much of it buried in the custom holster that had the look of being oiled and treated to conform snugly to the weapon and not simply hold it.

His knees came close to the steering wheel with no real room to move. The spit and polish shoes lost in the darkness near the pedals. His billy club was between us, pointing at the single dark barrel of the .16 gauge shotgun locked into its mount, its kick release at Carl's foot.

We were on a first name basis by the time we backed out from the driveway. The ten minutes went quickly, speaking about everything but shoptalk; not his, not mine.

"Carl. Got a question." I was looking at the .357.

"Nope. Never."

"Nope, never what?"

"Never shot no one," he answered.

"That's good for them, but that's not my question." I went on.

"Sorry. Usually is everyone's first question. Normal I guess. What's yours?"

"Two hands or one." I said simply.

"Two. Kicks like a mule first time. Second time too."

"Must be heavy."

He eased off the road, not really swerving, but I wasn't expecting the manoeuvre so the effect was the same. "What's up?"

The lights of a dozen or so hotel rooms showed through the darkness as distant patches. We'd just turned onto the hotel grounds when we came to a stop. Carl's hand went to meet the barrel of the freed shotgun in a blur, reacting to the quick release.

No One to Tell

"Looks like a good enough place. Let's go." Then he just got out, which was, to say the least, a complete brain fuck at 3:15 in the morning. I sort of thought I'd be better off in bed with Mae, with Luke in jail. Anyway, I got out. Like I had a choice.

Carl said, "This side, from behind, mind you," the fifty thousand-candle spotlight turning black into greens and browns.

The .16 gauge was in Carl's left hand, his right going for the .357, thumbing the leather snap. The weapon came out in one fluid motion into his hand and reversed, pointing at me.

"Ain't that heavy. Kicks like a mule, mind."

Holy shit! H-o-l-y s-h-i-t! "You serious?"

"Sure thing. I can tell ya'll, but that don't mean ya'll gonna know. This way ya'll will."

"Shoot it?" I verified.

"It's a gun, boy. Ain't no good for letter writin'."

I nodded over to the shotgun, "You're using that one?"

"Nope. Just holdin' it. Kinda ready like." He stepped back, to the side. "Feet apart, and ya'll might want to brace up against the car. Fix. Fire. Hold. Mind the kick."

"What do I aim at?"

"Don't much matter long as you're facin' that way and ya'll shoot before my battery dies out."

I fired. Holy shit! I was in the dark of Red Neck County woods near 3:30, standing beside an armed County Sheriff, holding his weapon and taking out innocent trees or whatever else was in the way and too small to see. I shot off five rounds, nearly taking off my face with the first recoil, taking about five minutes in all, enjoying the moment. Best of all: I was doing it. Worst of all: No one would ever believe me. I hadn't noticed, but the quilt work of light behind us had brightened, though I doubt Carl would have cared even if he'd noticed.

No One to Tell

I put the gun gently and with reverence on the hood of the jet-black Ford, backing away. Carl took it up like a toy, holstered it, raised the .16 gauge and fired, ripping a branch the size of my leg from a tree.

"Got to try them every so often or ya just won't know. Ain't no good if ya don't know." One more. Boom. Another. Boom. "Think we should go before we get arrested." He laughed. Boom. One more. Boom.

"That wouldn't be such a bad idea, Carl. At least I'd get out of a meeting tomorrow with my buddy Branes. I'm on his shitlist."

"We all got a price to pay, suppose. Don't know a Branes. He from around here?"

"Knoxville, but he spends a lot of time in the area. Hey, how's about a night in jail?"

"What's the first name?"

I didn't have to think about that one. "Shitfor."

He coughed a laugh. "I'd like to oblige, really would. But ya'll ain't done nothin' wrong as I can see and I'm the only one does any arrestin'." He paused. "Well, Burt does a bit, not much."

In the car he was still chuckling hard. Monday would be a day to remember, beginning with most people still sleeping while others peered out from darkened windows at the furious sparks of blue lights flickering through the woods in the distance.

Carl left me some distance from the main reception area.

The lobby of any hotel at that time of day is a lonely, unwelcoming place and the night auditors were probably working over the day's receipts somewhere in the back when I went unnoticed through the deserted and dimly lit space.

I was in our room near four, three hours before meeting a brand new day; but I didn't sleep and neither did Ihor. There was too much to say and hear.

*

Monday, March 26, AM: Tip speed Calculations, Capacities.

PM: Motor Data: Enclosures, Speeds, Currents, and Conversions.

Eight o'clock on day eleven came too early. Everyone was feeling the strain and stress of excess information, testing, food, booze, travel and thinking. Branes was up first boring us into a comatose state with tip speeds, RPMs and impellers.

A break was scheduled for 10:00 and we were in overtime at 10:45, Branes incredibly adept at numbing our minds. Guys were reshaping their eyes, pulling at their loose neck skin, pulling at earlobes and scratching. He was intellectually lethal.

I had two reasons for sitting as far back as I could that morning. Branes was one.

Carl's 2, 2 metres dressed in a black uniform and Smoky the Bear hat were a tight fit in the double doorframe. He stood like a silent and ominous symbol of authority; his eyes scanning the meeting room through silver aviator glasses. Nice touch.

Boss Man looked at him, then Branes. Branes clearing his throat, sticking out his chin with an exaggerated nod in the direction of the door to get Carl's attention. Carl stood his ground, saying nothing. No one said anything; everyone just watched.

Ihor's hands were clasped over his mouth. "This is too fucking wild. You are definitely fucking with fire."

Ihor had believed me about Carl but, seeing the cop, I could tell his mind was racing to imagine us in the woods a few hours earlier. One of the corporate cronies near the door got up and went to Carl to ask obvious questions. The sheriff whispered a few words before the man searched the room, pointing at me.

No One to Tell

There was a lot of talk that morning about the gunshots during a police shootout near the motel with robbers or druggies or rednecks or whatever, the number of cars and cops varying with the number of people talking. The few who'd been near their windows about 3:30 added their input, the ones who'd been sleeping added theirs as the crime worsened and the number of shots fired escalated to forty or fifty. I loved it.

Carl meandered casually between the tables like a big black wall, his mirrored eyes reflecting a miniature image of everything is his path. His right hand was on his hip, the thumb of his left hooked into the leather sling of his billy club. I wasn't laughing. This was serious. Serious enough for Ihor to slide back his chair to give room. He wanted to piss himself, but laughing would ruin my day.

Carl came in from the side of the table that was open, placing me between him and the corner wall. He hovered over me, shrouding me entirely from everyone's view. He was threatening, even for me, and I was innocent. I didn't do anything. That's what I told him. He whispered something near my ear and stood straight. I remained still, staring into my note pad. He hovered over me again, putting a hand on my shoulder. He wasn't asking.

I stood. Our movement seemed choreographed to no one and with one fluid motion he brought the stainless steel bracelets from his leather pouch to my wrists, locking them together. He was ignoring the thespian gypsy in the background, not responding to Ihor's nonchalant and caustic questions. He was preoccupied with his one hand at my elbow, the other pulling at the back of my chair. I scanned the room, my eyes locking onto Branes at the podium whose expression was pretty much conveying "you're fucked," or words to that affect.

Walking towards the exit I glanced over my shoulder at Ihor, looking plaintive, then again at the podium, completely satisfied with what I saw on Branes' face. We went through the double portal non-stop, maintaining the cop's pace through the lobby and out to the big black four-door with blue working lights.

The handcuffs were tight. They didn't feel good. I don't like shackles or restraints, not even soft, fluffy ones. Feeling the steel on my wrists was strangely unsettling and for the briefest instant I turned serious and held them up to Carl. He shook his head and said to get in the car; this time in the back. The pointed hat was tossed on the front passenger side, the gearshift clicked and we disappeared from gaping eyes ahead of a curtain of dust and blue lights.

We came to a stop at the back, at the entrance nearest my room. Carl got out to open the door for me. He was chuckling, the way one would expect. Guys like him never burst a gut. I tried thanking him, but he'd had as much fun as me. We spoke for a few minutes, neither of us in a hurry. I told him about my impending departure from the company, my thing about having the last word. We shook hands, said goodbye and he promised to stop in to see Luke and Mae for me later in the day.

I avoided the coffee break and spent those minutes in our room with Ihor, pissing ourselves. When the meeting started up again I was at my table in the conference room, sitting with Ihor, ignoring 148 guys who were answering their own questions instead of asking me.

Branes was at the podium for the second session. He glared straight at me. I knew he was thinking, "You're fucked." That's all he ever thought when he saw me. I smiled past him to where Mr. Fredericks was shaking his extended index finger at me. I smiled at him; what else could I do? No surprise. His fingers folded into a fist and his thumb came up. He had the biggest grin on his face I'd seen since telling him about the kid puking on me. Everyone except Branes saw him.

I sat back to half-listen and not take notes. Neither did anyone else.

*

We had five more days and nights. Monday night I understood why Luke and Mae weren't working. The bar was dead quiet. The HS had a few serious poker games going on and onlookers weren't welcome. Four of us were in the parking lot stretched out on the hoods of two cars facing each other; when I could easily have been stretched out over Mae. We were taking turns getting the few drinks that kept the part-time bartender busy, so he was tipping the bottle a little bit more in our favour than Luke might.

We were talking about Bill's new family, the guy who got canned for sleeping and Branes until serious swearing and screaming began happening in a room a few metres from us, whose bay window was scattered in shards around the bed that came through it, occupant included.

The landing wasn't perfect. One side of the headboard wouldn't let go of the window frame and the mattress left half the bed frame exposed. The sheets were intact and the pillows were childish weapons against the guy refusing to leave the bed. He was adamant, even as Boss Man marched closer.

This wouldn't be good. He was with the hotel manager and suddenly the partiers weren't having fun. Mr. Fredericks was shaking his head in agreement to whatever the hotel manager was saying. When the manager left the row of solemn faces along the outer wall became a row of bobbing puppet heads, all sorry, all agreeing to a punishment we hadn't overheard. Then he turned to us and bellowed. "And that means you!"

Say what? We weren't certain what he meant by that, fairly certain he didn't mean we should stay sitting on the cars, drinking and getting pissed. We slid to the ground and walked the other way. Thing is, the bar was behind us now, behind him.

We chanced to glance over our shoulders. The guy was still looking up at Boss Man from under the covers of the twisted bed. We kept walking. We had our own problems, one of the four reminding the others of a personal reserve. Someone we'd seen taking booze from the HS.

He was an old timer. The only one who could tell Boss Man he wouldn't share a room. The light was on and we knew he was in there. We pounded on the door, softly. He answered; swearing curses until he finally gave in. He'd been in bed reading and watching TV. He was buck-ass naked and swearing as he walked to the bed and crawled under the covers as he blew a long and loud wetness into the air that wasn't the first and not the last.

We were adamant. We made our mission clear to Theo who was born the year before God. The bar was off limits. Boss Man was lurking. HS was a dangerous place, and missing a bottle of scotch that we knew about and wanted.

The scene was comical, from the netherworld. His feet were first to come from under the jumbled bedcover to dangle before finding the floor. They were oddly shaped, disproportionate to the bowed and hairless legs they attached to at their protruding ankles; blue bulging veins wound their way to twisted toes capped with gnarled and thick yellow nails.

The head of his shrunken penis was a pelvic eye amidst a bushy afro, crushed under the bulbous belly that followed, his purple and hairless scrotum hanging like a sack of marbles over the side of the bed before swinging to and fro as he found his footing.

Gravity took over, everything dropping between bowed legs as he fell forward to open the dresser drawer where the bottle was hidden, bracing himself with one hand against the littered surface, his feet wide apart for balance. His legs, bent by the weight of a shapeless and ponderous gut, or naturally occurring from the unkindness of childbirth, were goalposts for his balls that hung between spotted knees as though ready for a game of croquet. His pancake ass completed the look, lacking sufficient meat to conceal a cluster of thrombotic, purple prunes clinging to their shrivelled orifice.

The man was a troll: A warped story-tale ogre with sagging jowls from years of bottled abuse and a swollen, plum-stained and pockmarked nose nurtured by good living or bad. His short spindly arms led to stubby hands and thick fingers that had greyish-blue veins dotted with clots running to their tips and he offered to pour.

We filled our glasses and left.

*

Tuesday, March 27, AM: Buses to Knoxville
    PM: Hands-on Workshop at the Turbine Plant.
    Dinner: Attendance required. (Come as you are)
    Another dinner with Branes.
    Knox. Knox.
    Who's there?

No one, they've all died of boredom and the only way I'd be going to Branes' garden feed was if I could stick a skew up his ass and have a weenie roast. What was with the guy that he needed us to see his house again, or for his neighbours to see the huge tour buses? The tour buses pulled out of the hotel parking lot at 6:00 PM, turning left onto the I-40 eastbound that would take them to the 640 and Valley View Drive. We turned right.

Our absence would be noticed. No problem, when you're with a gypsy.

*

Redneck bars are to regular bars what grits are to real food. We came off the road in front of a long brown, single storey, slatted building that was broken by one open door and a dull yellow static neon sign that wasn't blinking.

No One to Tell

Some down-home boys were on the deck leading to the door. Some were wearing hats, all were wearing belts.

I put the Impala into an unmarked spot and we got out, not having a real good feeling in my gut. He was going in and didn't hear me. He was a gypsy with a death wish, and I followed: an idiot with a death wish. They looked at us going through the door, at the only vehicle that wasn't a truck. We didn't look the part, but I suppose cords and sweaters were better than suits and ties. Maybe they felt sorry for us.

Inside the bar was as long as the building, with about fifty guys lined in an even row of worn hats, unpolished boots on the floor, most decorated with white stitching, and their pointed twins welded to a narrow brass bar. The lights weren't low. The place was lit up like a sunny day. Couples were dancing, some boy-girl, others girl-girl. Two pool tables were laden with quarters, bar tables laden with beer bottles empty and full. The music was blasting from four corners with foot stompin' tunes from the Good Ole Boy Collection of hurtin' this and hurtin' that.

Ihor nudged his way into the row of elbows and chequered shirts to order beers. Ihor had real big cojones.

"What beer do you want?" he asked.

"The kind he's just given you," I answered, seeing the possibly clean draft glasses dripping foam from the top that Billy-Bob pushed toward the edge. He was huge with coveralls that touched the bar and the counter behind him at the same time. His beard and moustache concealed his mouth, his nose, most of his face. The open collar of the requisite chequered shirt overflowed the sides of the coveralls, his black-haired bear paws covering most of my glass. His brother, Billy-Bob, at the other end, was his twin. What kind of female spawns that kind of thing, I wondered?

Redneck bars are where girls wear little short jean skirts over little white panties studded with little glass beads or little silver spangles that cover their little white bums. It's where men wear wide and heavy leather belts with big thick and heavy buckles studded with bigger glass beads and somebody's teeth from nights past, when someone chanced to peek at the smaller glass beads on little white panties covering little white bums. Little white bums are the only bums in the bars of Red Neck County.

Our Father who art in heaven; we're just two white-collar geeks in town for the night. Please don't let them kick the crap out of us for ordering drinks they don't think we should have or because we might take away two of their women. The women were wearing short, tight and pre-washed blue denim skirts, stiff white shirts and blouses with their collars positioned upward, black or red bras peeking out past undone buttons. Others opted to flash their wares with short and loose cotton dresses, with bare legs and mid-calf cowboy boots or bobby socks and sneakers.

Don't worry. Just look straight ahead when anyone passes by, especially a woman. Or better yet, close your eyes. Being in a place like that to pick up women was like going a fine restaurant with your lips stapled shut. Ihor went to one of the pool tables, putting a quarter on the edge. Some guy looked at it, then at Ihor. He picked up the quarter and put it in his pocket without giving Ihor a second glance. Message received and understood. I was gone. Ihor could die alone.

We arrived at the hotel long before the tour buses, by which time we were well-ensconced in the HS. We'd phoned a local garage to come and repair the two flattened tires on the Impala that sat useless in the bar's parking lot. We did try, we explained, to catch up with the buses, but they came too late. What choice did we have?

Boss Man knew better, despite the receipt.

*

Wednesday, March 28, AM: Multi-stage and High Pressure Services.

PM: Vertical Turbines, Corrosive & Erosive Applications

The day was full of low to high capacity, low to high headwater, high pressure, boiler feeds, and reverse osmosis. Fun Stuff. 4:57, 4:58, 4:59, HS and a night in a hotel bar which is safer than other bars, especially when you're responsible for a company-supplied vehicle, I was reminded.

A bunch of us were doing what sales reps always do: We were talking about sales managers, unfair quotas and the girls in the bar who loved us for our expense accounts.

She'd been sitting on the same stool throughout the evening, the constant object of our attention. We were paying for some of her drinks. Others were as well. Not because she was pretty, she wasn't. And not because she was available, which she was. We felt sorry for her, wondering who would finally feel desperate enough to sit with her.

We weren't sitting directly with any of the big boys, but they weren't very far away and bosses all have one thing is common: Mental notes held in reserve until needed.

He was talking like the rest of us at first, drinking like the rest of us, but before the evening was anywhere near over he was getting louder and more expert regarding every possible phase of management. The mental notes began. He was absolutely pissed to the gills and not all the booze he swallowed had leeched into his bloodstream. His roomie, Gutter Slut and I got him out with minimal ceremony, leaving behind someone to protect our table and our booze from marauding waitresses. We left him in his shorts on the bed, breathing and babbling, unaware he was doing either.

She hadn't gone, and we weren't paying much attention to her, not since cutting off her free drinks. Suddenly we were. The bosses had gone, as all bosses should, and she was at the bar trying to drink from one of those cheap bar-type lanterns that no longer had a candle burning in it, thinking she was drinking booze from a glass.

She was severely drunk, off the scale. She had nowhere to go, nowhere to stay. We didn't think to ask. Didn't need to. She began bartering for a place to stay, a place to spend the night, but there were no takers. She had all the right stuff in all the right places, but she was a double-bagger. Her fault, we assumed. What use was a nice body topped with a face scarred by life's many abuses?

Even so, she needed a place to stay and we had a place. We were serving humanity, helping another human being which made us feel good.

We had a plan.

The drunken know-it-all was sprawled across his bed in his shorts, booze still seeping into his bloodstream and oblivious to the world when we crept in, flipping the bathroom light switch for minimal lighting. The woman, we never did know her name, went into the bathroom, closing the door, which was good because she was talking too much and we had work to do.

When she did come into the bedroom she was naked, ready to party. That, we did not expect. She tried to play, but she wasn't sexy. Her face was a deterrent. She was also too drunk and we were busy. We put her in a cushioned chair so she wouldn't fall and whispered for her to be quiet. Very soon she fell asleep and we continued with our mission.

The room was crowded, three of us working diligently around two insensate and uncooperative bodies. Though we did check on her occasionally to see whether she was breathing, and because she was naked. She'd already crossed the threshold into her thirties with everything in the right place below her invisible neckline, though her skin was too white, her hair an unreal red, better suited to a cheap car. Her breasts weren't huge, but still perky and proud, prouder than her. Her features were muted in the half-light which gave her slim frame a faux-youthful look. I supposed her stomach was flat from dietary neglect, not from time at the gym, and she was groomed in an era when only strippers enhanced their appeal that particular way.

I wondered if she'd ever stripped for money. Probably, though not shedding silk or satin. She wasn't a hooker, I knew that. I'd met too many of them in earlier times when I thought social work might be my thing. I liked most of them. Who was I to judge? The difference between prostitutes here and now and German or Dutch Call Girls is about 100K per annum, social approbation and work permits.

We're the narrow, self-righteous thinkers believing the natural order of things is a crime.

In any event, whoever and whatever she was then, I felt sorry for her. I felt sorry about her face. Perhaps with another one her life would have been better, perhaps in the arms of a passionate lover and not in a room with three men and the shell of another. At least she was warm.

We didn't stay long. We finished what we'd come to do. We were leaving, our arms overflowing with sheets, blankets, pillowcases, his clothes and suitcases. The drapes, towels and bathmat also went as part of the spoils, though we left the sun curtains.

We turned our attention to the woman. She was slouched with her feet apart, her arms dangling over the chair, her chin pressed into her chest. Ihor took one arm, I took the other. The roomie hooked his hands under her knees. He drew the short stick. She was wafer-light. New friends naked and curled into each other on a mattress, not aware nor caring that eight AM was ticking its way closer and closer toward their wake up call.

We left her clothes on the bathroom floor where they lay: Shorts and a halter top with red shoes that matched her hair. Nothing else.

We did, however, empty the guy's wallet into her purse, mostly twenties, adding a few of our own.

We each took a last look, closing the door behind us.

*

Thursday, March 29, AM: Motivational Presentations.
Lunch: Boxed.
PM: Testing for all personnel in split groups.
Departure: 4:30 PM.
Late Night Poker: Amateurs Not Allowed.

The buses would depart on time for Dayton, Ohio.

As always eight o'clock came early. Be there, or else, irrespective of sore heads and threatening stomachs. He wasn't, particularly on Motivation Day. What was he thinking?

Do anything you want when you're good. If you're not good, you're a jerk. This guy was good, standing in front of us in GI Joe khaki boxer shorts, a matching undershirt and GI Joe boots. He was pasty-white, not a lover of the sun, in good shape and holding a quirt for a pointer. No laser beams back then; no PowerPoint either. He was the leader, the General; he needed all his troops, and one was missing. He was the guy who signed our cheques, Boss Man himself and eight AM was a thing of the past. So he went to find the MIA. The retrieval mission had begun and so had the countdown. Shit was nearing the fan.

The three of us smiled at each other from various points in the room. Everyone was smirking. Another public lashing, but we knew. We knew what Boss Man was walking into. It's certainly fun knowing what the boss doesn't…yet. Knock. Knock.

*

Boss Man strode into the quiet hall ten, maybe fifteen

minutes later. He wasn't smiling. Someone had stolen his moment. He wasn't pleased, probably wondering what else and when. Trailing behind him came the guy we'd put to bed, somewhat pallid, very humble, attired as though he'd dressed in a hurry. Question: Did Boss Man retrieve his suitcases as a humanitarian gesture, or did he stand there cloaked in sun drapes? We'll never know. What happened to the naked woman with the face, or how she got into his room in the first place, would remain a mystery.

Boss Man did stare down the guy's roomie, and us, as though he might have suspected us of some malevolent wrongdoing. He'd watched us taking the guy away the night before. But that was a good thing. And there we were, sitting patiently, waiting, eager to learn.

Planting his hands on the lectern, he snorted, shaking his head. He didn't know what to think, waiting for the guy to take his seat.

He began. His presentation was the best yet: two hours of good humour, nodding in agreement, not nodding in disagreement, leading into a boxed lunch and a beer. Then tests, an afternoon of proving we'd learned something, anything, and that we were good to go for one more year.

Calculations required open-book work and most of us walked out at the same time. No questions were allowed. You either knew the stuff or you didn't. Most of us survived. The HS was closed. The empty 18-wheeler was en route to Dayton.

*

The buses left at 4:30. We left at 3:45, with dispensation, this time with Frank. He had one call to make in Kentucky and we were volunteered by Boss Man, which we suspected was reprisal.

Five hundred kilometres on the I-75 north, with a stopover in Lexington where we arrived at 5:45. We could have gone for gas, deciding to wait for Frank who promised he'd only be a few minutes. We'd gas up on the highway. He took forty-five minutes to resolve the customer's issue while we waited in the blue-green, me stretched out in the front, Ihor stretched out in the back.

Frank came out in the low light of dusk, his teeth and hair cream gleaming in the frames of the car windows, bursting with pride about something we were going to hear about for the next two and a half hours. Ihor was smart. He sat in the back with his eyes closed as the blue grass of Kentucky turned black and we headed into Ohio.

The needle read ninety to where I-75 merges with the I-275, somewhere near Lakeside Park, where we stopped for gas and king-size hot dogs that tasted like the real thing. That done, we set off for the final 100K leg on the I-75. ETA Dayton: 9:30.

The night sky was clear.

Thursday night shoppers were still shopping, everyone else was at home. So the roads were ours for the ride through town. We headed onto the ramp at cruising speed to merge smoothly with the traffic until my brain started sending out alerts that all I was seeing in the side view mirror was blackness speckled with red dots, not headlights.

We were headed east on I-275 in the westbound lane, doing 130, eighty on the speedometer. Frank didn't understand metric. What saved us were the hour and the night. Frank squealed. He was somewhat of a worrier. He choked and coughed up food, causing me to say something appropriate for the occasion that had Ihor sitting up pronto. I swerved onto the soft shoulder, somewhat of a misnomer.

Frank had his hand on the crank, rolling down his window, yelling at me to stop. He was half out, ready to go, squirming, fighting against the grip Ihor had on his belt. The guy was going shitty in the pants and we didn't know whether to laugh at him or scream with him. Cars were speeding past us at a combined 260k/ph. We had two choices. One was to stop. The other would put us onto the eastbound, not talking to some state trooper.

We were travelling diagonally across the shallow dip of the median, slowing a little, bouncing a lot. Frank was half out the window screaming like his balls were burning; Ihor yelling at him to shut the fuck up, to get his ass in, Ihor bouncing off the car's roof, Frank doing likewise trapped in the window frame.

My head took a serious hit the same time my feet left the pedals, my teeth rattling when the front wheels hit a ditch or a pile of rubble. Seatbelts weren't PC in the 70s. The situation wasn't funny, but two of us were laughing hysterically, mostly at Frank slumping into his seat. I had to stop. Horns blared as we slowed: nervous drivers. Then, when our eyes dried, when Frank understood he wasn't driving, we waited for an opening and bounced onto the eastbound.

We took the first exit to stop for air and check for damage.

None. We were good to go. Ihor smacked Frank off the head, ordering him into the back while I checked the trunk to see that our neatly arranged filing system wasn't so neat. Not a big deal.

We were back on track. ETA Dayton: 9:35

The buses arrived just moments before us, confusion reigning. We drove straight to the main doors, parked, and lost no time getting to the reception desk while everyone was preoccupied with their luggage, standing to the side to avoid the fray, or waiting for instructions.

Frank went to join the confusion. No more freeloaders.

*

The TV was on for noise, our feet on one of the beds for comfort, and glasses in our hands for a toast to Desirée and Mae.

We were tired, but the night was young and our only

free time in Dayton. We didn't bother with the HS. We didn't want a crowd, smoke, or to watch serious cash exchanged in a game that had been included in the day's agenda. We went to the reception area to speak with the Bell Captain who sent us to Corby's Tavern.

The tavern was special, far from typical. Women were allowed. Ihor had found his heaven. The first floor was for drinking, light fare and dancing mostly to rock 'n roll. The bar stools were made of oak with high backs. They swivelled and had separate footrests to accommodate long and short legs. The wall behind the bar was mirrored, doubling the number of bottles. The lighting hanging from the ceiling was low-intensity pool table genre reflecting off bent heads and the shiny planked floor. Tables scattered around with no apparent formation were small and crowded. The place was alive with single women and single men who wanted single women, and couples who were single when they arrived.

I went upstairs, leaving Ihor to the scent. I ordered a JW black, neat.

Upstairs was a game room, less noisy. The bar was the same as downstairs, without stools, just a rail along the floor. Three walls were lined with inlaid game tables. The lighting and the floors were the same, but the mix and the clothes were different. Mostly men, sitting at the tables, and a few women who looked like men.

I sat at a backgammon table because I had nowhere else to sit. I'm not into leaning on bars.

I scanned the place. Sitting at a table was like putting quarters on the edge of a pool table. He sat in front of me and started lining up the grey and white disks.

He played well, the game lasting an hour or so. We refilled, lining up the disks for the second match. We began, each one confident, and somewhere into it I fell asleep. When I woke close to an hour later he was there waiting, with a different beer, the disks untouched. This guy was a serious player. I probably would have slept longer, but the urgency of nature's call exceeded my need for sleep and I followed his directions to the first floor.

The men's room smelled like a piss factory. The floor was so wet I wondered at the need for the trough or toilets. I went outside to where the car was parked. The corner was dark, out of sight, and anyone near would be doing the same thing at arm's length from the wall to avoid backsplash.

What does the shadow know? It knows I'm taking a leak on the wall. What do I know? I know the shadow is big, mean, one of Dayton's finest, and seriously lacking a sense of humour. As far as he was concerned, I'd just wet his boots and he wanted to know why, though I hadn't really wet his boots. I explained I was from Québec. I was in town on business and didn't understand what the problem was, Monsieur l'Agent. Those toilets on the inside, they were so crowded and they were so dirty, I explained. N'est pas? Eh, comment? Ah, this I did not know. I did believe that if I could do such a thing at my home, why I could not do it here, eh? I was so regretful that I was in so great trouble with him. I did excuse myself, of course. Non? Voilà.

The driver's license came out, was handed over and examined. Back then permits were paper, cheap, the size of a bus ticket. No photo ID, and mine was detailed in French. Oui, of course, this means the date of my naissance. Naissance? This is when your mother puts you out from her. Yes, oui, this is the number of months that I drive so far. Yes, I leave this Saturday. Hé, oui, I like your town, you know. Yes, it is true. The people, they are so nice to me. Oui, of course, je m'excuse, monsieur. I am so sorry, you know. No, never again. I do promise that to you.

Inside, my opponent wasn't interested in my story, a harbinger of my future. He wanted to win, but didn't, the second part of the second match lasting under an hour. He wanted a rematch. No, thank you. One AM was time to leave.

I went downstairs to find Gutter Slut who was writing napkin notes as the barman gave directions to Chez Discreet.

*

Chez Discreet was as unique as Corby's, a sophisticated telephone lounge with a subdued ambiance where strictly premium drinks were served.

The seating was plush armchairs, four to a table, and the tables were low. In the centre of each table was a period phone, suspended high over the table was a phone number. The idea was to call the number, get to know the person on the other end and, if all went well, hook-up. The drinks were expensive and the blank receipts would undergo the appropriate month-end consideration in our respective cities.

Ihor started dialling, not stopping until he found the right number, refusing to answer my question, which was: "If these women are so fantastic, how come they're here at 1:30 AM taking calls?"

The call was either the last he made or the last he could make, but she picked up and he was doing the Russian Gypsy, Gutter Slut thing. I reminded him that drinking anything pretty after 3:00 AM was highly unlikely and they were already severely disadvantaged. But the lighting was dim and he was undeterred.

Sales Meeting Math 202: 1:30 AM + two hours of drinking + one half-hour to the hotel + another half hour of prep talk and a night cap = 4:30 AM. Then comes the toss. Who gets the ugly sister? Why me? No way! Mange la merde!

Oh! He's French. And you're Russian…and a Gypsy. Can you say this? Can you say that? French sounds so romantic and Russian is so masculine. I was beyond tired, and she was pretty masculine herself...becoming more so.

These girls were too dumb to pour coffee in a doughnut shop and they weren't getting up to do the 'powder my nose' thing.

So adios, amigo. Hasta mañana por la mañana. ¿Comprendes?

The girls were enthralled. What did I say? What did I say?

Ihor understood he was taking a taxi.

I excused myself to visit the men's room, then to the car and the hotel for a private nightcap.

I woke four hours later when Ihor came through the door none the worse for wear. The man was resilient as much as he was insatiable. Or should that be incorrigible?

*

Friday, March 30, AM: Review of specific data (based on session test results).

PM: Free time.

Cocktails: 6:00 PM, Main Hall (Attendance & Jackets Required)

Dinner: 7:00 PM

Awards: 8:30 PM (Attendance Required)

We had survived to greet the last workday of the meeting when we would review all the technical points the various comprehension tests indicated were misunderstood or not clear to the group as a whole. We were given copies of the tests we'd done at the end of each session, minus the results. The day would be the shortest and the longest. Everyone wanted out. We'd reached the saturation point. We were exhausted with five hours to go and the more we looked at the clock the slower the hands moved. Till death do we part, only to rise again for the Boss' party.

*

We spent the afternoon packing, cramming our clothes around half-filled bottles from the HS. The wastepaper basket in the bathroom was filled with notes, spiral binders, copies of agendas and tests.

I'd called Monk in Montreal after lunch, confirming. Everything was set in place. I'd be phoning Boss Man from Montreal on Thursday, April 12, but he wouldn't accept the two weeks, which was perhaps another turning point in the profession.

I dressed at six o'clock, arriving for cocktails at 6:15. Once around the block: Hello, yes, thank you. What a great meeting. Excuse me. Back to the bar, then: Hello, yes, thank you. A really great meeting, thanks to you. And back to the room at 6:30.

Unexpectedly, Ihor came in a few minutes later, making my day. He had insider information. We didn't have much time, and we'd be walking in after everyone else to Boss Man's soirée.

*

The room was cavernous, seating 300 people that night. All the attendees were present, managers with their wives or girlfriends, secretaries were invited, plant supervisors, inside sales and marketing reps.

Each table sat eight, by assignment. The big wigs were sprinkled amongst the common folk, slumming, the single women distributed amongst the tables for balance. Or perhaps as a way to encourage proper decorum amongst the remaining 148 degenerates. The lights were airport-bright, not a romantic ambiance by any interpretation. Only three seats were changed at the last moment, by Ihor before he joined me in our room earlier.

The doors opened at 6:50, the invitees filing in on cue, the first few uncertain. By 7:00 confusion reigned, despite the presence of ushers verifying names and table numbers.

They filtered in through large double doors, meandering in every direction, holding their cocktails. Some let the ashes of their cigarettes fall to the royal blue cushiony carpet while others left their ember-red weeds stuck to their lips, their heads moving to and fro to avoid plumes of smoke inevitably wafting towards yellow-stained nostrils.

Finally, all were seated save the three.

The only other set of doors was straight across the huge hall, both wide open. No one was counting heads. Everyone was expected to arrive on time, be seated and ready for an evening of succulent food, fine wine and awards for the Best of This and the Best of That.

Neither Ihor nor I expected to hear our names called.

I was sitting in the lobby, seltzer water in hand, not yet ready to go in. Ihor had migrated to the other side of the hall by way of the outer corridor, unobtrusively swinging the tall panelled doors closed. No one paid attention to him as he waited.

He was the rep from Miami. At thirty-two he'd been with the company fourteen years, one of the more experienced, successful reps. Everyone liked Miami, even Ihor and I like him. He was 1, 8, not athletic, but trim, good-looking, but not outstanding, tanned everywhere but his ass to his knees.

He streaked like a bullet from the washroom where he'd been preparing himself, manning-up, so to speak, wanting, I supposed, to impress the ladies. He ran past me in a blur, cheering himself on, his arms out wide in a proud presentation of self, charging full tilt through the first set of doors, my doors. He was buck-ass naked, screaming his battle hymn "I'm the man! I *am*! I *am* the man!"

His bag of jewels was tucked in tight with cold excitement; its once arrogant guardian that he'd nurtured for temporary affect during his final moments of preparation in the washroom failing him, shrinking to anonymity from stage fright. The crowd went wild, clapping, cheering, waving and banging tabletops as he hurried his way through the serpentine path of tables toward the doorway for shelter, for his waiting robe.

Cameras were too late to flash, girls were craning for a better glimpse of the man's man and the guys were butt-slapping him or trying to. His arms flew out in a smooth motion, his palms up, aiming at the polished brass plates on either side of the near-invisible seam separating the closed doorway.

He bounced off them like an awkward and shapeless length of dazed rubber, momentarily air-borne with flailing arms and legs. He tried again, flashes capturing the routed road warrior, his battle hymn changing to: "Fuckers! Fuckers!"

I was witness to only part of the failed retreat. My job was to bar his only escape, heedless of the imploring wails for mercy. They moved, but not violently, beseechingly. He was on one side, pleading; I was on the other in tears, my ear close to the door, waiting as the clamour subsided and the hall became quiet as Boss Man stood to calm the crowd and order the dejected Olympian to his assigned seat: the vacant one directly in front of him.

Ihor and I walked in amidst a new and thunderous applause accorded to Miami as he took his seat, pulling himself close to the table. Dinner was served.

He spent the entire time from soup to dessert with his napkin as the most important part of his meal. The waitresses were commendable in their attention to his comfort and satisfaction with the meal. Would he like more water? Would he like more wine? Would he like more bread, perhaps a fresh napkin? Everyone who got up for a trip to the washroom passed by Boss Man's table, the men to slap his back, the women to lean in closer and whisper whatever.

The meal finished, digestives were served before the presentation of awards. Best margin, most sales, most sales of new equipment, most new customers, best overall performance, most initiative, etcetera. Seemingly, Ihor and I were the only ones whose names weren't called. The evening was at an end, with it the sixteen-day marathon killer conference.

To close the event Boss Man said, "Why don't all of you stand and give each other a round of applause for what was a great meeting?" A shuffling of clothes, chairs and feet responded obediently with an ensuing clatter of clapping hands as the final thunderous command of the meeting was issued through the PA system: "Miami! That means you too!"

*

Saturday, March 31, AM: Travel safely.

Perhaps too little, too late, we thought as the evacuation began.

Goodbyes were said the night before. We slept late, ordered room service and went to the pool for a good meal and a swim before our flights.

The white sparkling wine dissolved into the juice, the Danishes were tasty, the French toast was American and the coffee tasted like tea. So the good meal would have to wait.

We poured another glass of wine as a few departing reps passed by doing double takes, some with casual waves, but mostly the place was quiet and we sat discussing underwear and testicles. Ihor was wearing the usual baggy, knee-length bathing suit most Americans wear, the kind that makes swimming an extreme sport. I was wearing nylon straight-backs: Safe, light-weight, fast-drying and the boys were snug, not held captive in a mesh net.

Ihor defended the need for his boys to hang loose, free to get a good count at the end of the day. I claimed his point was moot, since, at the end of sixteen days, he likely had no sperm left, and that the only thing he ever counted was his conquests.

Besides, how do you get those things dry? How do you

stay afloat? We exchanged addresses and I promised to send him a few.

The morning flew by quickly. At 2:30 we were sitting on our luggage, leaning on our knees, toasting our time together with a neat JWB and Russian vodka. The buses had gone and the hotel was pretty well deserted, leaving the parking lot abandoned and lifeless for the two hunched over forms that stood and stretched with the false hope of rejuvenation. We were on the road one last time.

At the airport we stood staring into the trunk. The rental guy doing the return inspection peered in as well, not liking what he was seeing, as though that made a difference. We each gave him a five and walked away.

Somewhere between our respective departure gates we shook hands. There was no reason to linger. We shared a helluva two weeks and two days. Fabricated anti-climax had no place.

Ciao, Gutter Slut

*

I've worn aviator sunglasses for as long as I can remember, Ray*Bans, but I've always wanted the coveted Aviator Watch available to commercial pilots who laugh at and mock the rest of us. The time piece in question begins at 12:00 AM, losing five minutes each hour throughout a twenty-four hour cycle before resetting at the stroke of midnight. This means that by the first flight of the day the watch shows 05:30, not 6:00 like the rest of us. At 6:00 PM it tells the time as 4:30.

My flight was late, departing at 7:30, which didn't seem to bother the pilot.

One more phone call, one more drink to quietly nurse, hearing out of the blue from the guy on the stool beside me that if he looked the way I did and didn't know why, he'd go straight to the hospital. I waited seconds to answer, focused on his glass, not him. I said, "The thing is, I do know. So, fuck off." And he did.

The boarding began a general murmur of disbelieving appreciation by all. We sat, we listened, rolled away from the gate, taxied and were airborne with two stops and one flight connection. I fell asleep in the portside aisle seat of the last row to begin my recovery process. The one time I can remember sleeping onboard.

The halfway point was Philadelphia International Airport. I was the last of the disembarking passengers to leave the Jetway, searching for a phone. The carrousel stalls were located outside the gate, encircled with typically polite air travellers. I jumped in when space allowed, dialled, put a finger in one ear and kept my mouth and nose away from the receiver.

I was explaining where I was, when I should be picked up at Dorval; ETA: 00:15. Until a man was tapping my shoulder. I glared at him with a finger in the air, indicating one minute. He shook his head, tapping, trying to interrupt. I lowered the receiver to ask how I could help him.

He grinned ear to ear. "You ain't in Philly, young man. This here is Pittsburgh."

Shit! I handed him the receiver, bolting to the gate to see the Eastern attendant closing the door. I was in Pittsburgh at 8:45, not Philadelphia at 9:45. I was screwed, big-time.

No one saw me sailing through that airport, they just felt the breeze. At 8:55 I had five minutes to find them, get the paperwork done and get myself onboard. They were advised I was coming, waving me on. American saved the day, despite making it longer. The new routing would take me from Pittsburgh to Hamilton, Ottawa and on to Montreal five hours late and a pissed-off spouse.

I was landing in Hamilton after a sixteen-day journey, looking like a refugee without baggage and the Customs Agent took too long to understand the situation, which could have been because he was on night shift, or why he was on the nightshift.

My arrival in Montreal was no better where they did everything but turn my socks inside out when the Eastern rep met me with my luggage.

And, finally: Honey, I'm home.

*

I never did like and never did trust Bart. Early Saturday morning, April 07, I went to the Montreal office and worked with a purpose in Bart's office. When I finished removing all his personal and corporate information about me, my reports and forecasts, I left and American Durcast Inc. has never shown on my résumé.

Over the nine months I had increased sales by 12.8 % percent, an annually adjusted rate of 17.1%. Not bad for the new guy.

More to the point, my time with them expanded my contact base in key industries. I learned more about the sales process, the importance of planning. Most importantly, I learned more about people. Even now, so many years later, I would rather think badly of someone initially and reconsider later, than think well of somebody and get screwed. Some people might call that jaded; I prefer perceptive or intuitive.

April 12, I phoned Boss Man directly, ignoring the corporate chain of command. I thanked him sincerely for what I'd learned, and resigned.

No One to Tell

R.I.P.

I never did see the Gutter Slut again. We never stayed in touch, our short-lived friendship living on in vivid memories. I believe he remembers me when he recounts his version. Could be he's living in Macon, Georgia. I know he visited at least once, unless he broke a promise to Morticia.

Bart was unable to undo the impression he left with Boss Man the day of the run. Shortly after my departure he was recalled to the US and sent home. Michel went that same year to an inside sales position at one of the competitors where he wouldn't have to travel by air and would have more time for running. Bill was instructed to return the company vehicle. The rest can be imagined.

The Montreal office closed a few years later, unable to contend with ongoing staff migration, the product lines given over to distribution.

Desirée was for the longest time a measurement of femininity, class, elegance and sexiness to me; a Southern femme fatale par excellence, capricious and captivating. Morty was a charming Southern gent with a smooth manner and good heart. I hope they never stopped being Morty and Morticia.

Luke is probably still in Fairfield Glade with kids who are older now than I was then. I often wondered how their evening ended when Carl drove me to the hotel. What I choose to believe is that she left home very early the next day.

The woman with the unpleasant face *was* in the room when Boss Man knocked on the door in his GI Joe skivvies. At least her purse was a little fuller. Her bedmate didn't fare as well. He was court marshalled for contravening the 8:00 AM commandment, sentenced to the mediocrity of inside sales, though spared third place at the firing squad by virtue of his Regional Manager intervening.

Chapter Four
1979 - 1982

Murphy's red-faced contortions ended with the retrieval of a thin hardcover book. I don't believe the girl cared that he didn't retrieve her napkin that slid from her lap during the snack, though Murphy wasn't gay. He wasn't dressed well enough. He was simply rude, inconsiderate. Still, a young guy not checking out something that sexy violated life's natural order. Legs probably thinking what I was thinking, that he'd missed a perfect opportunity to take in the entirety of her designer and silky smooth namesakes.

Thirty minutes into the flight the wrappers were trashed. Then came the sani-wrapped and re-usable headsets, tantamount to using someone else's ear swab, though I did hold up a miniature Skyy for what I hoped was a good enough clue. Legs was fine with her Tía Maria and Murphy's face was buried in his book.

He was reading a Road Warrior book written by one of the most successful sales executives of the twentieth and 21st centuries, until someone else comes along, somebody unknown. But his picture was on the cover which meant he was an expert.

He was wearing French cuffs and a red tie, excellence personified. Ten Steps To Guaranteed Success In Sales (If You Suck Up *and* Don't Piss Off Your Boss) for $39.95, taxes extra. Or something like that. If you've read one, you've read them all, for those of us who can still turn a page.

I didn't hear her at the time. I saw her. Legs was standing, trying to. I didn't say anything. Instead we exchanged requisite in-flight smiles and I stood into the aisle, though Murphy was a little slow to catch on. Hello, Murphy. Pee-pee alert! And when he did stand he pulled hard enough on the seat in front of him to cause the man to crane his neck, then he ploughed past the guy in front of me, pushing that seat forward enough to annoy that already happy camper more than he was because he hadn't yet found a way to recline his seat.

She smiled a thank-you, squeezing past Murphy who was blocking her way while managing to invade the row behind him in order to give her enough room to break free. Murphy repeating the entire process, contorting himself into his seat. As I recall, I used the time to follow the hem of her skirt teasing her thighs barely a hand-width below her bum. Paying homage. Beautiful women are fewer and fewer, one prays not becoming extinct. They should be noticed and appreciated.

My vodka came late. Murphy ordered another beer, the lady attendant not very pleased with making a second trip when she could barely walk a straight line. The plane shuddering, groaning its way through a low ceiling of heavy, wet snow. Seconds later, a light tap on my shoulder, another requisite smile. She had nice teeth, an observation causing me to wonder why her ass couldn't have been the one in my face instead of Burger Boy's.

At that point, Murphy decided he was up next, before the beer came, lumbering along the aisle using each seat he passed as a crutch to help him arrive on time. Legs sat, straightened her skirt, fastened her seatbelt, slouched slightly, and closed her eyes to escape her surroundings. Her brow furrowed a little. She was thinking. So was I,

No One to Tell

about a Red Neck bar in Tennessee.

Murphy came back too soon; I believe specifically to spoil my view. I swear the guys in front were plotting to assassinate him as I stood to let him barge into his seat.

I remained standing, allowing the attendant to pass over his beer, but really I was letting him do his crotch and jacket thing, with one hand. His tray and beer held at forty-five degrees with the other.

The passengers in front exchanged wordless glances. They knew. I knew. Legs knew.

Murphy muttered something like "this is great stuff. The man knows what he's talking about." But my ears were plugged and Legs was Sleeping Beauty.

He thought I was interested. I wasn't. I detest 'How to' books, especially those discounted at seventy percent. The last thing I needed, or wanted from him, was a dissertation on selling. Murphy was a peddler, not a pro. Brushes and vacuums at the front door at dinnertime, that sort of thing, hawking his wares, trying to fill his quota by unloading unwanted crap on those too nice or naïve to say no.

Reading someone else's ten easy steps is a waste of time: Information in, information out. But he likely wouldn't discover that in time to save his career. Once a French-Cuff disciple for 39.95 plus taxes, always one.

Paul taught me a lot about salesmanship, discipline, product and application throughout my first three years, by osmosis. He was the boss and I was there to learn for a brief time when the word boss was a designation of achievement, not politicking. Nor was he some thirty-year-old hotshot.

All that went to hell in a basket as my career evolved. Vying, stroking and politicking would become essential to careers. Companies would no longer endure. People would become disposable, transient at best. Lifelong jobs would become intangible relics and those who succeeded were those who took ownership of their personal goals and objectives. Today's companies are mere stepping-stones along one's career path and it's up to each individual to choose which stones they step onto. Make the wrong choice and no one cares.

During that initial growth stage at W&W, I began nurturing a philosophy, a work ethic that became an integral part of me. I put myself first, my client-company second, and my employer third. Self-serving, but a logical protection against the corporate 'short-term pain, long term gain' mentality. Instead I fostered competence and value, strategic elements in sales. A reality Murphy likely would never discover.

*

Monday April 16th was workday number one at Monk Refractories, the company approaching its first anniversary of struggle for survival as a new entity in the refractory industry.

The company was a partnership insomuch as the Jesuit had borrowed money from a few people who decided that, in addition to second mortgages and loans, they would work at Monk for no money. He had three partners, including his wife who didn't count. The major partner, without whom the Jesuit would have remained preaching at W&W, was Jean-Guy. He ran the shop as a one man operation for the first year, that year becoming three.

He was a nice enough guy, if not somewhat unfamiliar with social graces. Some might say crude.

I went to lunch once with him, to a local brasserie, deciding once was enough when he decided he didn't like his meal. His steak was undercooked or overcooked or too whatever. In any event he made his feelings clear by whistling for the waiter, slamming the meat onto the floor before grinding a foot into it and spitting into the carnage. By which time I was standing, putting money onto the table and leaving.

I supposed he was in a bad mood, though, being that he wasn't lured into the fold to dine and dance, the flaw could be overlooked.

One very significant factor that helped Monk overcome competition from W&W was that Jean-Guy had been their shop manager, his resignation severely crippling them. He was good at what he did, and I only pissed him off every so often by going into the shop to complain or comment on work he'd done. For the most part, we got along. We just didn't go dancing and we certainly never again ate at the same table.

The other partner was Jacques. He migrated from pharmaceuticals to work in sales during my time at Durcast. His career change was a stretch, his transferable skills few in number, but he had cash and that's what Monk needed. Experience was secondary. He was nice enough, trying to appear significant in his newly unfurnished office; but that only works when you're noteworthy. He wasn't. He was having a rough time adapting to the rigors of industry after so much time spent with white coats and stethoscopes.

Jacques wore the same grey suit and black tie every day, which was fine with me when he wasn't beside me. We were in an era when sales people wore suits, plural. He also sported a black goatee and a moustache that gave his head a cone-like shape which he accented with black-rimmed glasses that matched his black briefcase.

Even on a sunny day Jacques looked bleak, and getting him to loosen up would be an unrewarding, long-term challenge.

Lise or Lizanne or Liette, or whatever the wife's name was, spent most of her time in the kitchen cooking Monk's lunch, washing Monk's dishes. That's what she was doing whenever I was in the office, so I had to assume she did little else beyond carrying on about the benefits of Québec separation. She was a political hippie; a French-speaking

Québécoise hippie whom I suspect wore fleur-de-lys bloomers under her multi-seasonal tie-dye peasant blouses and flower power wrap-around ankle-length skirts that never matched her open-toed sandals.

I doubt she owned a pair of nylons, though she was always pleasant, in an artificial way, always acquiescing to the wishes of a higher order: The Order of the Balding Pate.
*

I had no particular affinity for refractories. Pragmatically, the products were simply a catalyst into a wider range of industries, more so than many others, particularly in addition to my Durcast client list. What I did enjoy were my clients, most of them. The one element making Monk temporarily viable for me was recapturing Pontiac, which I had secretly negotiated with Bill some months earlier, without which I would have remained with Durcast.

Though the products and their range of applications were the epitome of Return on Investment, mine, a cash cow which was my single reason for joining Monk.

I was aware of his need to control by virtue of our previous association. He was aware of my need to do my thing without his interference. He also knew his one irritating habit made me crazy, which I'm sure he exaggerated in an effort to drive me insane. He made a snapping noise whenever his jaws came together to masticate whatever food was being processed inside his mouth, as though he possessed four extra molars.

My time with them would be love-hate at its finest, without loyalty feigned or real, my philosophy and education gained at W&W and Durcast in constant battle with Monk whose new methodology was go-go-go. Go do it; go get it; go do it again.

The rush and the pressure were on, my lack of loyalty balanced with his lack of appreciation. I was with them for the money, using them as a stepping-stone towards new frontiers and new horizons. That meant contracts, big contracts. All Monk had to do was fill them. There was no hidden agenda, we both knew. Above all, Pontiac was mine. No one else's.

I'd been to the unpretentious offices several times over the previous months, keeping tabs on their progress, initiatives, and the growth of their client base. None was as big as Pontiac, who were regrettably off limits.

Bill wasn't very happy with me leaving W&W, with me out of the equation. We had a rare synergy, though ethically I couldn't say too much and the Jesuit was under the same gag order. I did explain Monk to some extent, that I had plans to join them in the not-too-distant future. In the meantime crossing a bridge, so to speak, Bill understood, agreeing to give Monk a chance… once I was onboard.

We shook hands, wishing each other well. We'd had some good times together. On the other hand, he was pleased and somewhat amused when I strolled into his office days later as the Durcast rep. Hence the ethics.

Bill would now deal with both companies: One for any warranty work previously done, another for better pricing, quality, and service. Working with Bill and his team through the W&W and Durcast eras, I enjoyed a good deal of independence at the mill. Actually, I had a free pass. I knew the key personnel. Most often I would check in with them, do what had to be done, alone, invite them to lunch, continue my work, check in again, and leave at day's end.

We had a good relationship and soon W&W lost the business completely.

I knew Bill's maintenance and project schedules for each coming year, and I hadn't lost much during the previous nine months. In fact, he'd held off for the benefits I had sometimes alluded to during the many lunches Boss Man was financing. These were big dollar items and the business was being funnelled in my direction. Accordingly,

I was acting on my behalf, not Monk's. Monthly orders of thirty and forty K in 70's dollars were common to the alumina refractory business. Fifty to sixty K wasn't uncommon. Beyond that, well, Christmas came often.

My time at Durcast reinforced my philosophy on Sales Methodology, Business Plans and Preparation. In a word: Strategy. The positives surrounding Durcast, the formal structure of their sales culture, albeit somewhat modified, was high on my list. Requisite to the next three years.
*

Monk Refractories existed on paper well before the Jesuit left W&W. Everything was set in place to begin production on day one, though the initial orders came slowly. Their supplier was new to them and cautious. The working conditions were new, forced to contend with the 'new guy in town' fears of most customers both old and potential.

I had the same fear, which is why I joined them when they could afford me. Patrice-Alexandre and I got along well enough working together at a distance, not well enough for me to lend him money. In addition to which I would do my own thing without bullshit and be paid in full whether by cheque or from Monk's own purse.

I'd already been in all the pulp and paper mills and most of the mines in Québec and Ontario, soon to add the Maritimes, New England and New York, though my first plant visit without any hesitation was Pontiac

My first challenge: De-Monking Jacques, Jocko.
*

I was at the mines in Haliburton creating business for a new epoxy and alumina ball media compound for lining wear surfaces of vessels and casings with irregular shapes.

The mines were impressive and driving from office to office on the same private roads as off-highway 16-ton trucks, articulated and rigid loaders and haulers, was like piloting a dinghy in the New York harbour amidst ocean liners, tugs, battleships, aircraft carriers and garbage barges: an upcoming experience, albeit on a thirty-foot cruiser.

Seeing the yellow mastodon vehicles, grey with splattered slag and brown with caked on mud lumbering along precarious inclines and declines leading to narrow and well-compacted trails heightened the senses, and the gurgling in my stomach. The tires on those vehicles dwarfed the tallest man and would easily crush a midnight blue Monte Carlo.

I was hoping they'd be on their coffee break when I left. No such luck.

I stopped off for a fast supper before driving south on the 62 to the 401 that would take me home. By the time I wound my way to the main highway I was set for another coffee to keep me awake for the next 400 kilometres.

Somewhere near 9:30 on Thursday the place was typical of off-highway garage-restaurants. The tables were round, scratched beyond repair, stained, and either gum, snot, or both were stuck to the underside. The square vinyl cushions on matching chairs were torn and sticky, the coffee was served in cracked and stained coffee mugs whose handles were too thick to hold and half full or half empty with lipstick or brown smudges along the rims.

Everyone noticed when her car pulled up because we were only a half-dozen or so coffee drinkers in the place at the time. No one was eating, avoiding eventual death by clotting.

She came in through the main doors. She was wearing high-heeled leather boots that passed her knees in a wide cuff and gave her a buccaneer appearance. She was white as snow, her face speckled with red blotches. Her ultra-small tee shirt showed the shallow under swell of her breasts, only playing at covering her nipples. She'd probably flicked her reefer before coming in, but she was high on something and everyone put down his or her cup to watch the show.

No One to Tell

She was naked from her knees to her breasts, such as they were, floating around the room like they were filled with helium, which they certainly were not. She had some problems, discounting shyness and awareness, gliding along the sneeze-board covered self-serve bar, gyrating, flaunting matted and black pubic hair that resembled a used scouring pad and offering double-handed butt tours.

The owner called the cops, with no great urgency.

In the meantime she continued her performance. She stepped onto a chair and onto a tabletop where she was either gyrating provocatively or trying to regain her balance several times.

With her arms stretched out her breasts disappeared, figuratively speaking. Undeterred, she began plucking at her small and very dark nipples with the fingers of one hand while the other massaged the scouring pad; which is what the unsmiling cops first saw when they strutted in to bring her unceremoniously over one of their shoulders, pretty much cheek to cheek, while the other tried unsuccessfully to cover her with a raincoat.

Apparently they knew her. Perhaps she was a stripper having a slow night, drumming up business. Maybe she was the first frequent flyer in Belleville. Who knows? Anyway the tug of war ended at the door, neither the cops nor the manager checking to see what she might have left on the table.

Everyone went back to their cups, smirking, shaking their heads.

Gregori would have loved to see this one.

*

Jocko was having his first pulp and paper plant tour with me. Who better? He had the same protectionist outlook about his name as the Jesuit and had spent most of his first year in the shop learning about the product. Not so much that he was a slow learner, more because Patrice-Alexandre didn't want to hire another body to help Jean-guy. Besides, Jocko wasn't getting paid so what did it matter what he did? Most of their receivables were going to pay COD or net ten-day invoices from new suppliers, not shop staff.

Sadly, for Jocko, every once in a while Monk would take him on a learning visit, but I'd done some joint work with the Jesuit at W&W and the only thing Jocko had to learn was how to say "bugger off" or "foutre le camp."

We took a full day and went through the mill unescorted. Lunch came and went at the Italian restaurant that could seat four hundred, but never had more than twenty for lunch or thirty for dinner and they all came from the mill, with reps. No one joined us because the plant was in full maintenance mode and Bill had developed a coronary over the preceding year that precluded Lobster Thermidor, red wine and creamy desserts. Instead, he stayed in his office and practiced Keno for his annual trip with his wife to Vegas.

The shutdown gave us the opportunity to get into the rooftop chip cyclones, which wasn't by chance. Peering into one or being in one on the shop floor isn't the same as crawling in through an inspection port several stories high with howling winds as the unit becomes a conduit for external and internal noises and dust. Jacques didn't think much of the experience as I sat on the temporary twin planks running across the bottom of the six-metre diametre by fifteen-metre high unit to detail why I had selected one wear product over another, while he balanced himself against the sloping interior walls that were damp and smelled like cow piss.

The day wasn't over. We migrated to the elbows, walking along two fifteen-metre high by one-metre wide serrated catwalks, serrated for good footing in bad weather, which doesn't help much when you slip and take out the knees of your pants. Sorry, Jocko, but I wasn't the one who kept you locked up for a year.

Elbows often stand alone, but they can also have transitions for reduced forward flow from the elbow into smaller diametre pipelines and past the next elbow as chips or bark are blown around the mill unseen. This also serves to increase velocities and increase wear in particular patterns. At fifty K a pop, stainless steel cyclones were a precious commodity and at a fifth of the price so were elbows because there were so many more of them. All of this quickly becoming more apparent to Jocko who was increasingly anxious to take home money.

We headed over to the liquor recovery room. We didn't have to. Nothing was there for us, but they'd done it to me and I would do it to Jocko. Jacques was being initiated and the process lasted an hour. When he was sufficiently christened by the pungent fumes we made our way to the offices to ask the guys if drinks or supper was in order. They were ready, until Jocko interrupted to ask if we could just go home.

He never did learn to suck it in.

I wouldn't let him take notes. He always took too many to understand or read later and remember why he took them in the first place. He was trying hard, though he didn't have what it takes to work with certain client types: The ones with no mothers and no teeth, with missing fingers and spit cups on their desks, with no manners and no use for guys in white shirts and black ties. Jocko needed white coats and sanitation, not plants that often reek of cow piss.

Coming from pharma sales he was accustomed to joint calls every other week, having someone to answer his "but what if" and "may I" and hold his hand. Now he'd be working with people who didn't think that way. They wanted answers ASAP and they wanted good answers. Jocko was a butwhatiffer. I explained my theory to Jacques that doing something with good intention and good reason without permission is preferable to asking and being refused without reason. Or, grow some balls, Jocko.

He threw up when he got home.

*

Now that I'd given Jacques his introduction to Pulp and Paper, I was off the next week to New Hampshire and Maine. I was familiar with both states, so getting around would be easy.

Sister-in-law #1 lived in some horrible little New Hampshire town that I would bypass, quickly, more like a street: Hillbilly Lane. I never stopped in. I didn't like her, which was fine because she didn't like herself. She was obese, blaming restaurants and food producers instead of her hand-eye coordination. If she saw it, she would eat it. She also blamed motherhood. What a burden to put on your kid.

How fat? She once phoned her mother to beg that I be excluded from a family party. She'd put on such an amount of weight that she was afraid of what I would say. I can't imagine if she'd read *The Fatal Diners' Club*. I never saw her again. Imagine my grief.

She had a disgusting whiskey keg-type dog that leaked from the mouth and licked the slobber as a treat, so that I could never be certain whether the plates on the table had been washed or licked clean.

Her house was a dog-run: couches, bed, the bath, the laundry. Whenever I did visit, under duress, I was afraid of going to bed, fearful of waking dressed in dog hair, looking like the Sasquatch.

She used the smell of wet dog the way others use air freshener, but she loved dogs. She didn't care. She'd loved her other dog too: The Bichon Frise she'd taken to the shopping centre and kept in the car with the windows down, leashed to the steering wheel. The dog had fresh air and was quite comfortable until he jumped out. When she returned to the car Fido was hanged by the neck until dead against a backdrop of distressful scratches. Not a good day to Scratch and Win.

The advantage to working the New England area was the beaches and seafood restaurants. The day shifts begin early and end early, which meant I'd be at the best beaches by 4:00 to do my follow-ups and plan for the next day.

The small stuff came from New Hampshire. The plants in Maine had more impressive equipment and production figures, which is where I spent most of my time.

During my first trip to the States for Monk I booked my first night in Portsmouth, heading to the beach for supper, returning late, waking at dawn for a drive to Salem Mills outside Augusta where I would stay Tuesday. The trip took all day, stopping near Portland for a morning call and near Augusta for a PM call before getting into Waterville for dinner.

Thursday I drove the I-95 to US Pulp in Bangor, continuing on to the Lincoln mill before ending the week-long trip on Friday in Millinocket and East Millinocket.

AM was the East, PM was the big mill and both were strictly information gathering about specific applications and particular problem areas. I already had basic information from the Pulp and Paper Institute, though the meeting took a turn halfway through when more people were called in and one fellow was brought over from the sister mill in East Millinocket. Eight decision makers from two plants were ready to hear a full presentation expounding the virtues of the product, existing applications as well as good and not so good results.

I was in the right place at the right time. I'd be leaving happy. The meeting went on until six, no one accepting my offer of drinks and dinner. They were already late for dinner at home. I left them with a full array of drawings, sketches, new contact names at other mills, a tentative schedule for the next meeting, and I was on the same road heading towards Houlton for a night at the Wandlyn Inn in Woodstock before driving ten hours on Saturday to get home.

The 150 km trip took three hours due to some congestion in town, the border crossing that was always fun when working in the States, and just being tired. I was in my room, unpacked and at the restaurant by 9:30 for a fast feed, too tired to enjoy, and in my room by 10:30.

To say the least I was ecstatic about the order and had called the office from the plant, aware that even on Fridays the Jesuit would be working late at helping or annoying Jean-Guy. I had cut the call short because my side of the conversation would have sounded defensive or demanding, a different tone than the meeting I was in, so I gave the requisition number for the order, hung up and told the new clients how thrilled everyone was at home.

I didn't tell them I was pissed off to get that particular reaction from Monk, but nothing was taking away the feeling of walking out from a first call with 75K signed and sealed.

I was going to bed.

The sheets were threadbare, held together with something in addition to the warp and weft of the weave. I suspect the oils and secretions of previous visitors. The pillows were yellowed with age, underlying stains clearly visible. All that was fine, even the cigarette burns in the top woollen blanket that was balled, stiff in some places. But the hair was too much, particularly in conjunction with the yellowing butterfly shrimp stain that appeared damp.

Hair was everywhere. If the girl hadn't left as a smoothie, her friend did. Short and curly, the extent of my investigative work before calling housekeeping who didn't answer. The motel was full. Not my problem. No way was I sleeping in a feathered love nest, the lady manager not very pleased with her sudden drop in status, albeit happier than me.

Despite breakfast on the house, I never went back.

*

The crux of my meeting at the office the following Monday was simple, easy to understand: Stop bitching. I'd made reasonable promises to the client, typical of the industry as well guaranteeing a long-term relationship. So find a way. Seventy-five grand in '79 wasn't chump change, particularly coming from an influential corporation that pays on time. So, let's get it done.

*

Three months remained to endure before mid-winter of 1980 would melt away. During the winter months I continued leaving early for out of town trips, though not as early as in the spring or summer. I should have cancelled and rebooked. Hindsight. But I didn't and by 10:00 AM that Monday I was five minutes from the Vermont border and behind schedule.

The three-hour drive wasn't a lot of fun to that point, but conditions south of the border promised to improve and I was anxious to arrive. Inverse logic of the tortoise and the hare. The secondary road, normally well-travelled by truckers hauling logs to the US, had no definition. Neither did the soft shoulder, and that day I was alone.

I climbed the 30° grade to within a few metres of the summit, to a complete stop. The car was going nowhere on a fresh blanket of deepening snow. The brakes were useless, the car momentarily staying in place, easing backwards.

A car taking control is not good, so I shifted into neutral, stayed away from the brakes and hoped I could feel the lip of the road as I slid backward under the weight and momentum of the car.

I didn't. What I felt was my body shifting. That's when I braked, gently, sitting awkwardly on the side of the road with wipers clearing a line of sight with nothing to see. I knew I wasn't in the middle of the road. The better question was: How close was I to the ditch?

Crawling out was a treat. The passenger side was too iffy, too close to the ditch. Not a good thing. The driver's door, on the other hand, had snow beneath it, and road, despite a twenty degree or so angle that required a little squirming and cursing.

The flares were soon in place at the front and rear. I had thought of climbing the hill to place a few at the crest. I didn't. Instead I won a snowball fight with a tree. My first car phone wouldn't be installed for eleven years and would cost 1200 dollars. Too long to wait.

Soon after a farmer happened by. He had a tractor. He offered to hook me up and I'd be on my way in no time. I declined his generosity, because of what happened to me and Gregori while driving to Toronto in January '71, nine years and a few days earlier. The man was disappointed that I refused his good deed, however I wasn't about to deal with another chain dragging my car through the snow.

*

January 02, 1971 was an ordinary Saturday, apart from the snowstorm. I was standing in a downtown Drive Yourself office pleading along with Gregori for the best possible vehicle on the lot that needed to be transferred to Toronto. We told the lady anything and everything that sounded sincere, sweetened with honey and we got the brand new Lincoln Continental.

With papers filled out and a full tank we had thirty-six hours to complete the mission. We went about our day loading the trunk, buying cheap booze and making sandwiches that tasted the way blood pudding would look in the snow.

We were on our way. The adventure was beginning: A new life born in the swirling snow and dark grey sky of a menacing afternoon.

We'd driven forty-five miles, metric was a few years off, when we pulled into a gas station for a leak and Gregori said he'd like to take over the wheel for the next stretch. Sure, no sweat. I gave him the keys, sliding into the passenger side, slouching, closing my eyes. What was to see?

Not too many miles down the 401 near Curry Hill is a very long curve most people still take too quickly at any time of year. Throughout summer it's a favourite spot for athletic cops to sit in a blind spot and wait for the next unwary, grimacing driver.

Not our particular problem. Gregori was doing fine, apart from moving into the outside lane while taking the curve, giving himself a wider radius. He was driving, talking, staying up with the light traffic that wasn't slowed by the increasingly heavy snow.

He told me about the worsening conditions later, seconds later, about the time he confessed he'd never driven in winter conditions, when I pretty much discovered that reality on my own, opening my eyes to his "fuck me!"

We were in the outside lane, a vehicle passing us on the inside, Gregori's peripheral vision telling him the car was sliding into us. So he veered to his left while accelerating, careening our way up Shit Creek.

We were parting the White Sea in slow motion, burrowing our way deeper and deeper into the V-shaped median, coming to rest with the buried hood facing in the right direction, my door partially opened and Gregori driving somewhere imaginary at a good speed.

We were close to a truck stop that was too far and too dangerous to attempt on foot, certain some trucker would send word and we would soon be extricated from our luxury igloo. That didn't happen, and by the time the provincial plough happened by we'd crawled out through the revolutionary electric windows and were sitting on the roof waving at cars who either couldn't see us or didn't care.

The truck came to a halt on the outer shoulder, some big guy jumping down. He landed unevenly on the snow-packed surface before tramping through knee-high snow towards the Lincoln. He was pleasantly pissed; not fall down drunk, though sufficiently and euphorically pleased with life not to give a shit. He said nothing to us, not a word. He threw up a hand as a wave, searched for where the front-end would be, and returned to the truck. He trudged his way back with three shovels and the working end of a heavy-gauge tow chain.

We were in place, waiting for him, up to our waists, and, with three shovels working, he was able to connect the end of the steel cable under the car's bumper to the tow lugs.

Gregori and I climbed in through the windows, Gregori once again a passenger.

At first the car didn't move, but it wanted to. I gripped the wheel tightly. Gregori wasn't saying much as we ploughed through snow, this time in real slow motion, toward the cherished 0road. Thank you, sir, very much. Out came the hand, but not to shake. His next bottle was on us. Thanks again, and off we went; straight through to Belleville for another a piss break.

Gregori saw the damage first. The Lincoln's heavy steel bumper was twisted, mangled completely and entirely unreturnable in said condition, protruding outward and upward at odd angles that would challenge even the best body shop. We'd signed for damages and suddenly neither of us had to take a leak. That said, the tow lugs were in pristine condition.

We went to the rear of the garage, thinking we might work out something with the guy in charge, though he was gone along with everyone else at 8:30 on a Saturday. However, there were two yellow and very solid cast-iron posts that gave birth to inspiration.

We put our overcoats over the front right corner of the car, Gregori keeping them in place as I eased forward into the post, Gregori guiding me toward the contact that would push the bumper into place. We hoped. After several taps we began seeing measurable results. Yet the bumper remained pointing upwards, requiring further thought.

We discussed possible solutions while emptying our bladders against the wall.

We wondered if galvanized steel would hold up if we drove to the guardrail delineating the parking lot. Unfortunately, the railing was as high as the bumper. Shit. More thinking.

First, we flattened the front tires completely. Step two was for Gregori to stand on the radiator, inside the open hood, jumping up and down as I maintained contact between the two metals. It took a while, the railing finally snagging the bumper, both of us thankful for spongy American suspensions. Next, we jacked the front-end, both of us sweating in January, raising the car, lowering the bumper into a quasi-original condition.

We did a decent job, looking better as we began pelting it with snowballs before going into the nearly deserted diner for a coffee and mutual praise.

We'd done okay for a couple of guys who'd just met months earlier when we began working at a no-name printing company as sales reps. We were pretty much making deliveries, asking customers if they needed more supplies for the next week, and that was sales. Then, in mid-December, on our way downtown in the so-called boss' convertible, we noticed a wire stapled to the floor. When we jerked at it we found a useless telephone receiver at the other end and began looking through the console, the glove compartment, under the other front seat, and that's when we found the starter pistol and tin badge.

We parked the car, made the delivery without taking an order, phoned him to say where he could find his dilapidated secret service vehicle, and went to our respective homes by bus.

With the Lincoln repaired, Gregori and I headed for Spadina Avenue, to a hotel with cheap room rates and lots of women. Hopefully they'd still be there when we arrived: ETA: Midnight.

*

Discouraging the farmer from helping me was time-consuming. He was disappointed I was refusing his good deed, though he did promise to call for a tow. Merci. I had a full complement of flares, water, chocolate bars, shovels, and a first-aid kit. I was good to go. Sort of.

I'd eaten a few bars and my gloves were soaked through from undressing the white-coated trees with hard-packed snowballs by the time the tow arrived at one o'clock

The steep road through the Franconia Notch of the White Mountains at 1600 metres wasn't much wider than my car, blue sky filling my windshield at the summit, blindly plunging to 577 with too many breathless seconds before seeing the ribbon-like road. Not so bad in the summer, scary shit in the winter.

The guy was sitting behind the wheel looking stunned after his short-haul flight; though he wasn't injured, merely trapped. He'd flown over the deep brook running downhill between us, though the brook was more of a fast-flowing trench. We started discussing possible action plans.

I would throw him a line which he would wrap securely around his wrists; I would then attach my end to the side reinforcement beam of the car and drag him out. He was easily twice my weight and my idea was getting him out, not me in. In any event the line was too short by a metre and he'd come to the party empty-handed.

The ten-ton happened by fifteen minutes later. He did

that two-footed landing that truckers do, not smiling until he confirmed no one was hurt. Then, in a New England accent: "Road heaves." He pointed. "Says right there."

He crossed his arms, studying the situation.

His CB was out of range, nor would either of us go looking for a tow truck in a strange town near dark. My flares were depleted, though the trucker had a good supply and I started igniting them as he went about finding what he needed.

He was built like a brick shithouse in his one-style-fits-all blue overalls, red flannel shirt, beige work boots and leather fleece-lined work gloves. In the summer he could have cleared the ditch, no problem. That wasn't happening with the snow hindering his speed, needing more impetus to clear the banks, leaping as far as the shallow splash and the curse. 'A' for effort.

He was waist-high in frigid water coursing around him. We all said different things at the same time, laughing from the sudden shock.

He didn't wait long, his head and face shielded with heavy forearms against a possible blow from the steel hook at the end of the towline I was throwing at him. The one good thing about the snow bank was that I had something to brace myself against. This guy was no lightweight.

I held my end ready, waiting. The trucker taking an extra few seconds to fling his towline to the big guy standing with his hands in his pockets by the Fiat. Not doing much else.

Suddenly my line went taut, the trucker's weight spearing my feet deeper into the snow bank.

It took a few "Jesus H" and "Damn" before he clambered out and over, taking me under the arms, yanking me from my pedestal.

He yelled instructions to the Fiat pilot. Do this, do that. Don't do this. Don't do that. Before climbing into his cab.

No One to Tell

I moved the Monte Carlo ahead several lengths. The Fiat didn't have far to travel upward or across, but did have to get past the water trap where the sub-compact began resisting, burdening the truck. The guy inside looked comical, gripping his door, bracing himself against the other as the car twisted, dipped, rising up, twisting over the snow bank, plunging to the road.

The job was done. The car still ran, the guy on his own to choose his direction as we coiled our lines, stored reflective triangles and extinguished the flares. The Fiat pilot climbed out to thank us, offering us dinner in town. We declined, thanking him.

I followed the trucker for a cautious eighty km to Manchester where we horned our goodbyes ninety minutes later. The Fiat turned off in Concord and my day was shot.

*

I was well into my second summer with Monk, anticipating that our perceptions, our work ethics would remain fundamentally different and that frequent clashes would be the norm. The Jesuit spent too much time in Jean-Guy's and Jocko's faces, trying to get in mine, wanting to be all things unto himself and unto his flock. He thought himself the perfect man, in accordance with his own standard, leaving much room for opinion on the matter.

The transition from American Durcast was more difficult than I imagined. My rapid adaptation to the excesses of industry and the sales profession were well-engrained, making conversion to Monk's austere corporate culture impossible. Monk exceeded austerity to the point where he noted each phone call, each kilometre travelled, each mouthful swallowed. He should have known better, since we'd graduated from the same sales boot camp. He also knew that, to me, image ranked highly.

He was truly deserving of the Monk's cowl. The Jesuit was forming his own little cult. I suppose not much different from working in Jones Town. He'd forgotten I wasn't at the dark meeting when they all donned their hooded robes to swear his oath of fealty and vow to live in poverty. They all did what he did and said what he said, forsaking balance. For as good as Jean-Guy was, he knew nothing about sales and Jocko was in constant pain adjusting to plant personnel, getting dirty and being poor. I didn't have the input I should have, which I believe served to make their perspective very narrow and mine increasingly self-serving.

My frequent travels served to exclude me from decision making processes, not to mention that I was the devil's advocate and the Jesuit's preachings were too vulnerable to strong a contest. I would never learn anything listening to myself talk, a doctrine Monk never embraced.

Doing expense reports was always an exercise in what's your point, particularly after Durcast and W&W. I wasn't a brown bagger, nor was I about to start any bad habits. He expected high-octane performance from low-octane fuel, which wasn't going to happen. He was counting pennies, losing dollars, despite which I began flying to the East to avoid driving six or seven days, wasting my time.

He and Jocko had very small territories within Québec which they couldn't maintain because, again, they lacked any sense of logic relating to that decade's interpretation of Time or Territory Management. I was covering Ontario, one third of Québec, the Maritimes, Newfoundland, New York and New England. Something was definitely wrong with the picture.

That our relationship was going to deteriorate was a given, but would maintain itself awhile longer out of simple self-interest. I was growing as a sales rep as they concentrated on product cost, standard and cost-efficient applications which would eventually run out.
*

I'd wanted to begin my week in Maine, travelling through to New Hampshire to finish my week Friday night and Saturday AM in Hampton, but couldn't quite work it out. So I left not too early on Sunday, my new plan excluding New Hampshire. Though I would be at Hampton Beach early enough to spend a few hours by the ocean, have a late supper and head to the hotel in Portsmouth before crossing into Maine Monday with appoints in mills I hadn't yet visited.

Leaving home on Sunday or returning on Saturday wasn't a problem throughout my time at Monk. I had sister-in-law #2 living with me, so I could take those usually sacrosanct days and no one would care except, of course, when they needed the car. She was the sister; I simply came and went, though the thought did occur to me on several occasions that if she had invaded my space at an earlier time I might have spent my weekends with Zelda.

The bright gold-embossed printing on my credit card had long since been worn away and the bank had upped my limit twice. The beach was a good place to relax the body and soul after the five-hour drive and dinner at The Galley wasn't disappointing. Then the car needed gas and I fought the urge to wait until morning as some of the filling stations in the area would only open after my day had begun.

I always used full service, though this time my staying in the car cost me a few bucks. The pump jockey was doing his one-handed thing, tapping his foot to the music coming from the knob-less and greasy black box boasting a twisted and equally greasy clothes hanger. I was tapping my one credit card against the edge of the fissure that lowering the window had created. Until I wasn't tapping with my card, but drumming with my fingers to the clicking and clacking of the card tilting its way to the abyss of the door's interior.

What was the point in pretending an option existed? The panel came off, the pop of each retainer plug adding to the till. And, with no new parts in Little Town, the mangled originals were re-used. I thanked them for the speedy service. They smiled, and I was off to the hotel with blank gas receipts to cover the cost.

As usual the last plant visit of the week was at Millinocket, who were fast becoming a second Pontiac. Thursday would include US Pulp in Bangor, the Lincoln mill, and the late summer day was perfect. I was expected at nine, I arrived at 8:50.

The guard took my card, called up and asked that I take a seat. The people I'd come to see were in a meeting that was concluding. They apologized for the inconvenience, asking that I be patient for fifteen minutes which I spent reviewing my thoughts for the meeting. The fifteen minutes slid into my twenty-minute limit.

I was ready to go into town for a coffee, thinking that later I would meet with them together. The guard insisted they wouldn't be long, that getting them together might prove difficult, so I did the unusual and waited until 9:40 when I left a copy of my proposal along with a message that I would call later in the day and, if need be, I could swing back at day's end. I had an appointment in Lincoln and never jeopardized one call to favour another. Time was money.

Another good thing about working in the Northeast was country music stations, apart from dropping credit cards into car doors. I was just pulling off I-95 into Lincoln when the twangy music stopped for breaking news that froze my blood and stopped by breathing. Two men at US Pulp had been shot, both in serious condition at the time of the broadcast.

They were in a termination meeting, giving notice to a mill worker who apparently had a handgun concealed in his pants' pocket. Although severely wounded, no one was killed. I kept my meeting in Lincoln half-heartedly, during which the conversation had little to do with wear resistance and ROI.

The following morning was noiseless, still as I lay in my rented bed waiting for the wake-up. In those days real people woke you, not microchips. But the ring never came and I stayed in bed about an hour too long to make my day easy. Until I understood that not only did I not hear the phone, I wasn't hearing anything.

The phone did ring. I just didn't hear it. In fact I could only hear the sound of my own swallowing. I clapped my hands together, feeling, not hearing the sound. I spoke, hearing the muffled sounds of a voice inside me. I'd lost my hearing, my first reaction to phone the Front Desk, which was silly because I had no way of knowing when they would have answered.

Instead I wrote a note, dressed, and went to the Front Desk with enough information for the clerk to explain to Millinocket why I wouldn't be seeing them as planned. They blew me away when they offered to drive me home. Even for the early 80s that was beyond the pale, particularly for me coming from a big city and more accustomed to the "F" in finger. I declined, scribbling quickly that I would speak with them soon and that they'd be ahead of everyone else on my agenda.

Breakfast was quiet. The hotel staff called home for me and I set out at 9:00 AM for the eleven hour ride home.

Customs was interesting, always is, taking a while longer. They seemed not to understand my dilemma. Mental midgets. A personal opinion, of course.

Though driving to Québec City was a breeze, becoming a little more intense. I could have stopped in Québec to spend the night with the in-laws, the mother was nice, but I didn't. Staying with them would have been too much like a B&B, not my style, and there was always some family bullshit to contend with, not that I would have heard any.

No One to Tell

I arrived home on time to an overwhelming lack of sympathy. I didn't understand what was so amusing about my sudden loss of hearing.

Say what?

The note read: We've made reservations.

I went to bed, too tired for the ER. In addition to which the weekend was a double bitch because the dinner reservations were cancelled.

*

Summers, much like life, end too soon.

Fall was a good season for refractory work: never cold, never hot, and the time of most year-end maintenance shutdowns. Pictou was a big plant by any standard and high, very high. Nothing if not sixteen stories.

I was climbing the final flight of interior stairs leading to the shed and rooftop access with Jim, the Plant Manager, then through to the roof. This time without the breathtaking panoramic view of Northumberland Strait. Neither of us certain, Jim joking that perhaps we should hold hands.

On a clear day you could make out P.E.I, which wasn't the case in mid-October with high winds making breathing difficult and talking impossible. The torrential rain had calmed to a drizzle but the wind was throwing up water from the drenched rooftop, soaking our pants as we scurried to the ladder leading to the inspection port of the cyclone braced eight metres above us.

Jim had called me in for the year-end shutdown to determine the cause of tiles coming loose from the interior wall. We made it to the ladder with chins pressed to our chests, our safety glasses blurred with smeared raindrops, our coattails flapping wildly. In one hand we grasped our note pads, with the other our hardhats.

Jim was first up the ladder. I only made the third rung when a violent gust knocked off our hats that we never saw again and caused us to lose our footing. I landed clumsily, pretty much like my first time on ice skates, my notepad gone. Jim wasn't much better, finding his footing before dropping to his knees beside me, his notepad gone.

We were laughing. We looked ridiculous on our knees clinging to the vertical rails of the ladder, our coats snapping frantically with the wind. We were screaming, barely hearing each other.

We were thirty plus metres from the shed, the wind pushing us, tugging us, trying to loosen our grips. We spread ourselves eagle, holding hands, belly-crawling our way over gravel, wet tar, loose chips and other debris. Five, perhaps six minutes later, when we got to the shed, crashing through on all fours, greeted by some of Jim's crew, we could only sit on the grated steps and laugh ourselves silly. We were soaked through, drenched and dripping. I rescheduled. Jim went home.

On paper I took Jim and his lead hands out for a succulent dinner that night; in reality, I had a room service Club with a half-litre and bought new clothes the next day.

Jim was an entertaining lunch companion, though entertaining anytime is a crapshoot and you're lucky if you break even. I almost always tied in the Pictou visit with Port Hastings at the entrance to Cape Breton and, like I mentioned, you're lucky if you break even.

The one restaurant in town worth chancing was across the street from the Shielding Motel. I'd invited the Maintenance Supervisor from the Canso mill to lunch because we'd spent the morning together collecting data about various applications and he wouldn't go away.

He wanted lunch, I wanted his business. Case closed.

He had a beer. I had wine, thirty minutes passing without him saying a single word. When I attempted conversation he would grunt or grumble some Neanderthal response, saying nothing at all, which is when I realized I'd been talking to myself all morning. When the meal was finally served, his was a steak with a baked potato and canned peas. Mine was untouched.

He smashed the potato with one downward motion of his spoon, mashing until two halves were created, shovelling one into his mouth. The second mouthful was a spoonful of peas he'd scooped against a cupped hand, his jaws still working the potato. The steak was next, with both hands, sagging in the middle where uneven teeth tore away a sizeable semi-sphere to create a noisy shepherd's pie in a mouth through which he was apparently also breathing.

He had the etiquette of my sister-in-law's dog, a perfect dinner companion for Jean-Guy. I glanced at my watch, telling him I had to make a phone call. Not true, and that he should go ahead with his meal. I wouldn't be long, long enough for him to finish his meal and for me to see the waitress clearing the table. The downside was that he ordered another beer and wasn't rushing. I ordered a scotch, enduring the remaining forty and insufferable minutes with an in-depth monologue on wear-resistant refractories, barely escaping my own death by tedium.

No way ever again.

*

I didn't go to Sudbury very often, or to the uranium mines in Elliot Lake. I had this thing about wearing radiation level badges that told me if going to that mine was helping to shorten my life, but never by how much. When I did go, I stayed at the two-star hotel because the others in town were one-star. As well, the two-star afforded the best view of the city's moonscape scenery. At one time the town would have been a fair weather summer trip, but since I was flying to places God had neglected I had no seasonal preference.

Not enough snow had fallen to turn the black rocks white, or make the city seem more vibrant. Sudbury would never be vibrant. Sudbury was dreary and dull, blue-collar, where women worked their fingernails black and men smoked theirs yellow. Jeans were the code for breakfast, lunch and dinner, the same tee-shirt equally fashionable at work as for play. Sudbury was a place for those who'd chosen the wrong career or for those who had no career.

I arrived at the hotel before dinner, in my room with a view with my suitcase, briefcase and coat thrown across the bed before I could say, "Hey! Who the fuck are you?" to the big, naked, ugly and hairy guy standing at the bathroom door blocking my escape.

We took too long to work things out. Perhaps only seconds, but too long anyway.

Standing face to face with a 1, 9 tall naked guy who wanted to know why I was "fucking around in his room" wasn't a good way to end my day. But he had control of the door. I replied that he was fucking around in mine.

Anyway, he got to keep my room because he'd already dropped much of his body hair on the carpet. I got apologies, a pull-out in the conference room, a view of the parking lot, and dinner coupons.

I ate at the hotel because of the deepening snow, not the freebie, the sopping nudist sitting across from me in the full restaurant, probably pissed that his height to length ratio was known to me. I'm sure we both had the same thought: Eat and get the hell out.

Wednesday I'd been up to Elliot Lake for a dose of green glow, the storm putting me at the hotel late and road-weary. All I wanted was food, a scotch, and bed, now that I had the hang of the hide-in-the-wall pull-out sleep trap and no longer feared being flung into a drywall crypt.

In most cases the main decision when ordering room service isn't what to order, rather where to put the meal. No safe place exists in hotel rooms. In essence they're CSI training facilities, but I was in the conference room with a choice of forty seats.

The food was typical of a two-star: Better served to

someone else. Television wasn't much better. The management had brought a TV in for me, but I was in Sudbury, left with a toss-up between making finger faces on the overhead screen and flipping through the two available stations until my unexpected after-dinner theatre began with a bang. The adjoining door was a good three centimetres from the floor, dull light suddenly filling the gap.

The first bang came when they closed their door, followed by bang, bang, bang throughout the night. They weren't letting me sleep, so I joined the party half believing they knew I'd thrown cushions from a sofa onto the floor by the door, poured a nightcap, closed my eyes and hoped she was pretty. The guy must have had a battery pack to keep up with her and I don't believe a role of thirty-six (that would be camera film) would have been enough for all the "do this, do that, now this, now that, now this; no, not like that, like this. No! Not that. I said, not that!" But then, "Ooh, oh baby, oh, baby, uh-huh, uh-huh. Oh, baby."

The bossy control freak got laid more that night than I had all year, make that two years, three years. I needed a dental mirror, and in the morning I needed a chiropractor when I woke crunched against the corner wall and the door. However, when the clerk asked me as I was leaving for the day if I wanted to change to a proper room for my last night I said "No. Why bother?"

*

At the end of that winter, 1000 kilometres farther west in Thunder Bay, she came in wearing the essential two-piece of the typical '70s virgin bride and by the looks of her she was as untouched by him as by the sun.

The pool was the typical hotel variety: an eggshell blue concrete border scripted with 1m and 3m in black indicating the shallow and deep ends and 100-watt lamps that would turn any skin tone pallid. Such pools are used mostly by obese women who hang from the sides, kicking and thrashing to prevent drowning. Or out-of-shape, equally obese men standing in the shallows, avoiding the plump pods they arrived with, possibly hoping something nice might happen in.

Sunlight turned into sundown, converting huge steel-framed windows looking out onto the patio into a floor-to-ceiling and wall-to-wall mirror. Their marble-etched twins, across the bar, looked onto the interior pool.

She treaded water. He was twisting at the waist and doing jumping jacks, uncoordinated and jerky. No one paid any attention. They were alone, lost in a state of post-nuptial bliss, waving to each other as though coming together after time apart, blowing kisses, one asking the other to count time before submerging their heads. He came up for air. She came up for air, proud of her success, splashing her way to his eager embrace. He pulled her from the floor, spinning her around, attempting to swing her in circles, the water slowing her motion, the resistance causing her knees to surface from where Romeo scooped them up, sweeping her around and around. Oh, the unbridled passion of what we were witnessing.

We went back to our drinks.

He slowed to a stand, her arms clinging to his neck in the turbulent and ominous waist-high, heated water. Her hero. A kiss for her hero as their faces glued together in a soundless, water-soluble tangle of tongues, teeth and pushed-out noses; his whirlwind paws not knowing what to maul first.

There was no reaction to our chorus of moans and groans as we watched the mermaid bring up her legs, encircling his waist while she splashed and frolicked with her new legal closeness. We injected the words she was too shy to speak, reacting for him, booing when he cast her away. He went down, into the dangerous water, for her. She held to his head, praying for his safe return until, at last, he surfaced.

He was pleased, proud, raising her in his arms high above the water, her bare ass sparkling with dripping water under and beside the bright lights.

He pushed through the water to the side, lifting her onto the edge where she sat enjoying his caresses, his wet kisses, her eyes glued to the stairway. He tried pushing his face into her lap, but she didn't want to lay back. Instead she eased herself forward, her pretty pubes guiding her into and under the water before shooting up in a torrent of translucent beads.

He tossed her bottoms to the edge, lifting her, pinning her to the side of the pool, his back muscles straining; her arms gripping hard at his neck, her knees and shins clamped to his hips. The water around them was violent with surges and hectic waves. She released her grip, securing the edge, squirming her body higher, arching backward. She was beaming, pleased at giving him a better approach, which he no doubt needed.

He wasn't the biggest fish in the sea, a miniature moray eel not knowing whether to come out or stay in her soft fleshy grotto. He tugged at her top with a hand he could spare, baring her little and perfectly chilled breasts. We cheered, of course. Not to would have been rude.

She punched him. He probably thought for her additional nudity, we believed for his unskilled touch. He was on his toes, we could tell, his arms braced on the edge, her body convulsing against the wet carpet, one hand under her ass, the other mauling her breasts, pinching and pulling, though this time she didn't care. Her face was contorted, her mouth opened wide, her torso cramping with spasms.

The hero pulled out from her as though vacating a culvert, diving for his trunks, surfacing to fondle her satiated portal as she tried to manage her top. Instead he dragged her in, his arms pushing up her pinkish cheeks, grabbing her bottoms in one hand and her top in the other. She pushed him away, and under.

We ordered a round, saluting her, offering our services to the young lady since we deemed him unfit for the task.

She clambered from the pool by the edge, not the ladder, glistening, her legs parted extra wide to negotiate the ledge, teasing, letting him, us, admire her sparkling wet curves and secrets.

He watched from the water as she stood admiring her own nude sculpture in the mirrored wall, listening, smiling, pirouetting with her arms outstretched because he wanted to see her naked and naughty in a public place. Or so we assumed, seeing her coquettish smile, his hands clasped in a prayer we couldn't hear.

Didn't we all? No shit.

She sauntered to their chairs, bending, reaching for her toes, not her towel, offering a few eye-catching wiggles before wrapping herself into a fleecy robe.

More boos and, yes, more booze.

*

In defense of the barmaid, she did want to call the manager, but the six or seven of us at the bar promised good tips if she didn't. She hesitated at first, shaking her head, making tsk-tsk noises and calling us pigs.

The performance was over, an hour or so passing before the newlies strolled through the door holding hands, coochy-cooing each other, kissing as though they shared a single tongue.

They seemed disappointed that we hadn't been informed of their recent vows to love, honour and obey…at least for seven years.

No one turned to adore, applaud, marvel or pay homage. We'd already done that.

They stood for a moment, uncertain before agreeing on the darkest corner, despite all four being the darkest, ordering something like Daiquiris and Pink Ladies, unaware she was about to become the pinkest. The barmaid, filling the order, rolled her eyes, reaffirming in a whisper that we were indeed pigs. Though, deep down, she liked us.

The couple toasted their eternal devotion, clinked and blew kisses. One of the guys at the bar did the same to his buddy. Another called out, "Hey, have a looksee over there," and we all stared through the windows we knew were silver coated on the other side.

The barmaid, naturally, sighed loudly enough to ensure those good tips.

He stopped her from standing, not wanting her to be away for more than a breath. But she had to see for herself and stood at the window transfixed for a lifetime of seconds. Then she heard the applause and the cheers, gone through the door in a flash, deserting her hero in his chair.

Uncertain, he went to the window, running for the door just as quickly. They were gone from the hotel that night or early the next morning, I suppose without breakfast, though we did pay for their drinks and left the barmaid a better tip than any newlywed.

*

I was leaving Monk because my growth rate was exceeding theirs, held back by mediocrity and growing ostracism fostered by the dissimilarity in our methodologies and personas. Our time together was mutually rewarding to a point, though once the challenge and novelty of change began showing signs of mundane routine I was ready to move on.

I left Monk Refractories without ill-feeling, neither as a friend or colleague. In that regard I was never part of them. I worked and thought independently. Our mutual adoration was one of money. The fact is, I left with no feeling at all, which wasn't bizarre to me.

I would never see them again, and as I drove away I

realized they had never existed to me beyond a stepping stone. I can't think of anything worse to say about someone. They had no appreciation for life or for each other. I also realized that in those three years neither the Jesuit, Jocko, nor Jean-Guy ever laughed. Whatshername did once in a while, I suppose, though not in a way any intelligent person would trust.

They were each other's restraint as much as each other's purpose. Without one the other couldn't exist.

Those three years were unremarkable, in fact forgettable with a few remarkable memories, which was about to change. What saved me was success and the speed at which they passed.

April 22, 1982 stands out not for any sales success or personal achievement other than I'd be leaving them in eight days. The day stands out in my memory for the dinner at the Valhalla Inn in Thunder Bay, my farewell meal, because meals were a big thing with the Jesuit, a constant point of contention between us and we essentially agreed to disagree because that's as far as I would go.

Living a good life at home while existing as an indigent when travelling for business is incongruous, debilitating to morale, harmful to one's initiative and image. Monk never learned, never understood that wisdom.

The night wasn't the busiest of the week and being that most diners don't take time to enjoy their meals, even in fine restaurants, and this was a notch above, the staff was extremely accommodating when they heard my request. They had the area prepared and I believe they enjoyed the evening as much as me. The restaurant was a mezzanine, the lower section cordoned off for me.

Quite possibly the other diners thought I'd been stood up by a lot of people or that I was eccentric or wealthy. Wrong. Wrong. Wrong.

Driving wasn't a concern. I was nicely ensconced with a

No One to Tell

book whose title escapes me, certainly not 'How to Kiss Your Boss'. I intended to read. However the hour hand was touching 7:00, Happy Hour no longer in effect, though my double JW Black neat did become two. I was staring into blank pages, recounting the previous three years, wondering where Zelda would comb her hair in another six hours somewhere in Belgium, wondering why I'd never thought to help protect her skin from the sun's harmful rays.

I was into my second scotch they'd been kind enough to keep for me beyond the two-for-one curfew, becoming pensive, possibly philosophical, lamenting time lost, time wasted. I'd come to the realization that I'd wasted copious amounts of time in another's world, an increasingly distant world that was, in fact, a prison from which I engineered frequent escapes.

No villain or culprit was to blame, solely my original misjudgement camouflaged by time and frequent distance and, as I dined in a private dimension, I mulled over the ramifications of yet another philosophy inspired by solitude: Absence versus abstinence that may or may not make the heart grow fonder. My role over the previous eight years was one of an adjunct to a DINK relationship.

The waitresses spoke with me every so often, always laughing or smiling. Even Monsieur le Chef made an appearance which gave me the opportunity to thank him for the perfect meal and a memory that would never fade:
Johnnie Walker Black (2)
Consommé aux Xérés
Chateau Pontet-Canet (Paulliac 1979)
Rôti de bœuf au jus
Pommes de terre au four
Crêpes Suzette à l'érable
Courvoisier VSOP (2)
Café
*

There is no legacy in sales beyond exceptional events coming together to comprise personal portfolios. Individual contributions to industry become anonymous components of corporate success, losing identity and significance over time.

I brought to Monk Refractories substantial new accounts and solidified Pontiac as a premier client. I left them feeling accomplished. How they chose to maintain or neglect that success was theirs to decide.

We cannot advance by standing still; not in life, nor in business. Stagnation is the antithesis of well-being, not to mention upward mobility, which, at the time, was not in vogue.

As much as Monk was a valuable learning experience, the learning curve had flattened. The company was too small to allow for expansion. Advancement was impossible, stagnation looming.

Thanks for the meal, Monk.

R.I.P.

The Jesuit and Mrs. Monk renamed the company at some point over the years. I suspect neither one has learned to smile or laugh.

Whether he did or not, Jocko should have returned to his comfort zone in pharma where he could get the quantity of pills required to forget his years of speaking no evil and sufferance.

Jean-Guy would be retired by now, possibly still throwing meat on the floor if the two plus packs a day and the Jesuit didn't get to him first.

I saw Bill once more, soon after. I hope he's well, playing Keno with his wife in Vegas.

Statistically, the hero in the pool with his mermaid are divorced, or they have two or three kids in their thirties who won't leave home.

Gregori remained in Toronto where he met Ophelia whose Cuban family lived in exile in Florida. He called me from Fort Lauderdale a few months later with an invitation to their wedding. I declined, though we did speak at length one other time. He wanted to tell me he'd driven into and toppled a lamp standard on one of the city's bridges. He was sober at the time.

We never spoke again.

Chapter Five
1982 - 1987

I was certain Murphy was one of those kids in school who couldn't write one word without burying his face into the page, letting his tongue hang freely from his mouth, pronouncing each letter he scribbled, staring at each stroke with amazement and pride of achievement.

Everyone within hearing was aware that Murphy was teetering on the brink of a revelation that would transform him into the next hotshot wherever he worked, for the time being.

Bullshit baffles brains. Always will. I can't imagine the mental tug of war he was experiencing, his eyes glued to the chapter heading: Careerist: Doing What Needs to be Done.

And what the hell's a careerist?

Murphy would never understand that everything has a consequential value. Working Saturdays, arriving home late from out-of-town trips, the side effects of restaurant food all come at a cost that most often exceeds the reward. He was a peddler, the sudden urgency to get away from him, or his twitching leg, overpowering.

I don't usually stand in-flight, but I did then. He's made me want to scratch. I took a moment to empathize with Legs who hadn't opened her eyes, probably wishing she could stand.

No One to Tell

*

May 02, 1982. Two weeks of R & R remained before taking up my new position as Technical Sales Representative at RTI, world leader in plastic and castable refractories. Week number one was on the beaches of North Eleuthra for a week of diving, sunning, and JW Red or Black.

I arrived late on the Sunday by way of Fort Lauderdale in a sixteen-seat prop with two other passengers, newlyweds in love playing touchy feely. So when the pilot asked if I wanted to sit up front with him the answer was a no-brainer. We had a couple of laughs about the goo-goo gaga behind us, but mostly we spoke about travel.

Arriving, the lovers disappeared into a van and went somewhere. I flagged a cab.

My first acquaintance on the island was a small man who appeared broken, his black skin stained with salt lending a marbled affect, his bright white teeth keyed together with gold.

His hand was bony and trembling, yet strong enough to hold out to his new friend. The hand stayed empty; I didn't need a friend. Though I did take advantage of the service he offered, after we established his fee. All the shops had closed earlier, conflicting with my plans to enjoy a JW neat without joining everyone at the bar and the old guy didn't waste time.

The streets were uneven and narrow, paved with cracked asphalt or mud, bordered with white picket fences enclosing pastel houses in greens, pinks and blues with white slatted shutters and slopping whitewashed roofs. She was as big as he was small and seemed not to mind that we walked inside her white picket fence, past her shop and into her house. Of course she had JWR. In fact she had two and I took them both, first filling a large goblet for my bony guide.

The mornings were spent diving. My dive buddy was Walter from Norfolk, whose brother didn't want to dive with him. So I was quick to accept the Navy SEAL's invitation. We each had our own equipment. The others didn't know better.

The diving was great, the total escapism of the afternoons far better while most others at the dive club did PM dives. The vast expanse of white sand was mine to enjoy alone, checking every so often that my Hom hadn't blown away. The second afternoon particularly memorable.

I'd discovered after seven years in sales and 700 nights out of town that my time away was more fulfilling than my time in town. It's hard to know which is more telling; the fact that I'd gone away for a week without saying why I should, or her letting me go for a week without saying why I shouldn't.

The dull clicking isn't what prompted me to prop myself onto an elbow, rather the frequency and the particular sound.

She was squatting six metres closer to the crashing waves, an equal distance from me, bracing her camera with her elbows on her knees, her legs opened wide enough to show a triangle that, if not for the bright green ribbons at her hips, might have been an exotic 80s dye job.

I'd never been photographed in that particular way before, much less by a beautiful woman who was practically naked herself. I was staring straight into her lens through Ray*Bans, smiling. She stood, smiling. A green thong, her triangle top laced into the side ties. She had no towel.

What she did have were bare breasts, very nice bare breasts. Her hair was the colour of rich chocolate, slicked by the sea into a thick headdress; her body wet, beaded with lotion and the sea. Her eyes were silver, sparkling under the sun. I gave her late twenties, a graduate of the 70s. She was slim, sculpted and tanned.

No One to Tell

She had a Nikon view of me and I wondered if I'd end up with a staple somewhere that hurt, or on the wall of a ladies locker room. Sitting to put on my Hom would have been awkward, ridiculous. So I sat and didn't, waving. She waved.

She faced the turquoise water, squatting again into the sand. Nice. Standing, she slung the camera over a shoulder, reaching with one hand to extricate her top, the other tugging first at one hip then the other. Three green, shimmering triangles dangling from her hands, dancing in the sea breeze. She waved again, strolling away, a pale white arrowhead V barely visible.

She wasn't the only one with a Nikon. Click. Click. Click.

I stood, curious at what she'd scrawled in the sand: 118. No name, a stone's throw across from my room. I suppose what some might call a quandary. Zoom. Click. Click. Click. And she was gone.

*

The diving was a phenomenal experience, doing them with a SEAL was unique. On the last day Walter was onboard with his brother. So was Wendy from 118, though she wasn't a diver.

We headed to a place called The Channel where high and long underwater ridges formed a submerged narrow channel, creating a current that was pretty much like white water rafting without the raft.

Walter and I were cut a lot of slack by Captain Self-love because of what Walter was and I took advantage of his status. We'd all been given instructions about when and where to come up, duly noted and we dropped over the side. The dive went well, except when we were supposed to surface we didn't because of current and hammerhead shark issues. When we did we were a good bit off course and the dive master was being a hard ass about it, yelling that what he said goes and if we couldn't adhere to his rules we weren't welcome.

That's when Walter got into his face, staring him down from a centimetre away, making his point. Game over. I imagined him with black camouflage face-paint around steel blue eyes and rock-hard features doing his SEAL thing and making someone shit himself. Go team!

The PM dive was cancelled due to bullshit. We went our separate ways, regrouping after dinner. Then time to go home. The four of us, and two other girls we hooked-up with earlier, spent the last night lounging at the patio bar before heading out the next morning for different destinations.

Two weeks later I received a bill for several hundred dollars and a letter claiming I'd caused damages to a bed, a pillow and the linen: Guilty, with explanation and just cause, your Honour.

*

The sliding patio doors to room 109 had no lock, just a hole where it might once have been. This was an exclusive dive club, which meant nothing was included, including door locks. So I made a habit of sleeping with my dive and buddy knives by the pillow.

My buddy knife was a 12.5 cm stainless steel one-piece blade. Both top edges were serrated for cutting, the working end razor sharp. I usually wore the blade on my forearm in the event I might have to disentangle myself from a 'buddy' at depth.

The room had twin beds, likely purchased from a defunct prison or flophouse. At the early part of the week I laid out my dive gear on the one furthest from the doors, deciding to sleep in the other with my knives nearby. Clearly unaware at the time that my nights would be sleepless anyway.

Midway through the week I woke with my arm under

the pillow, my arm tingling with a myriad of sensations made worse by vivid imagination. I took a moment, my other hand reaching for my buddy knife, the sharper of the two by far, very good for shaving in a pinch, simultaneously tossing aside the pillow, uncovering a swarm of cockroaches.

Some died instantly, put to death by stabbing or squashing. Some scurried away. Others flew into the air in a flurry with the sheet. Many that had escaped with the pillow were later smothered or crushed.

Admittedly I made a bit of a mess with gut stains and more holes than roaches in the mattress, so what I did was flip the mattress over, replace the covers accordingly, and put my gear on that bed knowing that housekeeping wouldn't bother with it while I was there. They didn't.

I also made a point of purging my mouthpiece each morning to dislodge possible bite-size squatters.

So, you see, I couldn't very well hold myself accountable for damage incurred during a night of terror. As well, the day before, I'd trapped a palm-sized and fuzzy tarantula that had taken up residence in the bathroom. At first I considered imprisonment under a wicker basket, choosing in favour of capture under a spare blanket and my adaptation of a Celtic dance in order to alleviate future concerns.

I wrote a reply with a cc: to the Bahamian Tourist Board detailing my version, adding an appropriate footnote to the club's letter. Neither one replied.

*

I arrived home on the ninth, tanned and fit.

What's more damaging to the male ego than being accused of screwing around, is not being accused. That was fine with me. Ask no questions, hear no lies. The bags were already packed.

I was in Cape Cod on the tenth in time to see Blue

Lagoon. Life doesn't get much better. Driving 700km to watch a movie. Yippee. Payback for my week in the Bahamas.

Earlier in the day, walking along the shoreline of the tranquil bay side, we came across two guys setting up for a lunch. Two women in knee-deep water were splashing each other with cupped hands, giggling, having fun. Thing is, they were naked. So I suggested doing the same. I might as well have said, "I did sister number three last night, the pretty one."

Only then did I discover that, not only were those really good-looking and naked girls having fun in the gentle waves, they were lewd and disgusting. I also learned I was a pig. Go figure. We are what we are.

Well, if you can't join 'em, leave 'em. We could have had a good time, but I was on vacation and who has fun on vacation? Further along the coast another foursome was doing the same. One woman, tanned, easy on the eyes, was at the water's edge, her legs nicely separated with her bum nicely pushed up.

She was an early-twenties package of lithe sexiness stretched out, getting a burn on without the faintest footprint in the sand. Who wouldn't take notice of something like that?

The other three had seen us coming, not the least concerned or annoyed at the invasion. Once again I was tempted, knowing better than to offer the suggestion. Anyway, that would have meant missing the movie of…hello…a naked girl swimming.

Fill in the blanks.

*

Monday morning, May 17th. I was at the coffee shop down the road waiting for 8:20, early enough for the first day at RTI without appearing overly eager. Ralph always arrived early and probably saw me drive up.

No One to Tell

He stayed in his office until his secretary ushered me through the door. Ralph was all about Ralph.

I'd seen him on previous occasions. During the second meet, in the company of Scott who presided over Refractory Technologies from his office in Burlington, Ralph had told me that despite our age difference of thirty-three and forty-eight I could call him by his first name.

Scott laughed through his nose. I said thanks…Ralph, with little doubt Ralph was a pompous clown, much like an Easter egg: Colourful on the outside, filled with shit on the inside.

He was an affable fellow who'd done his time in sales, exclusively with RTI, given the job of managing the Eastern sales department because they needed him off the road and away from customers. He was the village idiot. He was also willing to trade substantially less money for prestige and a proud wife.

They needed him off the road because political correctness was burgeoning, becoming popular in business. Ralph, conversely, frequently and increasingly caused embarrassment to himself and others with questionable intellect and marginal language skills. His English made one cringe: a dialect of invented words and archaic expressions. His spoken French, worst of all, was a blatant criminal act against Francophonie.

He did however possess some qualities. Everyone did like Ralph, or pretended to, because he was charming in a 50s car salesman way. Truth be told, they didn't know what to do with an out-dated relic of simpler times.

*

I spent a week with each of the four other reps in their territories, with the exception of Frank who was volunteered to conduct the classroom portion of my training.

Frank didn't like the city. He lived in the sticks, coming to the office strictly for monthly meetings. He began his career as a 'travelling salesman' with another company, selling and delivering hardware supplies to customers in the northern lake region of Ontario, paddling his nine-metre birch bark canot du nord and wearing deerskin clothing. He looked ex-military, but wasn't. His white hair was brush-cut, each hair of his eyebrows cut uniformly short adding to his stern expression filled with crevices and colour when he laughed.

He'd once marvelled at the new technology of the telex, he'd loved an Indian maiden when there was such a thing, and swore he would never use a newfangled fax. Frank was frank and I never got to travel with him, which was unfortunate because he had a wealth of knowledge and a repertoire of incredible stories.

When Ralph's secretary, Gisèle, toured me around the office for the requisite new guy freak show, I asked her why a particular phone had such a large base.

"It's a fax machine," she replied, expecting I would believe that a phone could send printed messages instantly. Yeah, right. Good one. Not only was she cute, she was trying to mess with the new guy's brain on his fist day. However, it does appear at this point as though she was right, though I never used the thing and now I don't because they're obsolete.

*

Dean was charged with most of my on-road training; despite having as much do with the inside of bars as with the inside of furnaces, boilers and ovens. By the end of the week I'd been into most of the cheapest watering holes within a 200km radius of Montreal.

He'd come up through the ranks from bricklayer to field supervisor to construction supervisor, finally transferred into sales for the big bucks. Dean wasn't a good salesman, by his own admission, but he was an amiable people person who happened to have a client-refinery that kept him busy and affluent.

The applications were textbook and plentiful, requiring no innovation, just good pricing. He was successful financially and professionally, at the time. He had an intoxicating personality because he was always drunk, though one of the accounts where he did have to prove himself was Pontiac and Bill did not like him.

When I showed up with Dean at the mill to inspect their rotary kiln he was taken aback by all the warm handshaking and kisses; the kisses coming from Julie who'd begun as an intern a few years earlier and had become a full-time engineer. Hearing how much they regretted my departure from Monk was ego boosting, more so to hear they wanted me to represent RTI.

That wouldn't happen. That wasn't the way of the world and I never saw them again.

Travelling with Pierre was another thirst-quenching experience; the difference being that Dean liked bars where he could talk with anyone who walked in and Pierre preferred the smoky darkness of titty bars. His favourite colours of the flesh were black and pink and he got them both at the Le Hershey Bar.

Pierre led the wild life on expenses and didn't care about tomorrow. He liked to laugh and have fun. He also worked with a refinery that would eventually contribute to a permanent lifestyle change. The reason? He was regularly doing his client's wife…with his client's permission and presence. A little ménage à trois until things soured.

My time with Guy was the most rewarding. He had a more serious approach to his job. Like the other two he had a refinery, but also took care of a much broader base as security against client hissy fits, strikes, recession and bad luck. He enjoyed his job, the lifestyle. He was all about planning, listening, interaction and tangible results. He was professional without being arrogant or self-satisfied and the one I relied on for product application information. He was constantly enveloped by the calm assurance, never rankled.

Ralph never bothered Guy because he knew if Guy had lived closer to the office, the office would be his; though Guy never let that generally accepted fact affect his work, nor his attitude towards his boss.

We never argued, with one exception. Guy's claim was that Francophone girls wore sexier underwear than their Anglophone sisters. They wore high-rise backless, garters and lace, whereas English women preferred pantyhose, double-lined crotches six to a pack and undressed in the dark. The debate was difficult. As valiantly as I defended the Anglophone female, we both knew he was right. I asked him if his wife had a sister. She didn't, causing me to endure another year of double-lined crotches and shadows in the dark.

Avery was the Merlin of Refractory, The Oracle of Castables and the Purveyor of Technical Truth. He was the final indoctrination into the world of Interfacing and Graduated Temperature Reduction. Avery was a sales engineer; a special sales engineer. If he'd been rich he would have been eccentric. But he wasn't rich, so he was categorically insane. He was one of those guys that sales reps tolerate when critical engineering issues come into play beyond their expertise. He existed in a constant state of suspension and confusion, a technician emulating an engineer, constantly snared in minute details while neglecting the larger picture.

Avery was a chronic pain in the ass.

He would always wear stainless steel anchors around his neck when doing joint calls with reluctant reps. Reluctant not because he wasn't good, because of the anchors: A large tuning-fork shaped stud meant to support multiple layers of insulation and refractory in a furnace, not hang from a neck. They weigh a kilo, which is likely the reason Avery walked stooped over.

I first met Avery at the International Bar before getting him to his room, leaving him to clear my lungs and my head. He was heavily into the booze: a refractory staple. He was also into body language even though he didn't have much of one himself. He was somewhat of a troll.

As a female ex-office compatriot once said to me as she watched me admiring the marvellous derrière of another co-worker, "Small things amuse small minds, small pants fit small behinds." She might have had a clue as to what I was thinking at that moment regarding body language. I asked if she meant that her friend had a tight ass and wore small panties. She shook her head and walked away. But back at the bar, as our small table began filling with Avery's empty trophies, he got this stupid expression on his face. He knew something I didn't, good for him, and the stupid expression lasted a good couple of hours as I sucked in smoke and listened to the laments of a sad man.

Sufficiently contaminated with toxins and tales, I called the waitress over to pay the bill and asked her in French to help me. She looked as though she could give birth to a litter of nail-studded demon spawn and yank them out herself, so she didn't need my help. Nevertheless I stood for affect as we took hold of the table's edge and put my side in front of Avery.

He'd been attempting to discreetly move all his empties onto my side of the table to make a point. I was, of course, expected to cross my arms in a defensive gesture as the number of bottles increased, to cross my leg closest to him over the other, as my side of the table became more cluttered. Not so. Childish games. I got the last word, literally turning the table on the old coot.

He wasn't a likeable fellow. He was pathetic, dead and forgotten within the year from heart disease, though I'm sure the anchors around his neck didn't help the old guy.

No One to Tell

Unfortunately Ralph couldn't be forgotten. Not yet. He'd been Sales Manager a year or so before I joined the company. He was permanently unkempt, as though he drove to work every day on a motorcycle wearing his blue suit, white shirt, red tie and no helmet. His pants were always bunched at the crotch, standing or sitting, his boys huddled together in the cramped and clammy confines of his under shorts frequently attacked by mauling claws. Surprisingly, he never had blue threads caught in his fingernails.

He was a unique fashion statement, one of a kind, his sparse hair a yellowed-grey. He was bumbling and goofy, a spluttering 50s bird-dogger on the outside. On the inside he was cornered by the passing of time, or its encroachment on who he thought he still was.

You can never be friends with your boss, no matter how nice a guy he is, because one day he'll give you shit and there's the problem. Your boss has just pissed on your pant leg. So how do invite him to the barbeque? You can tell a friend to screw off and flip the burgers, but you can't do that to a boss-friend and still enjoy your meal.

I never involved myself in office politics and wasn't about to start picking sides, though on several occasions I wasted my breath cautioning Dean against his buddy-buddy familiarity with Ralph for which he would soon pay dearly.

Pierre lived in the past as well, thinking they were all still buddy-buddy bird-doggers. Guy however saw through Ralph, staying clear of him. He was nice enough and harmless most days, when he wasn't reliving moments of "What if" and "If only." Then, beware of dreams never realized.

I did my thing. Like Guy, stayed clear of him. One advantage of being a frequent traveller or, an infrequent part of the environment, is noticing change that others consider routine.

In my five years with them I never did a joint call with Ralph. Though I did tag along once at the beginning when he went with Dean to eastern Ontario, when the day's biggest event for Ralph was Dean running over a cat, Ralph turning in his seat to take in the red blotch for as long as he could.

He never promoted joint calls. Nor was he ever invited unless the advantage of his credit card outweighed having him with you. He had to know, as we did, that his years with the company were saving his bacon and not his technical expertise.

*

At RTI our incurred expenses, including the vehicles, were deducted from commissions earned, but the commissions and base salary were so high that no one cared. No one scrutinized beyond cursory interest what we expensed as long as receipts were submitted. Suits, car payments, weekend trips, Christmas booze, a pied à terre for the girlfriend, whatever. Nobody cared, as long as we could support the expense with paperwork.

We all used a system that Pierre was credited with developing and perfecting into an art. We each kept a file of blank restaurant and bar receipts which we would exchange according to language, location and type of establishment needed, recruiting secretaries or each other to fill in the amounts and dates so that the penmanship and colours of ink would vary. Numbered receipts were used according to the proper date and amount, though never used in the same sequential series by two reps on the same occasion.

This gave everyone an excellent after-tax income to where our net incomes exceeded the competition's gross incomes and I'd been elevated to the upper rungs of the top ten percentile, where I would stay. The one time of year expenses really came into play was Christmas when the 1:2 applied: One for you, two for me. All of it premium.

No One to Tell

*

I was the new guy in town, given the less glamorous side of the business which meant doing industrial furnace inspections on long weekends, doing northern Québec, marine boilers and crematoriums as well as the good stuff.

Winter came early in '82. The end of November was as bad as any January with snow and ice that made the A-10 to Sherbrooke treacherous, the inclined entrance to the funeral home unapproachable and I parked the car where I came to a stop.

The crematorium incinerator had failed catastrophically due to burning cadavers at temperatures well beyond the recommended 980° C. Also, they often used cardboard containers for the dearly departed, since much of their clientele came from limited means or penny-pinching families.

Rich or poor, visible body hair goes first in a flash of sparks, then the cardboard and clothing. With the body directly on the refractory, the skin chars into erupting popcorn-size blisters under the pressure of boiling fat, sizzling pools of body oils forming, leeching and causing a destructive chemical reaction.

Bodies were stacking up not only in the freezer, but in the garage where they'd left the door partially open to draw in the cold. That's where I saw grandpa laying in his cardboard coffin with his arms crossed and a leg that had somehow leaped or sprung from the box. The shoeless foot was firmly planted on the concrete floor, the leg exposed from the sock to mid-calf. So much for dignity in death.

Walking into the incinerator room, I briefly noticed a woman wearing something very short and very sexy as the maintenance fellow greeted me. Later, the inspection complete, he directed me to the Chief Administrator's office. Hers, I discovered.

Her skirt couldn't have ridden any higher, revealing the

tiny overlapping feathers of the off-white ribbon at the button-clasp of her garter. She didn't stand when I knocked and entered. A dollar to a doughnut she didn't want to upset the way she'd fixed her legs, her skirt and her ribbons. Had I sat in the seat in front of her, not to the side like an idiot, I would have seen a colour that wasn't the blue of her skirt, possibly mauve. Her lilac blouse wasn't transparent, though did allow for a generous view of her mauve push-up bra and resultant cleavage at the provocatively unbuttoned front.

Her office was modern, without the stuffiness of a funeral home with Danish-styled furniture, bright colours and sliding doors that opened onto a wide patio blanketed under snow and ice; perhaps a private café-terrace for the summer months. After fifteen minutes she reached for a file on the coffee table, uncrossing her legs, placing them far enough apart for me to understand that next time I should take the other seat. Which thereafter I did often.

She'd taken over the family business once her father became a client, though she preferred administration as opposed to the darker, more mysterious side of the business. She was a close match for Desirée whom I hadn't seen for three years.

She was in a panic, heading into the habitual December and January peak season. I explained why, that steel trays and longer burn times instead of cardboard boxes would save her thousands each year. I also promised the project would begin the very next day, thinking for a moment she might kiss me. She didn't. Unfortunate. Instead she kept the tease going for another half-hour.

The work lasted four days. As always, I visited the job site at completion. I was pleased, especially when coffee was served in the administrator's office. I can also attest to Christine's panties under her A-line skirt matching the colour of the bra under her open-knit sweater.

A popular rumour or myth from years past was that

during an installation a worker wanting some quiet time ate his lunch inside a furnace or boiler and apparently fell asleep. Unseen by his comrades, the pilot light functioning properly, they closed the door to conduct a test that would terminate the job, firing the burners to 1500° C, then to 500 to begin the curing process. They say no trace was ever found.

The guys doing my incinerator job asked a new recruit to go inside for some reason or other. Once in the cramped chamber, on all fours, the electric door closed quickly, and manually, the pranksters outside started yelling "No! No!" They began banging on the outer walls, which is when I hurried in from Christine's office with a quickened pulse, wondering what the hell was going on.

When I discovered what they'd done they lost little time raising the door. The guy inside was kneeling, purple with rage and white with fear, his leather gloves in tatters. He went at them with arms swinging blindly, kicking the crap out of them. I didn't get in the way.

After his complaint was filed, my comments were requested. The jokers were fired.

*

The train yards were another source of ongoing income, those maintenance people preferring tasks that didn't require crawling into room-sized boilers through impossibly small access doors to perform periodic inspections and easy repairs. Calling me once a year and waiting for the invoice was much easier.

The circular door was some 4.5 metres off the floor and slightly narrower than my shoulders. Squeezing through meant one arm followed by one shoulder, then the other side, scaling the pipes and steel tubes lining the front much easier and preferable to using a ladder. Although I always wore a suit and tie, such frequent inspections required that I travel with boots, coveralls, hardhat and work gloves.

Work lights were seldom in place for inspections, which meant carrying a pocketsize dive light with an adjustable beam, using a five-kilo hammer to sound out the hollows, verifying hot spots I'd determined with a thermal gun a few days prior to the shutdown.

I'd been inside for forty-five minutes to an hour, banging, picking, making notes and sketches with my light stuck in my mouth, aimed at the paper. Raising my head, I suppose as though that would help me with a particular thought, I froze at seeing the blue light; the pilot light that comes on seconds before four-metre flames would shoot out at 1300° C.

I had no time for "Holy Shit!" That came later. My head went straight through the porthole, both shoulders bearing the brunt of the collision with the steel rim. My hardhat fell away, my light clattering along the piping to the floor, everyone turning from what they were doing, staring at the guy squirming halfway out the hole, his hands grasping downward at the bars and pipes, pulling his lower half out with unusual speed and dexterity.

They said later that I shot out like a bullet, that they'd never seen that kind of determination. With my feet barely free of the hole, I was perfectly inverted, grabbing at whatever came first as my legs took over and I followed them in a semi-cartwheel to the ground before landing on my ass and hearing my own "Holy Shit!" as some guy passed me my hat.

They were concerned before they were amused. If they'd gotten to me any sooner they could have caught me in mid-flight, one fellow running to the controls to confirm all was fine with the safety still in the 'ON' position. The beam of my light had shone directly into the blue glass of an inspection hole over the burner, instantaneously very much like a pilot flame to my fast-thinking mind or overactive imagination.

Being in a furnace or boiler even at ambient temperatures has the effect of making bodies swell. When I recounted my story to Guy one day at lunch, he told me of an incident more comical than mine, at least to me.

Guy was about 1, 8 metres, weighing in at about 85 kilos. He was well-proportioned and fit from the rigors of the job. Guy was a man's man, in the fashion sense. He'd been in the furnace for over an hour doing calculations and notes. Finished, ready to leave, he couldn't get out despite all attempts at squirming, pulling and distortion. Short of cutting out the wall, Guy was entombed with only his head framed by the circular porthole while discussing strategies with the amused maintenance crew.

The decision was made. He had to strip to his underwear, throwing out his boots, coveralls, pants, shirt, socks and gloves. In return, they passed in a can of thick, pasty axle grease. He coated himself from his shoulders to his knees so that the men clinging to the piping on the outside could each grab a wrist and haul him out as best they could.

Finally, he stood on the ground in his shorts, greased, bruised and scraped, wondering why he hadn't passed out his notes and drawings first.

*

I'd previously moved into a top floor studio apartment of a downtown transient high-rise, commonly known as 2021 that was home to gays, lesbians, flight attendants, kept secretaries, call girls and old farts with red convertible sports cars.

I left with my clothes, personal affects, a mortgage, and maybe a bruise or two. Although I didn't see much value in keeping my bathrobe with the serious knife slash across the lapels that I'd been wearing at the time. The female condition.

The building was equipped with saunas, a pool, a gym,

two sundecks and interior parking. Not much different from 755, very different from the house I'd just bought.

April and May disappeared quickly into my ever-growing past and summer came at last, welcome as always. The women normally congregated on the top sundeck to sunbathe topless where men couldn't leer at them from a superior vantage. The building had a spectacular 360° view of the city, the river, and the sundeck was a calming place for my Friday afternoon paperwork.

She came to the deck wearing a sunhat, Bermuda shorts, knee socks, and a white long-sleeve cotton blouse with ruffles in the front and a high-neck collar, causing me to wonder why a nun would live in that building and be on a sundeck where eight of ten breasts were bare anytime.

I was on the top deck because the bum-boys were on the lower level. I'd commandeered the sunniest corner, laid my towel, cracked open a beer and worked; standing once in a while for a shower under the exterior head that wasn't five metres away.

After a few minutes she sauntered, swayed to the shower from behind a large concrete planter a few centimetres from my feet, her back to me most of the short journey. Show time. She was topless, wearing turquoise high-on-the-hip backless mesh panties with snaps. Definitely not swimwear. Déjà vu, or what? Her body was symmetrical perfection, one perfectly tanned feature joined tightly with another as she faced away while adjusting the hot and cold.

Her head tilted towards me, her front assailed with the full force of jet-like streams. After a few minutes she turned, heedless, doing her back, squeezing her shoulder-length red hair into wet tails that ended as her hands opened over her alert breasts with erotic slowness and remained there for long seconds, though not long enough, with the water spraying both of us. Definitely chilled water.

She brought her hands to her sides to test the snaps,

opening one then the other before sliding a steady hand inside the front, hiding the deeper red weaving through the open mesh with red-lacquered nails. She turned sideways, deliberately, closing the multiple streams, walking to her place at the other side of the planter. That was early afternoon and the showers continued on the half-hour until shadows crept over the deck.

Linda had seen the nun previously. She didn't believe me when I recounted the story, not until she saw for herself not very long after. The deck became my Friday haunt, my time for reflection, rain coming all too often on Fridays that year, not unlike past Fridays at 755.

Once, towards the end of August, I arrived at my sun-filled workstation to set up with paper, pen, beer and a towel. First showering away the stickiness of the early afternoon.

From that perspective I had a perfect view of where she normally ensconced herself, and her, the nun, facing away, topless, kneeling and rocking to and fro with her undone buff-coloured panties lying trapped between her legs and his. Come one, come all. So to speak.

Her ass was there for complimentary viewing, I assumed, with darkly tanned hands pulling and pushing at her hips with equal enthusiasm. Not even the sound of spraying water distracted her as she continued pinning him to the deck, firmly attached with her open weight. She didn't turn, stop, or hesitate. Very much the opposite. They accelerated their motion, her groans guttural, until she convulsed, gasping a shriek, collapsing forward, straddling the guy under her.

I stayed a few moments longer to show my respect, reaching blindly for the faucet.

But summer wasn't only to ogle pretty, redheaded exhibitionists getting laid, showing their tights asses or showering in the open air with perky breasts and see-though panties. There was more to life than that. Residents often had visitors who would go to the top deck to marvel at the panoramic view and the noiseless, miniature traffic twenty-four floors below.

That particular Friday I had a very late-day appointment which was a very rare event. I was on the deck dressed for business, doing a last minute pre-call. The two old ladies were sitting in their armour-plated beachwear adjusting the modesty skirts while ignoring varicose veins, loose skin and bent toes. We're talking eighty, eighty-five, not a day younger. They were having a good chat the way old ladies do, probably about the naked women who hadn't covered their breasts for someone else's grandmothers.

I could have gone and I should have gone, but they'd already begun the departure process and I wanted to avoid getting stuck in the elevator with them. I wasn't looking at them when they put on their muumuus, not even peripherally, avoiding them altogether when they began gyrating and shimmying out of their swimsuits. Spare me. Mission accomplished. I'd survived. Think so? Not quite.

The summer day was beautiful, very windy as well. Pleasant most days when the younger women stripped from their strings and tops under their towels to let them dry. After all, the building was a high-priced place for singles and how better to strike up a conversation? Particularly when dressed in a minimalist towel in an elevator.

At some point our age is expressed by how we bend to reach the floor, old age defined by legs being straight, feet wide apart and, from the hip, bending with one or both hands extended for protection against possible toppling. They both bent over at the same time, one with her back to me when the unruly winds swept across the rooftop and took the muumuu in various directions.

The ensuing and expansive surface was white and potted, painted with the blue markings of age and split with a fissure that was long and dark towards its core.

The frontage, more like spillage, hung in a series of overlapping, loose folds marked with large spots sporting smaller protrusions that served to centre a gap of various shades left barren by nature. The event lasted a nanosecond and I knew then why old men die before old women: By choice.

*

The one event I couldn't escape over my five years was the Annual Golf Tournament, 100 of the company's best clients congregating for a day of beating the crap out of tightly spun elastic balls and dislocating already out-of-shape bodies.

The first time for me was a 35° C day, my score winning me the dubious honour of what became the annual Lemon Award. No one on the committee had anticipated the score and the only award available was a fresh lemon that had previously decorated a shrimp platter.

Each of the four subsequent tourneys had similar temps, scores, and fresh lemons.

Scott had implemented a no-drive policy following my predecessor's drinking-related death. Anyone under the influence was to take a taxi home. The company would pay the bill, no questions asked. The policy also applied, company-wide, over the two-week Christmas period when some of the office staff took advantage, but never a sales rep. The single condition was that if you did not take advantage of the offer and were caught DUI, you were no longer at RTI.

The second month of my second year got me through another lemon prize because I refused to go into the rough to find one ball when I had dozens in the bag that came with the Spaldings I'd bought for the first tourney and would sell to Pierre after my last for the original 500. The month also brought me the second largest order in the company's thirty-five year history. One half-million for a project at a new plant on the Gaspé coast. The details had taken several months to prepare, revise and perfect, all in longhand because my PC was still ten years off.

At first the intermediary client-company, who was to supply the actual incineration unit, weren't part of any Client Business Plan. However I developed one subsequent to the initial visit with the engineering staff and production heads of both companies.

Scott stayed informed from a distance; Ralph dropped by once with his credit card. He left after lunch.

The deal was initialled on July 30th at 2:00 AM, I was sleeping at 3:00 and diving in the 1000 Islands at 10:00.

Monday morning was bright, the air was still. Inside was a whirlwind of shit and I was in the middle of the maelstrom. Ralph was showing his true colours and I would see him in that light for the next four years. If I'd called him that Friday night he would have meddled and made a mess of things. Everyone at lunch that day realized that truth. So did Scott.

Ralph wanted the glory, not satisfied when I mentioned for the second time that the contract was initialled, not signed by me. Anyway, I'd robbed him of the chance to take the credit that wasn't his and he was pissed. Not a big issue for me. He got on the phone red-faced and purple-lipped while I was in his office to tell Scott how badly I'd "fucked up," how much trouble I'd caused them. Good management technique, Ralph, meanwhile entertaining the entire office.

About an hour later, after reviewing pertinent data, a letter came through the rarely used fax machine to my attention, cc'd to Ralph. The brief note read: "J.T. Congratulations! Scott."

*

Ralph was blessed with low retention. We were walking

towards my car on our way to meet the other guys for lunch when he commented on how the black Grand Prix looked white with its thick layer of dust and he asked if I was getting divorced. Stupid question. Where the correlation came from I have no idea, though at the time I laughed it off and Ralph thought of something else stupid to say.

Dean was the only one who knew of the separation due to the terminal injuries of divergent personalities, indifference and lacklustre togetherness that grew disproportionately over eight years.

Moving from downtown to Longueuil was a function of convenience, a question of larger quarters. The studio apartment at 2021 went quickly from acceptably small at first to very small at the end. I was now ten minutes from the office that I went into on rarer occasions and Fridays were unquestionably mine. Linda, the lady I'd been seeing since moving out of my mortgage, moved to Ottawa. We would be weekend commuters for two years.

Soon after Ralph's hissy fit about the second largest order, I was at the Shell station in Casselman one Friday, en route to the capital when my beeper went off with a message from afore mentioned Sales Manager. I tossed it into the water bin before replacing the squeegee as a message of my own. Personalizing Fridays was never a guilt trip for me. In a word, balance.

To-date much of what I'd done in client meetings was with key figures at my accounts, the decision makers, though increasingly I included others who could have input regarding the final word on projects, or those who might be promoted to key positions sometime later. ROI was becoming increasingly imperative, more people responsible for seeing that happen, which meant more technically explicit and effective presentations delivered to anticipate objections based on perceived negative components while highlighting the need. Got all that? Always the need, not the want.

Larger meetings never appealed to me, in-house or otherwise. The average short span of attention combined with the tendency towards easy distraction didn't make large audiences an ideal or meaningful venue. Not my style. Of course there were in-house exceptions I had no control over, such as when Scott came into town, but by and large I stayed with smaller groups in favour of personal attention and attention to detail.

My favourite medium was eyeball to eyeball in a conference room. Flip charts were a nuisance, noisy and disruptive, apart from the fact my writing borders on atrocious. Power Point hadn't arrived. Instead I subsisted happily with telescopic pointers and overheads. Later, when technology did provide more creative tools, I would use them solely under duress. The reason? Simple. Vibrant colours and slick slideshows reinforce the sales' adage that bullshit baffles brains, which isn't my point.

Scott came in for a group meeting about twice each year, when the key personnel in each department would give him a full review of what was and what would be. Normally a dozen or so were present for a day of concise information and few wasted words. I never saw Scott tanned, but when he was pissed he got really white and that's when you hoped he wasn't glaring at you. One particular day he turned whiter-than-white, staring down Dean who said something perhaps a little too glibly that set Scott off and brought a response that began with "You fucking asshole…"

Guy was sitting beside me when I whispered, or thought I had, that Scott's reaction was uncalled for, which caused him to look away from Dean and glare directly at me. He said that if he wanted to call me a fucking asshole, he would. I countered without blinking, with a signature smirk that sometimes irritates people. I agreed with him, he should, with just cause. However were I to discover at any time that he was one, a fucking asshole, I would let him know. He wanted to smile. I know he did. Instead he responded that if I didn't I wasn't any use to him or the company.

Ralph coughed, sputtering wet flecks, probably messing himself while Scott turned to Ned.

Not good.

I kept my mouth shut.

*

The same summer as the beeper drowning I was waiting until 2:00 PM one Friday before leaving for Ottawa so I'd arrive at Linda's before rush hour traffic on the maniacal Queensway.

I was daydreaming, looking out over my seventh floor balcony at the passing traffic without seeing it when a man dressed entirely in black stopped at the intersection. The sun was blinding, the heat of the day blistering, which made his fashion statement seem all the more peculiar.

His hair was shoe polish-black as well, and he appeared reasonably fit from a distance. He was slim, tall, and had been walking with a gait that implied neither urgency nor distress. I thought he was about to jaywalk. Instead he sat on the curb, leaned onto one elbow and died, his body sinking the remainder of the way so that he lay on his back.

By coincidence a motorcycle cop arrived moments later, talking to the corpse, trying to stir the man, using cop logic. A popular bar was on the same block. The man was drunk, passed out.

Finally the cop swung from the saddle, first performing the toe test, followed by the prod with a billy club. After which, I suspected, a Merde! The body was taken away minutes later without fuss or ceremony. The cop sat on his Harley writing notes.

John lived in the same complex. He was the main

contact at the refinery I worked with and one of the main sources of my financial success. He had two habits solidly engrained as part of his character.

Passing by his private office one day with lunch in mind, and not seeing him, I left. This happened once or twice more before I mentioned to him that he was a hard guy to find at times. Seems I wasn't looking in the right place, under his desk. Every noon John would lie under his desk, take off his boots and snooze for twenty minutes. The other habit was chewing tobacco. Or, more precisely, the Styrofoam cup that became a danger to any nearby paperwork by day's end.

The night was another one alone in my apartment, with notes or whatever, when a serious knock came to the door that was followed by: "Police!" I ignored them. The knock came again. I ignored them. I didn't like being interrupted. Besides, use the intercom. Give a guy a heads-up. But cops are cops. They don't go away.

He was cool, a cop with a few questions. She had her head on a pivot. She was on a mission. She wanted desperately into the apartment, blocked by me.

"Are you alone?" he asked. Something like that.

"Why?" which seemed like a reasonable response.

"A neighbour reported a woman screaming."

I said, "You're late. She was screaming last night."

He chuckled. She didn't, probably straight from the academy, up early each morning shining her new badge with Silvo.

"May we come in? We have to make sure everything's okay." He explained. "It would help us."

I waved him in first, blocking her, letting her walk around me. I didn't like her. We didn't like each other. We didn't have to. She was a cop, not a lady, although she definitely had potential as a dominatrix.

He knew they wouldn't find anything untoward, asking

me about my photography lining the walls as she made a SWAT beeline for the bedroom, running in as she screeched at him to follow. He hurried, I didn't. He was leaning on the wall bursting a gut, seeing my vulcanized dive suit with its integrated boots pointing upwards.

I got nothing from her. She was pissed, disappointed. From him I got a "sorry for the trouble" and more chuckles that continued along the hall to the elevator.

I'd bet her steel-clad undies the rest of his shift was a tad chilly.

*

I visited with Christine a few times over each of the previous two years as a courtesy, and would in subsequent years, as well as more formal meetings for inspections and installations, a few of those occasions on her patio. She was never too busy.

The work was usually done in late fall, plans normally beginning in July or August. I was more expensive than her competitive options, though the higher grade of plastic I recommended gave her the flexibility of incinerating cadavers at higher temperatures without very much interim repair work.

Her problem was having a single incinerator and, despite her conversion from cardboard boxes to steel beds, and my warnings, she pushed the limits. This time teaching her a lesson. The extensive damage could not wait four months. Untreated corpses in July wouldn't go unnoticed for very long.

She always greeted me at the bottom of her private staircase at the rear of the building that had the double brightness of incandescent lighting and natural lighting glaring from the skylight directly over the stairs leading to her office. White-on-white. Yummy. The view could not have been better, or better illuminated. The girl was a vision. What I'd come to expect.

No One to Tell

Her double band summer sandals were white linen, 10cm heels giving definition and tautness to her bare legs. Her white linen sundress was sheer, short and flighty, the button-down front partially closed with only the most necessary buttons engaged above and below her unbelted waist. White lace decorated her white thong, perfectly detailed at eye level, disappearing nicely into a crevice parting teardrop curves, drawing particular attention to the fact, as she preceded me up the stairs, that her ass was bronzed and spectacular; one cheek caressing the other, exchanging shapes with each of the thirty-two steps.

She wasn't wearing a bra. Not needed. A simple pendant delineated faux-pockets filled with her breasts.

I declined her invitation to do lunch on the patio. Idiot. The season was busier than normal and, sadly, my agenda didn't permit. She used her patio at lunch and after hours for private tanning and spending the afternoon talking business would have been too easy.

She understood, though she did insist on lemonade. The day was sweltering, a slight breeze no relief at all. How could I refuse? I took a seat that put a low-rise wicker table between us, laying out blueprints as she filled crystal glasses. Classy.

Fact: The longer a beautiful woman takes to prepare and serve lemonade, the better it tastes. I know. She was taking her time. Her reach across the serving trolley for the jug was discreetly exaggerated, sheer fabric rippling across tanned cheeks, a timely breeze flirting shamelessly with the weightless material.

Christine stayed as she was, enjoying the unexpected touch of summer's heated breath across her bare skin. I could easily imagine the dreamy bliss she was feeling. I know what I was feeling. Her ass was spectacular, framed in fluttering linen, commanding or craving admiration. Both.

Seek and ye shall receive.

As she came to where I was sitting I was thankful for my Ray*Bans. Her dress was a matter of practicality, somewhat superfluous had we not been discussing business, though not exactly appropriate for meeting with grieving relatives. The view was exceptional, her half-open dress teasing her thighs and me under the prevailing soft breeze, my deserved recompense for the grannies on the 2021 sundeck.

She was inherently sultry, sexy and single, though I never asked why. Curious. Undoubtedly, someone was missing out big-time. Then again, who wants to share intimacy with a woman who oversees the dead? I do. I do. Or I did. Thank goodness Linda came along in time to save me.

Doing business with Christine was unlike other crematoriums, like the one on the edge of Mount Royal. That operation was much larger, centered more on production, forsaking personal attention. The place was a veritable bakery with rows of brick-faced ovens clouded in the eeriness of sombre monochromatic grey tones and the penetrating clanging noises of a foundry.

I enjoyed constant business with larger facilities with an endless need for repairs or major re-makes, though I never once went into any of the chambers fitted with rows of burners at the top and sides of their cramped interiors. My protocol for that particular clientele was a measuring tape, top grade material and PR. That was it. What counted was that I got the job done.

My day would come soon enough, despite the best wishes of the Sisters of the Holy Something or Other. I parked my car in front of their convent one day for an appointment across the street before my second rendezvous at the mountainside crematorium. Returning to the car, reaching for my keys, I saw they were on the wrong side of the door. One of the good sisters, seeing my plight, assured me that where there was a will there was a way. This, still a few years before my cellphone in a city with very few garages in the core.

Minutes later a gaggle of God's girls swarmed around me, smiling, giggling, staring at me, staring at the car, two or three taking turns with the coat hanger until the door opened. Their good deed done, I thanked them profusely, God blessing me eight, maybe nine times. The cop on the corner shaking his head.

I was at the mountain facility a few minutes late, wondering about the dozens of bodies waiting their turn for disappearance. Not all went to their fiery end in fine oak or mahogany caskets. Some went in cartons, while others lay exposed in open steel beds. Some clothed, others not.

The old blue-haired head attached to an emaciated body was on such a bed as I watched her gurney guided to the front of the blackened stainless steel door, her meagre and undressed mortal remains pushed in.

The door closed, the switch was pressed. Time was money. That I understood.

Bodies burn at different rates depending on bulk, now fashionably called BMI, and the lady had none. She would be a quickie at 980° C, and was. An hour or so later, workers brought out what was left of her on a fan-shaped spatula better suited to a pizzeria, scooping out the hollow skull alive with exploding sparks and a soft afterglow of blue flames that gave her head the appearance of a Christmas pudding.

I normally did those calls at day's end. Never before lunch.

*

I was in Sherbrooke and at the Auberge after dark on a Friday night, tired, parked as close as possible to my room at the end of the three-story hotel. I always asked for the same room and they obliged because I was a frequent guest.

The room was located conveniently to the pool in the summer, in the other seasons I was close to my car and usually no one parked that far from the entrance so the area was also quiet. I'd adopted the habit of dousing the headlights before veering in front of hotel windows to avoid bothering other guests with sudden glare. This night was no different.

The parking lot was black when I drove between the yellow lines, seeing the man and woman leaning against the grill of a car with Vermont plates.

I came in beside them. When I climbed out the man motioned politely to me to be quiet. I joined them to see what was going on, realizing why he'd silenced me. The drapes in one room were open; the bright lights no doubt making the windows appear mirrored from the inside where a woman was lying across her bed flipping through pages of a magazine. She was dressed in a camisole, her tap pants framing memorable cheeks, swaying bare feet sideways.

Her bed was separated from the one in the adjacent room by the thickness of a wall.

The drapes of the other room were half-drawn, another woman lying on her front atop her bed with the covers pulled back, also flipping through pages of a magazine.

She was wearing a garter and stockings, close enough to her cheeks to push them slightly upward. Her ass was bare, save for her dark blue thong outlining her curves, her bra laid out neatly beside her.

Her legs were in motion, her inviting contours immodest and enticing, raising and lowering one leg, the other, her ass rising and falling in an unbroken and silent rhythm, her panties alluring not meant to conceal. I knew; I bought them.

She reached once or twice for her glass of white wine, showing the profile of a breast that had the firmness of training. Watching her, them, seeing her, them, was like viewing a flat screen years in the future, each actress unaware of the other, yet playing the same role.

The guy gawked as though he'd never seen a near-naked woman lying on a hotel bed, and I wondered whether his lady friend would be the beneficiary of his increased heart-rate later on. Probably not. She was urging him to get into their car, certain the man working in the first window at one of those typically round coffee-work tables of the 80s would come out and start a fight. Besides, the women were disgusting. Like I said, probably not.

Truth be told, what was disgusting was her lime-green polyester two-piece suit from a nearly new store and her once-was white vinyl purse with a knotted strap that let the thing hang at the proper height. Finally she won out, with the nagging of a woman who would never think to escape the daily drudgery of her wall-less prison, her only achievement a series of polyester-clad abdominal streaks brought on by the boredom of winters past. Likely as not they were leaving because they couldn't afford the nightly rate.

I stayed outside the window a while longer, absorbing the views, though more as a comparative study, amused by the anonymity of what had just happened as the Vermont Polyesters drove to a more affordable bed. I was camouflaged by darkness, briefly tempted to toss a pebble at the window, to see her reaction. I didn't. That would have startled her, spoiled our shared moment. She was enjoying herself, as was I.

Instead I went to our room, smiling, not expecting more.

At the same moment as I arrived at the door, the man from the adjoining room came out, facing in, talking to the lady who'd changed her position on the bed, who'd caught my eye with a fleeting coquettish smirk. Nice. By the time he'd come fully into the hall en route to the ice machine, I was walking into my room.

The pages stopped flipping, though the knees kept slicing invisible air.

The guy from Vermont definitely left too soon.

*

Val d'Or and points northwest and northeast of the remote town was a region I went to from May to September. Even then I had no guarantee of not finding a metre or more of snow on the ground, like the time in June when girls were sunbathing on the lake in bikinis and mukluks. That would be *on* the ice-covered lake.

No guys. Northern guys stay pasty white. It's their thing.

By car the trip is punishing any time of year, with hours of gruelling driving on near-isolated roads that I did once. After which I flew, making an exception one winter to satisfy a client. Linda came with me. All she remembers is whiteness.

I included Lebel-sur-Quévillon into the agenda occasionally during summer months, when a specific need existed. Otherwise I had no reason to be in one of Québec's many northern hellholes.

The last time I saw Quévillon in my rear-view mirror was the spring of '86, late one Thursday that would put me into the relative civilization of Val d'Or by 6:30 if I didn't hit a moose or run into a Sûreté roadblock with two cop cars V'd in the middle of the road and four cops leaning over the olive-coloured hoods holding serious shotguns. That was a treat.

Québec's ultimate boy's club where being white, Francophone and arrogant gave you a better chance at carrying a gun and acting like King Shit. In the seventies, eighties and nineties tokens were meant for crossing bridges and travelling highways in La Belle Province. In the 70s and 80s it also meant being Anglophone, Black or female for those aspiring to wear provincial badges.

A hand went up telling me to stop, but the four shotguns had pretty much already done that. Two of them stayed poised while two others squeezed their doughnuts through the narrow apex, each taking one side of my car, searching the empty interior. All four were young, probably new recruits, being that novices in the green-shirted force were exiled to remoteness for as long as four years to prove their worth or their ability to remain sober.

They were searching for gold stolen from a mine earlier that afternoon, probably by guys who were wearing 600 dollar suits and ties and driving a rental car. I didn't have to pop the trunk, surprisingly, waved away without eye contact.

I drove off wondering how a .16 gauge shell in the back of the head would feel, not that I didn't trust them.

I did about 110, 120 along the isolated seventy-five kilometres to Senneterre in a 90 zone, slowing to posted speeds nearing and passing through the town, waiting a judicious ten km before accelerating to a speed that would get me to the hotel on time. I didn't consider my speed excessive, that at home was an acceptable infringement, since I hadn't seen a single car between the two towns. So when another Sûreté cop who was parked around a blind curve waved, I waved and kept going. Which isn't what he had in mind. He wasn't very nice about it and I believe those extra few metres cost me more than the 120 I was doing.

No matter. I'd expense the amount. N'est pas? Salut, Monsieur l'Agent.

L'Escale was a nice hotel with a comfortable bar, quiet ambiance, an above average restaurant for the area and quiet, modern rooms. The only inconvenience was going to my room from the restaurant or bar for latrine time, since an earlier occasion when I'd gone to answer the call and a queer followed me in. Back then they weren't gay, just queer.

I'd taken one of the stalls, not one of the two wall units, thinking of The Male Code. He went into the other stall, which wasn't a problem or unusual until moments later when his hand came in under the partitioning wall waving a business card with his room number on it.

I was surprised the reality of me pissing into his half-cupped hand took so long to set in. He wanted the hose, but got the water instead and, like eighty percent of the population, probably didn't wash his hands before leaving.

The next morning I drove to Rouyn-Noranda, an easy 100km drive for three meetings before a dinner and a late flight. I made money, which is always good, dead to the world as a result.

R-N at the time wasn't a culinary destination, probably isn't now, with one exception. The town's only decent hotel, where I would stay when not in Val d'Or, was owned by a man who was also a master chef from somewhere where food was an art. Then, a six-course meal with a glass of wine, or two, was under fifteen dollars. Incredible, and succulent. Except for the barbarian that night insisting loudly that his meal be returned to the kitchen,

He'd asked for his meat burnt, as in black, charcoal-crisp. Perhaps the cook should learn a few basics, he yelled. At which point Monsieur le Chef, a true artist, stormed into the dining room to personally evict the deviant, refusing him future privileges. When he asked how my feast was, well, I was rewarded with a complimentary glass of wine, which made me very late.

Again, no cellphones.

The Rouyn-Noranda airport was a small facility. Parking was a stone's throw from the runway, which is why when I sped in at 8:55, for an 8:55 flight, the props were blurred, the engines were revving, and the plane was pulling back from its position on the tarmac.

Perhaps the expression engraved on my face was sufficiently aghast at being deserted, or perhaps he noticed my outreached hands clasped in prayer, if only for appearances. But the silver thing jerked to a stop, the cockpit window opened and the pilot's arm shot out waving at me to hurry as another man came running towards me from inside the terminal.

He banged down on the trunk. I leaped out with the keys. He grabbed my bags and tickets, verifying the details, running like hell ahead of me, giving the forward section of the plane wide clearance. The steps lowered. I ran up, tossing the keys. Whew.

Those were indeed better days, the best days, and one of the few times I ever ran.

*

The first time I met Peter I was thirty-three. He was 133. He was old, bitter and rude. I had visions of his feet crossing in front of my face. He called me Charlie, changing my name to Buddy Boy until he thought Buddy sounded better. Then I was Charlie Boy.

"Charlie," he asked during our first meeting, "how long is a piece of string?"

"Pardon?"

"You heard me."

He stayed silent.

"What's the point of the question?"

"To get an answer. What else is a question for?"

He went silent again.

"There is no answer. That's my answer." I replied, half smiling, not certain whether he was a jerk or an asshole. "But I do know my name's James, or JT, or Mr. Barrett. Your choice. But not Charlie, not Buddy, and I'm nobody's boy."

No One to Tell

That set the tone for our relationship that lasted the better part five years.

He wasn't old, or as rude as he put on. He simply didn't like sales people and was bitter at his impending obsolescence. He'd kept up with the times, well-versed in the intricacies of his trade, which was purchasing, but retirement was coming ever closer. He was unprepared for leisure apart from perfecting his golf game which he practiced eight months a year, six days a week.

He never refused me an appointment. Nor did I ask for one unless I was bringing him the value of new information or innovation. He was accustomed to asking the questions and telling, not being asked or told.

I had, over the first several months, contributed in no small way to his change of philosophy about not seeing sales people. Essentially I convinced him that each rep he did not see left him with that much less information that he would otherwise have, that his competitor would have.

He was one of the few clients that I enjoyed kibitzing with, though he drew the line at going to lunch. He thought of lunches and dinners as time wasted, subliminal cajoling, when he would rather be working or golfing.

He played 18-holes each weeknight, 36 on Saturdays to compensate for time with his wife on Sundays, never accepting an invitation to a mid-week game or any company tournament that wasn't his own.

At sixty-five they gave him the Golden Kiss-Off and a watch. They threw him out of the company after forty-five years of dedicated service, which he took as a personal affront.

At one time I was the first person he would call for technical information, soon graduating to the only source of refractory-related issues, a confidence and synergy deserving of more than "Goodbye and good luck. See you around," and I was delighted when he accepted my invitation to dinner.

Dinner with our ladies at the finest restaurant in the region was all about fun conversation and laughing, no shoptalk, no glumness. I'd given Peter a gift a few days earlier, during our final business transaction, that I'd wrapped with just a piece of string so that the dinner would have nothing to do with work.

The meal was superb. The wine was excellent and dessert was succulent, most of which Peter managed to eat with one hand while squeezing and patting Linda's knee under the table all evening. Who enjoyed the evening the most is anyone's guess.

Ralph had a shit fit when I submitted the total bill for the equivalent of 1200 dollars in current day cash.

I shrugged, explaining the amount included a carbon golf club. There was just something about Ralph that made pissing him off enjoyable. What he didn't know, what pissed him off even more, was that the VP at Head Office not only approved the expense but that HO would absorb the full amount.

Ralph was getting increasingly cranky and this might have been the piss in his pea soup that made him snap. He was mid-fifties, looked seventy and felt eighty. He was washed up and knew it; though, I suspect what bothered him more was that we knew.

Scott was on his case for still being the industry idiot and Tony, the VP, was increasingly more interested in what Ralph was doing as much as what he wasn't doing.

I was getting pretty good at this last word peculiarity of mine and only at the end of the conversation did I explain that I'd been talking about Peter with Tony who insisted that I properly acknowledge Peter's large contribution to our sales.

*

Birds weren't the only things that flew over Ralph's head.

No One to Tell

He missed out on most conversations, not by exclusion, rather by oblivion. So I hadn't bothered to tell him that I would be unavailable for a couple of days while being poked, prodded and torn apart by a surgeon's scalpel.

The procedure was an annoyance, in no way serious, and I hated the fact of spending the night in clinical accommodations for the sake of a thirty-minute cut-me-up in the morning. They'd said to be at the hospital by 3:00 and I was. They'd said to follow certain procedures, and I did, albeit after annoying them with questions as to why. They'd said the operation would be at 8:00 AM, and that's all they said. They said nothing at all about what to do in between.

Coughing, hacking, moaning, groaning, spitting and farting generally annoy me about people. So even with a private room a hospital is not a friendly environment for me. The only place that smells worse than a hospital ward is their laundry facility where no distinction is made between your bedding and the guy who just messed himself through one orifice or another, or the one who died, or the one who came in covered with blood from a street fight.

Supper, a juice, was brought in at 5:00 by people unacquainted with local language and didn't much care when I declined the treat I was limited to. I'd already refused to wear the slit-down-the-back threadbare rag they'd given me after the millionth wash, so they weren't overly caring when I walked past the nurses' station in my jeans and sweater.

Looking out from my seventh-floor balcony was much more peaceful than all the clatter of trays, gurneys, and the gaseous explosions coming from those who seemed to wait until I was close enough to share in the event. Nowhere on the sheet of rules did I see any mention of scotch which I justified, as a liquid, was an allowable part of my clinical diet. I'd eaten my fill of real food earlier in the day and simply wanted to enjoy a few moments of alone time and a sip or two before being dug into like a Thanksgiving turkey.

The operation went according to schedule at 8:00 AM. I was at home by suppertime.

They had disagreed, arguing that I should stay one more night, but I was signed out and got on with what needed to be done. It's that authority thing again.

When I was eighteen I was admitted into a private hospital for some minor ailment. I spent the first part of the week operating the elevator, doing indoor messages for senior patients, one afternoon escaping for a downtown jaunt. That went pretty well, until I walked into a gaggle of my nurses who didn't exactly commiserate with my need for freedom.

I was escorted arm in arm to my room, and relieved of my shoes. Imagine, though not the severe punishment one might expect.

I had learned that, by sitting on the windowsill of my room with the drapes drawn when they came to administer nightly pills they said were vitamins, not only could I avoid them, I had a spectacular view.

I was across from the nurses' dorms, separated by a small courtyard, a lighted patchwork of girls wrapped in towels, sauntering around in panties and bras or naked. I suppose the fact that the hospital rooms had curtains obviated the need for the dorms to have curtains, though I can't say for certain that I was pleased to know as much about the nurses as they knew about me.

I was eighteen. They were naked. What else was there to know?

*

My fifth year had just passed and for unrelated reasons I spent an extra hour or so at the bar to toss a few back with the guys after lunch on a Friday before going to the office to pick up a contract that was being typed. Then home.

No One to Tell

I had left my briefcase in the sales area for no particular reason and when I got back old Ralph had put a note on it requesting my presence in his office, not worded quite that way. Uh-oh, this would not be good.

The door hadn't closed by the time his beet-red face streaked with bulging blue rivers of near coagulated blood, his ears red and twitching. The top of his head was so red I thought he was at the point of exploding its brainless interior.

Ralph never spoke, he spluttered. At first I thought he was just a sloppy eater, until I realized the ever-present marks on his ties were actually descendants of the dribble on his permanently wet lips. I had also always meant to comment to Ralph about his puffs, but this was clearly not a good time. He and I shared an affinity for the pocket fillers. Except that mine were Italian, in colours to match my shirts and suits. He had one that was white, plastic, streaked with blue to match his face, and filled with cheap ballpoint pens.

I've never understood yelling in a workplace setting. Words have enormous offensive impact or defensive resilience when used well, though sometimes silence is a superior weapon in a war of temperamental words.

It's a gift. Somehow I'm able to make angry people angrier and Linda stop talking, though she's somewhat immune now. It's an auto-mechanism I have no control over, an ability to convey clear and concise messages non-verbally, maintaining composure when others, Ralph, are losing theirs. Looking good when they look bad. And Ralph looked bad, he always looked bad.

One time he came out of the men's room in his suit, with his shirttails hanging below the hem of his jacket, walking past the women in the office, not aware I was walking behind him impersonating someone drying his hands on one of those public endless pull-down towels that never seem clean because they aren't.

No One to Tell

Everyone clapped, Ralph waving across the office, liking the adoration, not realizing what was going on. He never realized what was going on. For instance, when he attended an awards presentation with a few hundred others in the refractory industry who were to receive awards or applaud those who did.

As usual Ralph was in his own world confusing ridicule with recognition. When the name he was waiting for was finally called he rose from his chair, bowed deeply and beamed broadly, bolting to the stage for his plaque.

Thing is, they hadn't called out Goofball of the Year, or Village Idiot. They called another name and title, the owner of which came behind Ralph who was already at the podium accepting the silent praise of an audience stunned into disbelief and chuckling. Even when they got him to sit he wasn't exactly sure what had happened. Particularly when people came over to give him congratulatory slaps on the back. Well, then he was really confused.

He wore one blue suit with black or blue socks that always showed his pasty shins. His shoes were black, except in the back; his white shirts, or shirt, was always bent backwards at the tips of the collar; his front tails were always exposed to serve as hand or eyeglass wipes. His tie knot never knew which way to go, the tie serving to conceal open spaces that would otherwise reveal more than anyone needed to see.

My expression worked, as expected. He was screaming like a madman and I could visualize everyone stopping whatever they were doing to listen to the crazed monologue coming through the closed door.

I leaned over Ralph's desk calmly, stating plainly that I'd had about all I could take of his bird-dogging bullshit and that I'd invested too much time and energy into my career to be limited by, or interested in, his 50's peddler notions. He would have a copy of my letter in five minutes.

No One to Tell

I don't know how many times over those five years Ralph asked me if I'd closed a sale: The jargon of a true peddler. Nothing about a given phase or action as part of a series of actions completed over time. Client Business or Action Business Plans were as foreign to Ralph as thinking.

I walked out to compose the letter that Ralph's secretary typed, addressed to Tony, VP of Sales, and put it in the internal mail. Ralph got a photo copy. Not because of that one outburst, because of the widening gap between our philosophies, our mindsets. I'd gotten better at what I was doing while Ralph was locked in the 50s with no way out. His reaction was that, if I mailed the letter, I was fired. Good point, Ralph.

That was on a Friday. Monday evening I got a phone call from Tony asking that I meet with him Tuesday morning in the local South Shore office. He understood the situation entirely and didn't want me leaving the company. He wanted me in Vancouver at their expense to represent the company in the West where Québec's mounting tendency towards subsidies for state-supplied electricity, and a future of diminishing sales, wouldn't be an issue.

For that reason, not Ralph, I'd already researched other areas such as heavy equipment. Ralph was simply the catalyst I needed, deciding to let the pieces fall where they may. Tony might have been right when he said Ralph wouldn't be there much longer, and why quit because of a beat-up old-timer who dreaded each new day?

I agreed to weigh the pros and the cons, which I did before quitting.

The pro was the money; the con was moving to the West. Ralph was fifty-three, but with medical science advancing daily he still had a good number of years before he was put out to pasture or wrapped in silk and mahogany.

R.I.P.

Ralph probably isn't dead yet, though very likely comatose.

Dean was terminated six years later for failing to complete detox therapy. He went from a high six-figure income to welfare, ending our friendship when he began jumping turnstiles in the Metro to save the price of a ticket and crawling from basement windows to avoid paying rent.

Pierre was a victim of excess as well, leaving soon after Dean to work his way into retirement one stroke at a time as a house painter. His client's insatiable wife figured somewhat in the lifestyle change.

Ned was terminated as well. He came from a small town to live big, unable to deal with his wife once being the village whore, emptying a 2-4 each day to make things right.

Guy retired to his self-built chalet situated at the foot of a ski hill in the Eastern Townships.

Frank retired to his cottage up north with sufficient memories to fill a book that I would eagerly read.

Scott passed away during the mid-nineties, in all probability his legacy now forgotten. Avery might well have delayed his passing by virtue of having pre-pickled his organs. I believe he died from the sad loneliness of being the company clown.

Peter retired with hurt feelings to play two rounds of

golf each day with his carbon clubs, though by now he might be swinging them a little more slowly.

   Christine ranks highly in vivid memories. She belonged in a fashion magazine, though I'm certain she had a reserve wardrobe, something dark and sombre for each new client. She dressed the way she did for escape. She wanted others to see another side of her. Her way of distancing herself from life's final reality. Who could blame her? Not me. She was spectacular from any angle, a French-speaking Desirée…and still is.

   Some things must never change.

No One to Tell

Chapter Six
1987 - 1990

I never stand in the aisle. Not since the 747 en route to Spain in '75 with me onboard hit an air pocket, causing an impromptu version of musical chairs and airborne bumper-bodies.

Strange that, when an overweight clod crashes into your head, neck and shoulders, he gets pissed with you when you knee him in the face. Oops. So sorry.

Which is why I sat, my knees snapping involuntarily once too often, the captain once again apologetic for hurtling us through seriously aerated skies. Though I did enjoy the respite and better view of Legs crossing and uncrossing her legs, cramped for space and too polite to be miffed.

The guy in front of me was sleeping, judging by the angle of his head, unaware he'd cupped his crotch snugly in both hands and that his right foot was in line with the foot of the guy in front of him.

Murphy had gone through most of his book. I could read the rhetoric without straining. The font was baby-large with little text. His 39.95 plus tax hadn't bought him much wisdom. Forty pages so far of expert advice, Murphy plagiarizing his career by adhering to someone else's unsubstantiated keys to success, playing a crap shoot with his career if he hadn't yet read the best one, or hadn't read the worst one. Any distinction between the two indiscernible.

I didn't envy him. He was everyone I'd ever met in meetings and conferences with notable exceptions. He was forgettable, uncharismatic, unlike Legs. I'd done my time. I had days left, I knew. What I wanted was the ocean the sun and bikini-clad women.

Murphy had probably lived a third of his life in a box, directed, not guided, by teachers and parents. He probably thought because he was free from school that he was free from all things, that he'd paid his dues. Yet probably still clung to home. He had the definite look of a mommy's boy. Mommy still made his breakfast and dinner, while in-between he was told to follow the rules instead of thinking. I was damn certain he wasn't going home to anything resembling Legs.

Short-Term Pain, for Long-Term Gain, a chapter Murphy read in under ten minutes while underlining so many gems of wisdom the pages were as red as they were white. I might have been impressed if he'd made notes, without his tongue peeking out centimetres from the page.

The author was proposing nothing new. Old stuff: Crap. I hadn't heard that expression for years: The pain-gain theory. The reps I worked with at the time never bought into it, not the older ones anyway. The motto was strictly corporate driven, one-sided. You suffer for their gain until you quit, get canned for not buying into the programme, or die in a hotel room, or get divorced. Those who don't, stay on to play CYA.

Cover Your Ass, the rules of conduct prohibiting drinking with your boss. One earplug went in. Time again to de-Murphy.

Statistically we have eight job changes in our lives, those of us with good jobs. So where's the long-term gain? The theory wasn't relevant then and isn't now. The gain is in change and self. The sales world was and is too transient for mindless devotion. Those who don't adopt a "me-first, client second, disposable company third" attitude will face serious disappointments.

Legs reached to flick on her light, reaching under the seat in front of her to stow one book and bring out another, avoiding Murphy's fidgeting knee. She looked at the napkin, which was partly under Murphy's foot.

I had to wonder, who made breakfast for her?

*

In the name of self-preservation my transition into industrial belting was timely. The near demise of the refractory industry was underway and would never reverse. Individual prosperity in the industry was dead. Companies merged and sales reps were either sent home or swore unfamiliar oaths of servitude.

I'd done well by the company as they'd done well by me with double-digit yearly increases. My financial rewards were proportionate to my success, as were my experiences, intertwined dynamics I wanted not to change.

Bathing in the warm poolside sunshine of June's latter half was a perfect way to relax, to prepare for my new position as Technical Sales Representative for a division of a Swiss-based mechanical belting manufacturer. My meeting with them took place some weeks previously and I walked away knowing the job was mine. When Jon phoned me the following evening to ask whether I was still interested and, subsequently, to make the final offer, I wasn't surprised.

The job meant no more dirty hands, no more sojourns to the desolate north or taking two or three showers a day in peak season. Above all, no more long weekends sacrificed in the name of reputation and customer service.

Going into that initial meeting Gene met me at the door. He had a glass in hand. Behind him in the en suite, Mr.

No One to Tell

Wienerskin was seated with a glass in his hand. They never asked to see the letter of reference Tony had written for me, accepting at face value that I'd left RTI for self-improvement, because the industry was failing.

"That's what the Frogs have always done and Ontario's always expected to save the country's ass."

Say what?

That was Jon in a nutshell. Gene was no better.

They gave my résumé cursory interest, happy to finally interview a Frenchman who spoke English properly, "like the rest of us." I explained I wasn't French, but I lived in Québec and that made me French. Oh-kay. They lived in Toronto. What else need I say?

The process of tell me about this and tell me about that went on for the better part of the three drinks, when they began expounding on the virtues of Swiss, reputed to be the best and most expensive manufacturer of transmission and conveyor belts in the world. Both facts were later validated, or at least popularized.

I did speak Frog, though. Didn't I? Yes, I did. Good for me, said Gene. Which really didn't matter as long as I spoke English and was married. And why wasn't I married?

Bullshit baffles brains, especially small, narrow-minded ones and I got the job. Swiss wasn't really a family business, simply run by someone called Jon who had too many family members working under him and suffered under the illusion that *he* was the company and everyone working for him was family. Yeah, keep thinking that.

Jon was a member of Alcoholics Continuous. His leathery skin stretched to a slight 1, 7 metres and was smoked, not tanned, and I quickly learned that he hated all things beyond the whiteness of English Canada. He hated Blacks, though not exclusive of all other colours. He despised all non-English speaking earthlings and anyone who dared to live in sin, which is to say common-law fornicators who were the root cause of society's family woes and no one loathed gays and lesbians as fervently as Jon.

If I'd been a poor Black Francophone gay who just got divorced for coming out of the closet, I might not have got the job. Daring to be Catholic would have been a real ball-buster.

His stained teeth weren't so much discoloured by smoke as by caustic speech; though the real Jon shone through his eyes. He was fearful of life, made inferior by self-doubt, and homophobic.

His wife, Jane or Joyce or Janet, was a typical Torontonian female with pink polyester everything, hair that was too tight and a mouth that was too loose. She had hair like the sisters on The Simpsons, looking even more like them when she smoked, letting the lipstick-stained butt hang suspended from between cracked and smoke-yellowed lips as the smoldering tip spiralled upwards to stain one half of her face.

Sometimes she'd blow smoke through her nose as she coughed, creating a little dark thunder and hail storm. Happily, I'd only contend with Frau Wienerskin during three Christmas parties, one dinner and one branch opening, though she'd be aware of none of those occasions.

*

They were impressed with my credentials and my attitude towards sales as a profession, despite my impression that Gene hadn't understood a word I was saying and Jon didn't care as he passed his glass to Gene for a refill.

The Swiss HO had instructed them to establish a presence in Montreal as soon as possible and they had no idea how to go about it, but they were on the Swiss timeline.

They currently had a rep in Québec City who wouldn't relocate, another who lived in some little village in extreme eastern Ontario. They needed someone who knew the Québec marketplace as well as Montreal, someone who could open a new office and develop new business; Three of which I was very good at. The other I knew absolutely nothing about, though at the time I phrased that truth somewhat to my advantage.

Their Francophobia dictated that the person be English in order to facilitate communication, with them, though communication with Jon was never effortless. And whenever Gene would say anything he would either glance at Jon for approval or over his shoulder to see if Jon had heard. I was headed for another roller coaster ride that would broaden my experience and narrow my tolerance for people.

I would be responsible for the new office, from site location to stocking inventory, managing regional matters of regional importance. I would report to Gene regarding sales, to Jon regarding the office. Lucky me.

To-date I'd embraced the more formal sales methodologies of two companies, sculpting them to my needs and style. My philosophies and methodologies would soon prove diametrically different to theirs in that I possessed both.

In the belting industry month-end accountability was the single driving force, with sales experience equating to month-end values. At the day-to-day operational level the accepted methodology was to get out there and do it. Sound familiar? Nothing else was expected or encouraged. Don't talk about it; just go do it. That was a difficult stumbling block for me because I didn't work that way.

My work ethic was worlds apart. Working without a plan was an absolute waste of time. Neither Jon nor Gene understood the rudiments of sales because one was preparing for retirement, not knowing he would die very soon after, while the other had come up through the ranks without training or mentoring.

Gene was intellectually rock-like, albeit a friendly rock. He could have been very good. He certainly knew the product by virtue of his eighteen years, though he was limited by lack of professionalism. He'd chosen the wrong person to admire and emulate.

He was a Sales Manager lacking leadership qualities and skills, leading to an inevitable lack of respect from the sales team. He'd been Sales Manager for about a year, Jon's go-boy much longer, beginning as a gofer in the shop, working his way through production and installing to sales and his then current position.

The promotion was his when the former Sales Manager left to head up the local office of their main rival and natural foe, Euro ConTech, in the capacity of President, General Manager and self-infatuated prick.

I'd previously worked with a few sales reps that had graduated from production, such as Dean, but they were the exception. By and large that mid-life change precludes communication skills, persuasion, tenacity, negotiation skills and extroversion, feigned or real, which is why most engineers aren't allowed out alone.

Gene might have seemed like an extrovert, but mostly he floundered, too adept at saying "yes" to Jon.

Once again I was the new boy in town, with more experience under the proverbial belt. I'd spent time during my week in the Ontario facility with Brian, the bakery guy, recognizing his skill and talent immediately. Kerry I recognized a golden-hair wannabe, a suck, that I'd be quiet and cautious around. Pat wasn't a sales rep at the time, though I spent time with him in the shop to learn skiving, splicing, glues and cook times. I became proficient with the process, requisite because of the hands-on nature of the sales position, though nothing was rocket science.

Pat eventually graduated into sales with the potential of

being good, if he could avoid the mediocrity and short-sightedness of his milieu. But protégés are often wrongly protective, overly adoring of their supposed mentors, not seeing that wisdom doesn't come with age. That would be Pat's constraint for several years. He never understood the origin of wisdom.

Bob was a senior rep. What flowed from Bob's brain to his mouth and into the mainstream would make most sewage systems seem sparkling fresh. Even though his humour prompted occasional chuckles from me, he wasn't remotely funny most times. For the most part, I didn't have much to do with him.

Marc was the one who lived in Ontario not far from the Québec border, who thought his bastardized street French earned him honorary Québécois status. Wrong.

He lived to work, helpful when his involvement would serve to ingratiate him to Jon, his lord and master in all things. He always managed to get food on the back of his neck when he ate, often managing to tear his clothes simply by moving.

He wasn't overly large, though visibly on the hefty side, and three years is too long for anyone to wear the same suit day after day. The clothes didn't actually tear, giving that impression as they came apart at the seams. He was the only one to attend weeklong meetings and arrive without a suitcase.

Didier was Jon's pet Frog who gave the impression of previous military influence. He stood erect, spoke succinctly and conducted his speech with precise and martial hand gestures. He spoke English better than anyone in the Ontario office and defended his homeland and mother tongue with righteous indignation whenever Jon was fuelled with his favourite toxin.

Didier and I would work closely together over the next three years, matter-of-factly, most often by phone as linguistic comrades. As for Gordie and Kenny, I got to see them twice yearly at sales meetings which were notably good times.

Irrespective of their lack of organizational skills, Swiss was number one. No one suffered on payday.

Only two reps were ever fired: Kenny, and some guy called Marion. Jon had fired Kenny some years earlier for DUI, collapsing a lamp standard he'd driven into, which led to Gordie being hired in British Columbia. Gordie didn't fit the mould. He didn't care. He was excellent at what he did which gave him self-issued license not to give a shit about anything or anyone, which he frequently demonstrated when confronted with Gene. Kenny was re-hired sometime after the fiasco, relocated to Nova Scotia where he promised to stay away from street lamps if not his favourite brew.

*

The first days on a new job are like first impressions: They're everlasting. Though, really, my first day on the job was the interview. The second was in Toronto shaking hands, forgetting names, and heading to a titty bar at 5:00 for a few drinks with the new boss. No sweat.

That was Gene's thing: Naked women and damp knees. As long as they were eighteen plus a day, and bare, very bare, he'd go broke adoring them. The man couldn't carry enough tens in his wallet, despite his deep devotion for wife and family, his briefcase a veritable library of wife-replacement delusions or dreams.

That first after-hours drink with Gene was the last. Too much information.

About to order a second round, Bambi's bum off his leg, the bar exploded into a din of excitement and commotion, naked girls in heels leaving their ten-dollar stools, deserting their customers, scurrying with more naked girls up the spiral staircase. A wonderful sight to behold, all those bums.

Why? Because one girl was screaming from the mezzanine for help. Not for herself, for the girl who'd just slashed her wrists.

I stood first, Gene followed, each of us more accustomed to dealing with clients than cops.

*

My time at Swiss would be well spent, productive and profitable for everyone concerned. In refractory I'd been involved primarily with heavy industry; Swiss was the first step in the completion of a journey that would take me through virtually every major industry in Canada and the US as well as every worthwhile account in those industries.

Several years into the future, I would be the only sales rep in conveyor belting with pan-Canadian experience. Swiss experience, however, would be restricted to the Québec market.

Jon booked all sales meetings, held twice yearly in an all-exclusive retreat three hours north of Toronto because he was able to negotiate a weekend away for himself and Frau Wienerskin after each meeting. Why he would want that, I had no idea.

Objectively, the place was wretched only if you were accustomed to better, so Didier and I stood alone in our opinions. The place boasted a beautiful lake with watercraft and water sports, horseback riding, golf and nature trails. True. But the doors were rickety and a quick glance under the bed and the covers were always wise choices.

We spent a week on each occasion discussing new developments or successes, learning calculations that no one ever remembered, presenting, making promises of doing better during the coming two quarters that no one ever remembered. Mostly the week was a male getaway for those who needed a reason. Gordie and I stood alone in that respect and enjoyed the difference.

The first such meeting came at the end of September,

after a full quarter, so my participation was expected. By the time I arrived at Swiss Belt Tech I was very familiar with the rhetoric that was, and remains, the stuff of sales meetings: Go team go! All for one! Yeah! One for all! Yeah! You can do it! Yeah! Yeah! Together we can do it! Yeah!

Yeah, sure.

Nevertheless I noticed throughout the first meeting that no one was saying how to do it.

The participants were divided into three attitudes: Unaware, indifferent, and curious. I was in the curious camp, alone, understanding the limitation placed on us came from management's short-sightedness and their own limitations, which was not understanding the sales process. What's worse, they didn't know better. Because everyone was doing well, the issue never surfaced.

Never a groupie thinker, wary of novelty, skepticism dominated my mindset during the first meeting as a belt-specific application calculator was introduced. I knew I would never ever use the thing and saw no point in putting off the inevitable when I could piss off Gene right away.

Company loyalty wasn't an issue for me. I had none. I turned to Gene and said, "I can't see what's on the board. Either the print is too small or I need glasses."

I put down my pen and that was that.

Gene never swore; he thought not swearing made him a good person.

"Yes, you will do it. You have to because the rest of us are and, if we are, you are."

His logic escaped me. "I'm telling you, I can't see it. The print is too goddamned small. I'll do it next week when I get my new glasses," and my pen stayed put.

The next week never came. Actually, the tech data and exam didn't, though I did need glasses. I never made use of the calculator and, inside a year, the Switzerland office

No One to Tell

recalled them for recalibration. They were defective. Instead, everyone reverted to knowing what they were doing. Even when the recalibrated units were returned, no one used them.

There was one aspect of the company's bi-annual sales meeting that differed greatly from my past experiences. They allowed drinking throughout the entire day. The Boy's Club bar was open 24/7 and during the meetings the cooler was filled to overflowing. Some of us waited until at least midway through the afternoon, others didn't.

Curiously, filled with beer by noon, some would drink milk at lunch. Go figure. Then more beer or booze between lunch, dinner and breakfast. As Jon might say now, cryptically as he turns over: Vive la différence, without the accent, of course.

We each had multiple subjects to present throughout those weeks and at one such meeting Gordie truly excelled. This was a Kodak moment years before digital and cell phones.

We were all guilty of taxing our bodies' natural resistance to evil spirits the night before and the next morning came too early, as did the meeting on the day we were being videoed. Even the usually measured Didier was a little rounded at the shoulders. What can be said about those meets is that whatever transpired during our time together was left behind when we left. Hear no evil; speak no evil; see no evil, but pranks were always fair game.

Gordie was next up after Gene, taking his time to assemble his papers, a pen he wouldn't use and his beer. We were intrigued, waiting patiently, thankful we had at least another fifteen or twenty minutes before we had to think or communicate some semblance of intelligent thought.

Gordie arrived at the front of the room, standing, poised to deliver his presentation as we waited expectantly. Five minutes later he was there, standing, poised, and hadn't said a word, staring blankly as though he'd gone to sleep with his eyes open and unblinking.

We all pissed ourselves laughing, scaring the hell out of Gordie, jolting him from his trance, applauding. Yet, yet, the man started in as though he'd just gotten there, as though nothing had happened. And nothing had.

For some reason we sat in the same place at each meeting, not unlike school when some kids wanted to be closer to the teacher and others, the ones who usually got the strap, didn't. That would be me: Quiet, yet somehow always in shit.

Gordie sat as far as possible from Gene for his own reasons. He was next up again, this time alert and duly upset with what Gene had presented during his presentation moments before. They'd argued persistently, defending respective points of view. Gordie was adamant; Gene was management and things would be done his way. End of discussion, he thought. Because he lacked substance and enjoyed the power play. Good technique.

Bullshit. Not always.

Gordie simply responded that Swiss could "go fuck themselves." He was up next.

Gordie was succinct most times. He assembled his materials, went up without his beer this time, placing everything on the table in front of him in preparation.

He stood, pensive, beginning an impromptu presentation inspired by Gene's magisterial decree. He dragged a chair to the centre of the table where Gene had previously left his papers, proceeding to stand on the chair, positioning his back to us. We knew something was coming. We just didn't know what and still didn't as we watched his elbows working busily. We all wanted to laugh, in Pause Mode, not knowing what to laugh at.

He'd undone his belt buckle, unzipped his fly and, in one swift motion, had his pants and his Fruit of the Loom pushed to his ankles, presenting the hairiest butt I'd seen in years, or wanted to see.

He proceeded to squat on the table, grinding his butt firmly to and fro across Gene's papers without the support of his hands. Worse. As he stood, leaning slightly forward, he took up a single sheet in a final graphic gesture and wiped away Gene's presentation.

He pitched the crumpled sheet somewhere, bending straight to retrieve his pants. We applauded, Gene included.

He turned, made a final adjustment to his pants, and said: "That's what I think of your fucking ideas."

Go Gordie! We all kept laughing, Gene with us. He had no choice.

*

At one such meeting someone had thought of an activity we could all take part in and have fun doing, though no one in the Ontario office knew where to find the necessary components. Kerry would have volunteered, too afraid of being caught by his wife who owned him lock, stock and barrel where she kept his balls until family night.

So I became responsible for purchasing a rubber blow-up doll. We were all expert, or so we claimed, at undressing a woman. Despite most Canadian women undressing themselves, in the dark. Conversely, the competition was to dress a woman in the dark. Laura Latex was anatomically correct, complacent and compliant, and didn't seem to mind her arms and legs being bent or twisted this way and that.

I also purchased her new wardrobe: Nylons, garter, panties and bra which cost more than any of them had ever spent on their wives, with the probable exception of Gordie.

I thought the whole thing was too weird at first. Why not just bring in a stripper? Didier thought everyone was stupid, though we both acquiesced after the first few did so badly. We were timed and judged on tact, touch and sensitivity. The objective being to dress her while blindfolded. The outcome was hilarious. I empathized with the wives, particularly Marc's. We had to resuscitate Laura back to life with a foot pump after he got through with her.

At the end we agreed that women don't need bras or nylons, and if they were to wear their panties on backwards we wouldn't mind. Gordie came out on top, figuratively.

Before leaving at week's end I put Laura's panties and bra under Kerry's front car seat, with the best of intentions. He was terrified of his wife. He'd never been to a strip bar or cabaret because he thought his wife would smell naughty women on his clothing and scold him. He wouldn't go for a drink after work because he feared his wife's retribution for that sin as well. He needed to take a stand. He needed to become a man or, at the very worst, or best, confess to her that he secretly enjoyed wearing women's lingerie. I could see that working.

Any subsequent marital event was never made public.

I gave the doll to Marc when we got to his home where my car was parked, thinking he could use the practice. We'd taken his van because I didn't want him sitting in my new Taurus, new until I wiped out the entire front end in a head-on collision with some guy who did an illegal left turn a few weeks later.

On the way we passed through a highway construction zone. Marc drove the posted speed, I slouched into my seat holding Laura against the passenger side window. Even at work-zone speeds Laura was loved as one head twisted and yelled to the co-workers to drop what they were doing and look. I suppose the ultimate rubber necking.

Later we were behind the same car for too long on the narrow road. When we had a chance to pass the shiny new BMW that had someone's blonde secretary or special friend behind the wheel for a look-at-me drive, we did.

Laura jumped partway out from the window, waving

frantically at the woman who slowed, sped up, and slowed again with her head unnaturally close to the windshield as Laura continued flapping and waving. At a point I almost lost her, barely managing to grab her ankles as she began taking flight, pulling her to safety, tossing her onto the backseat.

Our speed stayed the same, the distance between the two cars grew wider rapidly.

There were two camps: One did something different every night at the isolated compound such as riding, golfing or fishing. Others played cards, drank and woke up broke or with an obligation to try again that night. Gene would always wait until Jon went to bed before bringing out the porno he watched alone for the most part; another of the many things the nasty little man viewed with disapproval. Though Jon might have been right. Not so much about the propriety of it all, but the quality.

The girls-on-girls, his favourite, were purple and pink, though not where they should be. Of greater importance was the girls' complete lack of pubic hair. Gene's well-known proclivity inspiring him to comment on the various beneficial sensations made possible by a woman's naked labia.

Bob, at the poker table, blurted out asking whether Gene's wife did the little-girl thing for him. And how was that?

The rage was obvious, Gene too far into his drinks to defend his wife's honour. Instead he told Bob to fuck himself. Sticks and stones...

Bob didn't give a shit, about anything, and the game continued, most of us believing Mrs. Gene was likely a traditional lady. We'd seen her.

The videos, though, were largely ignored by the guys. Many of us left the main salon while others played cards, gutted fish or thought of pranks to perform. Jon's son-in-law had fallen asleep wearing his newest and most favourite pair of jeans that, by the time he woke, had become an unfamiliar pair of shorts. I left before the final act, but heard about the outcome in the morning when Kenny was MIA.

He'd begun the card game with a bottle of rye and a Brador chaser. He'd forgotten about the tenth chaser with his eleventh and the eleventh with the twelfth. The made-up sign on his room door read: Sick Bay. Stay Out.

No one saw Kenny for thirty-six hours.

*

Much of my first six months was taken up with plans for the new office situated minutes from RTI and studying the Textile and Bakery industries that were Key Accounts for me. My contact base had changed from A to Z and I needed to once again work at developing relationships.

Both conveyor and transmission belts required a 'cooking' process in a calibrated press as part of the splicing process. We carried this equipment in our car trunks.

For installations requiring larger units we called in the big guns from the head office. The larger bakery companies were trained by previous sales reps, both Swiss and competitors, to buy the belt and wait for the sales rep to do the post-sale installation, free of charge and usually early on a Saturday morning. That wasn't good for me. Certain issues didn't make sense. One of them was waking up at 4:30 every other Saturday to do an install regardless of weather. If I'd wanted to do that, I would have gone to trade school for a career in blue coveralls.

Being around inanimate tools and machinery had limited appeal for me. Any hands-on portion of the job description would have to be very small as in "been there, done that, now what?"

Not as a question of technical skill which was mandatory anyway. I found install work mundane. I preferred planning and designing solutions and social interaction to a point. Every installer I've ever met has wanted a career in sales. I've never met a sales rep who's wanted the reverse switch, though I have known several who should have. The second issue was the amount of money I was leaving on the table.

Gene's interpretation of Return on Investment was a warm, fuzzy feeling after three beers. Mine was getting paid for working. I was always strong on ROI and business plans and didn't waste time preparing for the end of those weekend interruptions that came well before the official opening of the branch office in June '88.

The sale of equipment was a huge success, despite the resistance, cursing and threats emanating from King Jon. Recognition was not forthcoming when business significantly increased straight away. I'd acted on my behalf, Jon the beneficiary of good business planning and increased sales, the clients benefitting from immediate cost-savings. That's win-win, not to mention my weekends.

Jon went through the roof. Gene distanced himself as more customers wanted more equipment and, if we weren't willing to comply, they would approach the competition with my recommendations. He was between a rock and a hard place.

The plan was to give the larger, more dependent clients control and flexibility over their maintenance schedules, which would clear the way for the branch serviceman to accommodate more clients with less demanding needs.

Jon didn't see it that way. He was somewhat myopic. He remained disgruntled, proving that in certain cases time heals all wounds only when time ceases. Whereas Gene thought of the reps as select members of his Boy's Club, Jon thought of himself as a father figure and every so often felt the need to go to the barn for the switch.

*

No One to Tell

Marc and I had a different sense of work ethic. He'd been with Swiss for eight years and his blood was as green as the company's bright green signature colours. We agreed on very little, mostly in good humour, though sometimes decidedly on the stressful side of trying.

Living out of town and being responsible for the western portion of Montreal, he relied heavily on distributor activity, whereas I worked directly with most clients. Swiss had an understanding with MacLeary that their accounts were protected, but that didn't include the whole territory.

Marc overlooked any occasion when MacLeary would go into his accounts, but I made clear to them to stay out. When I came across something that fell into their jurisdiction, or made more sense for them to take over, I gave them a time frame and, if no contact was made within that time I took the business direct without explanation. Hence my many conversations and visits with Fred who was owner and GM of MacLeary.

There was nothing new about Fred or his company. MacLeary was a hundred years old, with old wavy hardwood floors, crooked windows and equipment that required the apprenticeship of each new shop employee regarding the workings of each because their operational manuals had been lost decades earlier. As for Fred, his suits pre-dated the 80s and most of his collection of wide-bottom and shiny ties had seen their best years when the suits were new.

He was basically a nice guy who'd outlived his era, who wanted to be called by his first name and lacked the ability to merge the merits of the old with the advantages of the new. His era was one of handshakes and loyalty, but his sales staff and Sales Manager didn't think that way. They thought about month-end quotas and commissions, respectively, and of suppliers as contributors to that end, fill-in sales people and someone to buy their lunches.

He was protective of them and didn't like that I was taking business away from his flock, preventing them from going into companies he was told should be theirs. My questions to Fred were: If those new customers should have been MacLeary's, why weren't they already? And why was his Sales Manager riding on my shirttails?

Then he became aware that I'd put equipment into the larger bakeries where they often did install work unrelated to my previous Saturday morning ritual. By which time Jon began adapting grudgingly to the new equipment sales, telling Fred the fault was mine, too late to turn back, and that he should find a way to settle the issue with me.

Dinner at the men's club was in order.

The private men's club was similar to where Paul at W&W enjoyed membership, though Fred's club was more like the antechamber to a mortuary. Paul's was affiliated with sports as well as wealth. This one was the end of the road for many of the city's privileged, a place for them to wait out their final days. The club was stale and dark, the people staid and somber, not an environment conducive to business for anyone under eighty.

The place was his comfort zone, his upper hand. He hoped. He needed for me to change my approach to equipment sales. The meal was fine, the wine excellent. The answer was no.

My insistence that customers be autonomous regarding their equipment pissed him off not just a little. Of course. He would certainly lose install business because of me. So what? He wasn't dedicated to Swiss, to me, and many of the belts he might install wouldn't be mine. Nor did he want to sign an agreement of exclusivity. So what did poor Fred expect?

*

The contractor and location were selected by the fall. Jon came in for an initial meeting and I spent several winter weeks visiting the construction site.

Product inventory was determined and office supplies were brought in from Ontario so that Jon could sleep peacefully knowing he hadn't supported a separatist government with tax dollars he could avoid spending.

The serviceman was hired and sent to Ontario for training, the truck was delivered and the doors opened in March '88 with a celebration of fine dining and fine wine because I made the selections. Their oenology expertise was limited to twisting caps and pouring until the rim of the glass disappeared under the red or white flow.

Jon was at the head of the table seating fifteen. We were with our wives or significant others, except Marion who was girlfriend-deficient when Jon welcomed him again into the fold. His social status wasn't one of choice. He was alone by the necessity of all Québec women to not have someone excruciatingly dimwitted in their lives.

He was to organize the official opening in June, which was fine with me, which included inviting clients. I wanted no involvement in the plans for the upcoming event, following his restaurant debacle in March. I'd thought at one time that people so unaware couldn't possibly be part of the corporate complexion at Swiss. Marion proved me wrong. He was comatose most days, existing in a private oblivion that no one thought to intrude upon. He'd once been fired by Jon for being drunk on the job, apparently rehired for that very reason because he was never anything but.

I was the one to select the restaurant, to make the hotel arrangements for the evening in March. Everyone had come in from out of town and, from the hotel situated a block away, hailed a few cabs for the five-minute walk. Marion, of course, had taken a room as well.

Linda and I arrived moments before the reservation time at the restaurant I'd visited on several previous occasions.

No One to Tell

We ordered aperos, enjoying the quiet as we waited. The reservation was for 7:30. By eight I was looking at my watch as often as the headwaiter. At 8:30 I phoned another restaurant in the area on a hunch. Sure enough. Jon's Marion of sunshine had led them all to the wrong restaurant that was five kilometres away, where they were happily ensconced.

Explaining the situation to the manager of our restaurant, leaving a very substantial gratuity to cover my embarrassment and their inconvenience, we took our time arriving at the restaurant where everyone was into a third or fourth drink, not caring a hoot about the mix-up.

Gene said something to placate me. I ignored the jerk, passing Marion on the way to my seat, leaning in close his ear, setting the tone for what was left of our time together.

Linda and I endured an evening of Jon's relentless monologue on the virtues of marriage, family, the shame of living together, the economic strength of Ontario and the bravado of establishing a base in Québec before Euro. Didier, our ladies and I spent the evening watching the other eleven heads bobbing like broken toys to Jon's perception of the world.

Gene was the worst of the litter.

*

The office was meant to ensure immediacy; customers would no longer wait three or four days for delivery from Ontario.

Marion was my predecessor in sales, brought back to perform simple inside functions: answering phones, forgetting about calls on hold, taking messages, throwing them out when he couldn't read his writing; managing inventory levels and staying away from me. He lived inside a constant shroud of forty-proof vapours and should have had a twist cap for a head.

Jon had asked Marion to oversee the open house event,

the non-son proud that daddy had noticed his good work.

Two hundred invitations were sent out, customers arriving that afternoon to tolerate unbearable heat, drink freely, eat freely and think of reasons to avoid Jon and Marion. Linda was the only woman present, bearing the brunt of unbalanced social interaction. Frau Wienerskin was fried by 3:00.

I poured myself a J W Black on the rocks. Neat and heat is not a good idea. Most of the visitors were my accounts, engaging me in conversation most of the afternoon, holding that one drink, and I hadn't eaten except for a few shrimp kept inside on a bed of ice.

The branch office was well-received, each of them expressing positive remarks, though soon after they'd gone I thought I was going to die. I couldn't put two words together. I was inarticulate, dizzy, believing I'd lose my breakfast. They understood, of course, what with the heat, the drinks and excitement. Go home and sleep it off.

Bullshit.

I puked out my guts for hours after Linda got me home, praying for death, a desirable alternative to shaking with the cold sweats and vomiting copious amounts of fluids mixed with tainted shrimp. I can count on one hand the number of days I've called in sick, exclusive of breaking my leg skiing while at Monk, and when I called the office word quickly spread that I was hung-over from the day before.

I was the subject of water cooler gossip, no one believing Marion had poisoned me, and the more I heard that I wasn't the only one the more pissed-off I got because I knew what saved the Ontarians was their alcohol content.

Everything has its time, as did their humour at my expense. The moron hadn't refrigerated the shrimp as part of the buffet in 30° plus temperatures for the better part of the afternoon, disguised by inadequate ice when served. The laughing stopped when clients began phoning to complain they'd taken the day off because of food poisoning, which wasn't the stupidest thing Marion had done. That would come a year later, though each of the twelve months in-between would have his signature.

Something else that had its time was making the first day of summer special. One of the highlights of my time at RTI was the way all the girls looked forward to the first day of summer when I personally delivered to each of them a half-dozen long-stemmed carnations with greeting cards wishing them 'Bonne été'. They never asked why, always gracious, and the event became a tradition dangerous to overlook.

I did the same for the women at Swiss in Ontario. Big mistake. The phone rang: "Why? What have you done? We don't understand. What do you need?"

Chill. Take a pill. What did I need? I fought the temptation. I needed to work with women who know the difference between feminine and female and my tradition went to hell in a hand basket.

*

Thursday was the final night of the meeting in Collingwood. The meeting went well, though the after-hours was another matter. I found something to do every night, including the previous night when Didier and I were discussing local politics and economy. Wienerskin took about thirty seconds to become a narrow-minded bigot, an obnoxious old man immersed in animosity.

Not words I used at the time.

Didier and I left, after telling Wienerskin that our business wasn't his, nor was our conversation. He was a bitter man, shallow. The next day was as if nothing had happened, though he'd been that way all week. Everyone was on edge, barely interested in the last dinner together.

Thursday's dinner was planned with a medieval theme. We dressed in period costumes. I was a friar in homemade garb of the era. Gordie was Robin Hood, the others were woodsmen, lords, jesters and troubadours. Jon went as King Drinkalot.

The hotel staff closed off a large portion of the restaurant for us because Thursday night in Collingwood wasn't a good time to be a waitress. Not many others had come in and the place was ours for a chunky "feast" that would require additional amounts of digestive juices to pass. The meal consisted of cobs of corn, whole chickens, roasted potatoes, bowls of fresh fruit, large goblets of ale and Ontario swill tasting like a fourteenth century vintage.

Eating utensils weren't the order of the day, nor were napkins and Bob produced frequent period noises that created an ambiance of olfactory realism.

A committee had been appointed to plan period games, no one exactly getting the hang of what those games might be. So they all agreed that playing a few rounds of mini-putt would save the day. Yawn.

First, however, Gordie went to the men's room located at the lobby entrance of the dining room, bedecked in forest-green tights, tunic and peaked chapeau with plumes. When he returned his path wasn't shortest line between the two points and not much about his condition had changed, except that he'd come back as Robin of Crotchly with his genitalia hanging out over the waistband of his green tights. Long live Robin's Hood!

The feast was passably good. The tables were cleared and the game was set to begin. I took that as my cue to take my leave, getting lost before getting trapped into playing golf ball into a hotel glass, though the characteristics of the game changed as quickly as boredom set in.

Four girls from the restaurant were taking care of us during our stay. Two worked the restaurant, two worked the conference rooms. All four worked the guests. Three of the four didn't require much makeup, blessed with nice figures under short skirts with no nylons and waitress-type blouses with enough buttons undone to show cleavage when they were hanging over you. All three hiking their skirts to make them much shorter for better tips or dates. This was Collingwood. Who could blame them?

The fourth one was ugly beyond the bottle. From a distance she appeared large and unshapely, closer inspection revealing she had a thick coating of fur-like hair. She had hair everywhere hair could possibly grow. She worked the restaurant, the lesbian lover of the bi-sexual girl who worked with her.

The hairy one admitted openly to not liking men, understanding that her friend did at times. This was one of those times. The restaurant was closed, other guests had gone.

I was on my way out when Brian stopped me to ask if he could borrow my camera for the evening. I should have said no, and Brian shouldn't have asked, though not for any obvious reason. Talking slowly to Gene, using small groupings of monosyllabic words, he understood that Swiss would be responsible for even the slightest scratch on my prized possession that only Brian would use. The one thing I can say for Gene is that he respected team rules, if not verbal contracts.

I left right after Gene's swearing in ceremony, committing him to my camera's well-being. I went to bed, woke early and left. The meeting was a good one in content, but home was home.

Normally I would have given my pro film to a pro lab, though for the meeting I'd bought bargain basement film and that's where I went for processing.

When I saw the photos I thought at first they'd given me the wrong set. Not so. What I had was a prime example of what people don't believe when I recount my experiences. So for that reason I showed them to Linda who didn't see me in any of the thirty-six images that Brian shot throughout the golf game.

There was one of Gordie after he'd tucked in his trappings. Everyone else was shot while at the green, for which the three pretties had volunteered their bodies as the furry lesbian looked on.

In some photos the girls were sitting in a row with their legs opened wide, flat against the floor with their skirts hiked to their waists. In others they were lying back, propped on their elbows, their raised knees parted, their hands grasping their skirts into tight rolls so they could see the balls coming towards them.

All three openly flirted during dinner, so I can imagine someone had an easy time getting them to participate in the par three.

A few days later I phoned Gene on some other matter, advising him of the envelope I'd sent to his attention. A small envelope was sealed inside a larger envelope, both marked Confidential. The outer and largest envelope was marked Personal and Confidential and I forwarded the package by registered mail. I never heard another word about it. I doubt anyone but Gene saw them and I suspect the most explicit are still in his basement.

*

Those three years passed quickly, the third year in particular. I had many fun times sprinkled with infrequent, minor frustrations. Other events were career-related, which weren't so minor.

Jon and Gene reneged on our verbal contract that was the basis for my decision to work with them. Worse, Jon cheated me arbitrarily, conveying the message matter-of-factly through his mouthpiece as I drove Gene to the airport. He said Jon saw more sense in Marion being the Branch Manager, being that he was always at the office, whereas I was too often on the road to be effective managing an office. Gene's comment was, "It's done, get used to it."

This all came about at the Collingwood meeting as Marion convinced Jon he could assemble belts in his spare time. Of course he had spare time, because he had nothing else to do. Didier, Marc and I had long since adopted an MO of excluding him from our affairs and distancing him from our customers.

Jon had accepted the notion too readily, creating a backlash of problems. Marion confused all manner of specific dimensions in applications requiring precision to the millimetre. He selected inappropriate glues, misjudged cook times, and often shipped prepared belts for orders that required a service call that never happened.

The true reason for the change was that Jon wanted his Marion to have a semblance of responsibility when, in fact, Jon was on the phone every day telling him what to do. Objectively, Marion was of no value to himself or to the company at any level. He was a buffoon, a village idiot, but you can't criticize a child to a parent. So once again I recalibrated my future.

The subsequent chain of events might have been different had Gene possessed any integrity at all. He didn't and Marion was given responsibility for the branch. Hence, instead of starting small and growing, they stayed small and became ineffective.

As the situation worsened, the office began costing more than Jon could justify to Switzerland. He decided to cut back on equipment, stocking only pre-measured transmission belts prepared in Ontario for high-volume users. The office would no longer inventory conveyor belts or equipment and, of course, Marion was mandated to organize the return of said equipment.

The carrier personnel carried out all manner of presses and unused inventory. As the serviceman stood watching his job carried away. On the bright side, not working meant not spending much of his day with Marion.

The documents were signed and the truck left. Marion locked the door and went home, though he hadn't always locked the door before going home.

The next morning when he arrived hung-over, he was shocked to see the equipment and machinery gone. He immediately phoned the police to report the theft, spending the morning filling out reports, answering the questions of curious cops who hadn't found any sign of forced entry. When that was done, when the cops had gone, Marion felt sufficiently empowered with all pertinent data. He phoned Jon to report the crime, explaining how he'd handled the situation. This as the shipment arrived at the Swiss loading dock. Marion was still with the company when I left some months later.

The last year was the least satisfying, and long. Challenges for the most part were fewer with each passing week. I'd already captured the big accounts, so when the phone rang a second time I agreed to a meeting.

I bore no resentment. I was progressing, taking care of number one. When Gene came into town for the sole purpose of handing me a final cheque, he took my car keys to prevent Marion from doing something stupid. Jon was severely pissed when he heard first about the black two-door T-Bird with mags I'd leased at his expense, more so when hearing about my decision to desert. Being a family man, committed to never hiring anyone but a family man, he had no idea what to do with a vehicle suited to rebellious fornicators. I was abandoning Swiss and going to Euro, or so he thought.

My desertion was the worst kind in his view, but to me Wienerskin was a liar, proving himself as two-faced. Neither of us saw the need for final goodbyes. Good riddance, Jonnie-boy.

No One to Tell

The vehicle was later locked in the garage to prevent Marion from potentially impressing an unsuspecting female during one of his frequent stupors. Gene took a taxi to the airport, but first he drove me home in the month-old T-Bird. When we got out where another new and shiny T-Bird with mags was parked. I thought he would pass out where we stood.

He asked when.

The previous week.

He said Jon would shit.

Jon should shit to cleanse himself.

And perhaps that's what Jon did need to feel better. Gene's last words were: "Please tell me you're not going there."

Okay.

We shook hands and I never saw him again.

I never told them outright, though they discovered soon enough. The car stayed in the company garage for months after my departure before ending up in Kerry's suburban driveway, probably after convincing his wife and Jon he could fit her and three kids through two doors, and that he wasn't a fornicator.

The branch closed a year or so later. Jon had entrusted its operation to someone who couldn't be trusted with car keys, Gene choosing not to intercede, which speaks volumes.

No One to Tell

R.I.P.

Jon refused to speak with me, once he suspected I'd gone over to his archenemy. I was a traitor.

Frau Wienerskin died a few years after Jon, probably because she hated drinking alone, death certainly sparing her the inconvenience of smoking through her neck or pushing a little caddy with an oxygen bottle alongside his.

Gene was demoted to active selling after Jon retired to die. He'd counted on taking over as president, but Switzerland knew he wasn't qualified. Jon II was hired from outside the industry, leaving Gene with eighteen good years to remember and eighteen more to endure with his gin and girlie magazines.

I wouldn't see Didier again for nine years. He called me once when he was let go by Jon II who had an unemployed friend in Québec City. I returned his call seven years later.

Marc cherished his company-green blood, despite very little ever reaching his brain. Jon's thoughts were Marc's, and for that he took my departure to heart. He never called.

Nothing more can be said of Marion.

Gordie went into business with his wife, Mavis. I never saw him after a trip to Vancouver immediately following my departure

Bob left Swiss with Pat to escape the supposed dictatorial rule of Jon II. They went into business together. In my later Yoakum years we would come together to negotiate a distribution agreement they would eventually renege on.

Brian left the industry: His escape from Switzerland. Kerry's end came with a serving of crow the day he had to ask Simple for a job.

Kenny died of heart failure and sales quotas. He was never replaced.

Chapter Seven
1990 - 1992

The cabin's lighting was muted, nothing to see beyond our immediate space save threatening streaks of silver-white. We were getting closer, neither our survival nor arrival guaranteed. The attendants were walking along the aisle collecting headsets, not saying anything. I suppose they had nothing to say, especially if someone might ask for a vodka forty minutes from touchdown, when finally poor Legs leaned forward excusing herself. Her voice was sweet, not submissive.

I had no need to stand. The leg room in the emergency row allowed her enough room and watching that little piece of pleated material sway by would be easy on the eyes. In spite of which I did stand. Murphy pulled in his feet, engrossed, nearing the end of his ten steps. But all wasn't lost, or perhaps my subconscious somehow suspected in advance. In any event I watched her sway down the aisle once again, smiling, ignoring the woman who sat judging me, sentencing me to purgatory. I doubt the old crow could have wrapped the girl's skirt around her wrist.

Besides, Legs knew I was appreciating as a man of discerning taste in women.

The book snapped shut, Murphy slouching into his seat with the holy text pressed between his corporate shirt and his folded arms. I'd read a few similar books, not many, all written by proverbial gurus, experts. The last one, which I later gave to a library, I used to smash a spider. Keeping any of them is like storing an empty wine bottle.

Murphy's face contorted into several funny shapes during Leg's absence, flipping backward through pages until he reached what he was searching for: the print date. Probably unaware the author had invested a few or several months writing, more months editing, even more months searching for an agent. And more months searching for a publisher who likely as not took a year to actually publish the book. So what was new or revolutionary about what he wrote? Nothing.

I turned my head, hearing Legs ask the attendant for another Tía Maria. I ordered vodka, letting her pass in front, watching her negotiate past visually impaired Murphy, lifting one leg, the other high enough to clear Murphy's outstretched limbs. She'd changed into pantyhose; reason enough to give her momentary attention.

With our drinks served, the in-flight caregiver was visibly miffed with Murphy. He'd waited until then to ask for another beer and by the time she returned he'd tucked the book under a leg, pulling a letter from his inside jacket pocket. Why not pull out your credit card bill, tax form, or your dick?

His knee was bouncing with anticipation, unaware that Legs or I had crossed ours in opposite directions to avoid the contamination of beer splatter.

I daresay Legs would have left us, had she discovered an empty seat elsewhere. .

*

When I answered the phone Sully Stephanovitch was asking whether I had a few moments to discuss an employment proposal. We spoke for an hour. Although he'd called a year earlier with a similar proposal, that conversation was exploratory, a superficial testing of the waters, both of us agreeing to continue the conversation at a later time.

Sully had left Swiss BeltTech four years earlier, assuming the position of General Manager at Euro ConTech, Jon's German-based competitor and nemesis. Very soon after a larger German consortium bought out Euro and sent hundreds of Germans home, rehiring the best. This worried Sully, nurturing a psychotic fear that transformed their competitive relationship with Swiss from a healthy norm to cutthroat antagonism.

Since our initial conversation he'd been promoted to president, mandated by the new regime to open the East that was thus far covered by one person and not very well according to the axe-wielding Herr Ledermann from across the ocean.

He was in immediate need of an edge, someone who knew the East, the key accounts, and could swing their affiliations in Euro's direction in the shortest possible timeframe. The Germans weren't as easy going as the Swiss. They were in number three position of three companies, instructed by Herr Ledermann to reach number two, if not number one. How better than to take a key figure away from number one? Me, which happened within a week with a substantial signing bonus.

I was the first Eastern Regional Manager for Euro. The job description was to hire two new reps, train them, assign territories, work with them and bring the company to the sought-after number-two position.

The mission began in November '90, the new team in place by the end of March, but that was after my own indoctrination into the company, one Christmas and a trip to Vancouver in January to meet with John, alias JJ who'd been with the company for several years prior to Sully's appearance. He knew the product and applications inside out and got along well with his competition, Gordie. Each one contentedly separated by mountains and time zones

No One to Tell

from bullshit in the East.

Vancouver is known for year-round wetness and warmth when the East is still shovelling out. JJ didn't hesitate recommending that I wear business casual, which meant no tie, with whatever coat I would wear at home in April. I arrived January 19th and stayed for nine days.

*

I took a taxi from the airport to the hotel, reserving a car for the weekend. I gave my bags over to the concierge because I was tired, hungry, and lazy as a result of the previous two conditions. I would have given him a much larger tip if he had carried me.

I'd never met JJ, but I liked him. He respected personal time and felt no obligation to extend insincere invitations to tour his adopted city. We'd get along just fine and he'd been right about the climatic conditions as well. Saturday was plus 10° C, sunny and windless through the Coastal Mountain Range en route to Whistler. I wasn't skiing, not since I'd broken my leg. I just walked around, had a pricy lunch and shot some photos of Japanese tourists taking pictures of me.

Whistler was an anthill of florescent yellows, blues, reds and greens, most people seeming to prefer pink, including papa-san. Everyone smiling, pretending that walking in downhill ski boots was fun. The ambiance was relaxing, far superior to a hotel room.

I was in Vancouver for dinner at a seaside restaurant, with a view of pleasure boats of every description floating peacefully in colder January waters. Mine was hauled three months earlier and wouldn't be launched for three more. Boats in the water didn't actually mean boating during the winter season, though I did see some hearty folk onboard larger crafts with extra jackets and cocktails.

Sunday I toured Vancouver. My mother had insisted that I must see Gas Town and the clock. So I did. Wow, a clock.

No One to Tell

Vancouver was Toronto by the sea: Polyester and sneakers very much in vogue and a little sandwich with a French name and English taste with a glass of viscous red wine that cost twenty-five dollars.

JJ hailed from South Africa. For reasons unknown or forgotten, he became a fixture in the belting community when he joined Euro some twenty years earlier. He would easily have filled the position of General Manager and President, but he preferred the freedom of selling to the political BS of management. Sully didn't. Sully thrived on bullshit. Especially his own.

We spent Monday visiting his distributors who gave him preferential treatment and open access to their facilities. Monday night I was on my own, followed by Tuesday that began with John being late. He called en route to explain. He was delayed in traffic that wasn't moving due to the worst snowstorm in fifteen years, according to the news.

John said the only snowstorm in fifteen years. Either way, the metre of white stuff that fell over the next thirty-six hours determined our week. If I hadn't been in town he would have spent the week at home. I was the fly in the ointment, thanking him for the extra effort and consideration, but not for the forecast.

Mankind is constantly plagued by famine, drought, pestilence, illness and first marriages. In my particular case, snowstorms that seem to happen wherever I travel.

We finally made it to a packaging company, the place was practically deserted, though the manager took the time to give me an exhaustive tour and JJ was obviously pleased as punch with the special treatment, if not a bit cocky.

We'd parked at the rear of the building. When we came out the SUV was encased to the wheel hubs with snow in a city of summer tires and anxious drivers with no experience in adverse road conditions. Not a good thing. Conversely, seeing drivers realizing their brakes are useless and steering wheels don't matter a shit was entertaining. I felt for the people who were everywhere they shouldn't be. In particular for the guy behind the tanker truck sliding his way downhill, all his efforts to climb making his situation worse.

JJ was confidant. He had four-wheel drive, still determined after ten minutes.

I was making a few suggestions that, in the male tradition, went unheeded. Until the mental lights went on! We trudged to the loading dock, making four trips, dragging four wooden pallets, kicking them into place in front of the wheels. We were home free, if he didn't stop and kept the wheels straight.

Wednesday was seafood day, as in a plant tour and dinner with John's family. The city still blanketed, worth the outing. Mrs. JJ prepared Pacific Salmon to perfection. I supplied the wine and happily the conversation had nothing to do with work. This guy had his head on straight. He did his job and got on with life. His job was a job. He had balance long before the shrinks recommended the practice for healthy living.

Being so remote, he enjoyed a great deal of independence and autonomy, coveting all accounts, big and small. He could have easily put Euro out of business in the West by opening his own business, which wasn't lost on Sully. He was well aware of the potential threat and knew how the Germans would react. For that reason, he let JJ do his thing.

The week was a great learning experience. When we shook hands at the hotel on Friday, I had two days left before heading home. We hadn't visited as many plants as planned due to the weather, but that information equipped me with sound knowledge for working with the seafood industry in Newfoundland.

The fisheries on the two coasts differed greatly, in

harvesting and processing, though when the East Coast fisheries discovered I was aware of the difference, I was accepted by an industry that's difficult to penetrate. I would see JJ only once more because whenever Sully asked him to come to the East he refused.

*

The snow had begun to melt everywhere that one could walk. The city was awash, so Mavis stayed in the car while Gordie puddle-jumped into the hotel to greet me.

I felt good seeing Gordie again, the evening dissolving quickly. He had good taste, in haute cuisine and the ladies. Mavis was attractive and, unlike most of the belting wives, she had a fully functioning brain. She also made the other women in the restaurant appear drab and plain.

We had the briefest conversation about the whys and wherefores surrounding my leaving, my explanation varying greatly from Wienerskin's. Gordie promised to take care of that at the next meeting and I knew he would. Then we got onto a more interesting subject: Our mutual love of boating.

Weather permitting they would set out Saturday mornings on their Carver flybridge for the Queen Charlotte Islands, find safe anchorage for the evening and return home late on Sunday. One sunny weekend that was the charted course and they wasted no time, which meant Mavis undressing and enjoying a full suntan throughout the breezy ride while Gordie navigated to a suitable anchorage.

Mavis was forward of the helm, au naturel as Gordie concentrated on dropping and burying the Dansforth. That done, with his shorts gone as well, he took up his binoculars to scan the surrounding waters. He stopped, coming across a man zeroed-in on Mavis sprawled on the forward deck from a half-kilometre away.

Being focused on Mavis, which I can understand as well as envy, the fellow, whose female companion was also nude, didn't seem to mind that Gordie was zeroed-in on her. The rules of engagement were set: You look; we look. In fact, let's both look. The girls are gorgeous. Why not? As any real boater will confess, boating's like being at a nude resort with a very large pool and the evening went on till closing recounting more memorable nautical encounters.

Gordie refused to let me contribute with digestives, signing the bill Wienerskin would pay.

*

I left Vancouver with a better understanding of industries we'd visited and a deeper understanding of Sully's thought processes. I arrived home Sunday with one stopover for an equipment change in Toronto. From there I was the only passenger on the L-1011 that had to be in Montreal for the first flight out the next morning, upgraded to First Class which was somewhat moot: A perfect ending to a nine-day excursion. Would you like another, sir?

The next morning began with a trip to the PO Box. Résumés had begun arriving in response to the recruitment ad I'd placed before leaving for the West Coast. Then Monday night a fax came in. I was to arrive in Toronto by 9:00 AM Wednesday to meet with Herr Ledermann.

My flight got me into Pearson late on Tuesday, though I ate in my room to avoid meeting Sully and Fritz who was staying at the same hotel. I had breakfast in my room as well and was in the office by 8:50 so that Herr Ledermann could meet the new Eastern Regional Manager and see for himself what he was getting for his money.

The discussion was philosophical. We spoke not so much about my past accomplishments, but rather how I accomplished them. More importantly, how I would transfer that philosophy and methodology in concrete terms to the new sales team in the East.

The meeting was closed-door in Sully's office, with him on the outside. The German had a way of lifting a puppy's paws from the floor. That done, I returned home to continue reading résumés, planning my first trip to Newfoundland in ten years that would be early in March to complete my initial cycle of sales calls to the entire eastern half of the country.

*

My past trips to the island were exclusively May to October, though no one I'd spoken with had scoffed at a March visit. Perhaps St. John's would have been different, but Corner Brook enjoys an annual snowfall of five to six metres and none had gone by mid-March.

The winter was another bitch. I hadn't seen snow like that since I was a kid. Many of the villages, towns and cities in Newfoundland are like a kid's playroom when they haven't put away their toys and everything is lying all over the place with no rhyme or reason. The roads are serpentine, twisting into graded curves in the most dangerous places, with Stop signs posted so motorists will know where they could have stopped had they been so inclined.

The choice is one of staying on the road and avoiding collisions, or reading street names and chancing the dull thud of one car impacting into another. One street becomes another without warning and the chance of anyone getting to their destination the first, second or third time without some degree of frustration is minute.

I was there to meet a potential distributor keen to represent our interests, also for direct meetings at pulp and paper mills, towering piles of snow hampering my week from the moment I arrived.

I got to the hotel tired and hungry, making the restaurant moments before closing. The menu was limited to moose burgers, moose stew and moose steak, probably from the same animal whose death wasn't recent judging by the burger that was either wet or greasy. I couldn't tell.

They had no wine, probably just as well. I had a beer

instead that tasted as though the moose might have pissed itself before the kill shot.

I began Tuesday by scaring the crap out of myself, seeing what came at me from the mirrored squares glued to the ceiling of the tacky Honey Moon suite. The room boasted a yellow shag carpet, a green velvet circular bed, a bathtub with handles I couldn't use by myself, chocolates on the pillow and a note from someone wishing me a good night.

Breakfast surpassed supper, somewhat, the only thing tasting like moose was the coffee. The switchboard operator put my call through to another hotel in town I'd found in the yellow pages, smiling when I checked out moments later. Packed up and ready to go with the best directions she could give me, I set out to find the distributor in a city with no visible street signs and hilly intersections resembling slalom courses.

They were a small machine shop with limited capability that would have a limited customer base. A good fit. I'd already checked him out with some potential users and everyone spoke well of him. Like all distributors he wanted more than he could handle and, in particular, the pulp and paper accounts. That wouldn't happen. When I asked him why, he didn't know, which worked out well.

He would soon get his presses and start selling to medium-size fisheries, bakeries and anywhere else that made sense. I gave his group a made-to-measure presentation, spending the rest of the day and Wednesday doing joint calls that I'd originally planned to do alone. I left them late Wednesday for a slow four-hour white-knuckle drive north that should have taken two.

Kenny at Swiss BeltTech hadn't done much work with industries in Newfoundland. Jon didn't want him travelling to where they were getting the business anyway. Nor had Euro ever bothered, which was about to change as I walked out the door with one commitment, several requests for quotes, and a firm handshake with an old acquaintance from Pontiac Mill.

*

Back home only the least qualified candidates were applying. The résumés were horrible. One was written on foolscap, another rolled, flattened, folded and stapled three or four times.

Some were handwritten with incredible mistakes, everyone fluent in English, of course, until they arrived at the bilingual interview. All made mention of their accomplishments, that might have happened, though no one indicated in their letters how their experiences related to the position in question or how past achievements prepared them because there were no letters.

I had advertised for Québec and Montreal simultaneously, choosing the oldest walled city in North America to interview in first. Québec was the immediate need.

The pickings were slim. One of the best was a sixty-five-year-old who'd retired prematurely and wanted a new career. Résumés came from several bearing peddlers as well, one managing his way to the interview stage. No further. He actually made the retiree seem promising. Until Gabriel, the best of the worst. He would need training, though he was eager. He said he was bilingual, which he wasn't. That would change in time and wasn't a major issue because Sully also thought *he* was bilingual, which he wasn't.

I must say, however, that for the longest time I did believe Gabriel was retarded.

"Welcome to Euro."

"Tank you. Tank you, mister."

The next phase was getting Montreal on line while Gabriel was in Toronto learning about splicing, skiving, and other processes. I'd travelled in with him for moral support and yet another meeting with Sully to discuss distributor possibilities in Montreal. That done, I went home for more interviews and head scratching.

The pickings were marginally better for a Montreal rep, with one candidate who had several years of belting and rubber experience standing out from the others. Though he was tainted by a distributorship mentality he'd have to overcome. Changing to a more professional discipline would prove difficult, the basis of several future discussions.

Gabriel went home to Québec as Gordon left for Toronto. When he came home we were set.

Gabriel did what he was told, nothing more. Not that my requests or Sully's were given as orders or instructions. He just said "yes" to everything. Gordon, on the other hand, always had a reason not to like all things positive, not to enjoy something good, or appreciate something helpful. He was too centred on self-deprecation and his hair shirt would never come off.

We would all work from home offices and I indicated clearly to them that setting up with top grade equipment was preferable to less expensive equipment that might malfunction and cause a disruption to their schedule at some point. Gabriel came in at a reasonable budget. Gordon, ill at ease with the idea of spending someone else's money, went to the bargain basement. I tried telling him that spending under budget wasn't the best option when a higher cost would give him superior performance and a justifiable ROI. But Gordon was bargain basement all the way, which also extended to his opinion of women.

Except for his car phone. For that I went with him. I didn't trust him not to buy a walkie-talkie, watching him publicly shit himself when the time came to sign the 1200-dollar invoice.

No One to Tell

My past training and experience taught me one all-important commandment: Do Not Make Cold Calls. Those who would say there's nothing to lose are wrong. You have time and money to lose. Arriving at a client's or prospective client's door to interrupt his day is fatal.

Bringing value to a customer is understanding *his* time is valuable. Whereas arriving without planning, without information, undermines that value and yours. You're a peddler, taking value as opposed to bringing value.

The sales reps at Durcast, RTI and W&W were intrinsically more professional, results oriented. Bringing value was their single purpose. They were top performers, big dollar guys. By comparison *most* belting reps I'd worked with for three plus years dressed and acted like peddlers, perched on the bottom rung, one step above bearing reps.

They had no interest in higher performance levels or long-term vision beyond each Friday, the month-end and "closing" that immediate sale. To Euro, five hundred was as good as five thousand. Small orders were easy, and the more they chased the better they did. They didn't understand the hunt versus the chase. The mindset was business by the month, narrow thinking that was industry wide, management inspired, and condoned.

*

Given that most belting salesmen are on the bottom rung and bearing guys are on the ground, distributors are subterranean creatures. There was existing and successful distribution in the Montreal region, though narrow in scope, dealing entirely with direct-drive applications in pulp and paper mills.

Sully needed more in order to cozy-up with Fritz and I was mandated to search out other possibilities. I knew the likely candidates, already affiliated and content with status quo: Bottom feeders. We needed a dedicated company who would think of partnership and long-term success, a company with clout and personnel possessing good selling skills. We needed a company that was a notch above.

I phoned Wiley & Wiley.

I was into my sixth month and had met twice with Gérard who'd steadily climbed the W&W ladder since I'd seen him thirteen years earlier. We'd set the groundwork for a promising relationship. The next step was bringing in Sully to cement the deal. They would be a fresh injection of talent in the industry and would set a new standard.

Sully came in the night prior to the meeting. We met over dinner and a few naked girls at a top-end strip bar to discuss the details and peculiarities of the proposal. Unexpectedly, his bullet list differed greatly in content from mine and Gérard's, which I made clear I didn't appreciate. Self-serving surprises have no place in business.

Gérard had the same reaction the following day, the add-ons and amendments giving rise to suspicion, making any discussion nearly impossible, setting the tone for a meeting that went differently than anyone anticipated.

On W&W's part the accent was on methodology and technique. Sully's concise input was "Just get out there. The product will sell itself." Gérard's reaction wasn't good. They didn't work that way, and the meeting ended with promises to speak again later.

For the last time, I knew, I was descending the venerable marble staircase I first used in '75. Sully, who carried himself with his usual synthetic urbanity, wasn't halfway when the heel of his shoe caught the step and he went the rest of the way as though he hadn't a single bone in his body with his legs buckled and his arms flailing in an attempt to grab an elusive handrail.

From the bottom looking up, all I could see and hear was a comical bumpity, bumpity, bump. He was somewhere between ridiculous and pathetic; all bunched up and folded at the door.

Shoes speak volumes about a man. His shoes were well-buffed on the sides and top, not at the heels that were scuffed and badly in need of polish, much like the man. Sully wasn't effeminate, not really, though he was far from masculine, overly gracious to the point of effusiveness, making excessive use of a lexicon better suited to soap operas or a toga party. His suits didn't fit well, oversized with cuffed pants dragging at his heels. The sleeves of his jackets hung too near his knuckles, his expensive shirts too loose at the waist, his expensive ties hanging incorrectly below ordinary belts never complementary to his suits.

He wasn't drunk, though he'd been working hard towards that end the night before, and would again that night at the purple strip bar by the airport where he would unknowingly drop his monogrammed pen.

Discovering the loss the next day, he asked me to go back to ask if they'd found it. They hadn't. No kidding. Not as bad as when seven or eight of us had gone to one of the classier cabarets near the Toronto airport and Sully refused to pay a girl for the dances she'd performed for him.

She'd gone to the bouncer instead of arguing with a drunk in front of other willing-to-pay customers. Seeing that, those of us still in possession of cognitive powers left after suggesting that Sully not fuck around, that he should pay the bill. He didn't, Kirk did. Then, in the parking lot, he wanted to go one-on-one with the bouncers who were at least fifteen years younger, twenty kilos heavier and thirty centimetres taller. No contest, though I suppose I would have enjoyed the event.

Gérard called me to advise that he'd discussed the new clauses with Mike the Marine. They regrettably had to decline. The deal was off. The new clauses included a scale, not a percentage on the dollar, newly added client-industry restrictions, higher quotas and deadlines that made the opportunity less attractive, if not exploitive. I understood.

I hung up the phone, angry, in full agreement with W&W. The contract was one-sided, delivered at the eleventh hour, loaded with unexpected revisions and I didn't like being associated with the affront. I diplomatically distanced myself from the changes, which Gérard understood. We ended the conversation with well wishes.

Life went on.

*

Joint calls had become a contentious issue with me. I didn't see the need to travel with someone who knew no more or less than me. For juniors, yes; for equals joint calls were a way to escape the office. Travelling with Sully was no different. The man was a drunk and a pain in the ass.

Travelling with Gabriel and Gordon was clearly different. Gabriel always seemed at ease, but wasn't. And Gordon did an inordinate amount of apologizing, making excuses for whatever catastrophe was on the menu du jour and by the end of those particularly fun days with Gordon I wanted to beat myself into oblivion.

My first trip with Gabriel took us through northern New Brunswick, ending with our final night in Newcastle and a drive home through the Matapédia Valley. I chose the hotel because he wasn't familiar with the area and when we arrived somewhat earlier than planned we had an excellent choice of rooms. The old section was fifteen dollars less than the renovated section. Gabriel opted for the old; I went with the new and we agreed to meet for drinks sometime later.

My room had a hot tub, a king, a new TV, a view of the river, and new oak furniture. I detoured by Gabriel's room in the older section because I was curious to see the difference and I didn't need long for the evaluation. The room smelled like animal piss, was dark, dank and he was already set up.

He was reluctant to change, even when I told him by morning he'd smell like animal piss and that could be bad for business. However his reluctance may have been due to his first ever hotel experience when he went to Toronto for training. The primary reason I believed he was retarded.

*

We'd checked into the hotel where everyone from out of town stayed, went for drinks and dinner, and to our respective rooms. The next morning I had an in-room breakfast and was waiting for Gabriel in the lounge. He came in looking lost. I pointed to the counter and the girl's smile pulled him in the rest of the way. I went back to my magazine article until I heard sounds one rarely hears coming from an adult. Not so much whining or crying, more akin to a final plea before the squad aims and fires.

Gabby Boy, that would be Gabriel, had spent the night enjoying the mini-bar the hotel had graciously put in his room for his comfort and convenience, while he watched the entire menu of adult in-room movies.

Here's the thing. There was a free, three-minute selection period for each film, after which an eight-dollar charge applied. However Gabriel hadn't understood the strange words that warned of those charges and, not knowing whether he preferred blondes or brunettes with their bums in the air, he'd spent the entire evening repeatedly flipping through each of them to discover his preference, exceeding the three-minute limit multiple times. The movies came to about 300 hundred dollars, his refreshment bill about one every other movie at five-fifty a pop, making the evening's entertainment not far from 400 dollars. By comparison, the room was ninety at the time.

It was one of those times when you can take a more relaxed stand because you're not personally involved. The worst-case scenario would be asking for two separate bills, with Gabby Boy paying the 400 on the QT.

His English failed him the more he tried explaining his way out of stupidity, which made my explanation all the more plausible. I told the girl he was retarded, that he had never previously travelled away from his family. I explained that normally he liked to sit and look at pictures of pretty women and that he thought the remote was a toy. She had no idea whether I was putting her on. And frankly, neither did I. Like I said, retarded. She fiddled with the keyboard for a while, occasionally glancing at Gabriel with an expression of comic tragedy, finally saying that he'd be responsible for the liquor and gave him two bills.

"Tank you, lady. Tank you. Tank you."

*

Back in Newcastle, checking out, my account for one night was something in the order of 600 dollars, the female desk clerk asking whether I was certain the bar charges weren't mine. I stared at her over the rims of my glasses, letting her know the question didn't merit an answer, meaning don't be fucking stupid. Turns out some guy had a party he didn't want to pay for. She didn't like me.

We had one all-morning call before heading home. On the way out from the hotel I sniffed towards Gabriel and said: "I told you so."

*

I did joint calls with Gabriel and Gordon when my input was required, or a free lunch, or to make a client feel he was getting extra attention.

At first Gordon and I shared the same thinking about joint calls, which was to get them over with as soon as possible and get the fuck away from each other. What he failed to understand was that I was working for him, not against him.

We did go through a metamorphosis of sorts into our second year, all that changing for the better, though he continued bringing his home life to work in a way potentially hazardous to the success Sully needed in order to appease his German god and keep his job.

The female of the cave had abandoned Gordon and his three kids to hook-up with a transvestite and move to Aruba. Shit happens. Still, every time he was asked to do something he'd bring up babysitters, groceries, stomach aches or the PTA. The whole nine yards. He thought because I didn't have kids, I didn't understand. He was wrong. I didn't care. When he said I didn't know what it was like to have that kind of responsibility, I simply replied that I did know. That's why I didn't have any.

I did however make concessions in terms of his territory assignment, frequency of travel and nights out of town. But once those terms were agreed to and signed my expectation was that he'd live with it.

Gabriel was given New Brunswick and half of Québec. I had Newfoundland, Nova Scotia, PEI and the other half of Québec. Gordon had Ottawa and the English half of Montreal because his atrocious street French would have lost business.

Travel requirements were a little lopsided in his favour, so when he started complaining about travel and the inconvenience of leaving town for some meeting or other, no one cared. Both reps had come in at above average income levels and excellent commission potential. The one thing I insisted on with Sully was that he'd get what he paid for. And the guys were being paid well.

For the most part belting salesmen worked the floor level of client companies, not with decision makers, which was unproductive, uninspiring, and a waste of their talent. Engineering, Plant Management, Maintenance and Production Management groups are where decisions are made, the fun of creating and bringing value. Most supervisors don't care squat about value, long-term relationships and ROI. He just wants everyone who does off his back

On the other hand, dealing with decision makers required decisiveness. The language and rapport were different. Telling someone you think they'd be better off doing something isn't convincing them that you *know* they would be better off.

Meetings with these people required preparation and confidence in one's own expertise. Seeing the supervisor on the floor was easier and had the success rate of a crapshoot. Meeting with management was more complex, requiring attention to detail, ROI and value, the payoff much more significant. But that wasn't Gordon's language. He lacked the confidence and self-esteem needed to deal with decision makers, despite his affable personality.

Gabriel didn't want to deal with management either. He felt unprepared, not up to the challenge. He felt out of place and he wasn't wrong. Yet, despite our divergent personalities, differing opinions and styles, the first year was a financial success after eight months as a team and we would have hit target if Sully hadn't adjusted our numbers upward near the end of the fourth quarter.

*

On several occasions I strongly encouraged Gordon to include his girlfriend in his out of town trips, occasionally work in a Friday night or weekend. I was talking to myself. He took her along for company functions, nothing more. He was afraid of Sully, possibly thinking I'd use it against him at some point. Too bad. Everyone needs balance. Without balance we have no perspective.

I never suggested the same to Gabriel. When he and I were together to sign his contract, he said he hadn't expected his salary to take such a significant jump so soon, to which I replied he'd be able to put more into his and his wife's retirement funds. Not so. She was on her own to find what she could from the monthly budget. Or she would be on her own. His money was his, not anyone else's. Nice guy.

Summer, the last Thursday in July, I was in Sherbrooke by the pool at the Auberge drinking a scotch. Linda was nursing a rum. She was on vacation, joining me once again for a week of poolside, shopping.

The area was loaded with textile and pulp and paper, so spending a week for what was a three-day trip was easily justified. The day was done, the sun still hot enough to melt the ice in my drink. Linda dipped into the pool every few minutes to get wet. I didn't because kids had been in earlier for too long without periodic sorties for personal maintenance. A shower would suffice before leaving for dinner at the Maison du Spaghetti.

We usually arrived when most other patrons were finishing or gone, leaving those who really enjoyed their meals and the quiet ambiance of a fine restaurant. The time wasn't far from 8:00 PM, with a bright sky producing a spectacular cityscape when I pulled into: Private: Patrons only.

To my dismay, standing at Linda's side of the car, I noticed I hadn't put a puff into my breast pocket. I put a hand out, stopping her from exiting. We had ten minutes before our reservation and not wearing a puff was like not wearing socks.

She had one leg out of the car, one leg in, which slowed my thinking somewhat. She was wearing a mid-thigh emerald green knit dress with a scoop neck and faux-belt. Her low-heeled leather sandals with twin bands were a dark tan.

"Why do guys call them puffs?"

She broke into my mindset. The dress was only mid-thigh when she was standing.

"They don't, I do. They're pocket hankies."

No One to Tell

Hankies: Something I always thought belonged in the back pockets of old men with big noses, who like to examine them after each use as if proud of a major triumph. She asked why. Why puff?

I hadn't thought of Janys in years, reignited memories giving me pause. I leaned into the door of the T-Bird, transported to a time of fanciful passion. I've worn coloured squares of Italian silk ever since, since that bitter day in High Park in January 1971.

*

Gregori and I arrived late in Toronto on January 02, after midnight at the tail end of their worst winter storm. We'd arranged to keep the Drive Yourself car till Sunday. A good decision. The extra day gave us the time, the snowstorm gave us the means to mask certain damages afflicting the vehicle before signing it over to the company.

We spent the first night at the hotel on Spadina Avenue.

The room had two beds, the lights too dim to distinguish any known colour. The beds sagged, the furniture at the point of disintegration. The closet had no hangers and the carpet was sticky. The bathroom reeked of gastric acids and urine, which we worsened with generous amounts of men's cologne sprinkled onto the tiled floor, carpet, beds and pillows to mask previous disease that hadn't washed out. The window faced a brick wall and the television was broken. We turned it on with gloves.

We would definitely sleep in our clothes and cover the pillows with our winter coats. Something I would do again on the shores of Lake Turd in not too many years. We'd thought of spending the night sitting atop the beds, leaning against the walls to sleep, but they were covered with the historical yellow of loneliness and the crusty browns of once green and stringy flickings.

Our luggage was in the car and would remain there for the night, safe from infection. We'd bought a bottle of cheap scotch to share over the evening hours, but that was also in the car. Instead we went to the bar on the second floor, conveniently close to our room, since the uneven door was no barrier to the laughing, shouting, and music. And we heard women. That was good.

Not quite.

The bar was no more than a larger room with a juke box, purple and green neon lighting, a collection of mismatched furnishings, a collection of insatiable and greedy whores and their low caste clientele who most likely had something to do with the décor of our room. The room was four dollars a night. I forget how much the beers were. But more than beer was on tap.

The guys who didn't have the four dollars, or didn't want to ante up, were openly groping the whores' tits and thighs, trying to cajole their way into chafed and swollen loose-fitting holes pre-lubricated by their more affluent buddies at a higher scale rate. Others were fucking their favourite releases on round vinyl stools that wobbled if neither was holding on because stools were cheaper than a room. Or less hassle.

Some were watching, some getting ready, those already serviced concentrating on their beers. We watched.

The whores wore their greased hair shaped into cones or stretched into tails, fake red or blonde, their faces thick with war-painted lips, their black and green eyes garish in the dim light.

Their skirts were pushed to their waists, potted and bruised flesh swelling from the edges of dark nylons and the straps holding them to thick waistbands. Their blue-streaked tits were half out, smothered by groping hands or slobbering, mouths. Sounds came from everywhere, some drowned out by the general clamour, sounds of wet thighs farting on slippery vinyl, thighs splashing and squeaking against thighs, belches before, belches after, groans of disappointment, groans of short-lived bravado and farts that were farts.

Some women looked our way, some smiling invitingly, some winking, one taking the time to saunter our way to show us her raw four-dollar special centred in its coarse dark wad.

We understood. We saw then why no one was snacking on the whores, which wasn't because she smelled of cheap perfume. Which she did, as we witnessed a large droplet falling free, splattering onto her black knee-high boots fitted with badly worn spiked heels, stained white with what we first thought was street salt. She left it there, adjusting her skirt as she returned to her stool.

We stayed sitting in our coats, nursing our first beers before going to the room an hour later with our second. Things weren't closing down. In fact our second beer lasted through several door closings before we dropped off with a chair braced against the doorknob. Pity. We'd had such high hopes.

Little did I realize at the time that thirty-something years later I would reawaken those ladies in *Family Lies*.

The next morning we sought the relative luxury of a two-star on Muir Street and spent the day pelting the car with snowballs, driving through slush and searching the Want-ads for jobs and better accommodations. I found a place in High Park. Gregori found what he needed closer to the downtown core.

We returned the car, hopeful yet expecting the worst. The guy signed off and, needless to say, we got lost. Each of us with a signed copy of the release form.

I took a taxi to my new quarters. Taking the taxi wasn't a luxury, more a necessity imposed by my inability to not get completely lost on public transit systems.

The home was located conveniently for job-hunting. The rent was eight dollars a week with no food or cooking privileges, which was okay at the time because I had no money for food anyway.

I spent three weeks, maybe four, coming and going, doing interviews, getting lost, being late and not doing very well. Jobs were available. Nothing great, nothing I couldn't get at home. Albeit preferable to selling printing for a wannabe lunatic spy.

I got into the habit of going into restaurants between peak hours, ordering water and the cheapest sandwich on the menu, reading through Want-ads and filling my pockets with soda crackers when I was finished. I bought a newspaper each morning from the dispenser outside the subway station, where a cop always stood. The honour system was in effect. Coins weren't required to open the door of the dispenser, though I assumed he was stationed there to listen for the clink of my coin manufactured the previous night from moulded and dried chewing gum.

The house had three floors. The main floor was private, the kitchen and parlour off limits. The second floor had three bedrooms, a shared bathroom and a TV room. The third floor had two bedrooms and no TV room. I was on the second.

At night, when everyone was in their rooms or gathered in the TV room, I stole into the sanctity of the kitchen, breaking into the fridge to borrow the ketchup I needed to mix with the crackers and hot water for a late-night supper. One late night, with supper over, I was in the bath behind a door I thought was locked, relaxing, listening to barely audible music from somewhere in the Victorian building.

The water was very hot, steaming, vanquishing another day.

I was quiet, pensive, staring at the discoloured brass faucet dripping incessantly, trying to staunch the drops with my toe. That's when she came in. She seemed surprised. I was. She wasn't drop-dead gorgeous, but definitely on the chart and very close to the top. She was wearing low-cut blue jeans, a sweatshirt that had lost its colour long ago, sneakers and a ponytail completing the girl-next-door thing. Except that she was in the bathroom with me.

In theory the conversation should have been brief, something like: Oops. Sorry.

Not quite.

She was at the house for the same reason I was, from somewhere she didn't like. She'd recently graduated from secretarial college with honours, arriving a week before me. She was on the same floor, but we'd only exchanged occasional words in passing. Now she was in the bathroom talking with me about everything under the sun while I was thinking about everything under the water. I was taking everything in, meaning her, leaning back, my toe gone from the broken spigot, enjoying her company.

She was a year older, and I wasn't trying to impress her, but my submerged preoccupation was beginning to surface from the shallow depths.

We'd been talking for much longer than we would have had I walked in on her, and she certainly beat reading Want-ads on vinyl stools and leaning on greasy counters embedded with remnants of past meals in the aluminum trims.

I wondered what would happen if I stood, just stood and said, "Pass me my towel, please." Or if I had suggested, "Want to get naked? The water's fine and there's room for two." I said neither. I was somewhat of an asshole back in the day.

My lips were turning blue. The suds had gone and I couldn't get any cleaner unless she was deciding to join me, which apparently wasn't happening as disappointed Dick was turning to Dorothy and she still needed to pee. I reached for the towel, stood, towelled-off and climbed into the fresh change I'd worn in. She kept talking, which I considered a little one-sided.

We met as planned in the TV room where, for an instant, I was about to drop dead. She was wearing a short mauve woollen skirt and matching cardigan buttoned to enhance her breasts. Not much cleavage, but sexy as hell. Her ponytail was brushed out, her legs and feet were bare, the fire was flickering wildly and we didn't bother with television. She was marvellous.

We spoke for a while. Then, without words, she put her feet up so that her legs crossed over mine, sliding into some old cushions, wiggling into a comfort zone, letting the unforgiving cloth of the worn sofa pull her skirt higher. She seemed not to mind. I certainly didn't. We kept talking, the touching non-committal, though somewhat requisite on my part given the dreamy mood. Her skin was smooth, warmed by the fire. She was relaxed and serene. I was horny as hell. Go figure.

The evening went on forever talking, laughing, feeling good, listening. We didn't have jobs. So what? The fire was casting out its heat; she was hot, and so was I. We didn't fall asleep. We were in a place of dreamy stillness, warmth without words pleasantly overpowering us. Her eyes closed, then mine.

My fingers locked into the softness hidden beneath wine-coloured silk, my thumb caressing the tiny firmness between moist and supple folds. Her breathing was deep and long, a sensual purr. She lowered one foot to the carpet, stretching, helping me, the apex of her panties widening, the lower and shadowed curvature of firm buttocks enticing.

I needed to touch her breasts, to feel their contours and rhythm, the fingers of my free hand plucking at the buttons of her sweater. She opened her eyes, smiling, parting the sweater to a mesmerizing path of flushed and undulating soft skin. No words were spoken; one breast covered by the warmth of my hand, the other by hers as she moved to the pressure of my other hand.

Footfalls in the hallway. A shattered moment.

I stood; she took my hand.

My room was not impressive, none were. They were functional and plain. The window was badly cracked, whistling winter wind forcing its way through. The ancient radiator worked hard to compensate, dripping and hissing. The window ledge was where I kept my dinner dishes: One cup with cold, dry clots that were once the stolen crackers for my potage du jour, a swizzle stick used for chipping, a glass, and a mug for my coffee and toothbrush.

That glass was always clean, for my scotch which I savoured because I only had one bottle. There was a mirror, a bureau, and wooden chair that once had cushions. The mirror didn't reflect and the furniture was painted pale blue. My suitcase was on the bureau, filled with clothes: Dirty on the left, clean on the right. I was in transit and needed to know that. The bed was a single and belonged in a cell. The blankets were beige with blue stripes along the top edge to remind me. They looked like hospital issue and belonged in a cell. I was living in a cell.

I lay propped on one elbow, my sweater gone, my cords straining. Janys stood assessing my surrounding wealth, smiling, unsure. She stared into the unseeing mirror, facing away, gazing beyond the window frosted and white.

Her sweater came away quickly and she hesitated. She hadn't meant to do it that way. She was a delicate silhouette, a feminine figurine in the semi-darkness of the garret that was my home, her bare back joining smoothly with the band of her skirt. I watched, studying her as she brought nervous hands to her hips, pushing the material to the floor slowly, sensually.

She was exquisite. She twirled and came to the bed, easing her fingers into the elastic of her glimmering panties, pushing at them, showing me what I'd caressed just moments before.

Our bodies were warm from the fire's glow and the heat we felt inside. My cords lay strewn somewhere in the darkness as we lay in each other's embrace, our legs entwined, our lips touching without insisting; my hands' journey across the small of her back slow and deliberate. Her hands were still, patient, clasped around me in a firm grip, clenching when I arrived at the roundness of flawless mounds, exploring, pressing, probing.

Our bodies imprisoned by the shackles of our embrace, we twisted, impatiently, grasping. Her eyes searched mine, obscured by the dark, her hair cascading so near to my face. Her fingers locked into my hair, demanding; my hands pressing into her hips urging her closer. I needed to feel her breasts lost between us, to kiss them. She refused to part. We became one. I could hardly breathe, her inner warmth engulfing me.

That was the fun part.

The door opened, amber light from the hallway warning us. The evening couldn't end so abruptly. We wanted more of each other. My head jerked towards the door. Dog-Woman, the unemployed athletic instructor, high on drugs or booze, wearing only a tee-shirt that came to her waist was invading our space.

She padded silently toward the bed. She was staring at us. She was homely and white with short grey-black hair curled tight. Her skin was scarred and dented from the abuses of picking and scraping. Her eyes were pinched together and blank. Her eyebrows were thick, untrimmed, her nose scooped, too undersized to be of any use. I watched her, dazed by sleep, reaching behind me for Janys. Where was she?

Dog-Woman clutched her top by its soiled neck, yanking it with both hands over her grotesque head. She was beside me, staring at me, her smile hideous. Her breasts were flat, her dark nipples bordered with grey stubble; her stomach was flat scarred with a dark line crossing from one side to the other at an angle. Her dog-bush was thick and matted: A scouring pad in line with my face, glistening with wetness, smelling of recent use or neglect.

I wouldn't let this slurring hag spoil my mood.

I threw back the covers, my hand pushing against her clammy skin, pushing her away.

She was the one whose footsteps we heard earlier. She was drunk, pissed, smelling of puke. I stood, naked, grabbing her arm, propelling her to the door and into the hallway, throwing her top behind her. She stumbled against the wall, but didn't fall. I stood in the doorway trading malicious stares.

I followed her drunken meandering along the hall, from wall to wall to the staircase, her bruised and sagging hind quarters a focal point as she dragged herself stumbling to the third-floor university students, naked and unclean. She was coughing, muttering curses. Apparently she hadn't wanted to fuck me after all.

Okay.

The bottom of Janys' door was dark. I wondered how she looked as she slept, what she was dreaming of, wearing, whether her skin was warm from the fire's glow. Intellectually we knew why she wasn't with me. Not that we didn't want each other. A woman's sexuality is linked too closely with her ability to reason. Or lack thereof. Whereas a man is able to easily disengage the corporal from the cerebral, though I wasn't certain whether I should. Better safe than sorry.

*

Thursday night, January 28, was closing a month that passed with horrible swiftness. Janys found work that day and I decided to leave Toronto very early that coming Saturday. I had intended to stay longer and leaving would be difficult. I knew I'd never see her again. However, something, a feeling, was calling me home. We stayed together in her room that night and into the next, savouring our time together.

Friday came early, lost to us in time blurred by the intensity of emotion. Closed eyes enhanced tender caresses; whispers lightly touching ears with messages of rapture. We spent the day entwined, embracing an aura, a feeling, a glow radiating from sadness and blissful contentment.

We were on the bed, wedged into a corner with cushions, Janys spooned against me, my hands cupping her breasts, hers cupping mine.

The darkening hews of evening eclipsed the winter sun. She squirmed; she wanted to see me, her face soft and smooth; her lips quivering. She was a mirror of sadness I couldn't peer into, unblinking eyes searching beyond the night, dampened and pink with unsuppressed tears, her breathing shallow. She grabbed at the bottom of her fleecy top, stretching its shape, pulling it over her head, tousling her hair, letting it crumple into her lap. She rose slightly, reaching for the drawstring of her flared shorts, pushing them away.

The house was warm and quiet. Gentle touches, oblivious to howling winds shaking the frosted panes. She looked peaceful, angelic and vulnerable. I wanted to remember her that way, flushed, content, not framed against the cold starkness of a frosted window mouthing words I wouldn't hear.

She sat quietly, her hand pressed tightly, urgently to the top of her inner thighs, seeking warmth or giving warmth to the downy softness under unyielding and undulating pressure. She eased from the bed, her hands grasping the delicate edges of her tap pants, pushing downward as she raised one knee slightly from the floor, freeing the fragile fabric from one leg, raising the other, kicking them away.

No One to Tell

She knelt against me, naked from her waist to her painted toes, her mauve camisole sailing into the air, her hands pressed against my chest. Our embrace seemed eternal, everlasting, yet suddenly fleeting once morning too soon vanquished the oblivion of reluctant sleep.

I steeled myself against the final touch of the soft, rounded flesh of her buttocks, her waist and her neck. She curled into me, pressing, my hands travelling a familiar path to downy softness, lingering, absorbing her warmth, tracing the delicate curves of her belly to the hardened summits of her arched and pounding chest. She slumped, pressing harder against me, sighing, urging my hands harder against her breasts, our time together at an end.

Sitting crossed-legged on the bed she watched me dress. With nothing left to say or do she stood, pulling my leather coat away from my corduroy jacket, putting her forehead to my chest, her hair and skin an intoxicating bouquet. I pulled her closer. Her embrace was hard, unyielding, but as she eased quietly away from me her fingers worked anxiously at folding the silky mauve panties deeply infused with the pungent scent of her body's perfume. She tucked them deep into the breast pocket of my jacket, tugging playfully at the rounded, uneven surface, satisfied, a silky puff of aromatic silk bursting from the tailored hollow. Sweet

Any relationship that would have come from those ten days would have altered my future in a way I didn't want. My time for 2.1 kids, a mortgage and dinner with the in-laws hadn't arrived and, for the most part, never would. That life wasn't mine. I'd grown up without deep friendships. Good friends were friends, and friends were acquaintances. I was a loner and I would remain one.

I needed to travel. I needed change and challenge. I knew I would never sit in an office from nine to five for the rest of my life. I'd seen that over the previous six years. People with their lunch boxes and no enthusiasm for work or play, young people who looked and acted old and older people who grew older prematurely; living out their time, not living their lives. That wasn't for me, too high a price to pay for any one relationship.

Easing from a wordless embrace, engraving mental images I knew would fade with time I walked into the bitter cold of artic air that bit at my skin, leaving a serrated path in blinding white and crisp snow. I kept my back to her window, opaque from the heat of her breath against the frosted pane. Not turning was the first leg of an unknown journey. I didn't look back, nor have I any time since. Looking back is regret; hope may only exist in the future.

I never returned to High Park. I never saw Janys again and memories did fade with time. I could have gone back. For a brief time I thought that I might, but going back meant not being where I was intended to be, been pre-ordained by who I'd become.

I arrived in Montreal on the second to last day of January, the day my father died.
*
That was then twenty-years earlier, the only time I wore mauve or scented puffs. Of course I gave Linda the condensed version, crossing into the reality of my dilemma, Linda smiling, her leg that was inside the car joining the other, her already shorter dress transforming nicely into a sweater.

She told me to move, standing with her hands at her hips. I retreated, watching the show, her fingers locking into the ribbons of a bright white silk thong. The small front panel showed brightly against the tan of her legs. She stooped forward, pushing them to her knees, raising one leg waist-high to release half the pure silky whiteness, her dress bunched at her waist as she sat into the car's bucket seat. She crossed the burdened leg over the one that was free of the panties, extending it fully before tugging the material past her ankle and over her sandal.

They hung from her red-tipped fingers, telling me we weren't going back. Otherwise she couldn't possibly dine without her panties. Good point. We didn't go back. She tossed them at me, grinning.

I had my puff, the first time I'd worn white and not the last, left to wonder whether she was the only woman in that restaurant with her bare bum on the seat. Possibly not. A quiet flashback to Christine and I was ready to eat.

Whenever we're together in a restaurant we sit on the same side of the table, or at right angles. We almost never sit facing each other. We didn't that night either. No shit.

*

The bells were ringing for me and my gal.

After one full year at Euro things were fairly stable, though Sully was having doubts about Gordon and I was having doubts about Gabriel. We invited Sully and his wife to our reception as a matter of course. Their gift was a bottle of Dom Pérignon, a touching and thoughtful gift from the company pocket that did more for Sully than for us.

*

The main difference between the management styles of Swiss and Euro was that Jon thought he was God and Sully thought he was God's gift, though nothing was really different beyond Sully's affected sophistication of French cuffs and motoring vacations in an entry–level German product. So he could say "motoring."

Management in the trade was uninspired, not solely in the companies I was attached to. The fault was industry wide at manufacturing and distribution levels. They lived in fear of their American and European superiors and when your boss is nervous about his, you have every reason to be nervous about yours. The one indisputable element limiting us to reasonable margins rather than more impressive achievements that would elevate us to number two in the

No One to Tell

industry.

With a well thought out plan in place that would allow for incremental and measurable units of success, achieving number one status wasn't impossible. No one at Swiss was better or worse than the personnel at Euro. In fact, growing discontent with management at Swiss meant significant personnel changes were imminent. The question was a matter of having a vision, both Jon and Sully were close-minded in their quests for success and when changes did come to Swiss they were under the single-minded reign of Jon II.

*

During the first year I brought over several accounts whose business I'd developed and enjoyed at Swiss and all was well until the German engineers couldn't leave well enough alone. Their changes affected a range of belt dynamics from splices to the percentage of elongation, the new series failing miserably. Go figure.

Stupefied sales engineers came from Germany, asking rhetorical questions of the savvy maintenance people in a way particular to Germans before returning home with nothing conclusive to report or recommend. The timing was the worst possible for failures in what was one of the key industries in Québec. The textile industry was feeling the NAFTA pain of losing business to Mexican labour rates. Plants were closing, moving equipment south of the US and the few who weren't didn't need the additional burden inferior quality belts and inherent maintenance problems that had no solution.

All I could do was watch a flood of cancellations and issue significant credits.

The meetings were endless, going nowhere because he needed to feed his ego or have companionship in the local strip bar. He couldn't fathom for a moment that the problem wasn't selling. The problem was product and he was afraid or incapable of relating that information to Fritz. Secondly, he had no concept of motivation, ignorant of the sales process: The value of bringing value.

He was an engineer. Or said he was.

What became increasingly apparent was that Fritz gave him the shits and he used the backs of his sales reps as his private rafts to stay afloat in waters he was polluting.

The nightly after-hour faxes became more regular, more predictable, Monday through Sunday, requesting information by the next morning, sometimes right away. Be there Monday morning, sent Sunday, revise forecasted figures for all territories by Monday, sent on Friday or Saturday. Of course, what he got on Monday was a phone call advising that he'd get the figures on Tuesday and Monday visits to his office were always late morning flights.

This puppy, me, kept his paws on the floor and his teeth sharp.

He was becoming a serious brain-fuck. He could adjust the figures upward all he wanted; nothing would alter the inevitable. Euro was destined to remain third.

He was no longer concealing that he was someone not to trust. His concerns about increasing sales, increasing the customer base, taking over the second-place position were secondary to his premier concern of keeping his job.

*

The conveyor belting actually came from an associate company in the US with ongoing communication between the two companies for different reasons. Belting was obvious, the second was Sully's support mechanism.

We flew to Chicago for a five-day group meeting at the spacious Arrow Head resort that boasted numerous amenities and luxury, a week of listening, nodding, writing and forgetting. Déjà vu, many times.

Gabriel wrote a lot, but anyone who read French would

have known he was writing irrelevant dribble. Gordon sat with his arms crossed as though listening, his mind at home.

I was sitting at the back, as usual, with countless unasked questions in my head because they would be construed as contrary to the spirit of the meeting. I would have stood out, which was contrary to my spirit of the meeting.

Our hosts had planned an evening aboard The Spirit of Chicago. I learned later that she was a cruise ship calling Chicago home after sailing the Atlantic from the Mediterranean. She was a sleek vessel, all the passengers cramming against each other to see the dirty waters churning beneath them as they were drawn from the dock.

I was inside arranging changes to my seating with an agreeable headwaiter.

The dinner cruise was for romantic couples wanting to enjoy the intimacy of their shared space, seductive music, gracious dining and the glittering lights of Chicago. And that's exactly what they got… until fifty belting reps got into the swing of things.

One couple in particular I felt sorry for. They were young, either new together or very happy together. He was a little gawky, dressed to impress his lady; she was cute, dressed to titillate her man, and a few dozen card-carrying members of the Gawkers Club milling around the deck.

She wore a white linen dress, unlined, with white backless panties. They were playing touchy-touchy trying hard to ignore the growing din of obnoxious sales reps. Futile at best. I knew what he was thinking. He'd spent a lot of money on a special evening with his lady that we were ruining, which would likely preclude any home-style dessert.

I asked their server to take them each a complimentary Rémy Martin, and to put their dinner and wine bill on the tab of the American guy paying for our corporate open-bar evening. I took a cognac as well, toasting them from a distance when he glanced my way, smiling. Then she glanced my way, and I smiled, leaving through a companionway leading past a private staircase and onto a portside deck.

I stopped at the staircase, enjoying the relative quiet of Lake Michigan rushing against the ship's superstructure, more pleasing than the music and clamour. I needed a break from witnessing the final race between Kirk and Gabby sucking up to the boss, each vying for the Quintessential Suck Award during a week of kissing up and stroking, certain one of them was about to win by a tongue.

All bets are closed. Quintessential wins by a tongue.

Every company has one, the proverbial BJ to a successful career. If Kirk and Gabby hadn't already been married to others, they'd have been perfect for each other. They were golden-haired sucks, Sully their Dominatrix.

I stepped aside for a steward who needed to climb the stairs. When he was midway he asked if I'd like to visit the bridge. That was a no-brainer and I began climbing with a smile wide enough to rub against the rails positioned high on either side. He took my drink before opening the door, placing it on a ledge.

I'd been into the engine rooms of most ships that spent their winters in the Montreal harbour for overhauls, but this was a first. This was frigging special. The wheelhouse was dark, the only illumination coming from the blue glow of the helm where the captain was seated with a subordinate on either side.

The captain's chair was a swivel, set halfway into the helm, any control within reach. In fact, the controls were few. I'd expected to see a wheel a metre across, yet he was guiding the ship with a single-arm handle small enough to cover with a hand.

He was hired by the cruise line to captain the ship

during its harbour schedule as well as during the Atlantic crossing, handling her as though she was a runabout. All three had their eyes working the many screens, the other two focused on the lake when he stopped to point out a few of the features, explaining their charted course. I spent ten minutes with them, thanking him with a handshake before my invitation ran out. Once outside I took my drink, returning to the din. Thirty minutes later we nestled against the dock.

Couples were anxious to escape the inebriated horde waiting in a shapeless mass for someone to tell them which way to turn. Quite some time passed before calm returned. When it did, somehow I was alone with Gabriel and got the immediate sensation of being in serious shit.

We weren't talking much when we started our way out of the deserted Chicago dockyards. At least I wasn't.

No visible sign of life, which I didn't think was a bad thing, though a taxi would have been good. We were seventy miles from the resort. The first driver that came along flipped us the bird and drove off. The second one laughed. The third had a brain, leaning over his passenger side to negotiate through a barely open window, telling us to get in.

We had forty between us, the driver calling dispatch to sign off from his shift. He'd pocket the cash, have a couple of drinks and a snack on me at the Arrow Head bar and go home to a small studio apartment that had no one waiting for him: Win-win.

I went to bed, leaving Gabriel at the other end of the bar to satiate a peculiar and bizarre propensity for maturity.

Gabriel was in his early thirties, though he'd developed a fetish for women in their late fifties and sixties. He'd discovered years earlier that older women seldom said no. Whatever Gabby was or wasn't, and whatever he would or wouldn't become, he wasn't good-looking by anyone's standard. He was an ugly little shit. His head was round, his eyes siting at the bottom of a low and wide forehead like glassy marbles. His hair was short, brown, tightly curled as though from contact with some bared electrical source. His ears were too small for their surroundings and his flat nose always seemed ready to drip. His clothes were shapeless, his pants too short, and he wore white socks with ankle boots. So his proclivity towards the aging female made bizarre sense. He would have had very little success with their daughters or granddaughters.

That said, his greater successes were those less blessed with beauty, far less sophisticated, far less erudite women. Social seconds.

*

Gabriel clearly had a hidden agenda by this time, working hard from the beginning to ingratiate himself and, when he failed with me, he gravitated towards Sully who was wooed by the new source of admiration and devotion. Sully was spending disproportionate time in Québec doing joint calls with Gabriel when he wasn't infatuating bar whores with company money.

I would have dumped Gabby Boy, by which time he was very well connected with, or to the boss, much like the spaceship Androgyny docking to the Mother Ship Hermaphrodite.

I always considered that I worked *with* people, but *for* money. I never fucked anyone, not once. I tried imparting that thinking to Gordon. He had to remove the hair shirt, stop talking like a deserted and forlorn housewife. No one cared, especially his girlfriend.

His wailing about the woes of life was beginning to annoy certain folk. He was well on his way to serious trouble with Sully and the only possibility of reversing that danger was a change of attitude. But because shit dripped from Sully's mouth like honey and, because he paid the bills, Gordon was more ready to believe him. He didn't trust me. I was the bad guy; Sully was the real boss. Better said, Gordon didn't trust himself and I was getting royally pissed that I was getting shit on by the sheep for trying to protect him from the wolf.

Sully instructed me to give Gordon his walking papers. I met with the sheep at a hotel bar to discuss the matter. He must have seen the day coming, but Gordon's way was to let events happen, the way he chased blindly, too fearful of hunting. The last thing I wanted to hear was what I did hear, which was that he needed the job. How would he take care of the kids? How would he pay the bills? Nothing constructive. What I wanted to hear was what he could do about it. Could he take courses in sales techniques or could he enlarge his territory by taking an area like PEI?

None of that happened and I was the one who felt like a real shit. Instead I asked him to prepare a document outlining specific steps he would take to improve his performance and increase sales, whereas Gordon thought I was manoeuvring him out of the company. When all along I wanted Gabriel out. He was the bad seed. Gordon just hadn't been planted properly.

*

Spring arrived, bringing its usual freshness that brightened and invigorated after months of lethargy brought on by prolonged cold, the gloomy darkness of winter, fatigue, and varying levels of seasonal affective disorder. The hypocrisy of the Christmas party was behind us, the '92 budget figures were in with the first-quarter achieved and we met for the dual purpose of imposing more demanding goals and placating the worried Fritz.

Sully wasn't a motivator. He lacked the ability to commend individual achievement. In fact, he only rewarded supplication once yearly with a gold ring which he regarded as a symbol of achievement. I regarded the thing as a symbol of cock-sucking. We were six sales reps in the company and only two had a ring: Sully, for being Sully, and Kirk, for being like Sully.

At that time we had car phones, not cells, which were prohibitive in cost and weight. Neither was there Call Forwarding. Oh, yes there was, at Kirk's. Whenever Kirk arrived at home he'd call the car phone to verify whether he'd missed any calls from Sully during his journey from the car to the front door. He did the reverse when leaving home.

Was he afraid? I suspect maybe so.

Sully also thought rich food and expensive wine were motivators, for guys who normally drank beer and scratched themselves.

The setting was in the foothills of the Les Laurentides, perfect for a romantic getaway if there weren't other options. The rooms were too small to be cozy, with beds too small for two, better suited to a penitent priest with a Gideon. We had no TV and no radio; the books were from another era, selected by a nun or a child. The muffled tones of disgruntled sales reps penetrated the walls of the rooms on either side, not the squeals of contented lovers.

We were there because the food was haute cuisine. His stuck-up secretary knew Sully had a preference for rich food, good wine, creamy desserts and arteriosclerosis, coming across the perfect venue while flipping through a gourmet magazine. He had a fondness for the good life, disregarding the bodily affects so obvious to others. Avoiding the same transmutation required abstention and serious gym time.

She didn't come along often, but when she did she was a fully-equipped mobile monitoring station with average legs in very short skirts she would hike or straighten depending who was near. She called herself his private secretary when there was nothing private about her, particularly when she was sitting at her desk or after a few drinks.

I was in the lobby, which served as a game room, sitting by myself at a backgammon board with the disks set up. Sully happened by, asking if I played. I gestured for him to sit, asking if he played at beginner, intermediate or expert levels. He was expert, of course, but backgammon was my game and I was about to swat the puppy's tail.

The first match went quickly, the second could have been his warm-up, the third took longer and the fourth took a good while as Sully's diluted mind struggled to put his four or five ousted men back in the game. When I returned from getting a fresh drink I asked him if I could make a suggestion that would facilitate my participation in the game. No! Then I asked if he'd like to forfeit, begin a fifth. No! Would he like some time alone to concentrate, perhaps call me when he was ready? Apparently not, because he stormed from the lobby and wasn't seen until the next day. At least not by the guys.

I was serious when I told the others to not touch the board. I wanted the game to remain as we'd left it until morning. After lunch the following day I saw him on the outside patio. I was sitting at the board as he came in by the only path open to him, which meant passing me. He ignored me. Go figure. The German might have lifted his puppy; I smacked it on the nose.

The meeting proceeded well enough, Sully's leggy life-support filling the coffee pot when needed, adjusting her skirt upward as Sully did the same to our quotas while eliminating performance bonuses. Ours, probably not hers.

And distribution was yet to be settled.

*

Another distributor in the Montreal area would have helped the cause. Even Ed realized that. The manner in which the search was undertaken, not the intent, was tactless. Instead of sitting with Ed to explain the need, getting his input, letting him get mad, then glad, he was left out of an equation that he figured into in no small way.

I dealt with Ed most often on critical issues, Gordon less often on routine issues, though with Ed most situations were critical. We'd broached the situation several times, my approach being that another distributor would certainly be good for the company but that protection for him would be written into the agreement. When he asked if I was actively pursuing the matter, I said yes. Was I close to cementing a deal? No.

The number of times Gordon, Sully and I met with Ed at his favourite rustic-styled restaurant boggles the mind and was like Thanksgiving with the family. Sully always wanted to impress Ed with extravagance, which was comical because Ed was the guy next door who didn't care how clean his coffee cup was, often confusing fuck with fine. He could have bought a half dozen four-door entry levels from Germany, preferring Caddies and Corvettes. He could have bought Sully, whose French cuffs were usually covered with the jus of his rôti de boeuf, who was usually into his second or third digestive after a fine meal and fine wines.

One night his tie was askew. He was on his fourth apero, his suit twisted in several directions. He was telling Ed in the crowded restaurant how much he loved him, that nothing would ever change that. Ed was stocky with rolled-up shirtsleeves, his collar open, slouched into his seat with a beer in his hand, looking around to see if anyone he knew was within range.

The restaurant normally had floorshows on weekend evenings, but that night the patrons were treated to a freebie. Sully was devoted to staying with Ed. Nothing would ever change that. Nothing would ever come between them. Their bond was too strong. Sully loved Ed, reaching for Ed's hand.

Ed looked over to me and Gordon, slapping away the girlish squeeze and said between clenched teeth that "I don't fucking need this. I can buy my own fucking meals. I don't have to put up with this shit."

"We have issues, Ed. But nothing we can't work out. I love you, man. You know I need you. Anything you want me to do, I'll do; just tell me, man. I love you, man."

"I already did. So shut the fuck up." He folded a fist, half joking. "I'll smack you, really, I will… fucking fag."

Words to live by. We were already on our way to the john and the girlfriend wouldn't go away. We had to get out of there, partly to relieve, partly to laugh, the first time I can say I went to take a leak while I pissed myself. We waited as long as we could. Nearing the table Sully was expressing his devotion to the well-being of their relationship, exacerbating Ed's resentment of being lied to and cheated, Ed leaning over the close quarters of the booth to take a shot at the blurry-eyed and wavering head.

One shot would have put him to sleep for a week and would have been fun to see, but Ed relented as we sat, signalling the waitress for the bill.

Sully was talking at the decibel level of a happy drunk, not loud enough disrupt other diners, sadly amusing to those who didn't know him. To us he wasn't amusing. Simply put, no one liked, trusted or wanted Sully. He was known by the industry as deceitful and untrustworthy. He was bad news and a liar.

The remnants of Ed's meal would be gone before Sully's hangover and we'd all return to the status quo of Ed dealing with Euro first, then with whoever would give him the best price and delivery that became more frequent. Ed always had his ear to the ground. He knew about our meeting with Wiley & Wiley.

When we left the restaurant, Gordon and I were fine to drive, Ed didn't care and Sully never could drive. Happily for me, Gordon drove the semi-corpse to the hotel, actually putting him into his room. I went home and poured another drink. Being with Euro was getting a bit much.

*

The frequency of nightly faxes worsened over the summer months. Very few of us could do anything right. Sully was panicking. Dave, my counterpart in Ontario, was having the same problem, never satisfying the German's puppy. His region, like mine, had grown substantially over the previous two years as a result of persistent and professional work. No good enough.

They were still in third place. We had to work longer and harder for less money. That was his thinking. Dave was given an opportunity to stay on under conditions that included swearing an oath of fealty and subservience to the Mighty Sully.

I was gone by September. Dave followed a month later.

During a final meeting at the Hilton, the official point of contention was my boat. He thought I spent too much time from Friday night to Sunday night onboard. I wasn't accessible enough. More likely, I'd never invited him onboard.

Not far from eleven I leaned closer. He was high on booze. He smelled despite chewing gum to combat the effects of nervous dry mouth. I could stay on I was told, but, but, and but. I stopped listening to the fool. He was babbling, repeating himself, making no sense.

His eyes told the truth, his trembling hands, his damp face and tense torso. I laughed when I realized why he'd chosen a hotel restaurant that would be fairly crowded, though I was tempted.

The meeting played out something like this: "Take your conditions and shove them up your arse."

The time had come to shake the German's puppy from my leg.

No One to Tell

R.I.P.

Sully now only had Gabby Boy and Kirk to comfort and adore him. Soon after, Jon II came in with fire and brimstone, turning Swiss upside down. That upheaval has kept Euro in third position to this day. Truly, if not for the ill-fitting suits, the expense accounts and European cars paid for by the German, I believe Stephanovitch would be a far worse person.

Gordon and I became friends after my departure from Euro, acquaintances, though he waited too long to heed my warnings about Sully and paid dearly for his lack of esteem with a lasting downturn in his career. When the day arrives his epitaph will read: Kick me again, please. He continues wearing a hair shirt, afflicted by a chronic indifference to his deserved unhappiness.

Gabriel stayed on at Euro and, if there today, I have no doubt he's the only "French-Canadian" proudly serving his English-speaking master's pleasure. He'd be nearing his sixties, so one must imagine he's currently screwing women in their nineties.

JJ called me as soon as he heard the news. Sully hadn't told him. He found out through the grapevine. Kirk was the only Ontario survivor, worshiping Sully Stephanovitch on bended knee. Nearer my God to thee, which is what Sully needed to complete his self-image.

Bill was terminated shortly after Gordon. He works for

himself in carpentry. I called him several years later to offer him a position as the Ontario rep for Yoakum, which he said he would consider. He never called back. I don't blame him.

Dave was a good Regional Manager in Ontario, held in check by the reins of inadequacy. Very soon after my departure he was unceremoniously terminated.

Ed doesn't care anymore whether or not Stephanovitch loved him, which I always interpreted literally. He's either long retired or dead.

Janys, I presume, has 2.1 kids and a picket fence somewhere in suburbia. She remains somewhat of a curiosity to this day…Linda's. Though, sadly, a gentleman doesn't kiss and tell. Unless, of course, there's something in it for him.

Chapter Eight
1992 - 1996

Murphy was gazing at the same page, apparently trying to focus; Legs was reading the French in-flight magazine. She was a step above, whereas Murphy in my view would spend his life never quite measuring up. He was biting his lower lip, shaking his head, nodding, doing both. He belonged on a dashboard. He was very impressed with something, or confused.

The plane's matriarch was hovering over us without a crease anywhere on her or her uniform, which doesn't mean she wasn't bent out of shape. I got the impression she wanted to smother him with the pillow rather than give it to him for the short time left.

He turned the thing repeatedly in his hands, squeezing, puffing, desiring optimum comfort, not understanding the in-flight incubator was used umpteen times that week under greasy heads and loose hair, loose skin and stubble when not used as mufflers for sneezing and coughing.

Legs' discreet grimace said it all: Yuck. The thing probably hadn't been washed in a year, if ever. Anyone using in-flight blankets or pillows shouldn't worry about what's under a hotel sheet or sharing a stranger's facecloth. Yet, undeterred, he leaned forward bringing the microbial platter over his head with both hands, with both elbows stretched out. Legs pressed herself against the window.

He was staring at the overhead bins, like an oversized and satiated sea otter basking in the sun alongside a mermaid, intrigued; Legs was staring at him, then at his hands. According to the captain we had thirty minutes before landing thanks to a slight tailwind. Slight tailwind. So this wasn't the fourth worst flight of my week or my career, and Legs wasn't put beside me to take my mind off our pending deaths in the midst of a raging snowstorm.

"Thank you for flying with us once again," he added.

Legs and I exchanged glances, her smile weak. Twenty-nine minutes.

*

R & R was onboard the B-Haven throughout the remaining weeks through to Thanksgiving, when I would traditionally take her out alone for a final run to enjoy the choppy waters of Lake Champlain before hauling her for the winter.

What better than a bottle of Dom Pérignon to celebrate a much needed career change? I'd saved the bottle for a special occasion and this ranked highly as one.

The pale yellow effervescence cascaded in a downward arc, penetrating beyond the still surface, instantaneously re-emerging as translucent bubbles quietly bursting. I shook the last drop free, dropping the bottle into the pail before flushing the toilet. Deepest apologies, Dom. I felt vindicated, I felt good. I felt relieved, as though flushing Stephanovitch. JW Black tasting much better: a real drink, for a real celebration.

That was day number two. From then on my time was spent reading and photographing the lake, sometimes cruising alongside the New York State Sheriff's patrol boat, swapping stories at a docile 900 or 1000 rpm with Cory and his partner. They were maintaining a late-season presence even though boating was virtually over for the year.

When days on the lake and nights at dock finally did

come to an end for me I explored possibilities of yet another segment in my career, unhurried. My seventh change in seventeen years, though Durcast was essentially a nine-month interlude of intensive training as part of my career.

The 90s began badly, initiating an era of depression and massive layoffs, fostering a new age.

Everywhere executives, top managers and high-income earners were being laid-off in record numbers in an attempt by corporations to cut costs. In fact what they achieved was an irreparable deficiency of talent and history within their organizations, ridding themselves of the short-term expense while leaving junior subordinates to flounder in a void they and their clientele were unprepared for.

The 90s transitioned into a time when younger managers lacked the experience of senior predecessors, foregoing the process of earning a position, lulled into a false sense of self- importance. Loyalty quickly became a critical fatality they didn't recognize or care about, genuine loyalty disappearing with professionalism forever as symbols of long-term mutual respect, synergy and value between companies. Replaced by desensitization.

Increasing numbers of women were joining the profession, bringing with them so-called politically correct titles. They weren't *salesmen*. They were Account Representatives, Account Managers, Technical Representatives, District Managers, Territory Managers, Sales Consultants, Sales Associates and Executive Account Managers, all meaning the same thing: Salesmen. Irrespective of which cheap labour, peddlers, became the norm reinforcing the adage that you get what you pay for whether in a skirt or Dockers.

When the time came for me to get back into a work mode, nine weeks after flushing Dom, the turmoil that had begun in sales had already left countless casualties. Those who once enjoyed long careers at the managerial level reported to under-qualified egoists who should have been their underlings. Sales reps who once enjoyed the privileges and perks of working in larger corporations with established clientele became agents or manufacturers' reps.

Companies didn't want to hire them. They were too expensive, when in reality those companies lacked the vision to appreciate an obvious Return on Investment. Others did the self-employment thing, competing with ex-employers for a piece of a smaller and less appetizing pie.

Overnight salaries plummeted, disproportionately low to the skills and competencies corporations were expecting, contrary to the concept of bringing value. For years I'd preached and promoted reciprocal ROI and value. So I would sit this one out.

*

LindArt became a reality several months later, after months of location searches, negotiations with suppliers and artists, legalities with lawyers and accountants, patience with plumbers, painters and electricians. The banks were the worst; the government in number two position. Dealing with grey-suited moneylenders was as much fun as eviscerating oneself or swimming with a cement block attached to the neck with barbed wire.

Equally critical were the tasks of selecting art that would appeal to those whose tastes I didn't know, and hiring competent staff acquainted with the industry. In effect they would train me in retail art while I would train them in selling techniques, my evenings taken up with The Study of the Human Form and Organizational Behaviour at my old Alma Mater where I hadn't been for fifteen years.

Caroline was the first employee hired, Nadine second. Denise was third. Caroline possessed the most experience, immediately taking responsibility for the daily operations while I went after corporate business. Saturdays and Sundays were my time to work retail, the girls rotating. I left the scheduling to them, never counted on except as a filler for vacations or emergencies. That said, when working with women there's always an emergency.

Initially I brought to LindArt a passion for photography, modest management skills, and an understanding of what I wanted to achieve. I relied on Caroline to guide me through the mechanics of daily retail, and to repair my occasional screw-up. So the girls were discreetly pleased when I was involved in corporate projects.

I established three concrete rules, which I viewed seriously: Be good at what you do. Do not pretend to know what you don't. And have fun.

Needless to say they took time to become comfortable with a mix of freedoms they hadn't known before. They were accustomed to being told what to do, and how, with no allowance for self-expression or criticism. They were well-paid, including their lunchtimes, and often I'd let them leave early on a Saturday afternoon or give them Friday or Thursday night off with pay.

They were paid to sell art, but when they got excited about something special, either phoning me or coming to tell me how they did it, ice cream or coffee and doughnuts were the norm. Not much, but those small gestures meant more to them than any gold ring and whenever I was away from the gallery I was free from worry when Caroline was working.

*

High-priced original oils were the domain of established galleries who had clientele with deep pockets, or American tourists with a tax-free status. We specialized in prints, watercolours, black and white photography and the original oils of talented regional artists with something distinctive to offer. We put a great deal of effort into uniqueness, which quickly became a matter of pride for Caroline.

The three girls were competent with past experience, but

never with any leeway to contribute. They put in their hours, made sales, or took payment from clients who believed they had an excellent sense of colour and texture when they didn't. Most don't. The results uninspired.

LindArt required a change of thinking on their part, all three quickly evolving toward the lack of restrictions and liberty of laying out imagery in unique frame-mat combinations that no one else would do, either for their galleries or for their clients.

We were a step above, and the most expensive. I didn't want a clientele coming in to hide cracks in their walls or fill blank spaces, rather those who sought to enhance their environments.

Dealing with the public was dynamically different for me, which I quite liked at the beginning, having lots of fun with the girls and clients alike. When customers or visitors left the gallery they were smiling, feeling good. We integrated a culture and synergy into the gallery that I had little to do with beyond hiring the right people and implementing three simple guidelines.

I'd heard nightmarish stories about working with women, often thinking during the pre-hiring stage that I should do something about that. From what I'd seen and heard in business, having them in sales wouldn't be a plus to a small company. What with periods, cramps, babies, pregnancy, maternity leave, not to mention female outbursts of emotions when least expected.

They pack too much of home in their purses when they go to work.

I was accustomed to plant personnel, production, maintenance, plant managers and mariners who wouldn't shed copious tears over minor issues, fret over the baby at home, or bring domestic grief to the workplace. Then cry more because no one cared. Not discounting the Gordons of the world.

Anyone who's ever dealt with women who can't handle their natural afflictions knows the no-win can be a pretty rough ride. But none of that happened. What we did have were individual plans to make each day different from the previous day. Making each day better than the last has no place in the real world. That's the rhetoric of over-paid gurus and junior managers.

I left the daily interaction to Caroline, while I endured administrative work. She had the authority and good judgement to do what was required. My involvement seldom happened, though at times she would ask me to take over when she felt her twenty-one years might be a shortcoming during a particular exchange, such as with the doctor and his wife.

I was in my office one Friday night determining by how many days each bite of the Montreal smoked meat and fries would shorten my life. Caroline came in with wide-open eyes, raised eyebrows, pursed lips and doing curls with her index finger. She explained her situation on our way to the stylish couple who were waiting impatiently. I welcomed them with a smile and slight dip of the head, acknowledging Madame first, then Monsieur. She was the decision maker, the one who would know about ROI. He was the family CFO who'd pay the bill and not understand why.

I glanced at the diploma attesting to their son's new standing in the medical community and the small pile of metal corners that lay to one side. They had to be kidding.

Doc was wearing a fur coat that weighed 800 kilos before it was killed and a Swiss watch that would never depreciate. His shirt, tie and suit came from a haberdashery we had in common, and he likely had as much cash in his pockets. She was wearing the female version of his coat, her diamond rings glittering indiscreetly under halogen lights. Her dress didn't come from a rack, her hair perfectly coiffed, though all I could say of his was that most of it was still there.

They were nicely tanned, easy to envy on that late November evening that was wet, cold, and too far from summer. They were privileged, as was I that they'd chosen my gallery, but they needed a little guidance which went something like this:

"Madame, you must let us show you another option; one more pleasing to the eye as well as better preserving the document."

He interjected with a curt: "This is the one we want. It will do just fine. Just tell us how much."

"Madame, please don't tell me this is what you want on that." I pointed to the document and metal corners, respectively. "That's an important document and what you're considering is under fifty dollars. The combination you want will eventually stain the diploma and the glass won't prevent yellowing or glare. In short, you won't be happy and you'll blame me. What Caroline is proposing will cost more, of course, and you'll have something to proudly give your son. However, if you truly want what you've unfortunately selected you can buy off the shelf at most stores for a fraction of the cost. I wouldn't feel right taking your money."

She nodded the way pensive consumers do when trying to appear decisive, now that she was confronted with new information and choices. Her husband was looking at Caroline, so it wasn't that he didn't have a good eye. She was laying out materials she'd selected from an extensive array of mats and corners behind us.

I swept away the pieces, Caroline already assembling her concept of the finished product.

"How much?" the man asked.

"As you would say, Doctor, we won't know until we're finished."

He looked over to his wife who ignored him,

concentrating on Caroline's attention to detail.

He kept looking at his wife, though she had too much persona to be just a Mrs. Him with a budget. I assumed she was a doctor as well. And now he was looking at me, seeming to regret he'd come in the first place. I was standing at an angle watching Caroline enjoy the attention and critical eyes. He was beginning to understand.

Caroline had earlier enquired as to the décor of their son's office, selecting double acid-free mats that would complement the mahogany frame under non-reflective glass. The glass was a standard, the cheaper quality strictly to demonstrate the difference.

When the temporary assembly was complete and tilted towards them, the lady smiled in agreement, flattering Caroline's work; Doc stayed where he was, resisting an obvious temptation to smile.

"Or, possibly this." I reached across the worktable for the original choice, theirs. I looked at him, they looked at each other. She giggled; he closed his eyes, shaking his head, accepting defeat.

"How much?" were the difficult words.

"Twenty-five dollars," I replied.

He jumped back so fast I thought he'd drag his wife with him. "For this one?"

"No. For this one. Not a bad price after a few hundred thousand for university and med school. Don't you think? Though not from us. We'll be happy to recommend another source."

"But we want that one." He emphasized, pointing to Caroline's work.

"Oh, you mean the beautiful one that will last a lifetime, not yellow and make your son proud."

The lady couldn't stifle her laugh, reaching for her purse. I believe she enjoyed her husband's uneasy transition from reluctance to acquiescence, which might have been spurred by the fact that Caroline had begun putting the diploma in a protective shield.

He sighed, signs of a painless smile forming across his face, though complete surrender would be unbecoming.

"Yes, that one."

"Two-fifty…plus tax, of course. Gift wrapped."

He closed his eyes, snorting a laugh through his nose, wanting us to believe he'd coughed.

When they returned some days later they were ecstatic and would become habitués of the gallery. She actually returned shortly after with two more diplomas to frame: Hers and his.

Such was the reaction we got each time clients saw what we'd done to transform their new or personal imagery. High quality was the value we strived to bring them, their ROI was lasting pleasure.

*

I also got to do fun stuff like hanging heavier artwork, sometimes positioned quite high for effect, hanging Christmas decorations and cleaning the storefront windows. The other big thrill was changing light bulbs, of which there were several dozen, which meant teetering atop the last step of a too-narrow aluminium ladder, barely able to reach the recessed fixtures installed for effect, not so much for maintenance.

Changing lights was normally done after hours, but one particular night two bulbs expired darkening an important exhibit at the peak of the Christmas period. So up I went, looking down at the heads of clients. The first one went in easily, pushing the second burnt-out halogen into my pocket, waiting for Nadine to pass me the replacement with the extension pole.

Both feet were on the top step, one hand stretched out flat against the ceiling for balance, then the second bulb went in and the job was done. The second phase was getting down, which was impossible without looking down. Though when I did, all I saw was the woman walking into the ladder while Nadine, holding the base, was staring at me balanced on a band of metal barely twenty by fifty centimetres, the nudge sufficient to create an expected fall from grace.

The lady was directly beneath me, Nadine not certain whether to run or stay. I was going down, the only question was how badly, aiming for the other side of the 2.5 metre stand-alone display between her and free space. That was the instantaneous Action Plan, both the plan and me falling short of complete success. I landed with both feet square on top of the unit, scaring the hell out of her, making each of the six people in the gallery turn and gape, balancing on the tight rope for a nanosecond before continuing my spur-of-the-moment pirouette that landed me on my ass, rebounding to my feet to see if anyone was hurt.

The lady who banged into the ladder, born the day before God, shook her head, scowling as though accusing me of intentionally scaring her. Everyone else gathered in a circle, concerned. I was fine, not even a little red in the face, though convincing them was an entirely different matter and several minutes passed before I was able to extricate myself from all the good wishes.

By the time everything was stored away closing time was an hour away on a Friday night after a hectic day. The next day would be yet another year-end battle of the fittest. The girls were pleased with their day and exhausted, so I told them to go home. I would do the cash.

I didn't have to tell them twice and I spent the next hour by myself, until a gentleman came through the main doors, stopping to use one foot against the other to ease off his boots. He trudged up the stairs to the main level, seeming too casual to be interested in art at 8:55 on a Friday night. His hands were tucked into his winter jacket and his hair was dishevelled. I greeted him with eye contact, letting him know I'd be pleased to assist him whenever he was ready, that he should take his time. He acknowledged the offer, proceeding to tour the place as though he knew where everything was. I went back to balancing the cash.

When I looked up he was standing to one side of me with a modern abstract nude in red, black and ochre framed in a lustrous hematite-coloured frame and trimmed with a dark and darker grey mats, a miniature to accent a bedroom or office. He had the piece under his arm with his hands in his pockets.

"Can you give me a hand here, please?" He slightly extended his hip and his chest.

Of course. I eased the frame from under his arm, laying it out on the counter.

He asked if I accepted cash.

"Yes, I do." I replied, enquiring as to where he'd be hanging the art.

"Study. Over the desk."

He was a man of few words and stopped talking as I prepared the invoice and certificate of authenticity.

There was nothing to sign. My invoices and work orders indicated clearly on the front that special orders were settled up front and pieces purchased from the gallery had a fifteen-day exchange period for any product of equal or greater value, a reasonable protection against those who would purchase an item on Friday for a party or event at their home on Saturday and return the piece on Sunday or Monday.

"Will you be paying by cash then?" was the obvious question.

"Yeah." And he thrust out his chest, his hands never leaving his pockets.

"Three-eighty-seven-fifty with tax."

I smiled. He stayed with his chest jutting forward.

"Do you mind?"

"Do I mind what?"

"Getting my cash. It's in my right inside pocket. They're a little deep."

I stood a little straighter, chuckling from surprise, uncertain how to answer. "You want me to go into your pockets for the money?"

"If you don't mind. They're hard for me to get into." He pulled his hands from his pockets, tugging at the front of his jacket with a chromed prosthesis, something like Captain Hook's with rubberized clamps at each end.

I went in. He was right, they were deep.

"Told you. You might as well count it out. It'll be faster."

I did, making sure the bills were singles, laying them out in twenties and tens in front of him. I took only one five.

"What say we round off to three-eighty-five and leave well enough alone?"

I put the balance in his pocket.

He hesitated for a moment, catching on, bursting into a resounding laugh.

We were agreed.

Laughing is contagious, even on a Friday night after a long week. I walked him to the door, wondering how to shake hands as I wished him Merry Christmas, wondering how he'd taken the thing off the wall, wondering how he'd hang it on a wall, pondering the enviable resilience of some people.

*

The only good thing about the day after Christmas is the smiles on the faces of those around you, if you've bought them what they wanted. Otherwise it's a bitch. It's always cold with only hostile weather to look forward to on the way back to the store to return the unwanted expressions of love, peace and goodwill. What's left is crap, store prices are exaggerated and families are moody after the arguments that soured their Christmas dinner.

Spending Christmas with family is bad enough, now they have to return their gifts to the store for exchange or credit. The reason I never worked on Boxing Day, affording that pleasure to the girls. The trade-off was that I would replace them at the gallery all day Saturday, New Year's Eve.

Boxing Day is to shopping what a buffet is to fine dining. You're never sure who had it in their hands before you, or for how long. We weren't a buffet and we weren't known for having discount sales, rather for having a specific Exchange Policy which made the girls' day an easy one. We could have remained closed for the day, but one never knows.

Saturday was fun and I spent most of the day rearranging art on the walls, so Caroline could come in the next day and re-do everything her way. My back was to the woman who came in, catching my attention by the swish of air as she hurried to the rear of the gallery. She went directly to a modernist and sombre interpretation of clandestine figures cloaked and sheltered beneath umbrellas beaded with raindrops and removed the piece from the wall.

I went to her, but she kept it in her hands and stayed in front of me until arriving at the cash. The one quirk I developed, for no particular reason, was studying the hands of women, surprised how even the best-dressed women with the nicest complexions had horrible, uncared-for hands. She had poise and was well-dressed, but her hands were rough and chafed. She was about to spend 500 dollars on an image, but wouldn't spend five dollars on hand lotion.

The only other person who came in that last day of the year was very well-dressed, possibly overly so for a shopping excursion. I greeted her with the usual sincere smile and offer of assistance, leaving her to tour the images and objets d'art.

I went to her once, enquiring as to whether I could direct her to something specific, or perhaps guide her through the large collection of fine art catalogues. She politely declined, turning to continue her search. I returned to my sorting and arranging. The next time I looked up she was on her way to the main entrance and I happened to glance to where she'd been, to where the objet d'art once was, a piece valued at hundred or so dollars I'd taken on consignment from an up and coming local artist who needed a venue to exhibit his work that would double in price within the year. She'd stolen something unique.

Legally and ethically I should have stopped her. However I was at the rear of the gallery, she was at the front, and running to catch her wasn't an option. What the hell. Why ruin New Years? And the artist would think he'd sold his work. She jerked as I called out, I suppose from nervous reaction, certainly not from any desire to wish me a successful season. "Bonne Année à vous deux, madame, et merci de votre dernière visite. Thank you for your final visit, madame, and Happy New Year to the both of you."

She ran, which was really comical, which is why I don't.

Tuesday morning was business as usual. I was in the gallery with Caroline and Nadine when the lady who'd purchased the beaded umbrellas came in. She went directly to Caroline, complaining that when she hung the painting on her wall Saturday night before her guests arrived, she noticed one of the corners was damaged. She and her husband were very upset, visibly traumatized by the embarrassment they suffered when their guests noticed the damage.

She wanted her money back.

Quite a few people were in the gallery at the time, the frame was wrapped and I was running late for an appointment. I wrote her a cheque for the whole amount, dated for a week later. She wasn't happy about the cheque, leaving quickly without noticing the date, and didn't return when the bank would have refused the premature transaction. The next morning I went in because Caroline had verified the condition of the framed art and called to say I should come in ASAP.

As soon as any print was returned from the outside framing shop that worked to our specifications, we would thoroughly inspect each piece. If even the slightest flaw was apparent the frame was returned. Absolutely nothing in the gallery was anything but perfect. I stopped payment on the cheque, receiving a phone call from the lady late Wednesday afternoon. The language of the conversation was plain. She'd lied, and I invited her to the gallery to work something out, being that she still owned the piece.

The next night this fellow came through the doors at closing time like a bull moose. If his chest were pushed out any farther he would have popped the buttons of his coat. He came straight to me with the index fingers of both hands pointing. Comical.

"You are Madame's husband?" I asked, before he could speak a word, looking beyond the storefront windows. I saw her coat sleeve clearly and couldn't resist smiling.

He began a tirade of accusations, criticizing the gallery and me from A to Z that incorporated the word 'dishonest'. When I asked him what his definition of dishonest was he stopped talking. He also stopped because by that time Caroline had laid the framed work on the counter and Mr. Man was staring at it with his mouth agape. The hand of defeat had just smacked him in the face.

"Your wife bought this Saturday to display during your New Year's Eve party, knowing very well she'd return it. We have a specific Exchange Policy, so she let the upper corner hit against something in order to claim unseen damaged merchandise. As you can see, she underestimated the results."

Whatever she'd done was enough to separate the frame. He said nothing, turning his head at my invitation to scan the walls lined with perfect frames.

"Your wife lied to me, and to you. What do you suggest we do?"

The ball was in his court. His chest wasn't out as much, his hands resting on the counter, and he clearly didn't want to be there.

"I'll take it."

"No. You won't." He looked even more nonplussed. "That would reflect badly on me. I'll redo the framework to the original state and charge you my cost, plus banking charges. Or, I'll credit your card minus the full retail value of the repairs, plus banking charges without benefit of the art."

He agreed to the former, though I don't believe his state of mind was very clear. He wanted to settle the account and get out, which he did, with the understanding that the piece would be delivered to him C.O.D. by courier. He understood the implication.

*

My enjoyment of the retail aspect was limited to occasional diversions. My thing was corporate sales and, although I'd gained considerable knowledge of the workings of the corporate mind, what was immediately apparent to me in my new role was the existence of an alter ego, a shadow lingering in the offices, corridors and foyers of even the most notable enterprises.

I'd always taken note of how poorly the walls of most offices were decorated with suppliers' calendars, bad snapshots of propped up children, or wives with bad hair days, their skin puffing out from excessively tight bathing suits; not to mention thumbtack holes, quarterly reports and ugly vacation souvenirs.

Office settings with the best equipment, well-appointed entrances with comfortable lounge furniture and well-designed offices or workstations also had the cheapest imagery imaginable. Faded prints lacking theme and colour housed in cheap or damaged gold-coloured frames with yellow mats that once were white when originally conceived by someone visually impaired.

Addressing the psychological need of the workplace was a challenge. The product was conceptual, requiring upper management endorsement. No buyer would ever put his salary increase or promotion on the line for such a frivolous expenditure and that's where my history with management came into play. However to a person they wanted a discounted price, replacing their business minds with their personal, domestic thinking, the private part of their persona, their out-of-office consumer psyche. Canadians had become a society of poverty-stricken beggars, expecting something for nothing, willing to purchase competitive trash for the sake of ten percent, treating retail as they would a vendor on some Caribbean beach.

That has never changed.

*

The International Art Exhibition happened every four years in New York. Trade members only.

The venue was the Javitt Convention Centre, a kaleidoscope of adjectives and superlatives boggling the mind, confusing the senses of the uninitiated. Artists of every medium, galleries from every known country, and the haute couture fashions of every imaginable designer on every possible interpretation of the human form were there to be seen, admired, critiqued or praised.

Security cameras scrutinized the every move of every attendee. Passes were matched to proof of ID; armed guards patrolled each of the dozens of intersecting alleyways and every conceivable entrance and exit. There were guards watching the guards. Hors d'oeuvres replaced hot dogs and champagne came before beer. Chic was the order of the day and I took a moment with my glass of champagne to acclimate myself to the high-voltage energy.

Each moment engendered a reaction, each new scene eclipsing a previous one. The energy was vibrant, alive, coursing through the humongous complex like a serpentine bolt of lightning.

The attendees were thespians on a world stage, there to entertain and be entertained by one another, to negotiate and relax amidst glamour and prestige. Gaiety mixed with poutiness, giddiness and haughtiness, flightiness and the gravity of decisions that would cultivate success or deliver disaster.

The fashions were trendy and exclusive, the living mannequins tall, short, big and small breasted with firm bellies and loose, with hair of every style and colour and all of that in any and all combinations. The women wore sheer silk dresses and see-through silk blouses with bras that did as much to outline the high contours of their breasts as those who wore designer jeans with delicate and indiscreet décolleté chiffon tops without bras, all with high heels and spangles.

Others wore demure outerwear that showed no lingerie, accented with exquisite jewellery. Some women were dressed like men, some men more effeminately attired than women and others I had no idea about.

Men wore jeans and overly tight silk shirts with open collars and chest hair groomed for effect. Others wore tuxes with satin lapels and patent leather shoes or a combination of the two and no one seemed to care, but they all did.

One particular and elegant gentleman attired in black tie with his hair coiffed to perfection, his tanned skin making his glittering diamonds and gold trinkets more glittery, was conversing with a woman elegantly dressed in a loose-fitting crossover silk blouse that went in a wide V from her shoulders to her waist, leaving the perfectly sculpted centrepieces of her mostly bare chest overtly admired or covertly pooh-poohed; a knee-length skirt with a high-slit at the front and back gave her the exotic appearance of wearing satin, silk-lined chaps.

Another lady, whom I'd earlier seen sipping champagne walked towards me, causing me to turn to see who was standing so close to me that she and I were on a collision course. No one. I was in a fantasy world trying to remember the real world, but I had no idea who she was standing with her arm through mine.

Her low-heeled and open-toed metallic gold sling-backs displayed a row of shimmering toes lining the bottom of her soft-silk, cuffed pants that hung loosely from the matching belt at her waist. Her bolero silk jacket was loose fitting, reminiscent of the 20s with a double-breasted two-button front revealing more than concealing. Any bra would have broken the smooth white lines, undermining her attention to that compelling detail.

Her hair was slicked back, adding to the 20's thing, sexy.

What was she doing on my arm, using my name, asking where I was staying? Somehow I had trouble interpreting this as miserable or bleak. She had the decency not to ask if I knew her name. She knew I didn't. Instead she mentioned the name of her partner early in the conversation. Indeed we knew each other. The last time I saw her she'd been wrapping prints for me after hours, wearing jeans, sneakers and a stained tee-shirt. She was one of my suppliers, and a prominent member of the art world.

I'd received her invitation to the exclusive soirée organized for the who's who of artists and gallery owners, but my return flight was booked for later that day. She knew of available accommodations at the hotel where the gala was being staged, but locating a good haberdasher at that hour for a tux and accessories, not to mention finding shoes, would be impossible. However another glass of champagne was entirely possible while she did her best to convince me.

Before leaving I took part in an international symphony of splashes and sounds that make all men equal, if not the white-jacketed fellow who no one tipped and everyone ignored. As I was next in line at the black-marbled sink devoid of clutter or drippings, the black-tied gent whom I'd seen earlier passed by, entered a stall with reading material in-hand and closed the door.

The guy behind me thought I understood when he urged me on, telling me in some tongue vaguely resembling English that the sink was free, washroom instinct rather than comprehension moving me forward.

I couldn't resist looking into the mirror at the floor of the stall where the classy gent had enclosed himself. His fallen silk-lined pants were covered with a crumpled coating of white cotton boxer shorts at the bottom of his bone-white legs, telling the true tale of his tan and covering his patent leather shoes. In front of his shoes were his deeply tanned hands crowned by silver links and bright white French cuffs protruding beyond the contrasting black borders of his jacket sleeves, deliberately turning pages of the newspaper laying across the moist octagonal-tiled bed of human particulate.

So much for elegance.

I left the convention centre late with a briefcase full of notes and phone numbers and went for a hot dog. I was in New York City. I was going to eat steamies from a street vendor, standing with my briefcase between my legs, devouring them as I listened to the hustle and bustle that defines New York. Street vendors weren't allowed in Montreal, a sure sign of civil disobedience, not tolerated by cops stuffing their mouths with doughnuts, particularly if people were having fun.

She stood about 1, 5 metres as well as diametrically. She was the colour of ebony with the brightest, roundest and whitest eyes I'd ever seen. She was dressed in sneakers, grey jogging pants and a blue fleece sweatshirt over the hooded one matching the pants. Her wool gloves were cut off at the fingers, her apron art nouveau with recent and mature streaks and dabs of mustard and mayo, ketchup and relish green.

Mustard and relish was my choice. What I got was a meaty tube of unknown animal offal liberally laced with regurgitated lettuce.

"This isn't what I ordered."

She looked at my open hands, then up. "I know, hon, but it's what you get."

"I wanted mustard and relish." I insisted, with a smile. "What is this stuff?"

"That's the stuff you get on my dogs, hon. That there's Sauer Kraut. You might want mustard and relish, but you won't get it. Not here, not on my dogs. Nope, not here" She scrunched up her lips, shaking her head from side to side, waving a finger in the opposite direction, possibly for balance.

"I don't like Sauer Kraut. How come you can have it on your apron and I can't have it on my dog?"

I pleaded with her. She didn't care, asking if I'd ever tried it, to which I said no, to which she laughed in a series of shock waves while turning to serve someone who wolfed down the shredded wet stuff before he'd even paid her.

What the hell, I was in New York with people pushing and squeezing past others who were standing, police sirens blaring, air horns of fire engines clearing their way as effectively as any battering ram, anonymous legs long and short scurrying across intersections irrespective of the yellow or red. The first bite followed a deep breath; the first swallow followed by a second. If I could get through one, I could pick up my briefcase and retreat. She was watching my progress, barely keeping up with the line in front of her. I noticed that no one spoke. They just paid and began eating, or maybe just swallowing.

The first one was down, and likely wouldn't be digested for several days as my digestive juices worked overtime to disintegrate the vinegary foreign matter laying like compost at the bottom of my stomach. The second steamie hailed a cab, the Sauer Kraut leaking down my sleeve as my briefcase came up from the sidewalk littered with the crumpled debris of on-the-run eaters.

The cab was bright yellow with gaudy billboard panels affixed to the roof advertising a bronzing cream. The woman was laying on her side, an untied bikini draped over her suntanned hip while the twin string was taut, held firmly by an anonymous hand.

The interior was a mini-gallery in its own right with wall-to-wall stickers announcing rates, rules, fines, districts, instructions for payment through the bullet-proof shield and a wallet-sized mug shot of the driver. The floor was a testimonial to the eating habits of previous riders with wrappers and cups covering every square centimetre of the cheap vinyl matting. The upholstery was torn with once-white stuffing hanging out in tufts, complementing a mosaic of countless cigarette burns that would scrape at overcoats, pants, and ruin pantyhose.

I remained still throughout the trip, unless he swerved or braked, throwing his fist out the window, cursing. I heard about everything that was wrong with New York. And the remedies, if only, if only. Whatever. The real problem was getting my hand free of the hot dog to pay the guy and I began appreciating the origins of historical clutter around my feet.

More importantly I arrived home to panties hanging from the chandelier.
*

Midway through the second year the girls left the gallery in a sequence opposite to their arrivals. Denise was terminated. She'd become overbearing with the clientele, ruffling a few feathers. She'd also begun implementing changes without passing them by Caroline or me. One particular time, coincidently the last change she made, she replaced all the pricing stickers with a new lot. The initiative would have been commendable if not for the fact that she inverted most of the prices.

The blunder was major and might have been extremely costly beyond the several hours required to verify and re-price the inventory. If she could have scratched my eyes out and ripped off principal appendages, she would have. I got off with a reasonably brief outburst of regional invectives, and curses intended to limit my reproductive capability. For those I thanked her.

Nadine was next in line. She'd begun taking advantage of a good thing. That she was paid for her lunch hours wasn't meant to imply her lunch break was indistinguishable from the rest of her day. She would come late, leave early, and began regarding Fridays as personal floater days to be used at her discretion.

Being ill on a Friday happens, being ill only on Fridays is something else, particularly when she'd call in sick but come to the gallery for her paycheque and leave immediately after. She was young, though I believed old enough to realize we were going through growing pains, that everyone's peak performance was crucial. She learned the hard way that caring is a mutual act. Bye-bye.

Caroline left of her own accord to dedicate more time to her final year at university, giving me her notice several weeks in advance. I replaced Nadine and Denise with

Shorty who came to the gallery from one of my suppliers. Now I had to find someone to replace Caroline and that would be difficult. She'd created a significant void.

Shorty had a friend, an idea I disliked immediately. She'd previously worked as assistant-manager of a gallery that recently closed and would be an asset to LindArt, according to Shorty. I reluctantly agreed to meet with her before placing a recruitment ad, partly to placate Shorty, partly because the friend sounded too good to be true. The interview with Christiane lasted three hours, including her doing layouts and selecting art for the coming month's inventory.

She started the week Caroline left.

The ladies took tremendous pride in their work. They worked well together, knowing intrinsically what was needed and when, knowing before walking in each morning what they would do, how they would make their day successful. They were far and away more organized and determined than most sales reps I'd met in belting. They enjoyed a synergy that required no supervision, which meant I could return to what I enjoyed doing and taking my first vacation in two years.

*

Beyond the world of oils and watercolours, we specialized in black and white photography, particularly tasteful female nudes. Bronzed or ceramic sculptures were one thing, but male paraphernalia wasn't what I wanted hanging in the gallery. Personal taste aside, almost everyone enjoyed the gallery's extensive collection of contemporary images of nude women, including straight women and gay men.

One day an older woman came in with a girl of pre-school age. While working at the counter arranging the layout combination for the woman's art, the little girl pointed to a beautiful black and white photograph, tugging her grandmother's sleeve for attention.

"Who's that?" she wanted to know, pointing at the image on the wall.

Granny looked over and replied. "That's mommy, getting ready for work."

The kid seemed satisfied.

The image was of a nude woman sitting on a velveteen bench at her vanity, pitch black hair cascading down the faultless symmetry of her snow-white back in long spiralling curls hanging suspended and uneven above the sensuous contours and shadows of her flawless buttocks. Her arms were cloaked in black evening gloves, framing her torso, her palms flat atop the cushioned bench. An excellent example of black with white and the human form made vulnerable by innocent simplicity and beauty.

I couldn't help thinking, if that was mommy, good for daddy. I liked that particular photograph so much that when Christiane heartlessly sold it to a client I composed a version of my own after my upcoming escape from reality and a couple of weeks of shooting photos with my preferred model in Cape Cod.

*

Ten days of good food, good wine, ocean views from the café windows of Provincetown, lazy walks along the deserted beaches, and visits to galleries dedicated to the distinctive work of artists who migrate to America's gay capital for the summer season. I saw more black and white, sepia and various other interpretations of male genitalia hanging on the walls of Provincetown art galleries than one would expect to see in all the bathhouses along the East Coast. Leaving me to wonder where lesbian artists hung out.

The weather system bringing a backdrop of theatrical thunderstorms provided an ideal venue for a once-in-a-lifetime photo shoot one could never duplicate and, for a brief moment in time, LindArt did not exist.

The first time we ambled around the main pier of the city harbour I knew the setting would capture the mood of the images I'd composed in my mind. The weather for the next day however called for clear skies, gusty winds off the Atlantic and moderate temperatures we hadn't felt for months at home. I could wait. Friday's weather would worsen.

Early Friday morning the end-of-season crowds wouldn't be there to clutter my background with strollers, beer bellies and out-of-date pink polyester pant suits. The pier would be cordoned off, trawlers at dock unloading their foul-smelling catches, men preparing for yet another day by mending nets, oiling winches and performing preventative maintenance in their powerhouses. The fishermen would be below deck or toiling topside with their backs bent into their hard work.

The larger private yachts granted docking privileges were relegated to the secondary pier, smaller private boats moored in the cradle of the arm that demarcates the northern point of the relatively calm waters of Cape Cod Bay.

Friday morning brought promised dark clouds and gusts from the choppy sea making the pier fresh. Breakfast was a fast coffee.

With simplicity comes the allure of sophistication, poise and confidence, the outfit selected for the shoot evoking all three elements against the disconnected background of manual labour, heavy equipment, commercial vehicles and laden fishing vessels. Her lightweight canvas jacket served as Linda's cover-up against the morning air, not the glances of the occasional male passer-by smiling at the mesh-covered legs extending past the hem while their wives pretended to look straight ahead.

The smaller craft were tugging against the braided lines mooring them to sunken blocks. Heavier displacement yachts and commercial vessels sat tied and motionless against tire-lined and sooty pylons as though in dry dock, their decks lowered to three or four metres below eye level by the morning tide.

    Linda got into it like a pro, flinging her outer jacket to the side like a cumbersome burden, taking ownership of the pier as her private catwalk amidst swinging blocks and tackle and overhead boom cranes. Her black kid leather shirt with black matt snaps was open, revealing a black one-piece bustier bodysuit sitting high on her hips. Black mesh stockings and high-heeled pumps completed the theme, a gold link belt slung across her waist to distract the eye. She did her thing non-stop for fifteen minutes without any direction, without stopping when I did for the film change or to argue against the wind's interpretation of what the lens should see.

    She was working the wind, the dock, and the crowd that began emerging.

    One head popped up, then another, framed by the curved top railing of the rusted and flaking ladders connecting the decks of the trawlers to the pier. We heard the voices, not the words. We didn't have to. Anyway, time for a quick break, and apparently not just for us. Linda was leaning against the grill of a Mack truck towering over her head, waving to the lady Coast Guard mere metres away who'd been leaning across the helm of her search and rescue vessel. The Coastie waved back with a smile and we knew she wasn't going anywhere.

    The pier was lined with tall, short, fat, thin, old, young, smiling and awestruck fishermen who needed a short break from their work, all sitting in yellow or black farmers with chequered shirts, tee-shirts or sweat tops along the makeshift guardrails that were soot-stained beams. A few seniors dressed in pastel-coloured windbreakers, bright white running shoes and tight-fitting white golf hats, who hadn't seen that much woman in thirty years, stood side by side transfixed, ignoring each other.

We were set to go again, the appearance of the unexpected audience bringing out the showgirl in Linda as she strode, extended, stretched, turned and titillated. Even I wasn't expecting the soft leather shirt to come off and no one seemed to care when I paused to change rolls or lenses. She gave a hell of a performance, matching the time in Cabo when she won the standing applause and catcalls of the entire crew of a US Coast Guard cutter and their captain during a bikini contest.

She'd missed her calling, much to the delight of a few dozen smiling fishermen who were quietly disappointed when I signalled Linda that I was finished, but she wasn't. She sauntered over to where her shirt lay across her jacket under the appreciative gazes of her newfound devotees, easing into it as seductively as she'd removed it. The smiling crew stood as she walked towards them, the wind playing with her permissive shirttails.

They elbowed one another and cheered a chorus of "thank you" and compliments. I took a few moments to catch up, crossing over from a different angle, looking to the foredeck of the Coast Guard vessel to see a big smile, a wink, and thumbs up. I smiled back. Aye, aye, Captain.

They were talking with her, wanting to know which magazine and which month. She told them The Fishermen's Weekly anytime soon. They didn't seem to know of it. They didn't seem to care. They were looking, waving goodbye as their crew leader ordered them back to work, cautioning them not to miss the first step.

As we neared the access gate to the secondary pier the pacemakers clicked into emergency mode and the old coots stopped breathing in order to heighten their visual senses. Just as well they weren't near the car when she slid into her matching mini-skirt. The pacemakers would have short-circuited.

*

There was no shortage of push-up bras, short skirts, bare thighs, sheer dresses, and bodies painted into Lycra visiting the gallery over the previous three years. Those delightful interludes were frequent, though I did miss the flavour that summertime Friday afternoons had once injected into my week.

Another Friday had come with me surviving almost a full week without Shorty and Christiane who needed the same two weeks for separate vacations, which was fine because those weeks were traditionally slow with most of the population on vacation with the ladies.

I was sitting at the front desk with my feet up, leafing through catalogues of black and white depictions of the female form, making notes. Suddenly I wasn't. I stood, thinking the woman was about to come in, overlooking the main entrance framing a wall-to-wall and floor-to-ceiling display window that also framed her titanium-coloured European convertible.

The top was down, the supple white leather driver's seat slightly reclined with perfectly tanned and very bare legs centred below the steering wheel. She wasn't in a hurry, adjusting her skirt. She eased out, one leg reluctant to follow the other, her skirt trailing behind with the same reluctance.

I went for a coffee, a little caffeine boost, not wanting to hover over her, thinking I should have stood a few moments earlier. By the time I came back she was lifting a foot from the final step and we stood facing each other.

Her summer stilettos gave her the appearance of being tall, but she wasn't, her blonde hair parted to one side, draped over a bare shoulder. Her sleeveless, ivory-toned muslin peasant blouse gave stirring evidence of a tan that was complete and travelled, not applied. As well as the firm conclusion that she wasn't wearing a bra.

The knee-length muslin skirt might just as well been pinched together by her fingers at the waist for all the good the one button was doing. The satin strings of the muted red thong she wore underneath were decidedly intended for viewing. The tiny V they held in place strived equally hard for attention as she stood with her back to the light, her chic sandals in red leather well apart from one another, her red lacquered toenails and fingernails glistening under the gallery's bright lights. Strangely, with all that, I noticed she had no purse.

She was smiling, scanning the gallery, asking if she might just stroll around, so that my recent acquisitions could be admired and appreciated.

"Yes, of course. May I offer you a coffee or a juice?"

"Thank you, no." She turned to see her car, leaning over the railing. "Is it quite fine as it is? Do you think?"

"Yes, indeed. It's perfectly fine," I had to admit.

Very fine. She sauntered from one image to the next, examining each one. I leaned against the desk to finish my coffee, available to answer any questions she might have. By the time the first question came, my coffee was cold.

"Who makes the final decision on choice and colours of private work?"

"The client does, though we assist."

"And what colours do they prefer?" she stooped forward, lifting a frame laying against the wall at floor level, the muslin conforming to the changing shape of her bared buttocks, the border of her loose blouse billowing to show the curves of her breasts.

The question didn't require much thought. "Earth tones, mostly."

"And why is that?" She straightened.

"It's safe, I suppose. They don't have to explain. Nor do we impose beyond their decision."

No One to Tell

"You mean they are afraid?" She held the image in extended arms, lowered it to the floor, pausing for one last glance before continuing. "Of what?"

"Fear, I suppose. Of being distinctive and spontaneous, yes. Colours represent who were are, is that not so?"

"You have many different colours on these walls; and who shall buy them?" She stood in front of a black and white image, compelling me to note the similarities.

I answered, "Those who lack colour or those who appreciate colour."

"Yet this is black and white."

She was drawn to an image of a nude woman standing at a full-length mirror with the beaded wetness of her recent shower glistening on her back and the sculpted semi-spheres of her buttocks facing the camera. Her towel was held partly across her youthful and firm breasts, her expression one of peaceful contentment and gratification. My visitor seemed lost in the image, transfixed or transported, imitating the pose. I think unaware that she was, her simple outfit not concealing the similarities of one near-naked woman appreciating the vulnerable serenity of another.

"Yes, both of them colours. Shades of blacks and whites are the colours of our reality. All others are the nuances of our dreams and expectations, our expression of self. Black and white show us what we truly are, the true nature of our flaws or our perfection; colours serve to mask what would otherwise be revealed to us by their absence, thereby bringing us the pleasure of escape we cannot find in our reality. That is the discovery that many fear."

She came towards me scanning the walls, fully aware my attention lay elsewhere. She hugged herself dreamily. "Yes, a splash of colour, a taste of life."

"Yes." I grinned. Life was all about colour, red in particular at the moment.

"Thank you. You have many beautiful images." She strolled to the stairs, turning to smile a goodbye. "Thank you again. I would like to come back to share something new and beautiful."

"I would enjoy that."

I returned the smile, sunlight filtering through her skirt, a soft aura encircling her every contour. The day was still, the door opening and closing without the slightest breath of wind. I leaned against the mezzanine railing, the woman briefly disappearing from my field of vision. I heard the trunk lid close, the car jerking under the shock seconds before she reappeared, sliding into her comfort zone, raising herself, freeing her legs from the twisted muslin.

Her seat was still relined. She wasn't in a hurry, releasing the single button at her waist, her skirt parting obediently to frame a beautiful demi-nue. I was right to think I should have stood a few moments earlier, blonde abruptly more appealing than red.

*

She wasn't the first, nor the last woman to enjoy or offer a private showing, reinforcing my belief that there's no point in buying or wearing enticing lingerie if no one can witness the enticement. Women, that would be good-looking, desirable women, aren't afraid to be seen in their panties and bras. Very much the opposite, I firmly believe, based on innumerable examples, all beautiful, all silky and satin. Nothing cotton. What would be the point? Those, the others, conversely, are afraid to be caught in six-to-a-pack cotton underpants or brassieres better-suited to post-op recovery.

The previous autumn something attractive and tanned, mid-thirties, happened into the gallery in boots and a long cashmere coat. Very stylish. We exchanged greetings and I left her to view the art at her leisure. When I next noticed her she was in a loosely knitted sweater dress, the emphasis on sweater that I doubt very much she was sitting on. She was perusing our catalogs, ensconced into the sofa, apparently unaware or uncaring that her free hand was caressing a very bare leg. She was enjoying herself. Coincidently, so was I. She actually seemed cozy, very much at home.

After twenty, possibly thirty minutes, she asked if she might use the washroom, which wasn't public. People seldom buy art with a full bladder, though I made an exception. Good decision, the sight of her standing, padding to the door was, to say the least, memorable. Her dress was a deep wine colour; what she wore under it was also. Five minutes later she came out, casually palming her hips, though any adjustment to her dress was impossible. The thing was impossibly and delightfully short.

Watching her slip into her coat was, to say the least, eye-catching. Then she was gone with an exchange of smiles and her promise to return.

Later, doing a check of each room before closing, I looked into the washroom. By the sink, neatly folded, was a wine-coloured silk thong. That I know of, she never came back. Pity. Though Christiane and Shorty, when they heard, weren't impressed. A female thing.

*

Charlene joined long enough before Christmas '95, so that she could learn about the gallery and help Christiane and Shorty over the peak period. It would be a fast study since only the two of us would work the Sunday, Christmas Eve. We were doing increasingly more work with designers and decorators, which was her expertise. She was a little snotty, and sometimes superior, but she had a charismatic appeal that worked well with clients.

I hadn't expected Christmas Eve to be very busy, but we were very busy and stress levels were high. I suggested to Charlene that a little cognac wouldn't put her into detox, but perhaps calm the troubled nerves. I asked her to serve each of the anxious clients a glass as well and, not amazingly, the ambiance mellowed immediately and people began talking with one another. They'd been a little frazzled also, but not because of us, more so for having waited too long to buy that special gift for their loved one.

The lady next in line was the epitome of elegance and propriety, somehow out of place amongst worried and unseasonably stern expressions concealing their real joy of Christmas. She had a dignity and serenity undiminished by the frantic mood surrounding her.

"Vous êtes Anglais, monsieur."

I smiled, thinking "not again." "Oui, madame. Je suis Anglais, as a result of my English parents, despite my pleas throughout the process of my birth that I was to have been French and six-foot-two. And, madame, as you can plainly see, neither am I six-foot-two."

My origin has often been the object of some interest by virtue of my accent when speaking French. Anglophones think I'm Francophone; Francophones think I'm British or American who think I'm European and Europeans have no opinion on the matter. Let's face it: Francophones who speak English with a French accent are cute; Anglophones who speak French with an English accent are English.

She chortled. But, really, making those people and others smile under duress was becoming a huge pain in the ass, subterfuge. Partly because I knew the smiles would disappear at the door. So what was the point? In industry I never left a client's office without either of us smiling, sincere smiles that didn't evaporate once out of each other's sight. That was the other part: Industry.

I had offers throughout that year to amalgamate with larger companies, suppliers who'd seen advantages in merging with an outlet such as mine, but that would have changed the chemistry and make-up of the gallery and that wasn't what it was all about for me. Though second thoughts about where I wanted to be, or should be, were embedding themselves into my very limited free time and space and I was experiencing a growing unease.

Looking back over the previous three years meant peering into a treasure trove deep within Pandora's Box. The treasures were plentiful; yet, the serpent that lay in the darkness beneath the lid defended them well and extraction of the valued cache became increasingly precarious. Better the chest be sealed and thrown beyond reach, than opened to satiate temporary greed and suffer a fatal sting.

That Christmas season for me was one of reflection, one of determining needs and goals. There was an unknown element that was key to my unrest that I had to define. I began the gallery to enjoy the freedom of my own expression. Though after three years I'd become involved to the point where my freedom was lost, my pleasure was synonymous with fatigue, and work was synonymous with life. Something I had always despised and abhorred.

My life was one dimensional in a three-dimensional setting, devoid of the passion needed to carry on. My reaction to that new awareness, which had probably lurked for some time in the subconscious, was one of immediate pro-action in response to a need. I began thinking as a citizen of industry, no longer as a visitor to art.

I would host one final vernissage, what was once the preview of an artist's work in his atelier as the final glazing was applied and the canvas was allowed to dry. That part of history was long gone. Showing an artist's completed work was all about immediate money, not the glazing or well wishes of friends, family, patrons, and the hoped-for benevolence of critics.

I left the month-long preparations for the one-day event to Charlene to manage and co-ordinate, restricting myself to photographing the artist's elliptical interpretations of human beings in their exaggerated daily circumstances and conditions once they'd been placed in the gallery. I made an appearance on the day in question, March 16, because I knew Jean-François wanted to give me one of his pieces as a memento. He was aware of my decision to make his showing my last, his way of signifying his turning point and mine.

Being in or near the gallery after my decision left me with no feeling of satisfaction, rather one of going through the motions for the sake of others. I had no sense of loss, only one of entering into a new phase. I wouldn't look back, but forward. I had nothing to lament. The day I handed over the key was truly a sad day, but like everything else LindArt had a beginning, a middle, and March 28th, 1996 was the end.

Linda came to the gallery with me to say our goodbyes and wish everyone well. I'd coached her prior to going in not to glance back when leaving. Wasted words. The ladies had been part of the negotiations. Their positions would be protected by the signed agreement and would all do well.

Part of being an effective communicator in sales is to know when to stop talking, knowing when to leave. Our moment to leave came quickly, bringing mascara tinted tears flowing silently to stain sombre faces. We kissed and hugged and said goodbye to the people who'd worked so hard for us, whom we would never see again, and as we turned to leave I cautioned Linda once more not to look back. She didn't listen, instantly making her day worse.

I smiled and said: "I told you that would happen."

She agreed, thinning the eye shadow that hadn't yet washed away. I shrugged.

As we walked out a man came in. I ignored him, hearing him say "Hey, is everything okay in here? Do you need help?"

"No, no," cried Christiane.

"He was our boss," wept Shorty.

"He's leaving us. We just said goodbye," sighed Charlene.

Shorty had managed to trip Linda's flood switch with a final goodbye, compelling her to look around again. I kept walking. Life is shit sometimes, mostly when we look back. I had nothing to add. I felt good. I was going home.

No One to Tell

Chapter Nine
1996 – 1999

I'd decided I didn't want to do this anymore, travel half the year or more, listen to corporate bullshit, watch small people act big and big people act small, watch people cut throats in or for jobs they wouldn't keep or protect longer than three, maybe five years for no better reason than low self- esteem.

That Monday, dying was a distinct possibility, and the week wasn't over. I have to believe the first pilot Monday morning soiled himself, and the last guy upfront on the Friday wasn't doing much better. Not to mention the Black Moccasin. All that to see for the umpteenth time what an asshole looks like in shoes and a suit. The last one in British tweed.

The generation gap was widening in sales and very few clients were like Michelle in Jacksonville. The days of carte blanche in plants were finished. Relationships were based on the best price, service and quality relics of the past. The here and now was the new credo, promoted by all-knowing thirty-year-olds whose flock adored them for their hard-earned knowledge gained after months and months of experience while still living at home with Mommy, like Murphy.

I'd gone through four sales managers in the past two years, about to meet the fifth at some point.

No One to Tell

A new breed of manager was emerging, chosen for the qualities of supplication and adherence, unprepared to lead those who knew more than they did, who possessed street savvy, knowledge and history.

*

LindArt was the end result of a passion created and maintained, not inherent. I felt liberated when I left. My passion for photography, the inspiration for LindArt, wasn't an obsession. Over the previous three years I had neglected the passions that were and I needed to reacquaint myself with them.

I hadn't been aboard the B-Haven for eighteen months. Ripping the blue poly cover from her decks fore and aft was the best feeling I had in months, and once onboard I felt as though I'd never missed the previous cruising season.

Gordon was sent home from Euro several months earlier, landing a job at MacLeary, by which time Fred had retired in advance of his obsolescence. Gordon believed he'd set his standards high, when in reality he'd redefined his parameters in very narrow terms. He wanted that *great* job, but the great job requirements were always well beyond what he was willing to give of himself. So he went to MacLeary to begin a sequence of unsatisfying and unrewarding jobs.

He always had his ear to the ground, hearing tidbits of information about the industry and its people before anyone else. Somehow he'd become the custodian of the industry grapevine. He knew a lot of people and had a lot of history, failing miserably to harness the benefits of either. His major shortcoming was that he couldn't distinguish between good advice and bad.

Arriving home one night at the end of June, a message was blinking. Gordon had called to tell me of an open position with an American manufacturer of plastic belting. The job required extensive travel throughout the East and technical ability. I told him outright to phone the guy and take the job. But Gordon was staying in his comfort zone and the next day at the marina I placed a call to Steve at Integrated Conveyance Systems in New Orleans. He could be in Montreal the next week and would be pleased to meet with "ya'll," if the timing was convenient to my schedule.

I was in the bar some twenty-minutes early. I ordered a club soda, sitting at right angles to a woman leaning to one side, toward her companion, affording a long and very nice view of one thigh crossed over another close to the sept in 5 à 7 and she probably knew the guy's condoms were beside the credit card he'd be paying with. Seems she had a decision to make, visibly more interested in showing passers-by her legs than in her conversation, unquestionably keeping her options open both figuratively speaking.

When the tall guy in the starched white shirt, dark tan, beige Dockers and oxblood penny loafers walked in he paid her the attention she warranted. Her eyes sparkled, her red lips curving. He smiled. She smiled, following his path to where I was seated. I could see myself working with this guy; the question was, for how long?

Steve was the quintessential Southern gent, his entrance into the hotel piano bar unhurried and casual. I liked the guy right away. His easy manner let him stand out against the electrically charged ambiance of expense account Romeos. So did I, the only guy in the bar sitting by himself, trying to balance between checking my notes and the lady's outstanding legs.

We shook hands and sat, reaching for briefcases we never opened. We ordered real drinks and spoke without noticing the time. Steve was confident, showing no temptation to glance behind him at the lady sitting by herself. I wish he had. He was blocking my view.

The meeting went well, a second meeting pencilled-in for early July in New Orleans with his boss, but for all

No One to Tell

intents and purposes Steve and I saw no reason not to work together by July 15th. When I left the bar Steve remained behind to order another drink before ordering two.

*

I arrived in New Orleans Monday night, July 08th, and into 48° C humid heat. Everything in my suitcase needed pressing. My boots felt two sizes smaller and taking them off would mean not getting them on again, my underwear soaked from sweat coursing from my neck and not stopping at my belt that wasn't expanding at the same rate I was.

The sky was black by the time I unpacked and I was in one of the most corrupt cities in the US, so I ordered room service, had a few hits, and crashed early.

The next morning Steve was at the hotel at 7:30. We were at the offices twenty minutes later, no official tour planned. Instead I travelled from one office to another as I met with nine separate individuals for hour-long meetings, non-stop over the next nine hours. I would finish at five, be on the plane at seven, and home anytime later according to the pilot's aviator watch.

Steve had somewhat understated the interview process.

Stan was first. He was National Sales Manager. Followed by Debbie, Customer Service Manager; Dave and Ernie, Technical Sales guys; Larry, Zone Manager for the South; Bobby, Sales Administrator; Lisa, Technical Training something or other; Steve, computer guru; and, finally, the Steve I met in Montreal.

I was exhausted and would have been at home by 1:00 AM if my flight hadn't been cancelled. Steve drove me to the airport, but the flashing sign behind the agent spoke volumes. After rebooking for a flight the next day I was in New Orleans compliments of Delta Airlines.

The hotel room was unremarkable; apart from the thirty-centimetre-long, locust-looking grasshopper perched on the edge of the window. Normally I would never look under a hotel bed. But I did, and under the sofa, chair, desk, toilet lid, inside the closet as well as under the sheets and pillows. Then, armed with a pillow and a phone book, I went after the lime green dinosaur-sized biblical cicada that had eyes as big as peas.

The hot sun coming through the open window must have lulled it somewhat, letting my foot slam the top edge of the frame to the closed position, the impact bisecting the creature into mismatching halves. The back half pinched between the window and the frame, the legs forced out at odd angles to the side. The other half that included the head and one pea eye that I could see lay on the outer sill, some translucent liquid forming tiny bubbles around what appeared like a crushed stick of celery.

Of course I felt sorry for housekeeping, closing the drapes before going for dinner, self-interest usurping any sense of propriety.

The day was an intellectual gauntlet. They wanted to know if I'd ever studied sales, if I had ever taken a course. No. In which case how had I become successful? Simple. I chose the best companies to work with, applying logic to the sales process. They wanted to know whether I'd be open to a structured methodology proven successful. Yes. If there were a logic and flexibility to the structure.

During the initial nine-man marathon they placed particular stress on the fact they wanted a self-managed and independent individual, someone who could get the job done without continually drawing from the intellectual resources of New Orleans. In which case, I replied, their search was over.

I went to dinner, the airline voucher barely enough for a pizza, which I used for drinks on the outside terrace before a real dinner I paid for.

*

What made me know the woman was selling something was

that my disconnection from reality had not inhibited her from sitting to talk with me, the scraping of her chair legs on the tiled floor jolting. She was good-looking, a marketing ploy much like the girls at the nude resort, and wore a smile that didn't seem fake. So I returned the smile, which changed pretty fast when I heard that God did in fact love me. What a relief.

"Are we taking sides, debating?"

"You mean you don't believe in God?"

"What happens if I don't?"

"God is love, and kindness."

"People love. People show kindness. God is an abstract. Therefore cannot be interpreted by one on behalf of many. At best it's a one-on-one thing."

Eyes wide, mouth agape. Maybe I should have flashed her instead.

"Oh, no. That's not right. That's just not true."

"Sure it is. Tell me, is hate the absence of God's love, or is God's love the absence of hate. And must one believe in God to love or be kind?"

She looked around; this hadn't come up at the pre-assault meeting with her sniper recruitment team. The wheels were turning, her smile uncertain, a little stiff. She was one of the faithful, or one of the lost and lonely. "Truly, yes. He is always there to love."

"Not what I asked. Must one love in order to be kind, or be kind in order to love?"

Her smile relaxed. "We're having a dance across the street later tonight. Please join us. We'd like you to come."

"Thank you, but I don't."

"Don't believe?"

"Don't dance." I lied. I'm a great dancer.

"You should come anyway."

"Why should I come anyway?"

"To meet new friends and neighbours, to feel their love

and compassion."

"Love thy neighbour, that kind of thing?"

She nodded, matter-of-factly, pleased that the wayward had finally caught on. I told her I don't even know my neighbours and, if I did, I was pretty sure I wouldn't love them. Canadians don't love their neighbours; they talk about them to other neighbours.

She smiled, undeterred. "May we send you information about our friends in Canada? What city do you live in?"

"Thank you, no. I don't dance at home either. But you enjoy your evening with your friends, sweetheart. And, really, I hope you find whatever you're missing."

I stood to leave when I saw the toothy reinforcements coming my way. What they got to hear were my wishes for a fun evening as I headed to the room to see if the dead bug had fallen into the basket. It hadn't, and I fell asleep in the Big Easy watching television.

*

A few weeks before knowing Steve existed I mentioned to someone that I'd like to visit the Big Easy once in my life. Over the next thirty-eight months I'd be in New Orleans on eighteen separate occasions, seventy nights.

Steve phoned the day after. Once we confirmed our agreement to work together, Stan signed the contract and couriered the document for my signature.

My twelve-day training began in New Orleans on the 21st, long days and the absorption of massive amounts of product and corporate information that began Monday morning at 7:30 in the hotel restaurant with Tom who was responsible for something called IC/SM. The restaurant, I learned later, because Tom didn't have an office.

I spent that time studying Tom who clearly didn't want to be there. He spoke the words, but lacked conviction. He wasn't believable Neither was Integrated Conveyance Sales Methodology, based on a recently published "Sales Expert" who alluded to what was the wash, rinse and spin cycle of the sales process. Tom either didn't know what he was talking about or he didn't believe in what he was talking about.

The meeting lasted until lunch, when I joined Steve for Red Bean and Rice. A New Orleans mandatory Monday meal from a time when housewives would slow cook red beans all day Monday while busying themselves with other chores, at day's end adding in chunks of leftover ham or sausage with enough spices to flavour the palate but not impair speech. The plates were enormous, one size fitting all: Man, woman or child.

That, and every other daytime meal, was accompanied by ice tea. I passed.

The rain began during lunch and we decided we could make it to the car without much effort or getting drenched. We didn't run. We walked quickly, reaching the car as the rain intensified. Good timing, though we didn't stand on formality. Steve ran to his side, pushing in the key, taking a while before looking up, bringing his hands up as blinders, peering through the window. "Jamie, this is not ma caw."

If I'd pissed myself laughing no one would have noticed because I was drenched through. We were in the middle of the parking lot, searching over the roofs of cars that were all the same colour in the grey rain. The second choice wasn't good either. The third one was Steve's.

I sat back, waiting for him to say something, both of us cracking up, looking as though we'd fallen into a pool. The hotel was twenty minutes away; Steve's home thirty minutes across the thirty eight-kilometre Lake Pontchartrain Causeway. Instead we went to the office, and immediately to the men's room. When we were finished we left puddles on the floor and no paper towels. When we left the building three hours later we were still soaked.

Steve arranged for me to have Old Blue, a twenty-year-old Buick kept in reserve for long-term visitors, giving me after-hours freedom and the ability to move around on the weekend. In exchange I taxied in a few others also staying at the Double Tree.

By quitting time the streets were bone dry, as would I be despite the night being mine. I only had to arrive at the office the next day according to my first appointment which was at the Jeffeson Hospital at 8:30 for a physical, corporate America's way of saying Drug Testing.

I arrived at 8:30 sharp. ICS must have been a major contributor to the hospital's fund raising because I went in before several others. When she saw the suit and tie she came directly to me, calling my last name first, my first name last, holding out her hand.

I didn't like her. Perhaps her tampon was spiked. Not my fault.

"I need your pee."

"In your hand?"

By her expression anyone would have thought I had.

"Did you pee today?"

"I did, did you?"

"Where is it?" She held out her hand again, moving her fingers to and fro like a traffic cop.

"The Mississippi."

She looked as though I was wasting her day, forgetting how much the company was paying to find out if I shot up or took my scotch intravenously.

"Excuse me."

I leaned closer, whispering. "Most of it's in the Mississippi. The rest is in my pocket."

She turned so quickly her torso took time to catch up with her head, barking an order to follow. When she got to the examination room she held out her hand without looking at me.

"Your pee, so we can get on with this. I don't have all

day."

I put the miniature ketchup bottle on top of the papers on her desk. She stared at it, lost for words, pushing it off her papers. "That won't do. First door on the left, and wash your hands first."

"What?"

She passed me a vial. "Wash your hands."

"For your info, lady, I can tell you I'm a whole lot cleaner than anything you'll find in this place. You wash your hands."

I took the little jar, walked out and went to the second door. The first one was barred. A woman's washroom in a hospital is only different when a woman is in it, so temporarily it was a men's room. I took no time at all to fill her vial from the little jar and put both in my pocket before returning to the white-frocked she-dog. Sitting, I removed the ketchup bottle from my pocket, pitching it into the garbage before putting the vial on her papers.

That she did not like, and I knew instantly the woman was not touching my balls.

The needle went in deeper than necessary, I'm certain, as though she wanted blood from the armrest. My arm was near blue as she took my blood pressure, but she somehow seemed happier so I stayed quiet. Until she ordered my pants off. Not a chance. I pulled rank. The only way she was squeezing my balls was if I was squeezing hers. She walked out without smiling. Bitch.

The doctor came in dressed like he was going to a trade show, his white coat hanging elsewhere, his stethoscope clipped to his belt instead of that arrogant around the neck, just out of med school look.

"How'd you make out?" He was studying a chart that must have been someone else's, because I'd only been in the place ten minutes.

"She's not having a good day."

"Wrong. She is having a good day. It's the rest of us who aren't. The good news is you get to leave in five minutes." He put aside the chart. "You know the drill."

All males over the age of ten know the drill, the real reason there aren't more doctors.

*

When Friday came I was ready for the weekend, Old Blue gassed and washed for the 110 km to Biloxi.

Saturday was fine with blue skies, a slight wind. When I left at 7:30 the temp was 30° C, by mid-day over forty with the index. What I was missing was cold beer, a beach mat, a towel, and some edible beach facsimile of food.

The drive would have taken two hours with the traffic and some unexpected signal lights in peculiar locations, but the closer I got to Biloxi the farther away it seemed.

I stopped in North Beach, Mississippi, I-10 hugging the Gulf water, whiter sand difficult to imagine. The other side of the road was lined with grocery stores catering to beach-goers who, apparently, didn't drink cold beer. The one I pulled into was no exception.

The full length of the beach was deserted at ten o'clock on a Saturday morning. So what did they know that I didn't? I waited, watching. Nothing happened, so I went toward the water, hidden from the road by miniature dunes.

Judging by its slant the sign was posted years or months earlier. The letters were in large black print across the international stop sign. NO FROGS ALLOWED.

Now, what did that mean? Possibly someone didn't want the homely amphibians spreading warts across the backs of bathers. Or they didn't want bare-breasted Frenchwomen and Speedo clad Frenchmen threatening the moral code of the local white supremacists in his and her matching pointy hats and goblin clothes. Or they didn't want this Québécois, French by association, on the beach that Saturday at 10:00 with a bathing suit imported from

No One to Tell

France.

I stayed until one, not leaving because of Whitie in a dunce cap. I left because I was bored. No one else had come to the beach, probably because of the water quality. I'd been in the water ankle deep and that was deep enough. Seeing my feet turn tawny didn't do much to persuade me to go deeper. I photographed the FROG sign, threw the mat, towel, wrappers and bottles in the garbage and left to plan Sunday in the French Quarter that really isn't French.

I'd gone there for dinner a couple of times during my first week with different guys I'd worked with, noting their suggestions with the exception of the plantation visit. The heat index was well over 40° C and death would have been a companion of that particular choice. I decided on an afternoon of barhopping, food tasting, art galleries, and a riverboat.

"Hey, mister, bet I could tell ya'll where ya'll got ya shoes." It was a hit. Four-foot nothing, black as coal with cue ball eyes and tattered shoes to match his tattered shirt and pants. The kid's teeth looked like icebergs in a tar pit cordoned off with thick pink rope.

"That a fact?"

"Yep. If I can't, the shine's free. If I do, its two bucks and no shine."

"Can we get this over with before I melt?"

"Ya'll got 'em on your feet!"

Shit. I discovered the northern brain doesn't function well at 40° C. If he'd asked for the two bucks just to leave me alone I would have paid.

After a morning of gallery browsing along Royal Street, Cathedral Square and a lazy walking tour of my own, the time had come for some barhopping. Some people call New Orleans The Swamp. Depending who was talking, the city was four to five metres below sea level, making New Orleans a veritable steam room, and in the blistering heat I settled for stool hopping on the corner of Orleans and Bourbon, listening to street musicians.

The bar was dark, quiet and cool, the evaporation process kicking in before my first beer was served. The place wasn't crowded. A few locals were into private conversations and the barman only nodded. The one view of the outside was through swinging glass-panelled doors forever stuck in the open position with full-length steel shutters to protect them after hours. The glass front of the firebox that once housed a fire extinguisher was broken.

Nothing was going to get me off that stool, my first beer evaporating as quickly as my sweat, my second ice-cold to the touch, the cold wetness on the outside of the glass as refreshing as the beer. I didn't want to move.

She walked by in the blink of an eye, my eye, crossing in front of the doors with a bounce in her step that was anomalous in the oppressive weather and that's what I had to photograph, not her tight and lithe body. No. I wanted to capture the mood, not her tanned skin, her blonde hair swinging in a ponytail behind her petite, slim body with its perfectly shaped half-moon ass framed in store-bought cut-off cords and perky breasts in a halter top.

That was all secondary. I wanted the mood and I set the camera for 3.5 frames per second, certainly more appealing than lacework balconies and wrought iron fences. She was America's latest perfect ten.

The next time I left the stool was to visit Saks Fifth Avenue before heading to the Steamboat Natchez, but not for dinner. I wanted a breeze and shots of New Orleans' skyline. They took a snapshot of me boarding, the image of a man clinging to life by the thinnest of threads. My shirt added considerable weight to my step, my pants felt glued to my crotch, my feet had more blisters than toes, my skin slippier than soap.

I changed shirts in the men's room, grimacing at the

sight of my hair, understanding why I was so closely followed in Saks even after I'd paid cash for overpriced lipstick and nail polish for Linda.

The cruise was nothing spectacular, filling my full quota for jazz over the next three years.

*

The second week was a repeat of the first with technical sessions, meetings with various staff and time spent working in the Customer Service Centre with my reps, Tiana and Gina. Tiana was essentially inside sales, doing reactive work. Gina would do my telemarketing proactively.

Tiana wasn't very good at being a CSR and we spent several months uncovering that fact. CS wasn't her thing and she eventually moved on, which is no big deal. We all do. But the way she was treated was a big thing. She didn't fit in with most of the CSRs because she was a lesbian and they didn't like 'dykes'. Neither did the guys. Tiana was a stigma and, for the guys, the ultimate male hypocrisy because there isn't a man alive who wouldn't be mesmerized by like-minded, good-looking women doing each other. Unless they're queer.

Steve referred to her as a dyke once, which surprised me. Bad-mouthing was not his style. Peer pressure perhaps, or lack of familiarity with the subject matter. In any event, he knows better now. He would soon discover that Québec City has more to offer than historic buildings and superb cuisine. He would look, and he would keep looking. Steve would be in love, again, this time with Les Twins. Though by that time Tiana had left, Gina taking over as CSR.

The women were all lookers, smart, alert, and protective in the extreme of their Sales Reps, alias District Managers. Except Gina who, for the first two years, lived with a stick up her ass that wouldn't bend. Larry, a Zone Manager like Steve, thought she was another man-hating dyke. But she wasn't. She just didn't know how to pull out the stick. She was a perfectionist, good at what she did. She was also a pain in the ass with dotting Is and crossing Ts, which I often neglected to piss her off.

IC/SM figured into the second week more than the first. I was aware of the need for methodology from as far back as W&W, particularly Durcast. Prepared as I was to visit the ICS version, I was not prepared to drop mine. The difference was conceptual selling; the process of selling perceived advantages/solutions inherent in a product, which was nothing new. The twist was in their insistence on growing the problem, the customer's problem, and therein grew the real problem with me.

I'd managed throughout the second week to avoid dinner invitations, taking advantage of the evening hours to relax, walk around Metairie and shop for gifts to take home.

When Larry first saw me come through the front doors of ICS, crisp and clean, wearing a new and rare short-sleeve shirt, he suggested jokingly that by the end of the twelve days I would look like shit. He was right. I did look like shit. I wanted to leave The Swamp. I wanted an arctic 20° C at home, arriving to German Night.

Despite the mostly Austrian meal and wine, when a woman in stilettos, stockings, garters, a thong and push-up bra under an open leather jacket tells you she's German, she's German. Das ist gut, ya? Ya, das ist very, very gut.

I'd be back in mid-October for my first National Meeting. In the meantime I'd spend a week at home organizing, one in Boston with Wayne, one in Wisconsin with Dennis, and the last of four in Toronto with Milton. After which Steve and I would hook-up.

*

Travelling with Steve wouldn't happen until December, the timing changing the venue.

In the meantime the mandate was a bitch in a territory left vacant for several months and, because of its

Francophone nature, not much was done to maintain current business.

The sales figures were at minus fifty-two percent from the previous year and the corporate expectation for all territories wasn't only double-digit growth, but in the twenties or thirties. By December 31st I was at minus six.

My time with the other reps was well-spent, particularly with Wayne and Dennis. Milton was a suck, too into gossip, and by the end of the week I knew a lot and he knew as much as he did on Monday. He was also younger in a double sense. Wayne, Dennis and I were months apart in years. We had our heads on straight. Milton, by virtue of his parents, mistakenly believed he was special. He wasn't.

Wayne took me into a lot of seafood plants, though nowhere as big as the ones I'd eventually work with. Dennis got me into the big breweries, juice producers and microwave applications.

Milton had pretty well a full range of industries, from large to small, from important to unjustifiable, and only with Milton did I have to upgrade my accommodations. He was into motels with shag carpets; I'd preferred four and five-stars for years. He had 150 km of linear travel to work within, home most nights or smelling dank like Gabriel. He had no idea about Executive Floors and Concierge Lounges.

*

By the time I was ready to leave for Ixtapa the territory was organized to my liking and I'd been everywhere in the territory except PEI and Newfoundland.

Integrated Conveyance Systems had a professional attitude that came across in their appearance and actions, as well as their reactions to given situations or circumstances. Suits and ties were mandatory in the office and casual Friday meant no tie. I fit right in to that mindset. I'd always maintained that we work the way we dress. Dress well, work well. Dress casually, work casually. Sloppy or careless dressers work in their respective fashions as well.

I was shocked at how the outer appearance and character of sales had changed during the previous four years. Suits were gone, pride was gone. Polo shirts, short-sleeves, open-collar cotton shirts, crumpled, washed to the point of permanent shapelessness had replaced suits and ties. Wearing a polo shirt with a company logo was casual dress, not lazy or cheap. Really? Dress pants that once accompanied sports coats or blazers were now creased Dockers. Shoe polish had apparently become a museum relic viewed curiously by kids whose parents lacked sufficient knowledge on the subject to answer probing questions as to its historic significance.

My transition was more discreet, but necessary all the same in order to maintain a modicum of inconspicuousness. My suits, dress shirts and ties remained part of my persona, as did my briefcase. That was something that did stick out, since I'd refused the one ICS had chosen for the sales reps' laptops. The sloppy and the careless had become easily identifiable by vinyl-covered agendas that took the place of briefcases, thirty-nine-cent plastic pens leaking into their pockets or staining their fingers, and canvas satchels better suited to a high school student.

Large numbers of former customers had been sent home, terminated by artificial redundancy called bridging. Snotty-nosed brats with certificates and pimples replaced people who once were operational managers, corporate decision makers. Some were demoted, their lesser-paid juniors suddenly their superiors; their retirement of paramount importance where once they thought only of work. I was shocked, above all by the blasé attitude and the striking lack of pride. Customers and sales reps alike had transformed. The sales representative was a peddler, the client a shopper.

No One to Tell

*

ICS was an international company, the National meeting bringing in people from all over North America, Europe, and the Pacific Rim. The twice yearly event was grandiose, well-orchestrated, at times flamboyant and always gruelling with little time to think of anything beyond what was at hand.

My flight from Ixtapa landed in Montreal about 11:00 PM on the Saturday, my flight to New Orleans departed Sunday at noon. Thing is, my luggage was misplaced in Ixtapa, sent to Venezuela. The airline offered to have it delivered to the Double Tree in Metairie, but I somehow thought explaining to Customs officials that I'd come from Canada and was in New Orleans twenty-four hours after a trip to Mexico picking up a suitcase coming from Venezuela would be awkward.

All I had left was meant for fall and winter and was black. The Swamp was hot, somewhere in the high thirties, though not as humid as in July and I spent the week pouring sweat from my boots. Naturally I was The Man in Black, Blackie, The Black Man, Dark Man, etc., which stuck with me for the remaining three years. I could have worn pink after that and they would have seen black.

Much like Durcast, the meetings began at eight and you'd be better off pissing on the carpet than leaving to go to the men's room. The first day was introduction day, like in grade one. "Class, this is James."

"Hi, James."

"James, why don't you stand and tell the class something interesting about yourself?"

Name, rank, serial number, city, country, marital status and, yes, I know I'm dressed in black fucking wool in a place hotter than hell. I'm looking forward to talking with all two hundred of you. Blah, blah, blah. Like pulling a bandage. Get it over with.

No One to Tell

"That was very interesting, James. Now class, sit up straight and pay attention to Tom who doesn't like his job."

By which Stan meant Tom's pontificating on the famed IC/SM. I got the impression Tom wouldn't live much longer. He seemed ready to pass on, despondent and victimized. He'd read the book. We all read the book, but he was the one chosen to put the ICS slant on it. We all listened patiently and politely as he demonstrated that he didn't know jack. He was out of his league, pressed involuntarily into service.

He was a senior sales rep, successful in his career, suddenly trying to impress his audience with the need for a new wheel: The ICS Sales Cycle. He didn't know how to present, not to his peers. Nor did he believe in what he was saying. A dollar to a doughnut says Tom had his first bourbon most days before noon. That day before breakfast. He was near sixty, taking the bullshit to see sixty-one.

Everyone was writing or talking about how to be the best, missing the point. Read this, read that, do this, do that, be this and be that. No one was talking about having fun or achieving balance. Interesting.

I joined ICS with intellectual baggage they closely scrutinized during the initial interview process with Stan, Steve and the others. Consequently I became defensive when ICS began failed attempts to redefine who I was. Nor was I alone. Other reps had successful methodologies suited to their particular environments, but ICS wanted uniformity.

Worse, all this came from clerical types kowtowing to a president who had a thinly disguised contempt of sales people. We were being told what to do by nine-to-fivers, the message coming from on high, indisputable, the closest thing to divine intervention. The Oracle.

Continuous Improvement had one flaw: The concept was pure bullshit. We can't continuously be better than the day before: An expectation of impossible standards. We can strive towards being the best; we cannot exceed personal limitations at which point we no longer perform at reasonable comfort levels. That's the reality not recognized by corporate cultures where slogans and shallow mission statements decorate the walls instead of fine art.

We can be different every day. We can perhaps make a difference every day. We cannot, as preached from the same mouth as "Short Term Pain for Long-term Gain" and "Don't Sweat the Small Stuff," improve each day.

The multi-millionaire, self-infatuated egoist with no problem beyond his obsession with superiority might presumably have a different perspective on what "Small Stuff" really means. Perhaps a nick in the Beamer or a piss stain on his pant leg. So it's not difficult to imagine whose pain and whose gain, believed by the young ones, silently questioned by the middle-aged, largely ignored by the older contingent who knew how to say one thing and do another.

My body was in New Orleans; my brain was in Jones Town.

*

The day came to an end. Even the young guys had trouble straightening when they stood.

When I got to my room to freshen and change into more dark clothes, I made the mistake of removing my boots and spent the next thirty minutes sitting on the edge of the bath with my feet in cold water and ice cubes, alternating the hair dryer from one boot to the other to relax the leather.

Cocktails were from six to eight. I arrived late, made one trip to the bar, meandered around the room, went to the bar for a refill and circulated once more before leaving. I was seen, and I was forgotten, believed to have been there for as long as anyone else.

*

Wayne and I went to dinner in the Quarter and got philosophical. He'd been with the company almost since day one, a very frequent visitor to the damp city, though he never acclimated to the climate. He'd sweat bullets in January, though not because of the climate. Because of Stan.

He was fifty, successful, and respected by all for his product and application knowledge. He was also a wreck because of Continuous Improvement.

IC/SM and IC/CI were the undeniable glitches in an otherwise informative week. The evenings were enjoyable, the camaraderie genuine between the guys, and Bourbon Street was remembered more some mornings than others. All in all the experience was positive; the only thing I threw out when I got home was a tape recording of The Oracle's long-winded dissertation on the importance of our allegiance to IC and Continuous Improvement.

*

I'd gone in with the mandate to reverse extreme regional downturns in sales figures, the customer base requiring the balance of several elements, not the least of which was blending a single-minded sales methodology with mine.

ICS was one of the best most times and *the* very best sometimes, though to say so was heresy and punishable by more frequent trips to The Swamp for programming. But minus fifty-two was still a formidable slump in business for one person to reverse, and devising a business plan was far from easy given their business plan.

They'd made a decision five years earlier to disband distribution worldwide, making the sales reps responsible for maintaining and developing any and all business. Distribution was a bad word, taboo, never mentioned for fear of a trip to The Swamp.

Newfoundland would become one large fishery account, other applications rare. However the time required to visit all the fisheries on the island was unimaginable as well as impractical. Newfies in outlying areas, which is most of the island, don't expect to see their resident sales reps more than once or twice a year, so mainland reps normally give attention to the very key accounts and leave the rest to distribution networks.

There was no distributor on the island, as such, though there was an important OEM. And who would know the difference?

*

Steve had never seen snow; Steve had never wanted to see snow, but he did want to see Québec City and arrived December 09th, for our first week of joint calls, in a beige summer-weight raincoat and rubber ducky ankle boots.

Steve had a good, subdued sense of humour and took my frequent bursts of laughter in stride, even the hotel staff took second looks and they were accustomed to seeing Americans dressed in their inimitable fashion. The plan was a good one that included getting the semi-annual review out of the way over dinner, seeing key accounts throughout the week, and enjoying Québec.

We got along well. Business was coming into the territory at an accelerated rate, the review a formality agreed to before dinner in the hotel because the Southern gent wasn't equipped for the frigid North that was buried under four metres of snow.

Tuesday began early, finishing early. I wasn't the type to fill the agenda to impress a visiting dignitary, nor did he expect that I would.

Tuesday evening had touring on the agenda, throughout the day Steve steadfastly refusing to outfit himself, taking my humour in stride. I'd never seen anyone smoking in the blowing snow, trying to keep a frail raincoat together with one hand while attempting to cover both ears at the same time with the other, all the while thinking that stepping on one foot with the other would keep one of them warm. He was quite a sight.

No One to Tell

We arrived at the hotel around four, in the dark, several bright spotlights illuminating already sparkling snow that had Steve mesmerized. He'd heard about snow blowers and on the way to St-Ansèlme he'd seen sheer walls of snow carved by road crews. Now he was seeing one up close and personal as he stood breathing in fresh winter air with tobacco smoke and holding his coat together. The equipment was sidewalk-size, big enough for one overweight city worker to sit in with his lunch pail, parka and radio.

Steve was awestruck watching the two-eyed yellow rotary-tooth monster slice a path through waist-high crusty snow, spewing an arc over the mound Steve was standing beside. He wanted to see more and he began walking ahead of the machine, on the far side, the operator watching Steve as closely as Steve was watching the blades work against the snow. The operator must never have seen anyone that intrigued with chunks of blowing snow, or he was thinking that the crazy guy in the raincoat with no gloves was going to throw himself in front of the spiralling blades, despondent over his lack of winter finery. Either way, I couldn't take all the excitement and told Steve I'd meet him in the bar.

He wanted to see the Citadelle, the Château Frontenac and experience local French cuisine, though the visit to the Château was cancelled when he discovered they didn't have indoor parking and that its architect had perched it atop a major promontory open to severe winds and bitter cold that would freeze Southern skin in seconds.

The Citadelle was even more of a fair weather destination and we decided on the low and well-travelled road to one of the local cafés that served ambiance and expensive morsels of exquisite sounding crackers, cheese and pâté. They served by the glass, Steve ordering Bordeaux, me preferring Bourgogne, already into our first story when our glasses clinked together.

Steve had been to see Denis in Wisconsin, to spend a couple of days travelling with him. One particular evening they had dinner, a couple of drinks, and called it a night because Denis wanted an early start the next day.

When travel becomes excessive, rest seldom comes with sleep. Steve had got up during the middle of the night in response to nature's call, making his way groggily to the bathroom where he stood ready to relieve himself, snapping to when he heard the door close behind him. He'd turned left instead of right, or right instead of left; either way he was standing outside his room in his boxers with no possible way to get back in.

He knew Dennis' room number, thinking Dennis might not like his boss knocking on his door in his underwear, choosing three or four flights of more a private stairway instead of the elevator to access the main floor and the Reception where a female night clerk was there to address his concern.

She called security once seeing Steve pad his way towards her in his diapers. He struck me as the cotton type, not silk, and not that I cared. Anyway, without proper ID the guard escorted him to his room draped in a towel to verify corroborating evidence. The event isn't all that rare, to which I can attest.

We were still on the first glass, sipping between laughs. My turn.

*

Coincidently, during my initial travels with Dennis in Wisconsin, we stayed one night at a two-storey motor court motel that had great food, reasonable wine, and rooms that were eight on a scale of ten. Though they didn't have a convenience store that sold bottled water and I'd neglected to stop by a store earlier in the day. So at two in the morning, knowing the place was deserted, I went along the hall to the vending machine in my silk briefs, the kind without front-entry capability.

The machine was twenty metres from my door, at the end of the hallway perpendicular to mine. There was no noise at all. So no surprise that I was as taken aback by the cops as they were at seeing me. A moment requiring confidence, self-assurance. I smiled at one, not the other.

They moved aside as I simultaneously explained my need to quench my thirst and jangled my room key. She wasn't bad-looking at all, easily an 8.5 or nine, and not fresh from the egg, late thirties, giving me the once over, smiling. He just looked like a cop. I wished her a good evening, ignored him, and walked to my room, turning to see one set of curious eyes and a wide smile before closing the door and laughing.

Funnier than the nude guy in northern Québec swaggering down the corridor, between my room and me, buck-ass naked. Upon seeing me he simply stopped, nodding before turning on his heels to walk in the opposite direction and disappearing around the corner. Hairy bent legs and a jangling scrotum under a ponderous gut aren't easy to forget.

I phoned the front desk and they sent someone to investigate, by which time the somnambulist was either fast asleep, or the exhibitionist was getting off, which reminded me of a similar event years earlier at the Laurentian Hotel.

I'd been working late as assistant to the manager, a title much better than the job. A number of guests had called to complain about a kook parading the tenth floor hallway wearing billy boots, boxer shorts with a singlet and a large pot on his head while carrying a baseball bat over his shoulder like a soldier on parade. When security went to investigate the disturbance they heard orders being shouted, absent troops admonished. A leader of men, a man accustomed to giving orders and shouting, a General, or a

No One to Tell

General Manager, their own boss, and somebody I didn't particularly care for.

Apparently he'd succumbed to some degree of stress and wasn't managing his medication very well.

*

We ordered another wine as we finished the first and Steve took us to Mardi Gras a few years earlier.

Mardi Gras, when women don't wear panties under short skirts or bras under short tee-shirts if they don't want to, or anything for that matter, though they did have to pay one dollar a head if they wanted to use the washroom at the top of the stairs in the bar owned by Steve's close friend.

The fee was a paper charge and Steve was recruited to make sure payment was exacted, payment for his labour all the free beer he could drink those evenings. The thing is that if a girl was wearing a tiny tee-shirt and tiny skirt with nothing underneath, where would the poor thing put her money and how could she pay to pee?

The guys barely made it up the stairs, most using the street corner anyway, but the poor girls were in a pickle and Steve felt badly for them. But rules were rules and his job was enforcement, so he came up with a compromise that seemed to work well for both parties. The girls could get a square of paper each time they bared their breasts and he encouraged them to take as many as they needed. Steve was a breast man, a connoisseur of the delicate feminine protuberances, though he did owe his friend a few rolls of paper.

*

The second glass came.

There's something about hotels that brings the best out in people, as in Trois-Rivières years earlier. Though it's not surprising. It's escapism. People like to be naughty when neighbours aren't around to gossip.

I was in Le Baron, a four-star with excellent

cuisine…and a pool whose fence I'd jumped an hour earlier. Near midnight a couple thought to do the same. The area was dark, lit by the moon. He was in underwear boys start wearing when they're six. She was in a tee-shirt sans culottes. I know because I was enjoying a JW Red in the windowsill gazing at the full moon until I saw hers as he helped her palms-to-butt over the 1.5 metre fence. He followed.

She was all excited, probably her first skinny-dip, tiptoeing across the deck to the shallow end as though not to disturb the people downstairs. They frolicked and dipped, dunked and twirled, piggy-backed, and I have to imagine a few breast strokes. Then time to go.

At the fence he was ridiculous in his drooping drawers. She was first over, one leg then the other swinging over the notched top. Then a little twist, and down. Oh, no! A naked and nubile body dangling on the fence by her tee-shirt cum hanger. That's what she got for cheating. She shouldn't have worn the top. Hello, skinny-dipping.

I was perplexed. I wanted to help, maybe take her a towel, a pair scissors. Perhaps drown him and bring her in for a scotch and a brisk rub to warm her.

He was laughing. I was chuckling. She wasn't, kicking.

He was lifting her, her knees pinned together. She was squirming, stretching, straining to break free. Her top ruined. She was on the ground, naked, lit by moon, leaning into him, whispering, her pretty face scrunching, that kind of forced whisper that isn't good, giving him shit. His dipping for the night at an abrupt end.

I tapped on the window, waving discreetly. The girl grew wings, and was gone.

Much better than the unclothed Brontosauruses in a Virginia pool bashing their groins together in a two AM relentless quest for release. That wasn't pretty, definitely not, my sleep ruined for several nights thereafter. Hell, I was on the eighth floor getting splashed. Not like the girl in Victoriaville, Victo to the locals.

Three AM. I wasn't sleeping. I wasn't tired, standing by the window.

The four-star was quiet, not a sound. The bar was closed, the parking half-empty, the staff had gone home and the night clerk was probably watching porno while balancing the day's receipts. The theme rooms had double doors: One leading into the hotel, the other directly to the outside.

The pool area was across the parking lot, some fifty metres. A good distance to run, skip or hop in the dark. She was naked, no towel. He was naked. She wanted to skinny-dip in a hotel pool. He was jogging behind her, enjoying the view.

She was the first in, excited, ecstatic, though she knew to be quiet. Not to ruin a good thing. She swam from end to end, standing waist-deep in the heated water, the immersed flood lights casting a muted glow. She looked up at him.

She said, "Come in. The water's warm, feels great. You have to do this."

"I have done that."

"Come in. Please."

"No." He exaggerated his scan of the pool, craning his neck. "There has to be a thousand frogs in there. No way."

Shock. Disbelief.

She peered into the water. The pool floor was alive. "Aghh!" And a few other sounds not yet with correct spelling available.

She was gone, in a flash, a tanned blur streaking across the parking lot. Not once since have I seen Linda run so fast.

Steve and I were enjoying our wine, but the food was a little too little for the Southern boy so we asked for the bill, thinking we'd do a restaurant on Grande Allée which was home to some of the finest restaurants in the city. It was time for Steve to say something, and he did when he took the bill. "Holy shit!" With tax and tip the bill wasn't far from a hundred dollars for the four glasses. Bienvenue à Québec.

*

Although we were expected to see ten or twelve clients in a week, we were also expected to produce. Most meetings with clients lasted near two hours, which required a reason, a need and preparation which is why one day a week was officially home-office day.

Though hired as a Zone Manager, Steve was a marketing specialist and managed by letting his guys do what they did best, exploiting each of their strengths to their best advantage within the zone. He was good, and the reps knew they could count on him which also made him easy to travel with. Not even Wayne hyperventilated when he travelled with Steve.

During Wednesday we discussed how to handle Newfoundland, Steve paling somewhat when I suggested we drop all direct sales and work with Sea & Double U as a conveyor OEM, but with exclusivity and preferential pricing. I'd already approached SDU with the notion and they were keen to enter into an exclusive, unwritten agreement. Not that the owner of the company was cunning or a smart businessman, he simply didn't trust anyone not born on the island and was generally suspicious of those who were. He would immediately reprimand anyone caught using his name on a cell phone, believing his competition had scanners that recorded his every word.

Paranoid? Yeah, maybe.

The payback would come immediately, the additional discount compensated by reduced travel costs. Also, they were Newfies. I wasn't. Newfies deal with their own before searching across the Cabot Strait toward the mainland. We would capture their OEM market, their after sales market and we would put all new business through them. We might also have a stocking facility that would help us compete with Danish competition, a subject for later discussion that would make Sea & Double U one of ICS's largest customers in North America, the second largest in Eastern Canada.

With that settled, we drove to Grande Allée and were met by Lise.

She was the demurely sophisticated hostess of the elegant Louis Hébert. She wore a simple heather-grey silk blouse with imitation black pearl buttons open from its rounded collar to the full lace border of her black silk camisole. The front slit of the understated black A-line skirt travelled to mid-thigh on one side, revealing an attractive silk-covered leg that I'm sure was toned even without the patent leather pumps she wore.

Steve had recently gone through a divorce, having replaced Kaye with Faye, but seeing him study Lise as she escorted us to our table I was as certain that he'd forgotten both their names as I was about her legs.

He was in love. She didn't speak English, he didn't speak French, which wasn't an issue. The issue was me taking twice as long to eat the succulent rôti de boeuf that I'd taken Steve there for in the first place. He did everything but ask her to join us.

The restaurant had a few couples, a few singles, and a group of three sales types who'd returned two opened bottles of wine. Americans. Sorry, Steve. Of course Lise was the carrier of those bottles, the courier of those complaints, and by the third bottle Steve was as flustered as she was, leaning over, offering to buy all three bottles when, finally, they seemed to find one that suited their boorish palates. They got the hint, Steve and Lise reigniting their three-way conversation about New Orleans and Québec as I ate between breaths.

During dessert, as Lise was attending to her other clientele, Steve and I talked more dinner trivia. He wasn't getting the hang of being in a car with nothing but white to see or the windshield wipers working all day, every day. He was amazed to see that city workers had wrapped trees and bushes in sackcloth, laughing each time he saw the electrical cord of a block heater disappearing into an office window or under the hoods of cars in the hotel parking lot.

Steve needed a life. What he wanted was a Lise.

The restaurant was closing. Lise would soon be going home, by herself, and Steve had needs. Steve needed a titty bar. I signalled Lise over. She was enjoying Steve's flirtation, observing him knowingly with a raised female eyebrow when I asked if I might speak with the owner for a moment. We required information of a personal nature.

The owner came to the table. He leaned over, standing for a moment to massage his jaw before recommending highly that we should go to Chez Carole.

As we were leaving Steve got the kiss he'd been hoping for. He'd seen so many women kissing since he arrived, women kissing men, women kissing women, that he wanted in. She obliged with one cheek then the other. I held the coats.

The snow was piled head-high, beginning to fall again, the twenty-minute circuitous drive, lasting an hour. The stories began again. Steve was going to see titties. Good times and titties. What a perfect, snow-covered world.

*

Back when I'd finished my road time with my three cohorts, my plan was to highlight and troubleshoot my way through to the end of the year while building a series of Business Plans which included a secondary process poultry plant located fifty kilometres north of Montreal in an area I'd never thought to visit previously. And I was late.

No One to Tell

One reason was the roadblock put up by the surly Sûreté; the other reason was my innate inability to follow even good directions. The guy was a smart-ass. He had a gun, a badge, watched too many American cop shows he couldn't understand, and probably thought he should be cloned. I just happened to be driving his way on the wrong road. Lucky me. Another cop.

"Turn around. The road is closed."

"Why?" Thinking there might be a flood or some other local disaster like a stalled car.

"Someone was killed."

"A car accident?"

"A shooting. Is that all right with you?"

"Better with me than the dead guy." I put the car in reverse, doing a one-eighty, waving goodbye. "Protect and serve," my ass.

The detour took time from my day which wasn't mine to spare, though I did have an alibi. I was in the general area, except I was in the boonies, each new road leading to somewhere I didn't need to be. Finally, not knowing I *was* on the right road, I pulled-in to where I saw the tall, pointed and weather-treated poles encircling the perimeter of what I thought was a campground. The poles were six metres high, made to appear as though skilled natives from another era had lashed them tightly together, though in reality they'd been pile-driven two metres into the ground and reinforced by steel bracing. The dark posts lost their definition as I peered deeper into the damp shade of surrounding woods on either side of the two-car gate wide open with arrows pointing to the office.

Three women, late twenties, early thirties, were standing around a desk, two facing me, one facing away. She was hunched over, arranging papers. Whatever. I was more interested in her body, her hypnotic ass, which, by any standard, was very nice.

No One to Tell

The two waved, the third turned. Delightful, very good-looking, very naked.

The one with the ass was charming, the Nude Resort's receptionist. She introduced herself. She was polite, cordial, giving me excellent directions to the company located not ten minutes from where I stood.

For the number of naked women I'd seen over the years, one standing at arm's length in an office environment amidst faxes and phones and computers, two others a leap away, was like being at the ideal Christmas party, or onboard an L-1011 alone in my dreams.

After the detailed travel information, she continued with information about their club and the benefits of clean living. I was late, but I did feel obliged to stay and listen since she'd been so helpful. Another five minutes wouldn't hurt. Not that being in an office setting with three naked women wasn't surreal.

I'd always imagined that type of resort frequented by those whose idea of 'natural' meant not doing their bikini line, letting various other natural growth areas go unattended, where people were naked because that was the one place they could get someone to see them naked.

As we spoke I flipped through the pages of a brochure as an alternative to looking at her breasts and the marketing duo nearby. They weren't in the office because they weren't perky and perfect. They were. I'd happened into orgasm central.

The receptionist took pride in her looks. That was obvious. She was about my height, slim and very tanned. Then I saw it, as she twisted slightly to one side to retrieve another brochure from her desk.

She didn't have a vagina, none I could see. She had a thick and furry sporran, a mass of hair a baseball mitt wouldn't cover and I wondered how long it would take to blow-dry. Any rite of passage into its darkness would require the agility of expert fingers, determination, and abundant desire.

She was a little too natural for me. Still, I listened, wondering whether she chafed on warmer days and how she would look wet. Her ass and breasts, I have to admit, were worthy of notice. Definitely easier on the eyes than her fluffy frontal filaments. Truly a pity, like a wart on the nose.

Most men would mentally undress a woman, though she'd done that for me. My quandary was imagining her in something sexy, skimpy, with that type of genital tapestry as a frilly border.

On the other hand, the women sharing the office with her did just fine with equally perky breasts of pre-motherhood and the tautness of cared-for skin. One's pubic hair a fashionable adornment, one would say eye-catching, the other's, well…She didn't have any.

So, something for everyone. That's fair. Join me up, right now. I could definitely see us in a place like this. I was dividing my attention as she spoke between the brochure, her, and the others who didn't seem very busy. Then she turned the page and what might have been salt-petered away. Beer-bellied men with no tone and more hair on their backs than she had between her legs, wearing sneakers, ankle socks, and gold chains while playing shuffle board. The pictures were small. Just as well. This had to be a joke, a test to judge prospective members, to weed out gawkers and opportunists.

Not my idea of a day in the park. As the pages continued flipping I began understanding that the prettiest at the retreat were in front of me that very moment. False advertising, but excellent marketing. They had no sagging back skin, no double chins, no baldheads nor stretch marks. Clothing optional was not an option, the law strictly enforced with the exception of women on their periods who were instructed by Rule Seven to wear shorts.

No One to Tell

I couldn't imagine Linda bare-breasted in shorts screaming, "Hey! Everyone! I'm a bitch this week. So stay away. I'm bleeding, and I'm permanently pissed off."

Not my girl.

Joining did seem like a good idea while standing in the office. Until I realized those girls likely had mothers or grandmothers who were members. Worse, much worse, fathers and grandfathers who could play croquet without mallets.

I pulled myself away, getting a warm send-off of smiles and waves from the three shapely nudes and a chorus of invitations to visit them again. But that wouldn't happen, not until Ladies' Day, young Ladies' Day. I took a few brochures with me as I left. I needed proof.

*

Chez Carole was purple under purple lights and purple one-way windows. When we walked in the doorman put out his hand, leading us to a table equal in value to what I'd given him.

The owner of the restaurant wasn't wrong in his recommendation. The girls were a step above, plentiful, and Steve wasted no time searching his pockets for Canadian tens. Our drinks came, we sat back, and did what erudite men do in strip bars: We paid homage, Steve content after thirty dollars when we forgot the girls to talk business. That is until Steve's revolving head came into visual contact with The Twins and his view of lesbians was forever be altered.

The girls were dancing for a gentleman slouched back with a glass in hand and a smile on his face. When they weren't facing him they were facing us and when they were facing him our view was no less pleasing. They bent, they straightened, they pushed out and they sucked in.

Steve loved the French, especially French nudes and didn't take his eyes off the performance for a second. He had no tens, though The Twins would cost twenties. As

No One to Tell

long as he was going to sign the expenses that was fine with me, even finer with Steve who was on the edge of his chair, waiting for the moment when he could signal them over.

He suggested I could put them on my card. I suggested I couldn't.

The second, third and fourth songs ended and the girls stayed where they were, giving their benefactor more personalized attention during the brief pauses, their panties and bras slung over the arm of his chair. If the girls dancing together made Steve weak, they made him fall apart when they began doing to each other what they'd been doing to themselves. They weren't hurrying their caresses, pinches and kisses. The real deal. Steve salivating.

Their hands glided, pressing over, around, between, and into all the possible glistening avenues each one made easy to the other, their intensity so animated they moved to the floor to avoid falling, their bodies barely separating. They were lovers, paid to play.

We lost count of the dances the guy put out for and two things were certain: Someone had his card and his hangover in the morning would be something serious. The girls' mouths were smudged, splashes of lip-gloss adorning them from their shoulders to their knees. Each time the music stopped they sank to their stool, embracing, glowing and wet, fanning each other with napkins while skipping a song or two. Their admirer reached into his shirt pocket each time, pulling out a wad of twenties, the girls smiling, continuing their erotic breezes with each new bill, the stack on the table growing.

Steve had his first drinks mechanically. When I ordered a soda he did also, to wet his mouth that had dried from sucking in air over the past hour and The Twins weren't slowing. Over an hour at twenty a crack, so to speak, meant this guy was in for at least a few hundred plus drinks.

I convinced Steve they would not be a cheap date and,

very likely, the date would be tired after working so hard at playing.

We left, though if Steve could have walked backwards he would have.

*

Surprisingly Steve didn't get frostbite that week, or on his tongue that night leaving the bar

Both business and after-hours surpassed his expectations. He'd go home feeling that his time was well-spent. One matter of curiosity remaining: Poutine.

I could have reminded Steve that if it looks like shit, and feels like shit, but he had to discover for himself and we went for his last lunch of the week.

Marie et Antoine catered to the intentionally obese with a menu that ensured indigestion, heartburn, tooth decay and eventual blood clotting. The menu contained no warnings, but did include a concoction of French fries cooked in low-grade saturated oil, generously smothered in thick brown, sodium-soaked, clotted gravy and topped with an unhealthy mound of cheese curds. With no guarantee the meal wasn't yesterday's leftovers mixed with tomorrow's leftovers. All this I explained to Steve, in spite of which his mouth watered for poutine.

She looked at me as though I was from the Board of Health. She looked at Steve as though he was the Messiah about to bless her. He wanted to know her name, another bizarre New Orleans custom, and she thought Steve was a masculine name. I thought I could barf without eating their food, Steve ordering his poutine and ice tea with the help of a picture.

He touched her sleeve. "Ya'll do have ice tea, don't ya'll?"

She looked at me, shrugging stupidly.

"Thé-glacé" was all I had time to say before she ignored me, nodding to Steve. We didn't like each other, so when

No One to Tell

my turn came I ordered a plain sandwich I knew wouldn't hide hair or bubbles.

Steve's portion was huge. Before his first mouthful I warned him that he was voluntarily shortening his life. Despite which he dug in, managing to swallow, beaming at her. She seemed pleased, until I checked the contents of my sandwich. Then she wasn't pleased.

Steve devoured his clumpy feast in a bowl with as much pleasure as watching The Twins. He loved it, but we were running out of time if he wanted to get home by midnight. I took the bill because I didn't want her getting fifteen percent. She got ten, only because she was bigger than me and had a thicker moustache.

On the way to the airport we stopped at a dépanneur so Steve could pick up a frozen poutine to carry home in his briefcase. His final glance at Québec City was Chez Carole, not looking as purple in the daylight.

*

I phoned Steve when I had to, not following the company rule of at least one weekly call to the manager. He was easy to talk with, but hard to talk to and often telephone calls for the sake of calling turned into difficult monologues so we quickly adopted a mutual 'call when necessary policy'.

This was necessary. Moving to Halifax made sense.

We were mandated to see ten clients per week with a minimum annual value of 50K over a six-week grid. Thing is, seventy-five percent of my business was coming from the Atlantic region and travelling was becoming an issue. We agreed to talk initially in Chicago and again in New Orleans when he would get Stan involved.

*

Medieval Times was in suburban Schaumburg, minutes out of O'Hare. Ten of us anxious to be served by wenches in medieval peasant dresses that showed their plump breasts pushed up by modern-day bras.

No One to Tell

John was from New Jersey, a nice guy, concerned all week about telling his bride-to-be about her moustache. He worried about the outcome, which nine of us didn't quite comprehend. Then the petite white foot came out from the passenger side of the compact car, followed by another after the first was firmly planted on the castle grounds. We were in direct line with the vertex of youthful and opened legs that left John gaping as though he'd never seen a girl's crotch covered in white silk. He stood transfixed, the girl climbing from the car and standing straight before tugging at her dress, allowing us a more rounded view.

She was performing for us, getting off. She was being naughty. She wanted us to see what we otherwise couldn't have. She was a tease. I left John with his fantasies and joined Wayne.

We were greeted by the lord of the castle who would entertain us with his army of knights doing battle for honour, perhaps winning the favour and affections of the ladies of the court, perhaps bedding a wench or two. Though not that we would see. His lordship was tall, imposing, and spoke with authority, commanding all who came his way to lay down their arms and pick up souvenirs. We opposed and picked up drinks.

We were ushered in by velveteen-clad boys whose moustaches weren't much thicker than John's bride's, seated along rows of benches separated by alleys that would allow the buxom beauties to serve us, thus allowing us the fleeting diversion of their ample charms so nicely accenting their frill-lined fronts.

John saw his dream girl once or twice more as we waited in the Grand Hall of the counterfeit castle, ogling her as though blessed with X-ray vision. Then, as we took our seats, he tried pushing past me seconds too late. I had no choice. I was sitting between Wayne and the girl in white silk panties.

No One to Tell

John was stuck between Stan and Steve. I looked over my shoulder and smiled, trying to understand what he was mouthing in conjunction with his two middle fingers. I cupped a hand to my ear, but alas...

The ale came first, followed by the meal served on fake or real pewter. Before my second sip of the unidentified brew the girl beside me, separated by maybe three hand widths, raised herself ever so slightly, pulling her already mini dress to her hips. Let the games begin.

Squires and trumpeters marched in regal procession ahead of the valiant knights mounted on imposing steeds, heavily laden with shining armour, weaponry of the day and proudly flying their colours at the tips of their lances.

Her knees applauded each clash of lance against shield and sword against sword, sometimes leaning toward her friend to ask a question he couldn't answer because he was dimwitted, out of his league and out of his century. She was wearing a Rio cut, one cheek was nice; two would be very nice and I turned to see John who'd progressed from trying to kill me with his fingers to begging me with a twenty in his hand. I didn't need his twenty. Cheap bastard. Maybe a fifty.

Horses charged, lesser knights collapsing under the strength of superior opponents, taking up the battle on foot with bola and mace against shield, sword and alabarda. The knights became weary, beseeching their lord for temporary respite, granted but a few moments as Milady of the Panties rose from her seat. For she, too, required respite. Either that or she wanted me to see her ass up close and personal, which I did, not having to imagine John's eyes trying hard to focus.

She'd adjusted her micro-mini downward as she stood, putting one foot on the bench, then her other, climbing over the back and into the aisle behind us. She moved slowly, deliberately, facing her friend, probably the way they'd practiced at home. They were getting off, being naughty.

If her bum were any closer to my face I could have cleaned my glasses with her undies, which would have required some tugging, her cheeks mostly exposed, the white silk nicely tucked in.

Her friend was looking straight ahead. I glanced at Wayne who seemed a little flushed. He was getting divorced. He hadn't seen that much so close in too long. John was leaning over his table, desperate, still with the twenty.

The guests of the realm had no more than a view of the heads in front of them, allowing a perfect view of the jousting field, and no view of Milady, save her immediate entourage and John whose neck was severely extended.

When she returned she took her seat in the same fashion as she'd left, adjusting her dress to our mutual satisfaction, allowing a single glance my way and mischievous smile before once again applauding her favourite knight.

The evening's entertainment came to an end, everyone easing sideways from their seats except her. A final review as she clambered into the aisle. I hadn't chanced leaving my seat for fear John would usurp my temporary right of ownership and I'd waited too long for the ale to complete its journey.

The men's room wasn't crowded, surprisingly clean, the urinals spaced with the usual elbow room. John was on the left, Wayne was on the right.

John: "Did you see her frigging ass? Did you see how gorgeous her ass was?"

Me: "Every detail. Very nice."

Wayne: "She was hot."

Me: "I know. I felt the heat."

John: "Did she smell? You know, perfume?"

Me: "She smelled of something."

John: You took my seat, you son of a bitch."

Me: "You didn't miss much, just her panties when she pulled her dress to her hips for the evening."

John: "What!"

Me: "Okay, I saw her ass, but only when she put it into my face when she climbed out and in. What was that, Wayne, three times?"

Wayne hummed a "uh-huh."

John: "Holy shit. Holy shit!"

Wayne coughed, hitting my elbow in strict violation of The Male Code, but I didn't catch on.

Me: "Going home with her would have been easy, if she weren't with him. He wasn't my idea of a three-way. Now if she had a sister…"

Wayne flushed and coughed, stepping away.

John: "She'd be a good lay. Shit, I'd love to get laid by something like that. Oh, man."

Me: "No kidding she'd be good. Just something you don't have to explain to the new wife. I saved you."

I flushed with my elbow, turning slightly to avoid touching the ceramic with my jacket, catching the profile of the dimwit. John was the first out the door. Wayne and I took time to finish properly, her friend still at the urinal, probably achieving the short strokes. I believe he was disappointed.

John was like a kid in a candy store. He'd seen a woman's panties. Oh, baby! He needed a drink and I paid the round as compensation for denying his best moment, telling him the girl wasn't an exception. We were in the right place at the right time, or I was, just like the previous summer in St-Jean.

I was inviting customers to freebie lunches less often, passing the point of enduring banal conversations in someone else's favourite restaurant with people who were there because I was paying, giving them added status at the office. I was having a hotdog and a soda by the edge of the miniature seaway and locking system allowing passage of pleasure crafts from the Atlantic to the Atlantic by way of the St. Lawrence through to Lake Champlain and the Hudson.

Two years had passed since the sale of the B-Haven, though I never tired of watching other boaters when I was near marinas or locks. Watching them negotiating the locks, handling the lines, waiting to be yelled at by the lockmaster, or yelling at each other because the whole thing was taking too long, reignited fond memories.

I was parked by the pedestrian walkway, observing, trying not to get mustard on my tie, the cheap napkin already used and discarded. The mid-summer day was pleasant. The air was off, the window down. A few pedestrians ambled aimlessly, window shopping across the street. They weren't interested in boats.

She was standing at the far side of the intersection on my side of the road where the bridge ended at a red light, waiting to cross, to continue in my direction. I wasn't paying attention to her until she started crossing over.

She was tall, straight, slim, and walking slowly, sauntering. She had no purse; either a local taking a break from her daily routine or she'd parked her car somewhere else and was coming to the canal to watch the boats. The second thing I noticed was the slight breeze coming off the water playing with the hem of her flared mini-dress.

When she got to the front of my car she stopped, facing the canal. She wore a pale green summer-weight bra-top dress, form fitting on the top and flyaway loose at the bottom.

Her hair was long and light, streaked with something from a bottle that put her somewhere between blonde and brunette. Her arms went up in front of her, her hands meeting at the nape of her neck, channelling her hair into momentary ponytail, the tease meant to shorten her dress or

No One to Tell

lengthen her already long legs, which was pretty much when I stopped watching the boats.

I'm an ass man from way back, immediately recognizing perfect filet mignons, the little fleshy part of a woman's derrière that peeks out from cut-offs or from bikinis pulled high in order to activate the appropriate male response. Mission accomplished.

The breeze was warm and gentle, the heels of her feet lifting away from her low-heeled sandals when she leaned forward to rest her elbows on the railing, craning for a better view of the boaters, the wind and dress working in concert to make my day.

I was in the proverbial right place at the right time, watching her hands move to the hem of her dress, positioning her thumbs upward, hooking them; bringing the hem to her waist. Holy shit! I had no time to put down the hotdog. She brought her hands around to below the small of her back, holding her dress in place, slipping both hands under the narrow band of her thong, tugging.

She had a gorgeous ass. A semi-professional, but learned opinion. Leaning forward again her hands travelled with no great urgency to her front, disappearing downward. She was pulling the front of her panties away from her skin, leisurely, teasingly, her hands slowly, precisely inching their way to the starting point, her right hand securing the dress in place, her left hand freeing the band trapped between tanned and firm cheeks.

The manoeuvre wasn't easy, requiring the slight extension of her stunningly tight bum as well as an imperceptible dip at the knees. Her ass was officially bare. I didn't bother counting. Why overwork an already preoccupied mind? Though perhaps she was, releasing the silk that eagerly slipped into the warmth of its familiar crevasse.

She didn't let her dress fall. She placed it, playfully, first making certain her skin was smooth and firm, each tanned cheek caressed and squeezed in turn.

Spontaneous or not, only she knew. In either case, she wasn't rushing the moment. Neither was I. When she turned to walk away, she paused, her smile wide and mischievous. If she was hoping she'd made my day, she was about right.

All that was too much for John to fathom. He left us and went to his room to dream of white panties, bare bums and moustaches.

*

Stan was gone, meaning that Steve was relaxed and happier. Stan was okay, though, like all upper management, best kept at a distance. We were nine at a golf course. I volunteered as beer caddy.

Being beer caddy is demanding of one's physical and mental resources, particularly when dealing with marshals who can't get real jobs and try to insist that you rent clubs, even though you've paid green fees and rented a cart, my foamy cargo beginning to flatten and warm during a conversation that didn't measure up to his expectations.

Before Steve and Wayne got to the ninth whole, however, our time had run out, leaving a twosome, something else for the marshal to bitch about.

Steve first wandered off towards the rough. We saw him standing there with his hands on his hips, facing away, so we went to see what the matter was. Unfortunately for us, before we could change course, eight of us were standing around Steve as he stood quietly taking a leak. Information overload, as Steve would say, though we did discover why he was popular with the ladies.

Our bags were at the hotel with the concierge, ready for pick-up before heading to O'Hare, which has a lot to do with a peculiarity alive and well in New Orleans that sets The Swamp apart from the rest of the free world. They're allowed to drink while they drive. Hence the need for

No One to Tell

Daiquiri Stands.

Driving home from work at the end of a long, hard day in The Swamp's humid heat, going for groceries or going to a biker bar, drinking a favourite cocktail behind the wheel was permitted. But Steve wasn't leaving work in N'Awlins, already relaxed, oblivious to that fact as he drew the beer from the clear plastic glass through his straw.

When we pulled into the hotel parking lot we climbed out, slammed the doors shut and stood talking girl-talk on the driver's side. Steve had put his glass on the roof, Wayne left his in the car where the air was cool, preserving what was left for the ride to the airport as we stood looking at the black and white cop car that pulled in four or five spaces from us.

Steve had a habit of turning red under stress, particularly Stan-induced, and he was pretty red.

Thankfully he was as tall as the glass sitting on the roof, standing immobile while Wayne and I stood laughing; but the cops never looked our way, driving off as Wayne and I came out with our luggage and Steve's who hadn't moved and hadn't finished his beer.

We would see each other again in a little over a month for a meeting with Stan who didn't yet know about why I should be living in Halifax.

*

When Tom smiled the cracks and crevices crowded into his grey skin darkened, giving him the shadowed appearance of a man unhappy in life, craving permanent relief from chronic sadness. He was out of his element, unable to tell anyone what everyone knew already. He didn't want to be there. The sales community at ICS was mature for the most part. They made a point of hiring experienced and successful reps, enticing many from competitors. Tom wasn't needed.

Senior reps were District Managers; Salesmen were very

junior reps who would apprentice in a DM's territory without benefit of commissions or a much higher salary, taking several months to a few years to become a DM, if he didn't quit first. DM's were elevated, so why treat them as though they were imbecilic know-nothings who lacked drive, initiative and discipline? That was IC/SM and its application was rigidly enforced.

My forte was consultative selling, working with clients to understand their operational processes and needs, bringing value through solutions based on that knowledge. Now I was being told I was wrong. Really? I was being told not to present, rather to grow the problem. Grow the problem? The guy already has a problem, why would I make things worse?

Given that the client was calling me, what need was there to grow a problem that's already apparent? People took notes. So did I. Mine read: Screw this!

Tom was flustered. DMs buried their faces and I kept my mouth shut. What they didn't know wouldn't hurt them.

Those who'd long since been removed from active selling at ICS, or never sold to begin with, were the single-minded proponents who set IC/SM in place. Those who might have had a say in its more logical configuration and application, said nothing.

Their enthusiasm was fanatical, managers taking up the banner without knowing why, or what the ramifications were. Then again, if The Oracle and Stan said it was so, it was so. Which comes into play with Mikey the British midget.

We were being told to conceptualize step by step, five steps in all, and report on each one. What crap! While I'd be growing the problem that was bad enough in the eyes of a customer, someone else would harvest the order. Certain elements were at risk in my view: Losing the order and losing the customer who always came ahead of number three.

We were issued cheat sheets reminding us of the sequential process required to grow the business and grow the problem. When I got home, I couldn't find mine. Wayne must have taken them, or John. And Wayne thought I'd taken his.

They were defining their strategy based on one book written by someone no one knew, someone needing fifteen minutes of fame at our expense. That's the book I used to squash a spider.

We would have mentors; other DMs who'd bought into the programme with gusto and enthusiasm, primarily because they lacked methodology and experience of their own. Good move. The zone managers were also pressed into service, which they accepted as a means of keeping their jobs and, every so often, we'd be questioned on our understanding and application of said doctrine.

Steve asked whether I understood IC/SM, I said I did. Good. I asked him if he did. He said he did. Good. And we went to Bourbon Street before the sun went down.

*

We agreed she could have been a cheerleader. We could see by her tank top and jeans that she had the body. The blonde hair was real, matching her Southern belle complexion, her ponytail whipping back and forth in a rhythm opposite to her hips as she walked away with Steve: An all-time record. So much for Kaye or Faye.

Steve had proven himself to be The Man. He'd picked her up in a record three minutes, leaving four of us standing with our tongues hanging out. The lowest we were willing to go was twenty-one, but her age was anyone's guess. She wasn't fifty, doubtful that her mother was. We wouldn't see Steve until the following morning and forgot about him once we turned around.

Another peculiarity within the confines of the French

Quarter is women raising their tee-shirts or opening their blouses to cheering crowds of eager onlookers perched on ancient and sloping balconies, throwing beads to the woman of their choice whose breasts they'd like to see. For the most part the women of New Orleans don't take part in the ritual that isn't strictly reserved for Mardi Gras. They take a more refined approach towards their femininity, or they wait until the famous celebration to wear masks or paint their naked torsos.

So for the most part the bare breasts in question belonged to out-of-towners, many of whom have never shown off their breasts with abandon in bars or in the middle of crowded streets, never giving them the requisite attention needed for superior viewing. So beware the spud-chested women from Idaho or the dairy queens who once thought that natural was better than formula. The key is in selection. Those beads don't come free.

We'd grown larger in numbers, walking along Bourbon Street, bumping into others who joined us and we ended up in front of some bar that blared out jazz loud enough to make one eye cross over to the other. We went in. I sat, for all of ten seconds, excusing myself to visit the men's room, walking out. The musicians were having a great toe-tapping time, but likely as not they'd been deaf for years and not able to hear their own music.

The night was in its prime and I would need most of the rest of it to get back to the hotel because I had no idea where I was in relation to it. Beads were raining from both sides of the street, girls giggling and smiling with temptation. One girl looked at her could-be husband, he nodded yes. She was mid-twenties, and maybe a sister, mother, a town doctor and a couple of boyfriends might have seen her breasts, then Bourbon Street was yelling their praises and she got so excited, twirling this way and that, that he ran to pull her sweater down for her, leading her

No One to Tell

away from cheering fans.

I stopped into a St. Louis Street café for a Po' Boy, New Orleans answer to a sub inspired by the depression when folk could buy the hearty sandwich cheaply to carry them through their day. I ordered "not dressed," which meant without lettuce, tomato or "mi-o-nez."

The crowd was putting a different slant on bead throwing. They were throwing them up, the object of their precision-testing a good-looking girl on one of the many balconies who was leaning over, teasing them. She wouldn't have won a sobriety award, no one on the street would. She was dressed in a black or brown ankle-length jersey dress.

The beads stopped when she stood straight, pulling the bottom of her dress to her waist to show her bright red panties. She pivoted to thunderous applause, draping her arms over the man behind her, jutting out her bare butt for the cheering audience. The man behind her, boyfriend or new friend, took up the task, pulling her dress higher, turning her, keeping the bunched material over her breasts as she swayed to an intoxicating rhythm that came as much from the exhilaration of release as from a glass.

The beads began again, the crowd demanding more. She answered them, flicking the quick-release tabs at her hips, squatting and gyrating, pulling her thong free, swinging it in an arc, hurling the moist souvenir into the crowd. Her dress remained high, those closest to her ignoring the crowd. She probably wouldn't remember in the morning that she'd got caught up in the moment, or maybe she would. The rhythm was easy to keep time to, probably why they call the place The Big Easy. Anyway, I'd had my fill of bare boobs, bare asses, and pussies I had no access to. I was going to bed after a quiet nightcap.

I always preferred courtyard rooms when staying in the Quarter, the muted lighting and quiet suppressing the raucous and flamboyant pedestrian traffic from the street that went on till the early hours, men and women throwing beads, women catching them. Though not all the booze-induced sexuality took place on the street.

Hotel courtyards in the Quarter came furnished with wrap-around communal balconies. Saunter at will past open or undraped doors, though I never did. I didn't have to. The rooms boasted French doors whose drapery or hinges often seemed not to function properly, often in concert. Given the number of times I saw women in towels, out of towels, dressing, undressing, laying on their rented beds, laying on their lovers, getting laid by their lovers, standing by their doors semi-cloaked in towels or unbuttoned shirts, or not, breathing in the still night air.

That night, early morning, on the third floor and what I recall was my second nightcap near 1:00 AM, the air was calm, most of the courtyard rooms darkened. One could hear a pin drop, or a woman giggling, or jiggling. Or both.

She was slightly pissed, half wearing a tee-shirt whose label might have read XXXXtra AND THEN SOME. Or DANGER! DO NOT APPROACH WHEN WET!

Her Lothario was nervous, scanning the perimeter, his shorts not much smaller than a sloop's spinnaker. If his neck weren't so thick he would have seen me hovering over them. He followed her in to the shallow end, first collapsing to his knees, rolling, plunging, his tidal wave clashing against hers. Male and female troglodytes blinded by the pool's muted lighting.

I was invisible, silent, nearly dropping my JW Black when her tee came off in a wet tug of war. He pushed away his shorts as far as he could, performing a watery ballet before somehow managing to shuffle his way free of them with anxious feet.

Her breasts might have required WIDE LOAD travel permits on most highways, her nipples sufficient in diametre to warn passing vehicles, though somehow small against her massive foundation afloat in troubled waters. I have no idea how he managed to lift and part her legs, or hit the hidden target hands-free. I daresay, if not for the water he might have broken his back.

He wasn't wasting time. He wanted to get in and get out, pounding her like a jackhammer, water rushing over all four edges. She looked as though she was in labour, water splashing over her, her face turned sideways, contorted, twisting the tighter parts of her loose neck and facial skin, the rest jiggling freely, her breasts in multi-directional mode.

I could tell, she wanted to scream with delight.

I couldn't stay. I was on the verge of pissing myself. I ran into the room, but couldn't stay there either, pouring a fast two-fingers, hurrying out in time for the explosive finale. A Kodak moment. She was adrift in a sea of love, gaping straight at me, blinded. Or perhaps not, doing her best to show me the little squiggly thing at the back of her throat. He was doing his best to finish, grimacing as though someone had run off with his triple all-dressed burger.

His ass looked like a bicycle rack, the folds falling from his chest to his expansive waist confused with hers, their bulk self-concealing as they parted, sparing me a hideous nightmare.

She stopped him. She wanted more, which wasn't happening. He was leaving. Once, twice, three times, finally rolling onto the deck, on his back, panting, feet in the air, down, up, rocking onto one knee, pushing himself with a gasp to something barely resembling a human form, leaning forward, reaching for her.

Whether she was coming out or he was going in, was a toss-up. Me? I was undecided between watching and stabbing myself in the eye. She pushed away, possibly realizing they were naked, possibly realizing they had nothing to wear at breakfast. Shit, were they naked.

Her tee had drifted from his untethered shorts on the pool floor, illuminated by the diffused and undulating aquamarine sparkles from the submerged lighting. She searched, fanning the water as though parting the sea. What a treat, an encore performance. Four-hundred pounds of untanned flotsam thrashing with feet and hands, grasping for the three-foot deep cover-ups.

She gave up. She was floundering, rolling. She raised her arms to his, a wall of water surging between them.

Witnessing the tug-of-war to get her land-based was too much, watching that much weight on auto-pilot swaying from side to side as they scurried to their patio doors would have damaged a lesser mind. I stayed as I was, finishing my drink, watching the shorts and top drift farther apart.

*

My plan to make Sea & Double U the main user of ICS in Newfoundland was accepted with reservation. My detailed plan for Halifax would again be reviewed after Steve's trip to the Maritimes in June.

*

Steve's reason for visiting the Atlantic region was two-fold: Measurement, gauging my adaptation to IC/SM, and to see a territory including Québec that was equal in size to all the US east of the Mississippi.

Steve flew into Saint John Sunday evening. Monday morning we checked-out by 7:30, circling the harbour, Steve marvelling at a fully-loaded freighter sitting in the glistening muck of low tide. He was in for a ride, during which we would do some business but mostly he was in for a ride and he was up to the challenge.

We visited seven companies, spending two half-days in two key accounts and one full day in another. The other four would take an hour or so each. We saw sixteen managers, did three plant tours related to specific needs and resolved each of those needs with a seven-day lead time without growing the problem.

Steve was expecting to see ten accounts, understanding why not. We covered 1400 km in four days on roads that were neither good, nor bad. They're slow, made worse in June by tourists who didn't care about our day.

Monday was a twelve-hour day with lunch from a hotdog stand that must have been a hair salon at one time. Tuesday we were at the hotel by four. Wednesday and Thursday were fourteen-hour days. Those nights we stayed in Fredericton, which did cause a few hundred extra kilometres, but the comfort was worth the extra drive time.

The week was non-stop banter and tales out of school. We also did some major problem solving and cementing of relationships that ensured future business. The end of the week brought us to Blacks Harbour and Steve's introduction to Acadian French that likely sounded like gibberish to him.

Peter was the stuff of sea shanties and caricatures. He didn't care much for fashion and not at all for the spoken word. He was friendly enough, outgoing towards a few, friendly and introverted towards most. He took for granted that you knew what he was thinking. He did a lot of pointing, after which he'd look at you quizzically, as though he'd made a point, and walk away.

With Peter, making statements that allowed him to nod was preferable to asking questions he might, or might not, answer. Of course, Steve was unaware of these fine personality traits and went on asking questions without much help from me. I was having too much fun watching.

The plant was one of the largest fisheries in the country, favouring me as I was also deeply involved with a new OEM that was developing a robotic system for his plant that incorporated ICS.

My first dozen or so visits to the OEM I'd noted as

phone calls because according to company policy they didn't fall into A, B or C. More corporate bullshit, until their first order came in for over sixty K USD causing everyone in The Swamp to float around on their own hot air, talking of reputation and quality. Peter's contract would bring that to over 150 K.

Steve went home happy, in full agreement that I should move to Halifax.

*

Friday, a couple of weeks later, checking my voice mail, Stan's brief broadcast message to the Northern Zone came as a shock. "Gentlemen, this is Stan. Steve is no longer with the company. Please contact me directly with any concerns, questions or outstanding issues."

Steve had never fit the mould, hired as a Zone Manager even though he was a marketing specialist with no previous sales experience. He'd survived the original nine-man gauntlet, heading a zone consistently ahead of the others. But he didn't fit the mould and never would because his opinion regarding the single-mindedness and narrow vision existing in The Swamp wasn't private. Besides which, he was an outsider, a Texan. He needed out and they wanted him out. He wasn't happy. He was suffocating in The Swamp.

Steve believed he could learn more from his sales reps than he could teach. Our combined strengths were greater than our individual weaknesses and Steve left us to self-manage our territories without intrusion; although his door was always open and he always responded with a sense of urgency to any request for assistance.

Acting as mediator between the reps and the corporate bog was Steve's self-confessed role in the company. The few who openly criticized Steve for his technique, one might say backstabbed, were the younger reps impressed by the structure of IC/SM and praised no other God but Stan.

Not only were they not self-managed, they weren't self-reliant. They had no history, no baggage, and I was back to square one.
*

In mid-July I listened to another voice-mail to the zone, from Larry, asking each of us to call him at our convenience. I called him the next day, giving the younger reps time enough to swear fealty to their new lord. I'd also been on the phone with Wayne and Milton much of the afternoon, convincing Wayne The Swamp hadn't done this intentionally to cause his anxiety attack, and to reassure Milton the company hadn't yet discovered that his usual workday rarely exceeded a few hours.

Larry was a type "A" personality who enjoyed life, people, and his work. If you worked with Larry you had to enjoy at least the latter. Anyone who had their ear to the ground heard Larry's footsteps first. He was a key fixture in most of the company's initiatives, an outspoken advocate of working hard, playing hard, and IC/SM. So I was pretty well screwed.

Neither did Larry waste time. He didn't know a thing about Canada other than I lived north of Vermont in year-round cold, kids played with tomahawks, and everybody spoke French. But he was willing to learn, his lessons beginning August 12 when I once again visited the sweaty swamp to give him an up-date on anything and everything to do with the territory. Larry never let anything ride. When he had a question, he'd ask. When he had a problem, he found a solution. He was a busy man managing two zones, insisting that all twenty reps be self-managed. The prerequisite to a happier life for all.

One of his attitudes was "if you don't want me to comment, don't ask me." Although not devout in his belief in IC/SM, he expected everyone in his zones to understand and practice the set of laws. He also understood that distance allowed for certain freedoms and what he didn't know wouldn't hurt him. Just don't be stupid, which is to say don't be obvious about oversights or omissions with regard to the programme. So, under Larry's regime, we were free to do what we wanted, when we wanted. We just had to cover our asses, paying obvious attention, if not true devotion, to IC/SM and make enough money to stay ahead of the previous year's sales.

*

I brought him up-to-date on current issues, had one dinner with him and one lunch with Gina. Larry didn't join us for lunch because he didn't like Gina. He thought she was the epitome of a bitch. Gina thought he was a spoiled tyrant who always got his way.

Larry usually did get what he wanted, but not because he was spoiled. He reinforced every want with a need and a benefit. He knew how to work the system. However, in defence of Gina, she wasn't really a bitch; she just acted like one.

Larry was aware of my letter to Steve regarding Halifax, my two-hour presentation to him supported by facts and figures, need and benefit. And once more everything made sense. He would study the matter, get back to me and probably come to Montreal in the early fall. He reviewed what he needed from me, as I reviewed what I needed from him. He asked if I practiced IC/SM. I responded that I couldn't imagine a sales role without methodology. Then I asked him a question, but not about IC/SM.

The meeting was meaningful. Larry and I would get along well. We understood each other. We didn't share a history, we'd never be close and we would seldom talk, but we knew each other. Our assessment of each other scored high. I was one of the few DMs who didn't freeze or sweat when Larry walked into a room. I liked the guy. He was honest, forthright and unbending in his beliefs until proven wrong or shown a better way. I believe most of them thought Larry was on a self-serving ego trip, self-infatuated. I believe he enjoyed and embraced what he was doing, what he was mandated to do, and had the confidence and dynamism the others lacked.

Larry always finished meetings the same way. "I have nothing more, do you?" If the answer was no, you were expected to leave. If yes, he expected something worthwhile. I said "no," and left for the airport late Friday.

*

The Seafood Show in Boston and the Atlantic Industrial Exhibition were 'must do' events, primarily for clients who were wined and dined. I went to the Boston show each year to help Wayne manage the booth; he reciprocated in Halifax at the AIE.

We stayed at the Holiday Inn on Robie Street, walking distance.

Early the second morning Wayne, usually far from apoplectic, called my room to ask if I had "taken a whiz", or had a shower. I responded in the negative, thanking him for his interest, but he insisted that I flush the toilet and run the shower while he waited. I told him I'd call him right back.

I took a shower, the water tepid at best, like standing naked in a hailstorm. I was being sandblasted. The water was grey, the tub changing colour around my feet. Climbing out, the towel I used turned grey and, looking into the toilet, the bowl was grey under the waterline with grey particulate clinging to the drying sides.

I phoned Wayne. He was into his second vodka to rid his mouth of the tap water after-taste from brushing his teeth, the damage done. The piping delivering water into the hotel from the city supply had ruptured and pollutants had infiltrated the hotel's system. The hotel restaurant was understandably closed.

We expected some sort of continental breakfast in the

lobby with doughnuts and coffee from across the street; perhaps some recompense for having to go outside for the coffee and doughnut, not to mention spending our day covered in a grey film. None of that happened. Instead we checked-out and I never went back.

The next year Gina came from The Swamp to work the show. Hearing that, Wayne declined my invitation. He believed she was a dyke, not because she was a lesbian, simply his way of expressing that she was a bitch. She'd torn a layer of his skin off once, much like she'd done with Larry, and he couldn't deal with a full three days of similar good times.

I had Gina to myself.

She came because the company had a policy of CSRs travelling with their DMs once a year. Gina didn't want to travel in Québec, although she was fluent in French. She wanted to travel the Maritimes, but I couldn't possibly travel for an entire week with her, not without frequent escapes. So I'd delayed until Moncton, a perfect and timely solution.

She was in the Maritimes, I could escape at will, and I could arrange the schedule to avoid excessive interaction. Three people can't be wrong and I was at least number 100 something. Gina was a certified bitch. She had a hate on for the world for no reason. Thing is, she waited too long to discover that reality.

She arrived Saturday afternoon. I arrived at the convention centre by mid-morning Monday because I'd hired a crew to assemble the booth, set up the equipment and have everything ready for the show on Tuesday. By the time I arrived, however, Gina had assembled the booth herself, leaving nothing for the crew to do despite the pre-paid contract, the rest of her day spent bitching, complaining about broken fingernails, a sore back, and DMs that arrive late.

No One to Tell

I'd made arrangements for her to stay at the hotel where I normally stayed in Moncton, on an executive floor and convenient to attractions she might have wanted to see over the weekend. She cancelled the room and stayed in a rooming house halfway across town, not thinking she'd have to come up with taxi fare because I wasn't a taxi driver. That news flash pissed her off.

The week was a preview of my eventual eternity in hell for my minor sins. She turned potential customers away with snarls, existing customers with equal charm. Unfortunately she didn't keep all of them at bay with her bared incisors. I should have known better, found a way, but the dinner invitation was unavoidable.

The men arrived at the chic restaurant in suits and ties. Gina arrived in jeans and sneakers. We sat with our feet on the floor. Gina sat with hers on the front edge of her chair, with her knees sticking up like a spare set of knobby breasts. We ordered red, she wanted white. We enjoyed the red; she hated the white. We were all bilingual, though my guests found difficulty with certain American expressions because Gina wouldn't speak French.

The owner of the OEM asked Gina why we weren't speaking French. He knew very well she could. She replied: "Why would I do that?" And we all stopped talking.

The evening wasn't drawn out, which doesn't mean what remained went quickly. We shrugged, physically or mentally, switching to French. Except Gina who remained silent throughout the duration.

Very soon after she was held accountable for what she'd done, unrelated to my comment to her manager that she wasn't meant to interact with people, that she should be fitted with a muzzle or transferred to telemarketing where she could do no harm. Her attitude in the restaurant was a gross insult that might have easily damaged future relationships with the client, the X on her personnel file reflecting comments originating from the clients themselves.

When the exhibition closed Thursday afternoon, I was at the airport inside one hour. The convention crew would dismantle, crate and ship the booth. I thought. Gina could do whatever she pleased, which she did. She did everything the crew was hired to do. Then she flew home to tell everyone I'd left her to dismantle the booth herself.

When Larry called for an explanation regarding the ungentlemanly snub, he understood the conversation wasn't happening. Instead I faxed him a copy of the crew's 1800-dollar invoice.

*

The October meeting was my third, orchestrated to the minute and the metronome of choice was Stan's timer. Of course jokes happened, laughter disrupting more than one presenter, but Stan's watchful eye carefully monitored outbursts, indiscreet taps of a pen returning calm and order.

The daily schedule seldom varied: technical workshops, computer workshops, strategy meetings with CSRs, individual meetings with zone managers, and messages from The Oracle. He spoke wisely of many things: life and commitment, strength of character, continuing improvement, opportunity, tenacity defeating complacency, the struggle for the common good, and short-term pain that all must endure in order to achieve our long-term gains that would make us successful and our contributions meaningful. And all this was available on tape, as well as video. Arrogant corporate evangelism at its finest, a bi-annual event of self-adoration and pontificating to the masses, the masses who knew another truth: the truth of sacrifice and burnout without recognition or acknowledgement.

The true corporate definition of short-term pain for long-term gain was made known. Major accounts in specific industries would transition over time into Industry Specific accounts. A few golden hairs would benefit greatly, the rest of us would lose big-time. I personally would soon lose the largest account in Canada along with another dozen or so important clients.

ICS recognized the golden hairs, the "yes sir" guys, the "please show me the way" guys, the "I know I'm inadequate and shouldn't be bothering you" guys. Certainly lip service was paid to those of us whose successes were undeniable, which happened to me twice when I was six and five, respectively, in margin of sales over the previous year. In any event, for guys like me who sit at the back and shut our mouths, it's a bit of a moot point.

At ICS standing alone, being independent, self-functioning, meant accomplishments went unrecognized, if, in fact, you weren't labelled as a rogue. But that was during the day, at night, especially Halloween night, all participants were equal. Though anyone who believed that was dressed as the village idiot.

Austin, my bi-annual buddy from Kentucky, needed a costume. So did I. So we spent our fifty-nine minutes and sixty seconds, timed by Stan, to forego lunch, to search for something cheap, disposable and thin. That brought us to a costume shop in Cathedral Square. We tried on hats, shirts, pants, faces, beards and moustaches. We considered hair colouring, wigs, fake nails, various other appendages and noise makers, body-noise makers: some good, some not so good.

Austin chose a plain black mask, lending him the appearance of a maniacal backwoodsman. Not exactly Zorro. I went with a gold face devoid of expression and life. We had thirty minutes and eighteen seconds remaining and went for lunch.

We sat eating our Po' Boys in the square, watching the girls, commenting appropriately. Austin was a gentleman, a smooth talking Kentuckian who could charm the pants off any woman with his paper roses and Blue Grass ease, but we were on a budget. Time was the currency and our environment had gotten the better of us with ten minutes remaining to walk what had earlier taken us fifteen at a good pace.

Austin began trotting with a never before seen energy that began widening the distance between us. The temperature was hotter than hell and we were both wearing black. We'd drown in our own sweat. Still, he was driven. He had one thing on his mind: Stan.

I called his name.

"Might as well slow down, Austin. We're going to be late whatever we do."

"We are in deep shit, man. Truly deep shit."

"Shit's like quicksand, the best way out is to relax. The more you hurry, the more you sink."

He slowed, mostly because he was dragging me.

"Get shit for one minute or get shit for ten... same shit. We can run, get there out of breath, soaked, red-faced, and still have to deal with Stan. Or we can finish our Po' Boys, walk in dry, be the butt of Stan's wit for a moment and enjoy the applause."

"Let's finish our Po's. But we are in truly deep shit."

We walked in seven minutes late, before Stan who was ten minutes late for his own meeting, He wanted to ask why we were standing by the door laughing so hard, but his meeting was more important and said "Gentlemen, be seated."

The masquerade party was well-planned, with no detail overlooked. Austin's mask would have worked better if he'd lost twenty kilos and shaved his full silver beard. My mask was another matter. I was wearing black, to offset the gold, but so was almost everyone else. Even Captain Stan had a black tunic over his pink tights and a black, wide-rimmed chapeau impaled by a long pink feather.

No one could be sure, but they had to know. He had to know. The Oracle had to know to whom he was speaking and it took all my will not to cough up through my nose. The condensation dripping past the front of my collar was bad enough. I was having a $1.89 facial.

He had no idea. I was the mute behind the black-eyed mask, the unknown, and not knowing pissed him off. He followed, staying near, waiting and listening for a clue that never came. And when he finally did find out, toward the end of the evening when I got my gift for the least imaginative costume, he was still pissed.

*

Christmas came and went, though spring was slow in coming. By the National in May I'd been with the company twenty-two months. For the previous fiscal year, my first full year, I ranked six out of fifty-two in growth based on the margin over the previous twelve months.

In that time I had gone from minus six percent to plus twenty. Those were only figures and success. What really counted was IC/SM fast becoming a bi-annual event of believers vs. non-believers, management trying hard to discern who was on which team and deciding on remedial treatment or excision. The non-believers had to be identified and isolated, brought back into the flock with supervision and nurturing. I escaped recognition, as did most of the more senior reps. Some of the younger ones weren't as fortunate, while others chose subjugation and security over pride and begged for clemency. Some simply disappeared, their departures explained by Stan's memorized broadcast on various Fridays at five.

Seemingly light-years ago, I learned that I don't learn anything by listening to myself. At American Durcast I learned to keep my mouth shut, curious when some young guy put up his hand for Stan's question period. He had a cause. He was righteous, fifty-one sales guys ready to beat him to death. This wouldn't be good for many of us. This would rekindle heated feelings. The kid wanted Stan to explain his decision that all Frequent Flyer Points earned by employees on company business be given to the company. The answer was simple: The decision stood.

When Stan finally finished with the upstart, he was inspired to discuss a matter close to his own heart: Hotels. The kid would be drinking alone that night. No one was looking at Stan, all eyes were on him and mild-mannered Austin was flexing. My views differed diametrically from Stan's on the subject of home away from home, and I cared not all about his. I had one golden rule: Always take my home with me. As for Frequent Flyer Points, I kept them.

*

Friday came at last. The final function was dinner with the Larry and the guys in his two zones. There were a recent series of territory changes affecting both zones, reps from one transferring into the other, spurred by the company's unstoppable push towards Industry Specific Accounts, a subject as dear to the hearts of the reps as IC/SM was to the hearts of management.

Larry always threw a great party. He was known for the best Zone Meetings, the best locations and the best food and drink. He loved a good restaurant and a good time. Work hard; play hard. Like Boss Man twenty years earlier. Larry was good at what he did. He was a tough nut and expected nothing less from his reps. He also defended them, though wouldn't hesitate to interrupt them in the middle of presentations to ask questions and if we didn't have answers the next question was: Why not? Or at the end of a presentation he would tell a rep that perhaps he should get an office job if that was the best he could do.

Not enough ice can be put into a glass to lessen the effects of scotch when the temperature's in the high 90s F with no air and your cigar is a ten-inch Cuban. What I was doing with an illegal Havana in my mouth, filling my head with smoke and coughing out good scotch, I have no idea. But I know I didn't get to my room until 1:30 AM and my flight was leaving at six-thirty.

I left Larry along with a few others in the HS, playing cards and watching movies the rep from Japan thought was really neat "fooooking", saying so a dozen times in half as many minutes. I wouldn't sleep, though I did have a nightcap that would help kill the next four hours of bad late night/early morning TV and packing. Sleeping four hours after a long day and longer evening was not a good idea, irrespective of a travel clock and a wake-up call. Still in my jacket, my tie loosened, my drink in hand, my mouth tasting like an ashtray, I watched TV.

When I woke, in my jacket, my tie strangling me, the empty glass in hand, my mouth tasting like a tobacco plantation in flames, the time was 5:50. At 5:55 fresh clothes were on without any thought to fashion, the rest packed. At six I was in the lobby, not certain how I got there, going through the main doors shouting for a cab with a twenty in my hand To Insure Prompt service from the doorman and my bags were in the cab before I was.

In good traffic the airport was a thirty-minute drive. I gave the driver his fifty at just after 6:00.

Yet another New Orleans peculiarity is that they don't bury their deceased. They place them in crypts. Seeing those grey-black homes of the dead, in all their shapes and sizes behind black iron fencing, in the grey light of early morning, blurred by speed and stupor, made them seem all the more eerie.

I have never been driven anywhere so quickly since, barely able to pull the bills from my pocket before we pulled in to Departures, very much to his satisfaction because at 6:20 he was popping the trunk and I wasn't

No One to Tell

waiting for change.

I was going to make it. No one was in line and the agent looked at me as though I'd crawled from one of those crypts. He made a call, stamping tickets, tapping his keyboard. The gate was an easy jog along the concourse, but I'm not a jogger. So I pretty much hobbled in a way that would qualify me for handicap parking. At the gate they waved me on, mouthing words lost over distance. Once they wave, they never close the gate. I was going home.

*

The structure of most organizations is pyramidal and managers are never free from downward or upward forces of measurement or politics.

The company's need for Larry to be all things to all people was wearing thin. Despite enjoying the limelight, Larry was feeling the agony and stress of constant short-term pain for someone else's long-term gain. He possessed qualities and values inherently destructive to Integrated Conveyance Systems' blind momentum. He had vitality, conviction and imagination. Corporations such as ICS require blind observance and obedience, the energy needed to fuel the machine and continuously drain the source.

The Friday following my return home, I checked my voice-mail at day's end. "Gentlemen, this is Stan. Larry is no longer with the company. Please contact me directly with any concerns, questions or outstanding issues."

The zone would report to Stan on any and all matters until such time as a suitable candidate could be found to take over the Northern Zone. In the meantime we were self-managed, which was fine with most of us, status quo, save those who saw an opportunity to ingratiate themselves.

The Industry guys were increasingly intrusive, creating not just a little friction. Not only did we have no choice in giving up our prized accounts, we had to escort the interlopers to their initial meetings with the companies to ensure a smooth and effortless transition.

One of the new "meat experts" lived in Colorado, taking over E.G. Blanchette outside Québec City. They were a prominent OEM in the North American meat industry and, until recent events, were my largest customer accounting for twenty percent of my business.

In June Québec is a magnificent place situated 100 metres or so above sea level. The temperatures are always pleasant, the winds always light, the women and good food unequalled.

I arrived by car late in the day Monday, early enough to enjoy a glass of wine by the pool and give thought to how I would deal with Corey of Colorado. The principals at Blanchette were aware of the changeover, the pending visit, which was likely the last time I'd be actively involved with them. They were an independent, self-sufficient company, seldom requiring more than PR visits or updates on new product applications. However, when a need did arise, they expected an immediate response and how would Corey to do that from Colorado? Not my issue.

The plane landed at 6:00 PM. I'd never met Corey; another boy named Sue, and had no idea what he looked like. He'd recently joined the company, had no previous experience in belting and was taking over one of the company's Key Accounts.

He had to be good, he had to have some quality or ability that would convince nine people to hire him.

A horde of unrestrained passengers pushed and shoved their way into the concourse, most stopping abruptly with no idea where to go next, possibly as a result of French signage.

More passengers filed in, a lady who was undoubtedly Québécoise standing out. She was well-dressed in a simple knee-length slip dress that swirled around her legs with every stride. She wore nylons that added sheen and sultriness and high-heeled pumps that added allure. Her hair was shiny and auburn, in contrast to her white dress, her make-up imperceptible. She was walking with a purpose, the click-clack of her heels growing louder, faster. She was talking with the man beside her without looking at him.

He stood about 1, 75 metres, looked about thirty, his skin the white of bleached bones and he hadn't seen his feet in five years. His laced shoes were black, his black socks stopping above the ankle. His legs were bare, white to the bottom of his black Adidas shorts that had a white stripe trimming each side to match his white singlet, his Hawaiian tie-dye shirt open. His gut was loose, his cap on backwards in a silly and pathetic attempt to imitate a teenager. She'd stopped talking. He hadn't, and when they passed I gave her more attention. Shit! No way! The stylized logo on the cap read: ICS. I called his name, watching her, seeing a definite change in her stride. She owed me big-time.

I had planned a full two days of plant visits that would include four companies, putting Corey at the airport Thursday morning. Not soon enough. Jerk Alert!

"You James?"

"Unless someone else knows you're here."

"Damn if your broads here aren't fucking gorgeous. That one was teaching me some French. She crawled on in Boston. Nice piece."

She was long gone. He was tugging as his crotch; the burp or its cousin couldn't be far away. He would require some serious and immediate strategy on my part to avoid spending any time with the offensive oaf. He woke when the front tires hit the cement block in the hotel parking lot perhaps a little harder than need be.

I left him to check-in and went to the bar where he joined me too soon, still in his shorts, wearing a Coors tee-shirt that might have been new when he could see his feet.

He was ready to see the town, like that would happen.

There would be no Chez Carole, nor Louis Hébert. The most this guy would get was a drive-through and a bag full of burgers the next day for lunch that he would eat outside my car. The bar was dark, though not dark enough, which is where we ate dinner that Corey had no trouble washing down.

With dinner over, so was the evening. Corey stayed. We met the next morning after my in-room breakfast.

He wore the same black shoes, the kind with thick rubber soles and heels vulcanized to simulate leather uppers. The heels were badly worn, the backs scuffed white from slouching behind the wheel in a car without carpets. His pants had no crease, though the crotch had more than a Geisha's fan. The points of the button-down collar on his once-white shirt were curled upwards and the tails had begun their journey out from his trousers held in place by a belt better suited to a pirate. His jacket had long since served its purpose, in too poor a condition to donate to the Mission, his tie shining under the bright sunlight. Not quite the sheen of silk.

During the one-hour drive I briefed him on all aspects of the client not found in the corporate database. Philippe came out to greet us. Laurent we met in the Engineering Department where his office was set up with five seats and where the VP of Engineering would join us.

Laurent was uncomfortable in English, Philippe and their boss had no problem switching from one to the other. As we sat I explained the situation to Laurent, the reason for the visit and that the visitor was language impaired. I went on to say that I would leave the rest to Corey, though I'd make sure he wasn't kept out of the conversation.

"We are in America, aren't we?" We looked at Corey; I came close to my first heart attack. "James, can you tell these guys I don't parlez-vous."

"You just have, and you're American. You're not

expected to."

"Shit, we're all Americans. With all the money we send up here to help you guys with your wars and stuff we pretty near own this country."

Philippe, on my other side, leaned over to get a better view of Corey.

"What war would that be, monsieur?"

Corey had his chair tilted on its back legs, against the open doorframe, one leg crossed over the other so that one of his spongy shoes was pressed against the upper front edge of Laurent's mahogany desk.

"What else, the one where we kicked your ass."

I was having a stroke. I could feel my entire head going numb.

"What do you mean, sir? Do you mean the Plains of Abraham?"

"The what?"

"Wolfe and Montcalm, 1759."

He shrugged. "Whatever. We're always helping someone kick ass, then we pay to clean up their mess."

The VP said: "Do you have any new information for us?"

Corey stayed as he. He began explaining that we had two or three new products, one of particular interest them. If he'd read my notes he would have known Blanchette had generated the product. The VP left.

Laurent asked me a question. I asked Corey. "How often will you come here from Colorado?"

He answered the way many Americans do when confronted with linguistic barriers, or when talking with the visually impaired: He raised his voice, answering that he'd come whenever a need was determined, at least every quarter.

"Determined by whom?" Philippe asked.

"By what's in it for us. We want to partner with you, be here when you need our input."

"We already have it under control, thank you. We have several large American clients already, also in Mexico with no intention of losing impetus."

"You'll never get the really big ones. Americans buy American. You'll need our help to get through those doors. I can work with you on that."

"From Colorado?"

"Damn straight."

"How many kilometres is that?"

"What's a kilometre?"

"How many miles?"

Corey blew air from his mouth, making a fluttering sound. "2000. Something like that."

"Then we can expect you in September." Philippe was still leaning forward, intrigued either by the sight or the sound. I couldn't be sure.

"Can't say. It's too soon. Hell, I got most of the US *and* up here."

Philippe nodded. I stood, Laurent and Corey didn't. We shook hands with a few words in French to sum up the visit and wish each other well. I wouldn't be back anytime soon. Laurent asked about my plans for the week, whether I'd be travelling alone. I explained that I'd planned for other joint calls but, as luck would have it, the three would be leaving me voice-mail messages that I would check later, asking that I postpone the visits until Thursday or Friday.

"These things happen, Laurent. You've done it to me yourself. C'est la vie, non?"

Laurent wasn't given to laughter. He was always calm and poised, making an exception, chuckling as he stood. We shook hands with the firmness of those who'd worked well together without being friends, and wouldn't again. Laurent would leave Blanchette the following month.

"So," The lout lowered his seat, standing to stretch, pulling his shirt farther from his pants before tucking it in

under the swell. "We grab some lunch? Meals are on me. You take the booze." He turned to Laurent, who gave the answer he always gave me, this time in English. "No, thank you. I am too busy."
*

Under normal circumstances I would never have said what I did to Laurent, but I had to distance myself from the intellectually deficient vagabond. What mattered was getting him on his way. In the parking lot I asked Corey about the foot on the desk, the reclined chair against the doorframe and his approach in general.

He answered that his body language demonstrated confidence, control of the meeting and its outcome. I asked what the outcome of the fifteen-minute meeting was in his view and he shrugged. I'd never spent less than two hours with them, at times entire days.

The messages from clients postponing visits, messages I'd sent to myself during lunch were waiting. Answering each one, I called the companies to confirm other arrangements for the end of the week. Corey had no one to see.

I'd hoped to get the loud boor gone by the next morning, though Lady Luck was on my side and he was gone by early afternoon. I drove home leaving Blanchette for whom I had no call report to complete. I no longer had access to their interactive file. That was his problem; though I did record the events. The week after I left on the Saturday for eight days in Newfoundland for business and pleasure
*

The business part was ten-hour days; the pleasure part was having Linda with me.

Dinner Saturday night was with Kelvin, one of the owners of Sea & Double U, the U standing for utility, the Double for their two divisions that were conveyors and mid-range shipbuilding. Kelvin was friendly, big, hardened

No One to Tell

by work and sports. Listening to him speak required a practiced ear. He spoke words three at time, when he was tired. If he wasn't he was impossible to understand, though he had a kind disposition towards mentally challenged mainlanders and would often enunciate especially for them. And I do mean- e-n-u-n-c-i-a-t-e.

Dinner was in a fine restaurant, somewhat out of character for Kelvin. Lunch with him normally meant going to the local grocery store, picking what we wanted to eat from the shelves, taking drinks from the freezer, bread and cakes from behind the main counter to complete the meal before sitting at one of the two corner tables to eat. The second phase was lining up at the cash, reciting the list of ingredients to the clerk as she punched in the corresponding amounts. Cod tongue soup was a favourite, when fin soup wasn't available.

He was more the pub type. After we finished dinner we headed to George Street, St. John's answer to anyone who ever had an incurable thirst: Newfie Mardi Gras and anyone on the street was a participant. The music was loud, the shouting louder, creating a din more like a deafening silence. The drinks flowed freely, some down the middle of the street; some through the doors of one pub and into another, but mostly into eager throats.

Kelvin often got lost, found soon after, a process he repeated into the wee hours, each time coming to where we sat or stood talking with someone different because each time he came back we went to another pub where he'd get lost searching for a woman he once knew or wanted to know.

Linda hadn't yet seen an iceberg up close, touching close, and somehow that came up during the evening's conversation. He would have his daughter Heather call me to arrange booking on a vessel owned by a small company she worked for a few kilometres from Sea & Double U.

No One to Tell

We left Kelvin at 1:00 AM, at the hotel by 1:30. He wasn't ready to go home. At seven the phone rang. Heather was calling, which went something like this:

"Are ye the pretty missus' mister from the night afore?"

Say what? "Morning, Heather." Half surprised I remembered her name.

"I have a booking for ye at nine. Right fine day here."

"No, you don't"

"Sure. T'is the best time of day and barely a chop."

"No. It's not; but thank you for the motivation. Anything later?"

"Could be eleven's a good time. More crowded, though."

"Let's say eleven sounds better. We'll be there. Thanks for the call."

"See ye then, then."

We had enough time for more sleep, breakfast and a thirty-minute drive. When we got there, so was Kelvin. The man had electricity instead of blood.

The boat was a twenty-metre converted trawler. Fishing in those parts had declined, the owner gravitating from fishing to touring with passengers from across North America. The only Newfies were at the helm.

June 21st. Everyone onboard was dressed for fall or early winter with gloves, hats, earmuffs and scarves. The sea wasn't the calmest I had ever seen, neither was it violent. The water temperature was 3° C and the wind had a definite chill.

A semi-circle of bodies craned their necks at the aft section of the upper deck. We sat amidships where the rocking was much less noticeable. We weren't interested in the frothy wake or people throwing up. The lines were cast and the Old Mariner, the Old Man O' the Sea was first to stand and start clicking photos of puffins and seagulls.

We'd be out for an hour, no sooner shoving off than,

"Now, look dear, isn't that so lovely?" Then some "Now, hold on dear." And finally a few "Oh my, I wasn't expecting that. Were you, dear? Gracious." The Old Mariner was no mariner at all and the first to go. Destination: lower aft. Purpose: Puking over the transom.

The lady who'd looked over to me at the outset, thinking she might want to change her mind about the whole adventure, stayed when I assured her the waves were nowhere near a metre, that the boat was certainly capable of handling the chop. I hadn't intended for her to overhear when I said to Linda: "This isn't any metre anymore, more like two. She disappeared. She was the last to go, leaving Linda and me alone on the upper deck getting better photographs of icebergs than I ever expected.

Everything I accomplished that week from St. John's to Corner Brook was put through Sea & Double U, further cementing their pseudo-distributor status. They were accustomed to ordering every conceivable width and style of belt, one belt for one conveyor. They were good at what they did, making money in the process, but I had a better way which was the purpose of my meeting with them. Always the sceptic, Kelvin's brother Terry wouldn't believe until seeing proof in black and white, my next reason for going to New Orleans. Or so I thought at the time, until…

*

"Gentlemen, this is Stan." His voice boomed with the hollowness of the hands-free option on his phone. "This message is for the Northern Zone. Guys, effective immediately, Mike is the new Zone Manager for your area. Thank you."

And we were supposed to have a good weekend. Thanks a lot, Stan.

*

I phoned Wayne; Milton called me. We were in agreement. We had to assume the midget was blowing Stan.

No One to Tell

I disliked Mikey from the very second I laid eyes on him. He was sinister in a rat-like way. He was a devious, mythological creature scurrying about in the dark with other parasites and pests, a sack filled with hidden agendas, huddled over the flickering flame that lit the hole where he wrote and read his notes, and rewrote them because he didn't write well.

He was once part of the Beverage Team, when I had him for a day, taking him to yet another account I'd lost to the Industry Specific guys: a worldwide beverage OEM with offices and production near Montreal.

Little Mikey asked questions and took notes. He answered questions with questions and took more notes. At day's end the client had learned nothing new, I was merely a fixture, and Mikey had notes. At lunch I ordered wine for our guests. Mikey ordered ice tea, taking notes while we ate. Mikey did drink wine, but if he had he wouldn't have been able to write his notes. The one thing he probably didn't jot down was: When in Rome...

He came to the States from the mist and foggy rains of Britain, though I never spoke with anyone who knew why. Even other managers didn't understand the reasoning. New Orleans was filled to the brim with experts of one specialty or another, and Mikey was a specialist in nothing, with a particular deficiency in Human Relations. He wasn't worldly, not in any way erudite. He was transparent, enough not to cast a shadow on a sunny day and he quickly created a reputation as a stroker, a yes-man. He was the butt of endless short jokes. In short, no one liked Mikey. He was, for the most part, unimportant to everyone.

The years with Steve and Larry were unconditionally good, successful, hard and rewarding. They were men who stood tall, worthy of the respect they received. Conversely, Mikey had a permanent stick up his ass that he couldn't hide because the stick was longer than he was tall. Which

No One to Tell

was his Achilles heel, not his minute stature, his minute impression of himself.

At this point I have to jump ahead from Stan's phone call in early July to the week before Midyear in October. I'd gone to New Orleans to officially meet Mikey and listen to his views on management. He spent the better part of an hour criticizing Steve and Larry, his objective being to get the Northern Zone into shape. That would be the Northern Zone that had continuously realized high double-digit growth over the past years and significantly increased their customer base and new business opportunities. Quite an objective he had set for himself, that little Mikey.

When I left his office, what he got was a single digit. No one understood why he'd come, why he was there. He'd done nothing significant or noteworthy. He certainly had no proven record of managing a sales team. He said little, and when he did speak he showed how little he knew. I'd be there two more days working on an extensive grid of Sea & Double U sales over the previous five years which included dozens of belt styles and as many belt widths with variations of as little as 1, 27 centimetres. This, wasting thousands of dollars a year.

I'd been to their customers. They needed only three or four belt types in a maximum of three widths.

Of course, Mikey wanted in on this and who was I to say no? Besides, I was in The Swamp. I spent two full days in Mikey's office using felt tips on his wallboard, writing, erasing, adding, erasing, changing, erasing, and editing some more. Only when I finished did I learn I had access to an electronic board he'd known about. I could have done the job in half the time, with printed hard copies. Instead one of the secretaries took a full day to transcribe what I'd copied from the wallboard.

Mikey came really close to losing his nuts that day. Figuratively speaking, because he didn't have any.

No One to Tell

I saved Sea & Double U thousands, increasing our business because they became a more viable, timely solution to many more plants.

*

I arrived home on the Friday night, back in New Orleans eight days later for the Midyear and IC/SM, the new in New Orleans becoming questionable. There were other questions as well. Was IC/SM understood? Were the cheat sheets being used on a daily basis? Was the process being embraced? Can I please die now?

I was nine weeks from my fiftieth birthday; I'd owned a company and had dwelled in the top ten percentile since '75. Now I was in mock meetings with mock customers practicing the fine art of IC/SM because the asshole Oracle who owned the company wanted to grow problems and no one with access to his narrow thinking had balls.

Nor was I alone in my thinking. They were robotizing the sales force, they wanted clones: a single mind in fifty-two bodies. The worst was yet to come. The Wondrous Oracle had yet to speak, greeting us much like one says, "Excuse me" when bumping into a stranger on the street.

They couldn't fathom the reality that methodology must be flexible, taking regional differences into account, especially foreign countries, mine and everyone's. They wanted us to swear allegiance to IC/SM: "I swear that I shall forever blindly walk the path of restrictive and narrow thinking and shall do no evil against The Oracle." Maybe not.

IC/SM as such wasn't the problem. The older guys had trouble with the allegiance, the all-out requirement of complete and absolute supplication and subjugation without deviation before the Lord of the Method.

Poor Tom had been condemned to prepare and manage the strict enforcement of the IC/SM code of conduct, standing before his peers, light years beyond where he

No One to Tell

should have stood and most everyone knew but The Oracle who was all-knowing and rather pouty when pissed off.

So nothing was said.

The joie de vivre had gone from the zone. The guys went their own way, had their own cliques, I associated mostly with Wayne and Austin and what was lost would not be found. On Friday, the final day, The Oracle pontificated at 8:10, following Stan's eye-opening address to the Bourbon Street survivors. Even Bourbon Street had its time with me.

At eight-ten the room was alert, a degree of feigned respect shown for The Oracle, a multimillionaire and, according to him, "just one of the guys." By 8:30 what was left was cynicism on the part of the sales group. Of the 200 attendees, 148 applauded, the other fifty-two were too stunned, the youngest of them looking at their more senior colleagues, uncertain.

We were to have sixty-five clients, maximum, no more, with a minimum value placed on the least of that number. All other accounts would be directed towards Customer Service and any exceptions would have to be approved by management with the minimum sales value being the responsibility of the sales rep to ascertain. They wanted only the big clients, the cream of the crop, the big money.

Such was the gem developed by the hierarchy of office workers.

The Oracle knew nothing of the sales process. What he did in those twenty-minutes was dissolve all the efforts and advances the sales force had made in their respective territories. We didn't even have to pick and choose. The monthly descending value did that for us. The one thought common to all the reps was "How do I explain this?"

He was into his short-term, long-term mode again. He really thought this stuff was innovative. ICS espoused self-management on the one hand, forbidding it on the other as they spoke of measurement which was monitoring. Each visit would be counted and categorized by dollar value, reviewed for content and purpose, measured against the performance of the zone, the company as a whole, the previous year and current year forecasts.

The best was "Be brutally honest." We would be accountable, which meant being monitored. We were told clearly that when on our way home early, any day of the week, and happened to pass a "smokestack" where we knew potential existed, we were to go home and "stroke the dog." But there was no sense in getting upset. Just do it, or pretend to. 1, 2, 3: Me, the client, them. Sales people, and or employers, come and go. For the most part clients remain.

At the airport, Dennis was livid. Like the rest of us he'd spent years developing relationships he was told to ignore. Several of us had talked about the same scenario and I waited until the others had gone before suggesting to Dennis that there was no problem, beyond working with a company that had no respect for what we'd accomplished. We were being blindly herded and where does "brutal" fit into corporate terminology?

The solution was simple: See the clients he needed to see, noting those not on the new list as phone calls.

Seeing the same sixty-five clients within that timeframe was a problem, taking me back to what Paul said at W&W about always having a reason to see a customer, always bringing value. I had five provinces and sixty-five clients, three-quarters of whom were at least a half-day travel by air from where I lived.

Halifax was critical to any future success, and I had to go through the process of explaining its importance once again. This time to someone indecisive, lacking cognitive powers, the same person who believed Newfoundland was in mainland Nova Scotia.

*

No One to Tell

A week later I was in Newfoundland, about ready for honorary citizenship, there to give a technical presentation to the fishery plants on the island. The meeting was held at the Hotel Newfoundland, but I was staying at the Delta where Mikey was scheduled to arrive from New Orleans close to midnight. I arrived around three PM, hadn't eaten and was ready for dinner and a glass of wine before reviewing the final preparations for the meeting.

The hostess was showing me to my table, and if I could have vaporized then would have been a good time. Little Mikey was sitting right there, sipping his wine. I despise sneaks. He'd come in early with Dave who'd come up to help with the presentation.

Mikey never participated unless someone higher on the ladder was present. Taking part would show him for what he was and he couldn't let that happen.

Mikey never uttered a thank-you, nor did he ever stand to greet those he considered subordinate, or shake their hands. Mikey was a humourless and unmannerly gnome who felt more equal in stature to others when he was seated, forsaking good manners to that end.

I explained that I'd come down for a cocktail, but the bar was too noisy. Apparently so was the dining room. I left, went to my room and ordered room service.

My forte was anticipating client need and their queries, each sales call prepared as a presentation, but this was different. The purpose of the presentation was to give generic information relative to the industry as a whole, denoting the advantages of plastic over steel for land-based operations as well as factory ships equipped to process onboard. There would be no growing the problem. The attendees were part of an extremely competitive industry and very suspicious of one another throughout the three-hour presentation.

No one would admit to having problems, though

everyone shared the ones they did have. Most had come to the meeting from trawlers moored in St. John's harbour, very few drove. These were weathered and savvy seafarers, not the usual audience of white and blue collars and if they were suspicious of one another, they were doubly so of us city folk from the mainland.

By noon I was hoarse, assisted by Dave when he was more qualified to elaborate on specific technical points or features. On those occasions I stepped aside, watching Little Mikey at the back of the room with pen in hand, his face lowered into his day timer.

By eleven I thought the presentation was going nowhere. Dave was a practiced and animated presenter. He also looked like a seafarer even though he wasn't. I held my own, but by that point gauging the interest level was extremely difficult.

Kelvin and Terry did ask questions they knew were on the minds of their longstanding customers, no heads nodding, Kelvin saving the best for a later time. We broke for lunch.

The afternoon portion was touchy-feely, the room filled with tables of samples, calculation programmes, mock-ups and one-on-one attention. Every one of the invitees took part, the interest level soaring. What surprised both Dave and me was that most of the questions were directly related to what we'd presented throughout the morning session. The few who approached Mikey were referred to us. What they needed to know wasn't in his notes.

The day was a success, Sea & Double U realizing substantial growth as a result. When everyone had gone the five of us headed to the bar for drinks, to recap the day and talk about subjects that didn't include catenaries, load and thermal expansion, though only four of us maintained a conversation. The fifth was being tutored.

He left the next morning after a trip to Terry and

Kelvin's office, completing a return 10,000 kilometres to attend a presentation during which he said nothing, and a one-hour plant visit that produced nothing. He'd seen nothing to grow. Kelvin's last question to me on the previous day was over drinks when Mikey had gone. "Why was the little fucker even here? He didn't do a fucking thing."
*

Our office days were Mondays, another dictum, one that was monitored, matched against the company and zone average. Mine were usually 1.5 days per week and those days were as long as any other. In the past our reports had been due sometime before the Friday of the following week. Then, in the Northern Zone, our reports were due Monday morning before 7:30 or the system would delay the transfer until the next day. These were reports varied in nature, not Call Reports that were expected every other day as part of the interactive upload/download.

Mikey was practicing his management techniques. I called him to explain Mondays were office days intended for follow-ups, paperwork, planning, etc., that Tuesday morning would give us more time to prepare.

"No. I need the information Monday morning. That's final. Or we'll have an issue." He tried to sound authoritative, two elements preventing that from happening. One, we were on the phone; two, Mikey was irrelevant.

Fridays became my office days, though most Friday afternoons always were when in town, which meant I would now arrive home from out of town on Thursdays. Dennis and Wayne followed suit

Very few trips didn't get me home after eleven or twelve PM, very few weeks spent locally didn't have fifty or sixty hours in them. So what's a Friday afternoon? Burnout prevention; some might say balance.

Mikey wasn't a good manager by any measure. He was

exceedingly ordinary and unskilled. He'd reached his level of incompetence and didn't know how to deal with the fear of failure. Apparently neither did Stan.

He'd been promoted by virtue of being the only candidate for a job that no one wanted, not for his talent, nor his skill. He was completely incapable of coaching and mentoring because he possessed nowhere near the experience of his so-called subordinates. He was the junior by any standard. To say wet behind the ears was an understatement. He was always out to prove something, particularly that he was as good as those who were taller. He lacked the confidence of the group as a whole, a poor communicator with no ability for the written or spoken word. He was inconsistent, often struggling to make a point, always wanting to fix what wasn't broken in an easy effort to appease, please and placate dwellers of the Ivory Tower.

Others in the Northern Zone and other territories were unquestionably equal to the position, but one of the stipulations was living in The Swamp. Mikey already did, the primary requisite. In Mikey's case the only one.

Most managers were figureheads, go-betweens with specific functions who brought a certain value and raison d'être to the position. Mikey constantly got in the way and brought no value. Although he was coy when Stan was near, he was caustic and terse in public, which came across clearly as his way of compensating for his diminutive stature. His style was to manage and suppress with his thumb, incapable of leading with competence and skill. Of course the key element to leading is to have someone behind you, whereas Mikey had no one behind him.

No one ever went to Mikey because everyone knew Mikey took notes. No one ever had anything good to say about him, though nobody stood up to him to challenge him. Not that they were individually afraid of the little munchkin, they were afraid of Stan: Stan the Man, the Evil

No One to Tell

One, the dark-tanned, tall and furry Stan.
*

Another year-end review, another visit to The Swamp in December, when I saw a difference in Mikey I couldn't at first discern. I was doing this wrong, and I was doing that wrong. I wasn't serious, I had to show more respect. I had no idea about IC/SM, protocol, teamwork, or taking my job seriously. This tirade as he pushed the report at me to sign.

I thought that was the difference. Mikey had grown a sense of humour. He believed he could raise his voice to me. Every meeting should include some element of humour. No. Not so after all. I was the one with the sense of humour. I was the only one laughing. But if Mikey was still a humourless gnome, what was different?

He needed me to say, as others had to his face, if not behind his back, that IC/SM was the way, that he was The Man. Slim fucking chance. He had a better chance of a miracle growth spurt. That was it! Yes! Mikey had grown since our time together in Newfoundland. The invigorating sea air of the North Atlantic had agreed with him. He'd grown 2.5 centimetres, maybe even five. Good for him. He had grown the problem after all.

He made very clear that he wouldn't talk about Halifax until he had an opportunity to travel there. I hadn't broached the subject, making very clear that Halifax was mandatory, not a subject for discussion. That was on him, not me. My views were documented. Going or not going had become a moot point. After two years of supplying facts and figures, and the acceptance of his competent predecessors, who was he to second guess us?

In fact my interest level was practically nil.

Back in Montreal, Mikey was the last thing on my mind. Of growing importance was the interest shown by Yoakum Industries in carrying the ICS product line. We'd discussed distribution for six months, which included my letter to

Larry in violation of the no-distribution dictum describing their history, potential, enthusiasm, the need and the benefit.

They'd been in business fourteen years and I'd come to know the owner during my time with Swiss and Euro, when they were both distributor and competitor. Timing was important to them because of buyouts and takeovers happening elsewhere in the industry that would affect them.

*

Joint calls and weekly reports had become surveillance mechanisms to the point of debilitating intrusion, though one time in particular Milton and I got an unexpected reprieve from Mikey's note-taking for an unexpected reason. The dumb bugger neglected to renew his green card. He could leave the US; he just couldn't get back in. Others weren't so fortunate, Wayne being one of them.

Wayne had experienced a traumatic physical event resulting from a serious fall, with injuries to his knees and the exacerbation of existing medical conditions. He required hospitalization and a subsequent recovery period at home during which he was on medication and instructed to stay off his feet.

He'd come home on the Wednesday, Mikey called him on the Friday asking that he be ready for joint calls that coming Monday. Wayne explained the situation; Mikey listened, before giving Wayne his flight information. Certain distinct problems existed: Mikey should never have been promoted to management and Wayne, as one of the longest standing members of the sales force, should have told him to fuck off.

By April my and Milton's luck ran out. We had to meet with him in up-state New York on the pretext of discussing distribution in Canada. We could have met him in N.O. Cost wasn't a question; the question was Mikey not yet having seen the North Country.

His main preoccupation in life was seeing as much of

North America as he could; his vehicle for the journey, ICS.

The meeting was preparatory to the May meeting when the three of us would meet with Stan, and Jayce LaPomme, The Oracle, to discuss distribution through Yoakum. In the interim Mikey and Milton would meet Mr. Hokum, forming their own conclusions.

Yoakum was about to lose their supplier of plastic belting, Hawk Industries, and two of the three principal suppliers had refused him. ICS was his only hope. He needed ICS and had spent the better part of a year trying to convince me the marriage would work.

The meeting was held at Yoakum. We met with Barnaby alone. His sales manager was absent. Not a big loss, which I kept to myself.

As usual Mikey was unprepared, his questions ordinary. Milton's questions were equally dynamic, meant to impress Mikey. He spoke like a valley girl with a permanent smirk on his face to disguise his nervousness, wanting to be at least as good as his miniature master, which offered a clear insight into his personality.

The meeting lasted three hours, ending with an invitation to lunch. As puppet and puppeteer made a few calls, I had a sidebar with Barnaby who was curious to know what purpose was served by having Milton there. His protectionist questions led nowhere, juvenile. And did Mikey have a full understanding of the mutual growth that would blossom from the relationship? I responded that Mikey was as full as he could be, best disregarded. I'd be the contact, and would get back to him after my next trip to N.O. with a yes or no answer.

That night I left them at a five-star, Milton all giddy. He thought he'd died and gone to heaven. But he was having dinner alone with Mikey, so he'd actually gone to hell. The next morning one was gone and the other remained behind for two days of joint calls. I'd told him well in advance that anywhere I'd take him would be French-speaking, which wasn't a deterrent.

Stuck with him, I made certain the clients we saw were French, uncomfortable with English. Mikey's input was nil, though not strictly as a result of linguistic deficiency. Unlike Americans who accept their linguistic limitations at face value, Brits have an imperial attitude towards foreign languages even when they're the foreigners. God is English, the Queen is English, sufficient reason for any of them to speak English when in the company of an Englishman.

So Mikey sat quietly taking notes. But what could have been in the notes? He hadn't understood one word, even the few times English was spoken in good will. I also made certain that all calls were within a one-hour drive of downtown Montreal, limiting my time with him and at dinner he was on his own.

The end of the second day was review time, in the hotel. Now that's professional. IC/SM, IC/SM, IC/SM wasn't going away. Neither was Mikey anytime soon.

"It's obvious to everyone that you don't understand IC/SM."

"Who is everyone?"

"Stan."

"Who else?"

No answer. He had no answer.

"What I saw this week shows me that you completely disregard IC/SM."

"What's your point?"

"That must stop. You must follow the guidelines." He brought out his agenda, opened to the IC/SM cheat sheet. "Show me yours."

"My what?"

"Your IC/SM cheat sheet."

"Do you really believe that after twenty-five years in sales I need a five-step cheat sheet to conduct a fucking

No One to Tell

sales call? You do realize that last year I was number five in the company, and this year I'll be number four."

"You don't even carry a day timer. You're supposed to carry a day timer and have your cheat sheets in it."

"Peddlers carry day timers, like that one. It's not a style I care to embrace." Mikey was visibly upset. He clearly didn't have full control of himself. "You're the only one who doesn't understand IC/SM and that has to change. I'm assigning you a mentor who'll work with you and report your progress."

"You're not assigning shit, Mikey."

"Stop calling me that."

"I was successful in sales when you were starting school. I knew sales methodology before you knew English. You don't tell me shit about selling." I stood, bringing up my briefcase. "What you can do, Mikey, is shove those cheat sheets and IC/SM up your arse."

That pretty much ended the meeting and we didn't see each other again until the National. Any interim communication was initiated by him via e-mail. Too bad someone hadn't thrown some self-esteem into the shopping bag when he'd bought those ridiculous elevator shoes.

The IC/SM process contained five steps from identifying a need to a consultative solution based entirely on 'growing' the problem. Presenting was a faux-pas. Therein lay the dilemma that went unspoken and unchallenged. The methodology was restrictive and blind to exception with absolutely no contrary opinion allowed.

Consultative selling wasn't new, the one credible part of the IC/SM process. Neither was conceptual selling. The problem was they confused the two because the wrong people were talking and everyone else was afraid. We weren't allowed samples or videos, or any sales aid. We were told to grow the problem, but not to show the solution and the only problem growing was mine.

No One to Tell

"Hey, buddy, you've got a helluva problem. And I've got the solution, but I'm not telling until you're really screwed."

Worse yet, no one ever once mentioned or questioned that what we were selling was profit. Reduce a plant's maintenance costs, or increase the production capability: That's profit. Do both, and you're his.

We were confused and discouraged. We'd been hired for our strengths and competencies, now told to forget what we knew and embrace IC/SM by those who lacked the requisite competencies, skills, and foresight to include senior sales people in the equation.

They were telling us to follow and complete a schedule of predetermined events before discussing a solution with a client, growing the need, the problem, while the competition was harvesting the order.

Unfortunately, unlike Steve and Larry, Mikey had to prove to Stan and LaPomme that IC/SM was embraced by us. In that way IC/SM and Mikey would be linked with our success. He'd be a hero, which was never the case. Very much the opposite: We were successful in spite of him.

Larry really should have been the one to oversee the implementation of the IC/SM concept and consultative selling. He had the motivation and the respect of the sales force. Tom was tired, made weary by the momentum of change he couldn't keep pace with. Larry, on the other hand, had the two well-defined. He understood that IC/SM could be a worthwhile tool if administered properly and he understood the long-term advantages of a consultative approach.

*

Wayne and I hooked-up in Boston, flying to The Swamp together for the National Meeting in Biloxi, Mississippi. The final leg of the journey was by chartered bus, Wayne already sweating bullets at the thought of spending five days with Mikey. National meetings always ended on Saturday evening, following award ceremonies and the usual company dinner speeches.

Mikey and I were somewhat at peace with one another, the calm before the storm. He didn't bother with me, and I contentedly ignored him. The only time during the week we had to tolerate one another was at the breakaway zone meeting and sidebar with LaPomme about distribution in Canada which would be taken under advisement. They didn't see it as a primary concern at the moment. Mikey, per usual, said nothing. When asked for an opinion he deferred to Milton and me.

Mikey had no sense of self-worth, with good reason. He was worthless. He had no sense of belonging and he certainly had no sense of sound reasoning. His only sense was that of accountability to upper management, never to his zone when he should have had both. He was a puppet, never understanding that a sales force can help promote their manager as much as the manager can assist the career of an individual. He wanted to dictate from the top down, incapable or unwilling to lead by organizing the thoughts and contributions of all the team members to everyone's advantage. Incapable. For that and other reasons no one trusted him. By and large the zone relied on one another. If they didn't visibly distance themselves from Mikey, neither did they encourage closeness.

I'd known for some months that I was number four. Wayne was number one, based on increase in margin over the previous year. Thirty-four months earlier I'd begun at minus fifty-two percent, I was then at plus thirty as a result of consultative selling.

Mikey had his own presentation to make to the zone. He gave each of us a golf shirt with the zone designation embroidered on the chest. Wow. Thanks, Mikey. A company shirt like yours. We all left with words of appreciation…until we got outside. Well, not everyone.

Six AM the next morning I was up and travelling to the Louis Armstrong airport on a half-empty bus with most of the Northern Zone. I'd be home by four from my seventeenth trip and sixty-third night in the Big Easy, five in Biloxi.

*

Two months passed before I heard what the powers in New Orleans had decided about distribution. In the meantime status quo prevailed. Mike didn't bother me and I didn't give him the time of day. Out of sight, out of mind, and the territory continued its upward climb, showing continued growth in sales despite a reduced customer base.

Sea & Double U quickly realized increased sales, and due to the fact they were now using recommended sale price strategies, their overall profit margin was improving as well. All of which was accomplished without sales people, other than my direct contact with clients that I put their way exclusively. Not that I had a choice. Dealing directly would have meant many more trips to the island, which wasn't self-serving, creating one more competitor which was self-defeating.

When I arrived on the Monday, I'd planned to be home on the Thursday.

By late Wednesday afternoon I was in my hotel room, cancelling more appointments, reviewing notes, entering detailed information into the database to reflect commitments and upcoming business from the plants I'd visited while strolling George Street or sitting in the hotel bar. The fog had made driving impossible. The week was the second worst of my career, the first was five years away. Anyone with a car old enough or expensive enough to have a hood ornament wouldn't have seen it from behind the wheel. It comes in without warning like a huge blanket of cotton fluff, almost tangible.

No One to Tell

It was expected to lift, all flights departing on schedule according to the pre-recorded airline message at eight the next morning when the fog was just as thick. Turned out the airline rep was in Toronto or Winnipeg with no idea what was going on. I extended my stay through to Saturday, maintaining contact with the airport each morning. At noon, in the lobby, people were milling around complaining, squawking into cellphones, searching for rooms. The airport was closed.

I called Linda, telling her not to keep dinner. I'd be home Saturday. Saturday I called, suggesting perhaps Sunday. Then Monday became Tuesday, when the flight was delayed due to a moose on the runway.

In the meantime, drinking in Newfoundland is a respected and respectable custom, though even the bars on George Street were mostly empty. Kelvin in particular conspicuous by his absence, though I did my best to survive despite the 'Montreal smoked meat' served like a dog's tongue dipped in yellow goo and served between slices of white, doughy bread thin enough to see through. Then came the woolly mastodon while shopping for weekend attire.

*

She was getting on the escalator before me, carrying bags that weren't heavy, albeit large and clumsy. A vinyl jacket was slung over her arm. She was wearing tight, one-size-cannot-fit-all mid-calf spandex pants women wear outside their homes when they need to wear something, but want that feeling of being naked. Her cashmere sweater was loose-fitting, matted with tiny clusters of miniature woolly balls. She was bigger than me, way bigger, my brain determining that managing her dead weight would require Olympian strength that I likely did not have as I switched into alert mode.

She wasn't holding the rails. The escalator jerked once, destabilizing the woolly-clad lady. She came back at me,

No One to Tell

her arms rising and flailing for balance, not letting go of the bags. I reached out to grab her, to break her fall. Big tits! Why me? Big tits! They weren't breasts, or boobies, or hooters; these were the mammoth mammary glands of a mastodon shopper, intended for maternal labour and wrapped solely in a thick woolly sweater.

They were big woolly tits, woolly mammoths with their mammillae already responsive to my grasp of the situation; though if I had let go she would have fallen, taking me with her. So, I had those malleable woollies in my hands for the next fifteen metres of angular descent as I stood stooped over with my chin on her head and both my arms pinned against her sides. She was in the birthing position without the benefit of stirrups, her legs and feet unruly, slipping, her bags taking priority over dignity.

When we finally got to the bottom she righted herself by the movement of the steps and me pushing against her from behind. Only then was I was able to release my hold on her bulky bundles. I asked her if she was okay and she was, if not somewhat crimson. I didn't apologize for my rescue technique, some things are better left unsaid. Who knows? She may have enjoyed the impromptu attention. I smiled at her and left. We shared a moment, a new memory like so many others. Or not.

Finally, departing on Tuesday, the man beside me spoke of a time he'd been stranded for thirty-five days. Serious or not, I never returned to Newfoundland in May.

*

I spent much of June and July achieving some balance in my out-of-town travel, putting off Mr. Hokum who was becoming impatient, worried about his place in the world of plastic. His loss of a supplier was imminent; he needed an answer. So Mikey's invitation to once again fly to The Swamp was timely, as well as a waste of time

Nothing happened, nothing of importance. I was in NO

for two days, three nights, flying home Thursday. In the interim I had a review with Mikey that I didn't sign, I met with engineers to discuss certain applications, and sat with Gina in Customer Service, listening in on phone calls that meant nothing to me. Though she'd changed. She'd become more outward, more relaxed and friendlier.

The answer was no, which they could have told me on the phone, so I concluded the only reason I'd gone to New Orleans was to visit The Biker Bar, which was Bobbi's idea. She was a CSR, easy on the eyes, hard not to pay homage to as a female of outstanding good-looks.

I did have certain images of the my earlier days in Chicoutimi, Québec, a town incorporated only twenty-six years before my first arrival, where the only hotel was a staggered row of trailers with no restaurant and pump-out toilets. The place was rough and tough: Miners, woodsmen, and bikers with tattoos they probably etched themselves with switchblades and the blood of some guy they killed. They were riding Harleys and hogs, I was in a Malibu Classic painted baby-blue.

I stayed one night, walking to the restaurant, thinking that parking somewhere between fifty or sixty bikes might be a tad life-threatening, eating Salisbury steak and guzzling beer from the bottle while waiting for a fight to break out. Nothing happened.

Not like the night in Kingston, at Lino's, where my all-dressed and wine was interrupted when some biker guy from the bar across the street came in to bash in the face of some other guy who wasn't doing so well. Something about the first guy's bitch.

Anyway, Bobbi had long dark hair and tanned skin, which was an anomaly in The Swamp. She was slim, tight everywhere that showed and nicely rounded everywhere that didn't. She put into short shorts what they were intended for, and when she offered to pick me up at my hotel, well, what choice did I have? I was in.

I had seen photos of Bobbi in her cheerleader outfit, which was no preparation for what I saw at seven that night. It boggled a mind barely able to form pertinent questions. How did her boyfriend let her out like that, en route to pick up some other guy? And who cared?

Her legs were bare, but for ankle socks and sneakers, leading to matching filets mignons, soft and smooth, at the tattered edges of her shorts. Her midriff was bare, her tank-top neither tight nor loose, her bra straps delicate and disappointing despite being expensive. Her hair was in a ponytail, her lips bright red, curved into a bright smile.

The Biker Bar was fifteen minutes away. Other CSR ladies who owned bikes were expecting us. Bobbi told me she was more into cars, this one a Camaro convertible, though her shorts would definitely do any bike saddle justice.

The Daiquiri stand across from the hotel was our first stop. A daiquiri for Bobbi, scotch on the rocks for me, after which we made our way to The Biker Bar talking about anything and everything unrelated to work. The evening was memorable, sipping scotch while stopped at a red light beside a cop car winning second place. Patricia took first prize, tied with Bobbi, which would in itself be memorable.

There were 300 bikes or more, and more bikers, strewn around a little shack of a place that was practically empty. Everyone was drinking outside, sitting on their bikes, leaning on them or admiring them, bikes more desirable than girls in tank tops, bikini tops, cut-offs and chaps over bikini bottoms. Cops were in their cars at every corner, watching as bikers came and went, either holding their own beer or having their passenger hold two.

What truly amazed me was seeing Gina standing by the entrance of the shack, waiting for us. One never knows.

She didn't have a drink, Bobbi had finished hers and mine wasn't worth holding after so many minutes in swamp heat. I left them to correct the deficiency, to check out the inside.

The girl came to my shoulders. She had black hair ponytailed on one side, loose on the other. She wore stiletto heels, a once-piece backless and sheer teddy with a push-up bra she didn't need and spaghetti straps.

"Hi, I'm Patricia. May I model for you this evening?" She twirled. I didn't. "I'm wearing a one-piece design with very modest embroidery across the top edge of the bra and eyelets laced with silky ribbon that also enhances the centre front. It's American-made from a blend of spandex, viscose and nylon with a bottom snap for comfort and a lady's convenience. The price is forty-nine even, tax included."

She twirled once more, reading my mind.

"Does the bra have an under wire?" I knew about this stuff.

"It does have a removable under wire, and comes with inserts for affect, though I am not currently using them. I do, however, have other styles in various colours. May I change for you while you order your drink?"

Oh, yeah. Then, crap.

Gina and Bobbi came in together. Seeing I was involved in a business discussion, they interrupted. Gina looked at Patricia like she was a hooker; Bobbi looked at her as though tempted to touch what I wanted to touch.

I excused myself. I'd be right back. I ordered three drinks, paid, and went to where Bobbi was talking with Patricia.

"I also have a full line of reasonably priced and seductive chemises, panty and bra ensembles I would enjoy modelling for you and the ladies."

"Thank you, I normally take something home after a trip. I'd certainly like to see more."

And I believe Bobbi wanted to see more as well, but not Gina. We smiled, Patricia smiled. I glanced over my shoulder at Patricia. So did Bobbi. We smiled at each other, Gina ignoring us.

I had no idea ICS was home to so many Biker Babes. If there was one bike with dust on it, I didn't see it. There were muscles and tattoos, decals and mottos, pink bikes and blue, black bikes and white. The ladies knew their bikes as well as they knew their plastic belts.

Bobbi's boyfriend showed up later with other boyfriends. My flight was early the next morning. So after getting pink, red, mauve and mahogany kisses from the Biker Babes, Gina drove me to the hotel. I did invite her to an après-biker snack, but she'd made plans to be home. She did however make a small detour so I could jump into Hooter's and pick-up some requisite tee-shirts for Linda. The much sought-after orange shorts still beyond the average man's reach.

If I thought seeing Gina at the bar was surprising, nothing could have prepared me for the big hug and sisterly kiss when she dropped me off. Nearly three years had passed, but the ice had broken.

*

August 02nd was the first day of a new week after my trip to New Orleans, and I met with Mr. Hokum in the afternoon. The day was sunny, bright, warm, and I happily agreed when he suggested that we meet for a glass of wine at an outside terrace. Not his office. He wasn't one to ask questions prematurely and nothing regarding the decision to decline his distributorship was discussed until we sat with our glasses clinking together in good health.

I cut to the chase. ICS was indifferent, the decision disappointing. Discussing the illogic of the decision was pointless. The more important and immediate questions were: From what source would Yoakum Industries acquire plastic belt, and what were my plans?

Barnaby and I had formed a solid relationship over the previous year, one of mutual respect and measured openness. After all, we were competitors as often as not. He knew it was a matter of time before he lost his current source of plastic, and I knew my time was limited as well. I was reaching the saturation point with Mikey, wondering at what dark spot along which New Brunswick highway I'd throw him from the car the following week.

ICS was progressing steadily towards a telemarketing system: Internet belting, the way of the future. They were transmuting into a very high tech, human-indifferent machine powered to-date by multiple expendable sources, and those sources were becoming increasingly redundant.

Their pep rally slogan of short-term pain for long-term gain was wearing thin with those who'd become chronically pained. Within a span of fourteen months from Larry's departure, Boston, Chicago, New York, Philly, Charleston, New Orleans itself, and Vancouver had lost their sales reps one way or another.

They wanted customers to call them, to work with tech reps in Customer Service or with Sales Engineers. They envisioned a near future of three-dimensional imagery, of applications sent to them, possessing the capability to make recommendations interactively. They didn't want sales reps and their focus was increasingly national accounts.

I'd be gone by August 12th. Spending a week with Mikey in New Brunswick without stuffing him in the trunk or leaving him stranded in the dark in the middle of nowhere would be impossible, I told Barnaby. He'd met Mikey once, which was enough. He understood, offering me a job as Plastics Manager at Yoakum.

We poured more wine, shaking hands across the table.
*

Tuesday afternoon I called Gina, thinking I'd be pushing

the envelope, needing very much to satisfy my curiosity. She had no idea whether Corey was still travelling to Québec to see Blanchette. They were no longer her client.

The one way I could get that information was having Tom's code changed with mine, but I needed the help of someone who could switch the codes. We all knew each other's code, our initials, but information in the main database could only be read by a computer whose ID matched the user's initials. Seek and ye shall receive, if only for one hour, which was enough time for me to scan the files, print hard copies for later review, and make a few minor adjustments.

In fact, I saw nothing to review, nothing to print. There had been no activity for over a year, not since the joint call I'd made with Corey. Their largest Canadian customer purchased 500K annually and no one had visited them in over a year, when I was a three-hour drive away. The rest of the week was somewhat relaxed.

The following Monday I met my passenger at the hotel. I'd made his reservation for a standard room. I saw no need for him to know about the Executive Floor offering peace and quiet, breakfast, and a private lounge until 10:00 PM. The day began when I arrived from the airport and met him in the parking lot, popping the trunk.

Our first call was in Florenceville, an hour's drive from Fredericton where he should have flown into. But he'd listened to the corporate travel agent I never used, disregarding me. The agent said flying in and out of Moncton was less expensive, so we were in Moncton with three additional hours of unnecessary driving ahead of us and my first day wasted.

I arrived at his hotel at 12:30, arriving in Fredericton by three-thirty, much too late to get to Florenceville, Mikey waiting until I was turning into the hotel's entrance before asking if he could get some cigarettes in town. This after we'd driven the 300 kilometres on shit roads jammed with tourists in absolute silence. Not a word. They were too expensive in hotels. So, a U-turn and into town. Cheap bastard.

He wanted a tour, and dinner in town.

"Not a fucking chance."

He wrote a note.

At the hotel entrance, again, he began talking nervously, like the sneaky little thing he was.

"Why did you go to Nova Scotia for two weeks in July?"

"It was convenient. What's your point?"

"It was an unnecessary expense and one not approved by management."

"What management? What approval?"

"All unusual travel has to be approved, by me."

"It wasn't unusual. It's where most of the business is and the cost of the hotel was defrayed by the cost of a second airfare the following week. Also, are you at all aware of the business generated during that trip? What point are you trying to make exactly, Mikey?" I found myself leaning on the centre console, which probably accounted for the greasy smudges on the passenger-side window I noticed the next day.

"It wasn't your right to make that judgment. That's why there's management."

"Do I look fucking stupid to you?" Of course he wasn't going to answer me.

"There's no need for that."

"For what?"

He took a deep breath, turning a page in his day timer. He said: "If you want to move to Halifax you may do so at your own expense and if, after one year, we determine that you were successful and that your observations were correct, we'll reimburse you."

No One to Tell

He was on meds, the only plausible explanation. Any verbal response would have been pointless, a waste of good expletives; any other response, like throttling him by his little chicken neck would likely have been illegal, though in retrospect I'm not so sure. He was nervous, close to wetting his pants which was good enough for me. The time was right for me to make provisions for moving, though not to Halifax. Not yet.

I have a proclivity for order, uniformity and organization. I detest the opposites. Once, very early on at ICS, Gina had admonished me for organizing and streamlining the files in my computer, saying whatever changes I'd made were downloaded to the main database and irreversible. No different from saving a smaller file into a previously larger file, thereby deleting the excess data. Oops.

We drove in silence to Florenceville the next morning, spending the better part of the day in meetings during which Mikey said little. But he did take notes, all sorts of notes, one meeting lasting through to 12:15 in a town where people go home for lunch. Our next appointment was at the same location, though a different division, much of the forty-five minutes taken up at the guard house. Mikey complained. He was hungry. I commiserated, for the umpteenth time reading the inscriptions tacked into the frames of corporate portraits.

We left at three, at the hotel by 4:30. I wasn't stopping to eat. Mikey wrote notes. I was alone five minutes later. I would need all the privacy available. The following morning we would pass Florenceville once more on the way to Grand Falls to see yet another three divisions of the same company. There was a motel across from that plant, known for thin walls, giggles and other sounds of the newly acquainted, but I was going back to the capital for a drink, an in-room dinner and work. Mikey wrote notes.

No One to Tell

Silence is golden. He was in a part of the world he'd likely never see again and didn't ask one question, not gasping one breath at the expansive, wild and panoramic scenery.

The drive was 200 km on a two-lane highway, three hours of driving and we got to the plant close to ten. The first division I lined up brought us to noon, knowing the Plant Manager didn't accept invitations for lunch. He hated going home, but I knew he did like to talk. Perfect! And he was French, they all were. We were in northern New Brunswick, home of the want-to-be Québécois and Mikey was adrift in a sea of Acadian expressions that must have sounded like a dog barking gibberish. We left the divorcé at 12:30, went through guardhouse protocol and arrived at the second appointment moments before one. I spent the few minutes reviewing facts I knew the contact would have questions about.

When he came in he was friendly enough, completely ignoring Mikey. He didn't like tagalongs wasting his time with questions they already should have the answers to. He also knew in advance, as did the others, not to offer a plant tour. We were at the hotel by five-thirty.

Pulling into the entrance, I made the point very clearly, stopping in front of the main doors, making no attempt to get out.

When he did, he made no eye contact. Mikey didn't like other people's eyes; he liked his crotch. That's where he looked most times.

I couldn't choose my manager, but I could choose my dinner companion, so Mikey ate alone one last time. I returned a few hours later after a relaxing dinner in town, a view of the Saint John River, good scotch and where I could remember better times and smile a bit. My project was all but complete, with no need to rush the evening. Tomorrow would come soon enough, and be the last of four very long days and three longer nights.

The only thing missing along the old route #2 from Fredericton to Moncton was the occasional amphetamine outlet. It's near 200 km of narrow, twisting and potholed asphalt with nothing to see beyond a few beat up shacks and the occasional car that speeds by and disappears in front or behind.

During the drive I thought to a time twenty-years earlier when I'd been driving at 120 km on route #108. The road was mostly used for logging, unpaved with a gravel surface and 150 km from one nowhere to another. My Monte Carlo was brand new and shiny when the trip began, not so when it ended. Not even halfway along the road a semi loaded to maximum capacity or more with logs tore by in a cloud of pellets, dust and wind, delivering two spud-sized missiles into the car. One rock lodged in the windshield, creating a fist-sized decoration in line with my face, the other took out the entire driver-side headlight assembly. How nice it would have been to see Mikey with a made-to-measure stone gag, with no malice intended.

We arrived in Moncton not long after one o'clock for a meeting lasting until two, the second until three. The third was a bottle plant for beverages. Mikey's supposed speciality with nothing more to talk about during the one-hour meeting than the home life in Britain that he missed so much and the golf prizes strewn across the floor.

The Plant Manager was British, but could have given a hoot. He was more interested in the 1.14 litre of Johnnie Walker Black I'd given him as a prize for golf his golf tournament. The bottle was tucked into his drawer, won by him in a tournament not yet played.

At 3:30 I stood to leave, explaining that my flight was in an hour. The visit was strictly PR. In and out. We shook hands and I left, footsteps following me down the staircase that I assumed were Mikey's. If not, he was going in a taxi.

No One to Tell

*

I stopped for gas before dropping off the car, Mikey standing well over to the far end for a cigarette. Perhaps he was thinking that I'd douse him and he didn't want to take a chance.

Over the previous four days we'd driven 1400 kilometres, the only conversation when pulling into the hotel before and after he'd bought his cigarettes. He was looking at the ground, or his crotch, ignoring me until hearing the engine turn over. I wasn't waiting.

I parked the car. He went to the men's room to gaze at his crotch. I went to check-in. When I went to the rental counter, he was standing like a sightless person in rush-hour traffic. His head was swivelling, like one of those dashboard springy-neck ornaments. My flight was leaving in ten minutes, sufficient time to return the keys.

"We need to talk."

I was already talking with the rental agent.

Fourteen-hundred km with his Mute on and little Mikey needed to talk. "What about Mikey?"

"Outside would be better."

"No." I tapped my watch. "Five minutes, Mikey. No can do. Besides, think that's really a good idea?"

When I stepped from the counter he handed me a scrap of paper, scribbled reminders, his week's work torn from his day timer, a list of what I was to return to the company without delay.

Oh, Mikey. I crumpled it, the ball landing between his feet. "Fuck you, squirt."

He stooped to retrieve it. What kind of man would do that? A Mikey.

I moved a tad closer so the world wouldn't hear, though I could see peripherally that a security officer was a little interested.

I said, "Listen, Mikey, you sneaky shit. Shove it up

your ass."

"I need your computer."

"In your dreams, little guy."

Then he yelled out, "Nothing personal! Nothing personal! You will not say anything personal! Do you hear me!?"

"They do, Mikey."

He looked around, his face red with rage. Like that mattered. He'd lost control, attracting a crowd, many of whom would be on his flight because the passengers on my flight had boarded.

I wanted to tell him that I'd yanked his chain all week, that I was very soon joining Yoakum, but this was more rewarding, more of a payback for all his bullshit.

"I'll courier it, Mikey, with the rest of the list that comes type-written and signed from Stan's office. Not his go-boy."

I walked into security.

Poor Mikey was having a seizure. He was at the end of his leash. He left his suitcase and briefcase, following me through security. Not because he wanted my computer, because he was terrified of telling Stan he hadn't accomplished such a simple task. He hadn't grown the problem. Of course, the guards halted him. Two, with a backup not far off.

The lady scanning me stood ready to check my briefcase as I removed the laptop, tossing it to Mikey across five or six metres past the guards' desk. Five-minute Mikey could have caught it between his eyeballs; they bulged out so much when he saw the empty thing flying his way.

"Don't bother reading it, Mikey. Moot point that you have it, really. Regards to Stan."

Onboard I felt good; massages on the beaches of Punta Cana kind of good, and the Johnnie Walker Black was good, for medicinal purposes.

R.I.P.

Steve returned to live in Texas. He flew home onboard his brother's private jet. So let's not worry about Steve.

Larry took up the position of North American Director of Sales and Marketing at Shenandoah Belting. He was Floridian by birth, eager to escape the still, wet air of The Swamp.

Wayne left shortly after me, demotivated with no intention reporting to a village idiot.

Mikey was a fool; still is wherever he is. Fools don't get better with age. They grow the problem while waiting too long to expire. His contribution to the company was equal to Mikey's significance as a person. Somewhat meaningless. The industry's grapevine was very aware that Mikey was applying for one job after another at various competitors and OEMs, Stan's five PM call coming too late. Mikey was crossing the street to Swiss in Georgia. Though knowing the Swiss proclivity for intelligence and substance, Mikey would have been wise to rent in Georgia.

Gina left shortly after for a job in Communications, though she did call me to say goodbye, just a little curious about her files. I chuckled, telling her to check Tom's.

Stan was, Stan is,

Corey was a five PM message soon after his last debacle. Beyond that, who cares?

As for The Oracle who loved to say "be brutally honest," perhaps it's a good thing he wore Dockers and not a uniform.

As for John, he's probably divorced, or sharing his shaver.

As for me, I switched to premium vodka and swore off cigars.

No One to Tell

Chapter Ten
1999 - 2002

Eighteen minutes. I felt like a kernel in a carnival popcorn maker, pissed with Murphy for personal reasons. I wasn't sitting beside Legs.

I'd always promised myself, Linda knew, that if I was going to die in the air, or because of it, that I'd die smiling with something pretty either in my hands or slapping my face. What the hell. Legs would be screaming anyway.

We were close to the airport, not close enough. That's where most shit happens.

We were about to land, my last business flight. Somehow I knew, an overwhelming gut feeling, a good feeling. Audelle had hired someone that week whom she believed was perfect for the job of managing a sales team. She was very good at hiring the right people, which is why she'd gone through one rep a month and four managers in two plus years. She was decidedly not a good businesswoman, nor was she human. No doubt, that at night her fangs came out and her eyes glowed red to prowl dark streets.

He was an economist, the new guy, who'd never made a sales call, who'd never had anyone tell him to fuck off to his face, at least not yet, who'd never had an old rosy-cheeked fishwife chase him around an office trying to grab his balls like the chubby cherub what chased me right quick-like around a client's desk in Cape Breton. The first time I'd swung a customer in circles trying to save the boys.

I'd won, however. Victorious. The day was mine. I thought.

The meeting went well. Time to go, time to stop talking, time to cover my ass. Agh! Too late. Chubby and eager hands squeezing hard enough to brand me, half a cigarette pinched in her stained lips like a thick skewer in raw beef.

"If not yer balls, yer arse'll do just fine, dearie Are ye busy fer dinner?"

Oh, yeah.

Over the previous two years air travel had become increasingly mundane, the best hotels boring, my schedule exceeding fifty percent. I wasn't allowed to develop business at home, strictly in the Southeast where I travelled every other week, at times more often.

At home, weeks were spent booking hotels, flights, cars and writing my first novels. Travelling, I seldom exceeded five, possibly six appointments while working on *The Viewing Room* and *The 4th Man* at night and the occasional late-day poolside.

I'd never had such an easy sales job or such an easy product, deprived of challenge for two reasons: The product was the best, and I was. What I looked forward to, what elated me, was the travel, the experiences, the people. Well beyond Murphy's capabilities, the challenge wasn't selling, rather to whom I sold. That set me apart; that made Audelle money.

Murphy hadn't spoken a single word to Legs. Perhaps he knew. I certainly did, reminiscent of Corey from Colorado and the chic lady in Québec.

*

I left ICS behind August 12th, the moment I boarded the plane. I received a letter from Stan, signed, a few loose ends

No One to Tell

were dealt with honorably between us and a severance cheque above and beyond for an amount considerably in excess of what one would have expected for only three plus years. That alone told me I'd done something right, the reason I didn't kick Mikey in the tonsils at the airport. The car was returned, another one acquired, and I was once again free to breathe.

Whether or not the chicken came before egg is irrelevant. The inevitable is a function of time, and my time had come once again. The whys and the wherefores don't matter; but the need for change did matter, as evidenced by what had begun to peer at me through the mirror.

Current events in The Swamp clearly didn't have the best interests of the sales force incorporated in their design. The pep rally slogan of short-term pain for long-term gain had transmuted into chronic pain with no relief in sight.

I had one phone conversation with Barnaby Hokum to confirm my availability, and one lunch meeting held outside the office. We agreed on the terms and conditions, shook hands, and the contract was signed later. Barnaby's handshake was as good as ink.

Yoakum was a company of twenty-three people, from Barnaby to the shipper. A far cry from ICS, the reason I accepted Barnaby's offer the day I delivered New Orleans' negative response. Yoakum was what I needed to reawaken the senses and bring a value to me equal to the value I would bring them. The sales force was small, three outside reps, one of whom was the Sales Manager and two inside reps. That would soon change.

They weren't a technical sales force, unfamiliar with formulae and calculations.

Barnaby wanted them brought to a higher level that would equip them to compete in an industry increasingly more technical and more controlled by manufacturers, which was half my mandate. The other half was developing the plastic line itself, once we determined whose product that would be.

Césaire was the senior inside sales rep, with the company fifteen years. He was extremely conversant with their existing products. As was Marcel, who'd been there a few years less as number two inside. Elmer was an outside rep with the company for eighteen months with no previous product or application experience. He'd left his job in a tire store when the position became available, his father convincing Barnaby to try the kid. His father, Henry, was the Operations and Purchasing Manager. Clément had been with Barnaby for two years, ex-military, with no previous selling or belting experience. Félix was Sales Manager, though he preferred being called Perfect.

One of my questions to Barnaby concerned Félix's probable reaction to my position and mandate in the company. He responded that Félix was given his chance. The time had come for new blood, a new way of thinking.

I wasn't expected at Yoakum until 100 years earlier, October 04, 1899: how I felt the day I walked through the doors for the first time as Plastics Manager.

*

The company building looked like an old country-styled cottage nestled in an idyllic setting between widespread farms dotting the side road leading to Vermont through the scenic wine region. In the winter the landscape was postcard white, in the spring and summer lush and green. In the early fall, an artist's palette of rich earth tones mixed with reds and gold before the stark bareness of late fall.

This particular October 04th was unfriendly and cold, snowing prematurely in the Cantons of Québec. The usual gold and red leaves of autumn were monochromatic white, sagging under the unexpected weight. Driving required caution, as did treading from my parking spot to the front door at Yoakum Industries. Once inside, mental agility was

No One to Tell

requisite.

I'd been there many times over the previous several years, particularly over the past twelve months, so walking through the door wasn't unfamiliar to me. What surprised me were the expressions on their faces. At 8:30 Monday morning the sign read: Welcome James T. Barrett. When I might well have been warned to: Run! Get Out Of Here! You have been lured to Goonieville! Get out while you can!

I wouldn't know for several months that Barnaby had waited until the previous Friday afternoon to tell them I was coming to rock their quiet and idyllic world.

When I joined Yoakum I was the only rep in the industry with pan-Canadian experience. I had a lot to offer them. My role was four-fold and not strictly related to the growth of plastic sales or the acquisition of new business. I was also responsible for modernizing the sales force, introducing a methodology and implementing a sales training programme.

I was in sales for seven years before the introduction of fax machines; twelve before my first answering machine; fifteen before my first car phone; seventeen before I had a PC and cellphone; twenty-one before my first laptop and voice-mail; and twenty-four before hooking-up my scanner. Then, I joined Yoakum Industries and had to start all over again.

Félix was with the company fourteen of its eighteen years, Sales Manager for most of that time without training. Neither was he aware of my pending arrival until the Friday, or of my mandate. Or who I would not report to. That stipulation was one of my pre-conditions, the other was that I'd have carte blanche to do what was necessary to bring their sales team to the higher level Barnaby needed.

To cushion the blow Barnaby promoted Félix to VP of Sales, an honorary position at best.

Félix would continue overseeing traditional flat belting,

distributed on behalf of a half-dozen manufacturers. The two sales reps and the two inside reps would report to him regarding those products. All five of them, including Félix and the new hires would report to me regarding plastic, expected to embrace new technologies and processes. I wasn't usurping Félix. Nor did I intend to, but the shit was already en route to the fan. I endangered him; he knew he couldn't keep up with the momentum. Nor with me. I also knew his dirty little secret, reawakened on the Friday. I didn't hire him. He wasn't good enough.

Eight and a half years earlier, interviewing potential Montreal reps for Euro, Félix was one of the applicants. At the time we knew each other by name and reputation. He asked and I invited him to interview as a potential candidate. He didn't make the second round. Strangely, throughout my time at Euro, and the number of times I'd met with Barnaby while at ICS, I never saw him. I imagine his jaw hit the ground pretty hard that night before having a few too many.

Barnaby was wrong to bring me into the company that way. For someone supposedly thoughtful and considerate of others, he was incredibly insensitive to the feelings of a very tightly knit group. He should have known better, despite his desperation, and should have foreseen the consequences.

That said, he did need to lift the puppy's paws from the floor. And did a fine job.

Barnaby owned the company, whereas Félix had come to own the people who were too naïve to see through him. That changed when I walked through the door, and Félix knew the precise moment his protective bubble began to chafe, a bubble that would burst completely seven months later.

Because Félix had dominion over his minions, his believers, in a benevolent, mesmerizing way, Barnaby needed help regaining the control he'd lost. He didn't possess the vitality to revitalize his environment. He lacked familiarity with methodology; he wasn't skilled at mentoring, unable to shape the sales force he envisioned. Neither did he have the technical expertise. By his admission he'd been out of active selling too many years.

*

Barnaby had a penchant for privacy. Very few outsiders ever got to see the inside workings of Yoakum, me included. I'd seen his private office and the conference room adjacent to Félix's office. Nothing else.

I hadn't thought to ask where I'd spend my time. I took for granted they would at least have a chair for me, if not an office. Not quite. Apparently Barnaby hadn't thought about that particular need and for the first three months I made use of the conference room, which delighted Félix to no end.

At the end of the first Monday, Félix advised me in Barnaby's office that he'd scheduled a one-hour meeting for the sales group the coming Friday, which he believed would be a good time for my first technical presentation to the group. I agreed immediately with a smile. No time like the present. If they were going to get their feet wet, they might as well jump in, though I advised Félix I would require three full hours, not part of one.

I spent the following three days in my home office preparing a presentation comprising competitive data sheets, printouts of calculations and conversion and cross reference sheets I'd designed to show all the available products in relation to one another. They would also hear about applications, successes, failures, and the reasons for each.

When we met in the conference room Friday, there was no need to take notes and no one did. The presentation was complete, each one with a binder containing current data in a format they could reference any time. The questions came steadily, some for the sake of knowledge, most for the sake of challenge.

I'd prepared and conducted the entire meeting in French as a courtesy to them because everyone had French names but Elmer, everyone speaking French. No big deal. Very near the end, before the shop segment, Félix interjected that I could speak English if I preferred because everyone understood English but not the French terminology used in plastic.

So he tried to make me appear stupid. Virtually impossible. And he berated them, though no one realized. From then on I spoke French strictly to Marcel, the ladies and the guys in the shop.

When Félix spoke to me I answered in English, when he answered me he did so in French. Sort of a mutual flipping of the bird.

During the shop session, he asked me how I would determine whether a module was polyethylene or propylene. I told him to take note of the PP or PE imprint on the underside of the module. Or, if he preferred, verify the specific gravity with a water test. Then he pulled out a lighter, put the flame to the plastic and inhaled the spiral of toxic smoke, claiming PP had a lighter, less dense smoke than PE. I asked him if he performed at parties and, if he did, did he remember those parties the next day, which pretty much set the tone of our relationship.

When the meeting finished, I thanked Félix for the opportunity, suggesting the following Friday would be an excellent time for me to learn more about the guys, and for them to learn more about me. So, let's do lunch, Félix…in Montreal.

During those first weeks I'd also been in contact with my previous key accounts, most of whom weren't aware I'd left ICS months earlier, explaining I would see them as soon as possible with information on a new source of plastic distributed by Yoakum.

I wasn't late arriving at the restaurant; they'd arrived early. I was interrupting their meeting in progress. Félix, Elmer and Clément were drinking beer. I ordered wine, we ordered lunch and began with little preamble. I'd met previously with Félix to give him information on the content of the meeting, certain the others were fully up-to-date. The previous Friday they had a few questions, now all they had was attitude and resentment towards Barnaby.

First they had to understand what the status quo was. They asked me what I meant. Good start. I asked what they didn't like about the company, what they would change. Elmer said "everything," confirmed by Clément who claimed Barnaby never listened to them. I asked for an example and they both looked at Félix who was Perfect in their eyes.

All they could come up with was their car allowance.

"When was the last time you spoke with him?" They looked at Félix again.

"I talk with him often, with the same results."

"You talk with him. What about these guys?"

"Uh, they're new. They don't know him the way I do."

Meaning Félix would sometimes meet with Barnaby to discuss matters, reporting back to Elmer, Clément, and sometimes Césaire and Marcel. In the years he'd been Sales Manager, he'd never invited Barnaby to a sales meeting and Barnaby never thought to attend. We didn't speak much about territories, sales figures and quotas, which would come later when doing joint calls with all three to help them develop plastic business. In the meantime of greater importance was knowing about me and my mandate.

I spoke about Territory Management and grid plans, the ratio of sales calls to sales dollars, Pre-Call Planning and Action Business Plans, which would eventually be interactive. To work with engineers, plant managers and vie for capital projects and large-scale maintenance projects they'd have to develop a sense for consultative selling and long sales cycles. They were accustomed to taking orders of four or 500, not forty or 50K, one of the reasons ABP and Pre-Call were mandatory. What did I mean by interactive?

One of them lived over 100 km from the office, the other about twenty and Félix about sixty. Each one went to the office every day and, most times, stayed or returned to have lunch with Barnaby at his favourite restaurant. When I had earlier asked Barnaby what the deal was, I sat stupefied. The routine was to leave for lunch near 11:45, spending an hour or more at the restaurant, then driving to the office before setting out again.

I asked how many calls they made each week, all answering nineteen or twenty with no idea of how long the visits lasted. The answer was: not very.

I told them that as soon as possible they would be enjoying the freedom of working from remote home offices with new computers, interactive Account Management software, faxes and e-mail. They looked at Félix, all three laughing.

"You need phones for that," said Félix, splitting a gut.

"What's your point?"

"Our phones are outdated. We can't even dial directly. We need to place a dial tone box over the mouthpiece each time we call out to create a dial tone before we dial. We don't have voice-mail and we can't connect an answering machine."

"How do you know whether someone's called after hours, on the weekend, or while the lines are tied up?"

"We don't."

"Then we get new phones and voice-mail. No problem."

By this time they thought I was an absolute asshole, an outsider with absolutely no clue about what was going on, and to some degree they weren't wrong.

Félix put down his beer. He hadn't finished drinking; he just couldn't drink and laugh at the same time. "I've been asking forever for computers and new stuff. Good luck. The old man will never spend the money. He's too cheap."

"It's not luck, Félix. It's ROI."

"What's that, ROI?"

"It's what will get you computers and a new phone system with voice-mail."

Well, they thought that was hilarious. When I left they stayed, no doubt laughing, though before leaving I gave Elmer a list of companies in New Brunswick and PEI whom I'd contacted to set up meetings to introduce him and Yoakum. We left two weeks later for a week of enticing ICS customers over to Yoakum.

Another project was hiring someone to represent plastic in Ontario. Barnaby had visions of becoming a countrywide firm, and he wanted his first step westward planted in Ontario. I'd been in the company two weeks and already Barnaby was getting a big bang for his buck; I was on a high, enjoying the moment.

*

On the Tuesday of the third week I called Elmer to ask what airport I should meet him at in New Brunswick the following week. The air went quiet. We weren't flying.

Say what?

"Barnaby doesn't want to spend the money."

"Did he say that?"

"Nah, we just know."

"How do you know if he didn't say it?"

"It's always been that way. Félix knows all that stuff. Ask him."

"What's the plan?"

Elmer spoke in a monotone, said "uh" before every second word and sucked on his lips as he spoke. He wasn't ready for large crowds. He was a Gomer, and I made a note to speak with him about taking a public speaking course.

The plan was to leave by car Sunday morning, arrive in Grand Falls by dinnertime and at the food plant across the road by 8:00 AM Monday. We would stay a second night, drive to Florenceville, call on a number of people, stay at a roadside motel I didn't stay at with Mikey and go through two other small towns with limited potential before arriving in Saint John late Wednesday. Thursday was all about Saint John and Friday we would drive to Blacks Harbour before returning to Saint John. Driving home Saturday he would arrive home after dinnertime, me an hour later. I wanted to choke the little fucker.

The plan wasn't bad, if one could disregard wasted driving time, leaving on Sunday, driving on Saturday and staying in cheap motels. He only had to change one appointment and we left early Monday morning to arrive in Grand Falls by noon. Friday we left Blacks Harbour at four and got home after midnight. He had those extra days with his family, between which we did good business and he even cracked a smile.

I thought we'd be out of the plant by eleven, maybe twelve, but there was so much to do we stayed until the evening shift began. The only break all day was the thirty minutes we took to grab a few sandwiches from the local supermarket.

We both began eating the sandwiches before getting to the cash. Elmer was first in line. He handed his sandwich in its open wrapping to one girl who scanned it before passing it to the other who bagged it, putting her hand into the bag to make sure the sandwich wasn't squashed. Elmer watched all this thinking she was pretty efficient. He paid and left, wondering why I was laughing. I'd peeled the label from mine for scanning, declined the bag and followed behind him.

"What's so funny?"

He pulled the second half of his sandwich from the bag and began eating.

"She had her hands all over your sandwich."

"It's wrapped. What's the big deal?"

The side of his face was bulging with food, like a deprived squirrel.

"While you were watching the girl at the cash, the one with your bag had her finger up her nose like she was scratching her brain before bagging the sandwich. Good thing she didn't have a hangnail."

The mush in his mouth hurled out with a single cough.

Peter gave Elmer the same tour he'd given Steve a few years earlier, only this time the robotic system was complete, working like a charm. His main concern was a belt that had been in operation for fifteen years, completely unidentifiable and in need of change.

Like most fisheries, they waited until the last minute and wanted the replacement yesterday. We left Peter with a request to quote. ICS and Sea & Double U's Newfoundland competitor were also quoting. We were third, with equal opportunity, Elmer balanced between ecstasy and despondency throughout the 1100 km to his home

The following Monday his euphoria was replaced by too many negatives to enumerate. Elmer's father had all the reasons why we wouldn't get the order all but alphabetized. Félix agreeing the contract was beyond the capability of the people in production and Césaire didn't know if he could get his hands on enough belting from the then backdoor source. Barnaby looked at me.

"What's the probable value of a belt like that?"

"Forty-five to fifty K, US."

"When does he want it?"

"Two weeks after he places the order."

My response had Henry gasping for air. Seeing a living

person's face that purple was rare.

He was having an anxiety attack and I left them to work things out. I had to get a recruitment ad into the Toronto newspapers, plan a trip to Newfoundland, plan a second trip with Elmer to PEI and New Brunswick and spend two days with Clément. I was most looking forward to preparing for a meeting one week away with the Director of Sales and Marketing at Shenandoah Belting.

Clément drew the short stick, not very pleased about spending any time with the asshole, me.

*

Clément came from the military, with a brief stop at MacLeary where he worked in the shop.

He knew squat about sales, absolutely devoid of any redeeming qualities as a sales person, and many normally considered as requisite for being a human. He was the classic village idiot. He wore a brass belt buckle the size of a flagstone, black jeans permanently bowed from repeated wears and thick-soled shoes that were oily more than polished.

Irrespective of season, an array of colourful shirts opened down the front would frame a white tee-shirt held in place by the brass flagstone. That is until he was gripped by the desire to yank it out to reveal and massage the giant white pod beneath. He could also pick at any orifice while carrying on a conversation, discarding the various findings against himself or onto the floor without any pause whatsoever. His outerwear most days was a shiny, multi-coloured, polyester baseball jacket with blue and white ribbing one the sleeves and a frayed elastic waist. He thought because he spoke French and English, he spoke them well. He didn't. He was a monosyllabic moron with an unusable hole in his face. That's what waited for me on the Wednesday of my sixth week, which could have been the Tuesday, but he was unable to make any appointments at nine in morning.

The receptionist wasn't Madame; she was toi, as one would address a girlfriend.

"Yeah, yeah. He'll see me. We're like that," crossing his fingers to indicate to her the closeness he shared with the supposed contact. "Yeah, yeah, he's with me." He looked at me. "What? How come? I had an appointment." He put down his box. "I know I had one, I'm pretty sure. Call him back, c'mon. I only need a minute."

One minute. Really? Maybe I'd underestimated this guy. He must be good if he could conduct business in a minute, and I noticed he was confident as well. The box he'd used to carry in samples was covered with the name and advertising of our competitor. Nor did he need a briefcase. His writing pad from yet another competitor was sitting atop the mound of samples.

I'd never done a lobby call, having surreptitiously joined in on many. On the few occasions that talking business in a lobby was the only option, having an appointment, my reaction to clients was to thank them and say I'd come back at a more convenient time. Nor would I ever do a sales call standing or with my coat on.

As Paul said to me twenty-five years earlier, describing those who do cold calls, Clément was proving himself the Village Idiot. He had just enough time before the client came to stretch widely with both arms, yawn almost as widely, scratch himself where the men's room might have been a more appropriate venue, stoop for the box and stand semi-erect.

When the client arrived they shook hands for the sake of convention, the client shaking his head, looking at his watch as he pushed through a door with Clément in tow.

The man wasn't expecting us. He didn't want us there. Worse yet, his need was unknown to Clément, to himself, and to me. We were together not five minutes from top to bottom and when I shook hands with him I apologized for the inconvenience. I wasn't aware. He commiserated.

Out by our cars, Clément said he thought he could have one more call, maybe two. Better calls, guys he knew. I didn't say goodbye or bugger off before driving home. I had nothing else to learn about Clément. Whereas he was about to learn a lot about me.

*

When the industry became aware of my departure from ICS I received a phone call from Jon II at Swiss BeltTech asking if I'd be interested in joining them as Plastics Manager. They'd taken on a new line of plastic manufactured to their specifications and needed someone to spearhead the effort. There would have been a time when Jon II and I would have worked well together, but that time had passed. I declined the offer, saying I'd already agreed to join Yoakum, which was certainly the main reason; though rejoining Swiss would have contravened my lifelong credo of not going back, never looking back.

Unexpectedly, the week before my meeting with Shenandoah, the Montreal Swiss rep who replaced me when I left, called me at home to discuss on behalf of Jon II whether I would reconsider. No. The marriage would be short-lived and the in-laws would have much to do with it. I knew I wouldn't be well-received by Gene, and I could see my personality conflicting with Jon's. Too much had changed. Also, I knew Ken didn't believe what he was telling me.

*

Larry was again in the picture, as debonair as ever, complete with silver hair, blue suit and red tie. He sported a wide-brimmed hat, comfortable in his Dick Tracey coat. As usual, when he walked through the door into the room, the room became Larry's.

He was in his second year at Shenandoah, ready to

implement projects he'd developed during that time. He'd brought with him to Shenandoah a suitcase of intellectual goodies that included my plan for the Maritimes, the document that spoke to the need for distribution, and Yoakum was his primary choice. Along with that baggage he brought the guys he'd stolen from ICS.

He called Barnaby for a meeting at some point during my ICS negotiations with him, understanding that Barnaby was waiting for the final decision from me, all the while knowing what that decision would be and that Barnaby would soon invite him to the table.

Those preliminary negotiations took the direction Larry expected, though I only became aware of that on October 04th when I called Larry to arrange a meeting.

The negotiations lasted a few months, the contract making Yoakum their exclusive distributor across Canada with the first shipment of plastic delivered at the end of the month. Sufficient in quantity for Félix to sniff.

The deal was a win-win, but demanding, requiring that we also represent their steel belting, most everyone at Yoakum convulsing. The reason was pricing, and more work. They were expensive, one of the most expensive. Félix, Elmer and Clément the recipients of more bad news: They could no longer sell on price. They could no longer trade goods for dollars and Barnaby was committed to going beyond Ontario, into Manitoba, Saskatchewan and Alberta. British Columbia was on hold.

Marty was the Shenandoah liaison. I was the Yoakum counterpart. Dual communication barriers primarily preventing Clément and Elmer from making a mess of matters they weren't privy to.

*

Even though we signed the contract in January, the agreement in principal was set and the rest was a matter of fine-tuning the document. With that I went to

No One to Tell

Newfoundland to meet with Terry and Kelvin, taking Barnaby along for the ride.

He'd been to the island once before, when he'd tried to meet with Sea & Double U without success. That's why he was there: Terry wanted to see who he might be doing business with. I was in the unique position of knowing Terry's company inside out. I knew the requirements, the customer base, their pricing and competition. I'd even begun conversations with the president of the Danish company who was their competitor's source on the off chance Shenandoah would fall through.

Shenandoah's product line wasn't as extensive as ICS's, Larry's main objective during his first year in Virginia. His solution: Create a product line made up of styles common to the widest number of industries and applications. All of which Sea & Double U required.

Preferential pricing was based on a pre-determined volume, the lead-time was cut in half, and I continued working on the island on their behalf. In addition to which we stocked for them in sufficient quantities to maintain promised deliveries and emergencies.

The trip was brief. We saw a few key accounts, Barnaby put faces to names, and I made more headway for and with Sea & Double U. In that sales is a self-serving career.

At night we did our own thing, except for one evening at Linda's bar in Quidi Vidi.

*

Linda was 1, 25 metres in all directions with arms like sides of beef and a belly that created a convenient resting place for her not so tiny breasts which were level with the countertop and teat-like. No one would ever think to call them titties. Her hair was thick and black, her eyebrows like thick black caterpillars dead on her face. Her cheeks were red, her nose redder, her mouth opened onto unmatched rows of yellow and jagged teeth interspersed with gaping holes. Her ears were large with black sprouts of untrimmed hair growing from within at all angles and various lengths. She was a looker in her tight sweater and tight black skirt, her one good eye fixed on Barnaby.

"Well, now, aren't ye a fine lookin' man. I loves a man what has a beard, I do. What's yer pleasure, Dearie?" She laid her arms across the bar, winking at Barnaby who hadn't had such an invitation in years, her other eye wandering behind a greyish fog.

He stepped back, giggling, bringing his hand to his mouth to cover the glitter from his partial.

"Do you have red wine?"

"It's a fuckin' bar, Dearie Of course we have fuckin' red wine, though not the fancy stuff you be used to." She turned to me, staying near Barnaby. "And you, sir? What be yer pleasure?"

"Johnnie Walker, Red, neat. Please"

"Red JW, neat. Now that'll straighten the hairs on yer balls. And, please." She turned her neck, not her torso, looking past Barnaby, managing to tighten the loose skin on one side of her neck and bunch it up on the other. "Did ye hear that, Patrick? Please, he said. When was the last time ye heard please in 'ere, then? Quite the gent, he be, this one."

Patrick put the book he was reading onto the bar top, joining us. He stood erect, his face craggy with the worry and weather of his years, coloured with fine red lines from his many nights at Linda's. He was wearing a lightweight raincoat with its collar up over a heavy wool sweater and a wide-brimmed fedora angled for effect. He was the local gentry and very much the bon vivant in a village of fifty fishermen and Linda. He left his empty glass behind, asking Linda to fill another, in fact three more if we would join him in a toast to our beautiful barmaid.

She looked at us. We both said "beer." He was paying.

Asking what kind was pointless; it was bound to be the "fuckin" best."

Patrick was a writer of some renown. Everyone in town knew he'd written a book about his family and friends, his acquaintances and public figures. Perhaps we'd read it? Perhaps we would like to? Even Barnaby who didn't get out much knew we had to escape, Linda sliding steins in front of us by the time introductions were made.

"Linda, Love. Sit with us. Take a load off yourself. You've been standing all the while."

"I'm fine where I am. Me legs are strong enough to hold this fine form all day and all night, if needs be."

"Aye, that's no lie. It's truly a fine figure of a woman that you are, my love."

She gave him the finger. "Up yer arse with a pick for that, Patty boy."

"Thrombosis, Love. Give your tired legs a break while I guide these fine gentlemen through the pages of my adventures. Relax your garters and sit with us."

I didn't like the sound of that "pages of my adventures." Oh, shit.

"Thrombosis me flat arse. Me legs are just fine. And just so's ye know, I don't use no fuckin' garters. T'is the stiff hairs what stick out from the back of me legs what sticks through and holds the fuckers up."

Barnaby was choking on his beer, with more on his face than in his mouth. Patrick began with tales of his cousin in Gander, his mothers here and his fathers there. My beer was half gone; Barnaby's still full. Which wasn't helping us escape any faster.

"Linda, love, would you be so kind as to get me two copies of my book for these kindly gentlemen." He raised his glass to our health a second time; the first was when we came in, Barnaby nodding too quickly to acknowledge him. Seems I had a few things to teach Barnaby as well.

She didn't go far, groping under the counter.

"Gentlemen, allow me." He opened one, pen in hand.

"How much?" I asked.

At that he put a hand to his heart. I'd crushed him. Go figure. He would never think of charging such worldly gentlemen for such a simple and modest work, his gift to us, his brethren in a callous and changing world, men of honour and propriety charged with the responsibility of upholding decency, defending gallantry and good manners.

"Gentlemen, raise your glasses." He raised his to his mouth, draining the contents.

My glass was beside Patrick's who turned to Barnaby, whose glass was stuck to his face like a respirator. He was a wine drinker. Chugging beers was new to him.

"Gentlemen, another I say! The evening is at its conception."

"Yeah, but we're not." I interjected, pulling out my billfold. "How much for the beer?"

"That'll be a fiver, eh." Linda held out her hand at right angles to her forearm mounted vertically on the bar.

"For the three."

Patrick looked my way. "Oh! Sir, that thou be so kind." He stepped back, bowing deeply from the waist, somewhat unsteadily. "Your most humble of servants, kind sir."

"That'd be two more of these fine blue bills, then." A little bit of spittle hit the bar that she wiped with her forearm, standing on her tiptoes.

I put two tens over the damp smear, picked up the book, said goodbye and shook hands with the local celebrity. Barnaby took a final sip, shook hands, took his copy and we both got out before Linda decided she might like a goodnight kiss from Barnaby who was the quintessential family man. But easy money says he could have swooned Linda that night.

*

December took me into New Brunswick and PEI with Elmer. Most of his territory was in the Maritimes and meeting with ICS key accounts while I was still fresh in their minds was crucial.

Not trusting Elmer, I booked the flights. He booked the car. I thought he'd be pleased with an early morning flight that would get us in by mid-morning Monday. Not so. Not that I cared. He wanted to leave Sunday, driving, which was a thing of the past.

I'd given Barnaby more examples than he cared to have of how driving, hotels, meals and time lost were losing him thousands each year and Elmer was taking his first of many steps into a new era that he would fight against all the way.

I asked him to meet me in the VIP lounge where we could go over our plans for the week, have something to eat and relax away from the bustling crowds. I also thought he'd like that, but he didn't. He came in dressed like a small town Bubba with brown-laced shoes that Barnaby was too young to wear, white socks, blue jeans that hadn't been blue in a while, and a chequered shirt with a white tee-shirt underneath. He was quite a sight, several passengers in the lounge pausing a moment to study the spectacle that Elmer completed with his coat when our flight was called.

He was 1.9 metres in a coat that would embarrass a sixth grader. The apparent hand-me-down was cinched at the waist with drawstrings; the cuffs were easily fifty centimetres above his wrist and the bottom came to the pockets of his jeans. He looked goofy. He was goofy, a Bubba who'd borrowed Pa's wagon to come to town for the supplies on Mama's list, and maybe catch a peek at some of them there city folk, maybe even a peep show. What he did like, however, was that I'd pre-booked both our seats well apart from each other. Imagine how happy I was.

I have no recollection of why he wanted to book the car, but he did. He reserved a sub-compact that wasn't ready when we got to the airport in Moncton. When he came to explain the delay I said: "Just as well. Get a full size," and he started sucking on his lips and making noises reminiscent of a clogged drain.

Not quite my reaction at day's end when I discovered too late where he expected me to spend the night, causing to contemplate where I could bury him.

One of these carriage places: a misnomer at best.

The only thing worse than not having a restaurant in the motor court, or any hotel, apart from watching Elmer eat, was the next morning in the lobby lost in a horde of touring retirees questioning each other on the quality of their previous night's sleep, their pills, constipation, their need to wear a sweater on the bus, and probably stealing a banana or two. New and squeaky sneakers shuffling on the carpet, nylon sleeves scratching against nylon windbreakers.

On the positive side... *There was none!*

That joy lay ahead of me. My shower came first, disregarding the curtain once seeing a cluster of toe and fingernail clippings at the edge of the sofa moments earlier. I wondered at the towels on the rack, threadbare, dull-white. Were they possibly not laundered, simply dried?

The water was hot, my mind and eyes focused on the towels, the restorative affects barely beginning when a piercing siren blared; probably some old fart smoking in bed, the sound intense, almost painful, louder as I dripped my way from the steamy bathroom into the sitting area, cursing all geriatric backpackers. Shit!

The steam from the shower had infiltrated the entire area, masking stains on the ceiling, hovering over the bed, enveloping the plastic dome, triggering the smoke detector with no indication of stopping anytime soon. The first expletive barely wasted before I was bouncing up on the bed, pillow in hand, vigorously fanning the mist, clearing the heat from the sensors; not doing very well, visions of some burly maintenance guy or Swedish housekeeper bursting through the door to see a shampoo-covered head attached to a dripping and naked madman swinging a pillow and yelling at the ceiling.

A final effort. Silence. The yellowed and brittle assembly dangling thirty centimetres from the ceiling, swinging by red, black and white arteries, mocking me. Son of a bitch. The centre of the bed was soaked where I stood palpitating, listening for any outside disturbance, shampoo burning my eyes. No one had heard, or no one cared; or, perhaps the grannies hadn't yet turned on their hearing aids.

I wasn't touching the towels, opting for the hairdryer, planning Elmer's suicide.

Checking-out after escaping the lobby with a coffee, the female clerk asked how I enjoyed my stay. I did, I told her politely, apart from the body parts on the carpet, the threadbare towels, the sticky hairdryer and the smoke detector I'd noticed hanging from the ceiling when I woke. Happy the entire assembly hadn't fallen while I was asleep.

She gave me a coupon towards my next stay, Elmer twitching as I tossed it in the garbage. That night I checked into the Delta, Elmer managing to follow despite his involuntary convulsions.

In any event the time spent in PEI was time well-spent. Elmer was certainly familiar with his traditional flat products for his twenty months with the company. I'll give him that much. Plastic was a separate issue. He wasn't catching on. Even when they carried the Hawk products they hadn't done much and that's what Barnaby wanted to change. What I wanted was Seaside Systems as part of that change.

I'd enjoyed working with them over the previous three years and still maintained "drop by anytime" privileges, though Elmer had phoned to arrange this particular appointment without telling me.

No One to Tell

Frank and I knew each other well. We were casual with each other, underscored with commitment and mutual respect. I believed what he said and he believed me.

His proviso was that Yoakum and Shenandoah would have to maintain quality, price, delivery, and Elmer would have to maintain the service they'd come to expect. With that said, Frank agreed they would give us a try at the first opportunity. But he'd looked at Elmer very seldom, pretty well excluding him from the conversation, which wasn't good.

Elmer sat in Frank's office as though trying on shoes. He slouched, he kept his boy-jacket on, and took not one note. He didn't have to; everything was in his head, he told me later.

The next morning he spent ninety minutes talking about sports and babies before getting us into the plant where his client, my ex-client, had major problems. The client had done everything wrong he could possibly do and I gave him the points list. No fault of the ICS belt they believed was no good, Elmer reinforcing that thinking. In fact their in-house installation was improperly done, which we corrected.

The belt they wanted to toss lasted another year and Elmer might have learned a lesson, which I doubt. Never knock the competition because we never know when we'll be working with them.

Elmer challenged me on not taking advantage of the client's perception of the existing belt to sell them a new one. He was wrong. I was there, ICS wasn't, and the huge plant was loaded with ICS I'd previously sold. Get the point?

Once back at the office I'd speak with Barnaby about enrolling Elmer in a professional sales course to help kick start his career, modify or erase the many bad habits he'd learned to-date. Also, I was dying to broach the subject of etiquette, with no idea how. I'd never wanted children and had no idea how to tell someone to get their elbows off the table, sit up straight and get their face out of their soup. In short, Elmer was better suited to feeding with his face buried in a trough. No doubt a frequent winner at hotdog and pie-eating contests at the fair.

I was amazed from day one watching Elmer consume food in restaurants. I don't believe I ever saw the stems of the implements he used as tools to bring food to his mouth. He never used a knife, though he did use spoons and forks, seemingly confused by their traditional uses. He'd use a spoon to butter his bread, a fork to cut through his meat, whichever was already in hand to scoop up the selected item. His face always so close to the table there was barely enough room to slide in the bowl or plate when he could have easily sucked his food in.

Napkins were used solely for wiping up food that had splashed or bounced its way onto the table. When eating with Elmer, all one saw was the top of his head.

His manners were atrocious, easily filling the momentary voids in any conversation. What was curious to me was that his father's sense of etiquette was fine and his mother might have learned hers at a girl's school. Somehow Elmer got left behind and someone had to clue him in, just not me.

We were back in Blacks Harbour by the end of the week, meeting with Peter, going over some details, getting his input on some product suggestions, and meeting more key people.

Before leaving we called the Plant Manager of the third plant. Sonny worked twenty-four- seven and was happy to see us. He'd once worked on Grand Manan, coming home to Blacks Harbour on the weekends to rejoin his family.

Arriving home after one of his weeks away he'd found "the wife" with one of the company security guards who had his pants down and his gate up at the time, making

No One to Tell

Sonny a confirmed bachelor.

Elmer walked away from the meeting with information to quote on for Sonny that turned into a substantial order for traditional belting and many more in the future. I'd wanted him to meet key people we hadn't seen in October, which we did with the exception of Richard on Grand Manan. The next step was Nova Scotia in the spring, by which time he'd be more at ease with the products and possess a better understanding of their applications.

I was such a dreamer.

*

The Christmas Party was the Friday of the following week, at six o'clock. Elmer filled me in during our trip to the East. The party was for company employees, everyone expected to dress properly because of the women in the office who normally wore dresses and did their hair.

That Friday I stayed home, leaving for the party at four-thirty. I lived an hour's drive from the company in good weather and that day's weather was anything but good. I arrived at ten to the hour, hung my coat, met Mrs. Hokum for the first time and went to the bar for a JW, neat. Then I stood, watching. By 6:15 all were present and accounted for. The men with their wives or girlfriends, the women with their husbands or significant others. The women were dressed well, for a house party, in a farmhouse. Barnaby wore an open shirt with a jacket, Félix wore a dark suit with a starched white shirt and a power tie. Every other man wore jeans, sweatshirts and winter boots.

I made several attempt to catch Elmer's eye without success, excusing myself to my hosts moments before ten, leaving unnoticed, getting home before eleven. Whatever the weather conditions might be in the Cantons during Christmases to come, snow would always be falling too heavily in Montreal.

*

No One to Tell

One peculiarity about Yoakum was that no one, with the exception of Barnaby, ever said thank you, not for anything. They never said thank you for lunch, not for opening doors, not for small favours done, not for new digital cellphones, not for a new high-speed fax machine with all the bells and whistles that one would expect of the twenty-first century. Nor for computers or email. This after Félix had the reps convinced they would never have computers, never be modern; convincing them the old man was irreversibly set in his ways.

Even Barnaby stepped back to think about that lack of reaction.

All my time would now be taken up with the Shenandoah contract, hiring the Ontario rep and Yoakum's first real sales meeting in eighteen years which wasn't received well. When they read the four-page outline of what was expected, Félix and his duo went into a catatonic state.

Félix was successful in developing his key role in the company, to the point where people were dependent on him for as little as rebooting the desktops in the front office. He needed that dependency and didn't want to lose his status. When he heard of the sales meeting, he laughed, insisting it wasn't necessary. His format of meeting with the guys every other week for lunch worked well, without notes. What he needed to know he remembered, everything in his head.

I asked him to arrive on time.

Félix was always down in the mouth. He never smiled. He never laughed and would always speak openly about Barnaby, when Barnaby wasn't around. He was contrary to everything a sales manager should be. He had no contacts, he had no training, always negative and never upbeat. He lacked the creativity to think of rewards and incentives. He lacked the confidence to realize he could sometimes stand back and learn from others.

No One to Tell

My plan was for quarterly meetings, two of them during off-season weekends in resort environments where girlfriends and wives could join us. We would have half-days of work and half-days of pleasure. Of course Félix snickered, saying the guys would be out of their league, overshadowing Barnaby's enthusiasm. Making me realize I was blowing smoke, wondering who actually ran the company.

Instead I reserved the entire condo spa where I lived, which gave them access to the pool, sauna, whirlpool, sunroom and fitness centre. I also suggested to Barnaby that new leather briefcases for everyone would put a positive edge on the meeting. He agreed, adding that each attaché should have a solid brass name tag and company logo. Done.

January 14th was the day. They all came late, even Barnaby on a beautiful day. I fully expected the snub from Félix as a power play, but the fact that Barnaby reinforced the behaviour when he was so insistent on having a new and improved sales force surprised me.

Félix couldn't allow his sales reps more experience, product or application knowledge than he possessed. He garnered the best customers for himself, brokering knowledge and company information to his advantage. He was also so paranoid someone would discover any weakness he might have, including his inability to manage, that he coded most of what he stored in his computer. It wasn't unusual for him to reference a third hidden file to obtain a second and access information on the first, which was about to come crashing in on him.

Everything was to become interactive over a six-month timeframe during which they would have to adapt to Time Management, Pre-Call Planning, Action Business Plans, Call Reports and ROI. They'd be required to modify their habits and their routine to meet Barnaby's expectations.

No One to Tell

To their way of thinking they had jobs with paid car expenses, not careers. Sell belts or stock shelves in a tire store, no difference. Now they had to change their thinking, learn to work within a process, long cycles with a purpose that brought real value, not just three percent at the end of the month. They would have to grow into Consultative Selling, not just Johnny on the spot, from which juncture anyone in the company would have enough current information to assist any client at any time.

They each did their presentation from crib notes on scraps of paper torn from a loose-leaf, without distributing copies, including Barnaby, though his was marginally more professional.

His presentation was primarily about the company's flat yet stable financial status and his projections for the next eighteen months. He wanted to see an increase of 1.5 million dollars by that time to which Félix said "impossible." Then came my turn.

Félix openly argued the methods and procedures I wanted to implement were unnecessary, to which I responded that if any of them were to start with a new company they'd be expected to be already familiar with them. At that point Barnaby interjected. If they didn't learn, they *would* be starting at new companies. He'd invested a considerable sum in new computers and peripheral equipment, which would become part of the daily routine, and quickly.

Félix chortled, asking how we could possibly use an interactive reporting system with the antiquated phone system Barnaby had done nothing about, losing his colour when Barnaby took obvious pleasure announcing the installation of the new system, including individual voice-mail, would begin that month. Things weren't going their way. Time for me to chortle.

The content of my presentation was the explanation of

various procedures, using the KISS principle. Time Management meant the pre-selection of ten or twelve customers to meet with over the course of a week using a grid dividing a given territory into five or six smaller territories as a guide, not written in stone.

Clément argued he was doing twenty calls a week and needed that many to fill Barnaby's quota. I answered that he was filling his time, not his quota. Quota wasn't the issue. He wasn't aware I'd done a complete evaluation of every call he'd made over the previous year. His average was 14.9, many of which were deliveries of low-value, non-critical accessory goods that could have been delivered by courier. Eliminating those from his reports brought him to 9.8.

He told me that was "crap." I told him I wasn't finished.

Pre-Call Planning was simply knowing the reason for a sales call, being effective and bringing value to the client.

They would be required to prepare four or five Action Business Plans outlining specific companies, measurable objectives and measurable actions leading to the objective within a stated timeframe. There would be a provision in the ABP to change or cancel the objective altogether if it became unworkable or unreasonable. The intention was to get them to think about determining client need, bringing value throughout long-term relationships, working on a consultative level and not going in with an order pad for a fast buck.

Call Reports thus far were submitted to Félix with details such as: "Saw Joe, talked about belting. Nothing now," or "Saw Joe. He had a problem. Sold a belt."

Now I expected, "Saw Joe to discuss the downtime problems he's having on his #3 line. We determined the problem was slippage caused by premature sprocket wear as a result of improper tensioning. I resolved the issue, suggesting he upgrade to series XYZ, ASAP. Subject of next visit: Performance advantages of the upgrade and ROI."

I have no doubt they would have stormed out, if not for Barnaby. When I went on to say that from that point forward they'd be expected to make use of their equipment and work from their home offices that was too much for all three. The inside guys kept their mouths shut. The changes meant no more lunches with Barnaby, no more daily trips for Clément to the office 100 km from his territory.

He said we were only a small company, too small for methodology and technique. "This isn't ICS, we're a nothing company. What do you think you're doing with these big ideas?"

"This isn't a small company. What's small, Clément, is your thinking. The success of the company isn't relative to the number of people, but the quality of people. Care to challenge me on that one? Please."

For every hour spent with a customer they would need equal time to prepare for the call. They would also have an office day of their choosing, when no travel was expected, and sales meetings each year in addition to what Félix thought was appropriate from his perspective. Which I wouldn't attend.

They were beyond reaction, until Barnaby continued with: "I want a meeting like this four times a year, the next one in April. Clément, if you're not up to the change or the challenge, we can take care of that right away."

I couldn't blame him. He'd seen up close and personal just how poor a sales force he had and how little they thought of his company.

Nothing was said, no comment made, but they were unanimous. They would resist any change. When they left they went with new leather briefcases and brass tags they would never use. I saw Elmer use his once, tied together with household string. The meeting was a disaster, the spa was a flop and the single beer each one had at the end of the meeting was sucked back so quickly I was surprised the bottles didn't implode in their throats. Neither Barnaby nor I had the energy or desire to tell them their car allowance had been increased by a hundred dollars retroactive to January 01st.

Upstairs in my condo, I poured myself a stiff JW Black with little to think about.

*

A week after the meeting I met with Barnaby to review the résumés I'd selected as possible candidates for Ontario, the sales meeting too obvious a subject not to discuss. I made clear to him that Clément would forever be a backdoor peddler and that a separation should be made as soon as possible if he was serious about the 1.5 million increase. As for Elmer, he had potential, but without training and coaching he'd go the way of the other. He had to be distanced from the peddler ASAP and Félix's influence over him had to be held in check.

He agreed. Clément was out.

I suggested hiring someone in the industry whom we both knew, who could do the job well. The only consideration was timing. I still had to hire and train a Toronto rep, and in view of the new association with Shenandoah that took precedence.

Following the meeting there was an immediate worsening of the attitudes in the office. Félix was once again established as their leader because now they saw him as their ally in escaping the new order of methodology and professionalism, though they wouldn't have been so enamoured of Félix if they'd ever discovered what he really thought of them: Clément was socially dumb and rude, a man of little talent, dimwitted with no manners and no initiative. Elmer was quick to catch on, but slow nonetheless and would never aspire to anything great.

Barnaby had his time, was uninspired, deceitful and miserly.

Barnaby was dragging the company down. Francis had no understanding of her own language and translated Barnaby's letters at an elementary school level. She was unable to grasp the ordinary. Césaire was a country boy, unmotivated and content with status quo. Marcel was there, nothing more, and would always be there. The guys in the back were uneducated. They were simple country folk and if they couldn't work with their hands, they couldn't work.

All the while they followed him like puppies, not knowing or caring that Félix was in no way equipped to mentor or educate because he had no learning experience to bring to the table other than those he'd created within his own cloistered world. He'd spent his years since his promotion to Sales Manager as a recluse, hiding from innovation and new ideas, riding on the shirttails of others.

Félix hadn't made Yoakum a name in the industry, rather those who had left. While I was at Swiss and Euro Barnaby had sales reps that excelled. But they'd moved on to better their careers and those who replaced them weren't of the same calibre, the loss either going unnoticed or camouflaged by someone who had something to lose himself.

Barnaby wanted to believe Yoakum was bigger than it was. He was President, Félix was Sales Manager, then VP which meant nothing. Eugéne was VP of Operations and Comptroller. Henry was Operations Manager and Purchasing Manager, Francis was Office Manager and Jacques was Production Manager. I was the Plastics Manager.

This in a company of twenty-three people when what he needed was a good work ethic. Hello. I once asked him what the office hours were.

"When we're finished we go home." That's what he

No One to Tell

said, which cost Barnaby the loss of control over his own company, creating his need to rely on others to regain what once was his, though Barnaby's worst enemy wasn't Félix. Anthony held that position.

Félix had zero contacts in the industry. None. A fact that floored me when he first volunteered that information. He had no training nor comparative concepts to rely on, no way of judging good techniques from bad. All he possessed was influence over those he considered inferior, creating the impression held by everyone that Barnaby relied on him for virtually everything.

When he heard of the upcoming weeklong meeting with the four reps from Shenandoah, and what their individual histories were, Félix became absolutely dejected. He told me later that he'd parked in the cold for a few hours that night before going home to be sure his kids were asleep. He didn't want them to see him that way. The momentum of change at the office was making him sick; he was becoming more and more despondent at his loss of control.

Why not tell me he had his balls amputated? I told him it wasn't about control, simply about sharing information and ideas. I wasn't usurping his position. We were intended to complement each other. Elmer and Clément were in their early thirties and forties, respectively. Thirty was a borderline age for starting outside sales and the forties was irresponsible on his part and Barnaby's. What were they thinking to hire a forty-year-old moron?

The reason for Shenandoah's visit was to give us an edge, including the inside guys whom Félix never included. So pull out the stick.
*

Larry arrived with Marty, his Marketing Specialist from Virginia, Pat and Charles. Clint was lured back to The Swamp. The accommodations at the lodge were superior: private rooms with whirlpools, an equipped game room

No One to Tell

reserved for the week, excellent dining room facilities and bar privileges. The only one to decline the room, preferring the one-hour drive each morning and every night, was Félix.

No one at Yoakum had ever taken part in a sales meeting like the one planned by Larry and me. His team came in with product and application PowerPoint presentations and videos, case histories, not hypothetical possibilities, ready to jumpstart our respective territories. The meeting wasn't large by many standards, but planned to run on schedule, be meaningful and effective.

Shenandoah wasn't coming to see what I could do. They wanted to see what the rest of Yoakum was about, Larry' expectations based largely on my original letter.

I'd asked everyone to talk about specifics, including numbers, current plastic sales, potential sales, specific concerns, competition, lost orders and existing proposals. I asked them to be professional, to do their presentations on acetates because PowerPoint was foreign to them. I also asked that they line-up two clients for each of the last three days.

I told Elmer and Clément I'd help them with the format, if they wanted. They didn't want. They were capable. Good. I wasn't a nanny. Henry was asked to present Operational questions because Eugéne refused to speak English. Césaire and Marcel discussed inter-company communication questions, lead times. That sort of thing.

I started the twelve-person meeting at 8:30, by which time everyone had already met over dinner the previous evening or breakfast.

I first presented a general overview of Yoakum Industries, Larry following with the same content about Shenandoah. Barnaby followed with his presentation on expectations, growth, working together and co-operation. Those presentations taking up half the morning.

Pat and Charles were up next, presenting Food

No One to Tell

processing applications, Beverage and Containers through a working lunch. Then we went straight into Félix's blurb on the subject of past sales performance, past supplier-related difficulties, the crux of his presentation revolving around the difficulty he foresaw convincing existing customers to change from Hawk, and new customers not to consider ICS.

Félix had a little work to do on his motivational approach.

I stood to close the day's meeting, asking if anyone had anything to add before we headed to the game room-HS. Larry did, standing, staring straight at Félix.

"Felix, with an attitude like that, why do you bother getting up in the morning?"

"I feel that we had…"

"What you had wasn't as good as what you have." He took the floor. Larry was in his element. "Understand that we'll give you the tools to help you sell these products and understand the applications. What we need from you is commitment and an interest level that surpasses the competition's It's all about methodology; having something to talk about, knowing whom to talk with, knowing when, and knowing why he should listen to you. Hell, J.T. knows all this; he was in enough meetings." He turned to me. "Damn. How hard is that?" He turned to Félix. "It's all about consultative selling. Ain't no big thing."

"Larry, our customers don't care about that. They just want the belt. This consultative stuff is good in books, not in sales. We know what our guys need. We just need to know the product and be at their door when the order is ready."

Larry grew a tumor. If Félix had said that as an ICS or Shenandoah rep Larry would have fired him on the spot. Larry was a fervent believer in consultative and pro-active selling. This peddler-ese spewing from Yoakum's so-called

VP of Sales was as foreign to his thinking as poutine was to his palate.

In frustration he turned to Barnaby. "I don't see how we can get to where we have to be with this kind of thinking. In fact, we should probably be re-thinking our position with Yoakum."

"Félix has some particular issues that concern particular customers. I don't believe he was talking in general terms."

"Pretty much," Félix answered, saying something without saying anything.

*

Félix was convinced for weeks that we wouldn't retain current business with the Shenandoah products, arrogantly choosing the wrong person to tell. To be fair, Larry also had a piece of Charles for not having the visual portion of his presentation in sync with the text, which is why everyone who worked with Larry was as good as they could be. Charles knew Larry got mad, then glad; Félix went home pouting.

The standard sales technique at Yoakum was promoting their products' features as superior to the competition's, attempting to close and hopefully selling a product or service for a given price that would be adjusted according to the level of competition. A dollar-fifty today, a dollar tomorrow. Beating the competition was as important as getting the order, never about what they'd accomplished for the customer who was secondary in their view.

That thinking had to be modified.

The next day began at eight, a full ten hours with more questions from Shenandoah than Félix, Clément and Elmer had answers. Clément's presentation was done sitting down, reading directly from a torn sheet of paper; Elmer did his standing, reading from scrap paper, words dribbling from his mouth. Each presentation slated for an hour lasted five minutes, which gave the rest of us more time to ask

No One to Tell

questions before lunch. The second afternoon was product data and more applications.

Joint calls began Wednesday with Elmer and Charles flying to Nova Scotia. They ran into a severe blizzard, stayed one night and returned. Charles took the unforeseeable in stride, making use of their time to share information; for his part Elmer had a great learning opportunity that was lost on him, failing to make the best of a bad situation. Larry and Marty went to Blanchette with Félix; I went with Pat and Clément as a buffer and damage control.

He'd only made two appointments for the three days, both at Key Accounts I'd developed at ICS. The first was an engineering firm made up of young go-getters who were building a fine reputation for talent and innovation. Everyone in the company dressed for success and carried himself accordingly.

I'd given Pat a heads-up. Clément hadn't needed one because he'd been there with me before Christmas when they called me at home, asking that I visit them to discuss some comparative belting information. I called Clément as a courtesy, because they were officially his customer and he hadn't seen them since because he was out of their league.

There was very little to add. We had no reason to see them other than Pat's interpretation and confirmation of what we could do for them as an alternative supplier. The call was a waste of time for Pat and me. As for Clément, he had something to write in his report.

Pat drove with me to our second call; Clément got to the client near the nude resort on his own. I knew every application in the plant; Clément barely knew where the reception was, where I would have preferred him to stay. I'd begun taking my own car for joint calls, alone, once learning that Félix had a driving-related death wish, Elmer was better suited to driving a covered wagon and Clément lived out of his car.

Returning to the office, Clément decided for whatever reason to call us. Pat shifted, peering through the rear window, gulping an "Oh, shit!"

Félix's mongrel was trailing us by a metre in poor conditions.

Pat was eating potato chips from a cellophane bag, digging for remnants. I put my cell close to the bag, calling out to Clément that I couldn't hear him, at which point Pat crunched the bag and I pressed END. Clément went into the passing lane, I took Pat for lunch.

When Thursday came Charles and Elmer were still struggling with snow that Charles had never seen, a Nova Scotia blizzard not a good way to start. Larry had plans to visit key meat plants with Félix and I'd set up Pat with Césaire and Marcel for the morning so the inside guys wouldn't be lost in the shuffle and to partially disguise that Clément hadn't set up appointments.

He and I would go to Sherbrooke in the afternoon, when Marty would spend time with the inside guys. I told Clément to go home. His portion of the sales meeting was finished.

Larry was very high on Time Management. I'd sent him an agenda that included a certain number of joint calls and we were falling very short of that number. Nova Scotia we all laughed at. Shit happens, though justifiably upset about Clément's indifference and now where was Félix? His first appointment with Larry was scheduled for nine, 200 kilometres away, and at ten o'clock the first call to his home wasn't answered. We called once more. He was stuck in his driveway, shovelling out his car. I hung up, saying something appropriate to the moment.

Outside, Larry was taking in the countryside, enjoying the white serenity. The setting was so peaceful and quiet he'd actually put on the radio to sleep.

"That's complete bullshit. Ain't no way he's stuck. He just doesn't want to work. This damn storm finished before breakfast." Larry trudged into the restaurant, shaking his head. I followed for a coffee and a little reminiscing before getting serious.

Our conversation consumed most of the morning, by which time Barnaby was back from a quick trip to the office and took over the conversation while I went to Sherbrooke with Pat. Félix had messed up big time, and would never recover from the slight. He'd lost face, and he'd lost hope...to himself. No one else cared. They just wanted to get things done.

The week was a success in spite of a few drawbacks, and Larry went home to the States with his guys feeling optimistic about the future. Marty would be back on several occasions, not Larry, though I would see him again in Virginia, Philadelphia and Chicago.

*

Professional sales reps invest time and effort developing requisite skills and competencies, not so peddlers who wake up and open a book of addresses. Soon after the meeting with Larry, I approached Elmer to talk about enrolling him in a professional sales course. Yoakum already had one peddler and didn't need another. Elmer had potential, a bright future, but not on his own.

We discussed the matter on previous occasions. Both times he refused. Hokum would have given him the time, paid expenses and a tangible acknowledgement I hadn't mentioned. But the course meant going to Montreal on Friday nights over a three-month period or one full week of intensive studies in Montreal or Toronto.

The 100 kilometres was too far, he said, and wouldn't benefit him. No course could make him a better salesman. Nobody would know anything about belting and Félix was teaching him what he needed to know. His customers were happy with him. So should I be, so should the old man be, and I should stop making waves.

So I discovered you can lead a horse to water, but you can't make it drink. Except I believed that all horses were smarter than Elmer, so what chance would he have in a world that would know that and pass him by? He'd missed his chance, proud that he'd taken a stand against being better. He certainly got the better of me. Congratulations. And from that moment, whenever I saw Elmer, I saw Bubba.

He came into Barnaby's office the day before I left for a week in the Shenandoah Valley of Virginia with Césaire, with news that Blacks Harbour had ordered the complicated 275-metre belt from the company in Newfoundland. He wasn't upset about losing the order, explaining that the Maritimes worked that way.

"Have you kept in touch with Peter?"

"Well, yeah."

"To say what, exactly?"

"What else? To find out when he was giving the order."

"That's it?"

He looked past me to Barnaby. "We already gave him the price. You even said there was no way to cut it down. Those guys deal between themselves. That's it, that's all. We lost the account to the Newfies."

He shook his head, Barnaby mimicked, and they both shrugged.

"No, we haven't." They both looked at me. "We haven't lost the account, and by the way, Elmer, it's my account. It's just on loan to you."

"Since when is the account yours?"

"Since four years ago. You've known them barely four months, submitting a proposal for a major once-in-a-lifetime project. How many times have you called Peter?"

Apparently he had tried a few times, but Peter never

picked up and never returned the call.

"What did you tell him was the reason for your call?"

"To know if he was getting ready to place the order."

"He phoned you to tell you?"

"Well, yeah. When it was too late."

"So what? He phoned, and he told you what you wanted to know. That's all you wanted, and that's all you got. What about what he wanted to know? You had no reason to phone him. You weren't giving him new information, you weren't reinforcing the benefits to him and you weren't prepared. I bet Rick was on the phone to him every week, in the plant once a month. Personally I think he's a shyster, probably bullshitting his way through, but he beat you out."

I don't know any Rick."

"He's the Newfie you lost to. And just so you know, this wasn't lost on price. The Danish manufacturer gave special pricing on an already bargain basement belt that was perfect for the job. They had everyone beat, ICS and Hawk included. So we haven't lost the account."

"Says who?"

"Says Peter, when I spoke with him last week and the week before that. If anyone's a loser here, you are."

During those trips to the East with me, then Charles, Elmer was led through the sales process of who, what, where, when and why, but he was so influenced by his surroundings on a daily basis that he was unaffected by reason. That's why he needed formal training, to interact with others who would influence him differently, give him exposure to new ideas and concepts. He'd dwelled on losing the account without knowing whether he had. He'd forgotten or trivialized the business he'd achieved with Sonny and, when asked whether he'd made initial contact with Richard on Grand Manan the answer was "not yet." No surprise there, Bubba.

And what was with the jeans and chequered shirts? The

office staff wore jeans, sweatshirts, crumpled chequered shirts and sneakers, nothing designer, everything sloppy. The jeans were loose and their shirttails always hung out. Barnaby agreed. He didn't like the fact they all wore jeans, especially the salesmen, but that was Félix's domain and if he intervened they'd all quit.

What was his point? I asked.

He knew Félix would never question what Clément and Elmer wore, nor would he ever criticize the lax dress code in the office because he always wore a suit and tie. The fact his inside and outside reps wore jeans and sweat shirts, walking around like Billy Bumpkin and his brother Billy, was fine with him. They made him appear all the more sophisticated…in his eyes, enhancing the image he carried of himself, the image he needed others to see, which Barnaby should have realized.

I broached the subject with Félix one day when we went for a rare lunch together. My stand was that when you dress better, you feel better; when you dress better, you work better. When you dress a notch above for the job, you perform a notch above.

Félix's claim was that they were too simple with no understanding of these concepts. They would never be more than they were. I was wasting my time trying to improve them.

I asked Félix why he enjoyed working with losers. They would have to learn to work with engineering staff and plant management, front office people who decided on capital projects, preventative shutdowns and had authority to implement changes or probationary tests, which wouldn't happen unless they improved their skill and appearance significantly.

In business we are how we appear to. First impressions count, your image directly correlated to success. Or the lack thereof.

No One to Tell

*

I went to Virginia to discuss product brochures and joint advertising programmes with their marketing staff and several one-on-one sessions with engineering to learn more about steel belting. Césaire went with me to learn assembly techniques for modular belting. When I stopped into the assembly shop to see how he was doing, he was standing around looking at various pieces of equipment, grumbling that we'd stayed one day too long, that the day was pretty well wasted. Was that so?

One particular piece of equipment he was studying was a Dado saw used to cut polypropylene rods and modules. What they did in thirty seconds took Yoakum ten minutes to accomplish. When I suggested he should note the particulars of the saw assembly because we could definitely benefit from having one, he shrugged and said the old man would never go for it. Then he finally understood about ROI, time saving and cost effectiveness, although it took the better part of an hour.

The saw would cost 1500 dollars, the arithmetic too easy. The machine would increase productivity and produce a better end product. Somewhat of a no-brainer and Césaire was the one to know. He did the assembly costing for plastic belting. What better person to do a selling job on Barnaby? I told Césaire to figure out the rest and present his argument Monday morning, Césaire expressing doubts all the way home, spending much of our wait time at Dulles smirking at me, shaking his head, convinced he knew Barnaby.

Monday I went to the office at noon. The Dado saw already up and running. Césaire had done his thing. Then, after a few moments of conversation with Barnaby, he called a local metalwork shop to initiate work on new workstations and a new piece of equipment that would roll and wrap, something else we'd spoken about during his wasted time in the Shenandoah shop. The Dado unit paid for itself a week before the net 30 terms of the invoice.

Those innovations borrowed from Shenandoah greatly reduced cost, improved efficiency and increased the safety of the assemblers, though the equipment for rolling and wrapping was discarded after a couple of weeks. But that was positive as well, because for the first time employees felt they could approach Barnaby and voice opinions, good or bad. For Barnaby, having those guys come into his office to say they would prefer not using the new equipment probably outweighed the five or 600 dollars the thing cost. They weren't going through Félix.

*

One of the biggest challenges confronting me was converting a particular client over to Shenandoah from Hawk, who they'd been buying through Yoakum as a matter of routine for years. That McCann's average annual purchase exceeded fifty K. Until Shenandoah we'd supplied that one Manitoba client with Hawk products acquired through a back door arrangement with a third party, but that practice was contrary to the spirit of our agreement with Shenandoah.

No one thought it would happen, from Barnaby to Henry, to the sales reps. I said it would, telling Henry to have sufficient material in stock for the first order that would be placed during my trip the next week to Winnipeg. The material ordered thus far was reserved for Sea & Double U, untouchable and two weeks late.

I arrived at the plant with one sample, put it on the Plant Manager's desk and told him that was the product we'd be sending him from now on. He refused outright. He wanted nothing but Hawk, proceeding through a barrage of reasons based on information given to him by the Hawk rep that had visited the plant years before with Henry who was Operations Manager in name only, better suited to farming.

No One to Tell

He knew nothing about applications, his knowledge of plastic belts based on second or third hand information from Felix. No one had visited the plant since, leaving the Plant Manager with absolutely wrong information and myths.

Think Henry mentioned that?

He asked how much I knew about potatoes. I said as much as he knew about belting, and he stared for a second before choking on a laugh. I told him how I'd done all Florenceville, twice. I told him I knew enough. Florenceville was his Head Office.

Because the previous information was wrong didn't mean the belt was wrong, but this one would work better and we began talking about loads, speeds, design, rod and sprocket migration, product fallback and angles. Fun stuff. At the end of three hours he was convinced, but he had inventory and the slightest misgiving that something might go wrong, that his production would suffer as a result.

Would I give him the belt? No. What good would that do if the belt failed and his production stopped? The cost of the belt was inconsequential compared to his lost production. And nothing is ever free. Somebody somewhere pays for those freebies. The issue was whether the new belt would increase performance, reducing downtime, lost production and maintenance costs. The answer was a definite yes. So why would the belt be free?

The remaining glimmer of doubt was for show. He would pay full price after three months and, if the belt didn't perform to his satisfaction, he'd pay a pro-rated price based on a normal life of one-year.

Inside of eighteen months the entire plant was converted, the delay due to their existing stock. Shenandoah was ecstatic, whereas Yoakum had no reaction at all and I left for Toronto to work with Charles who'd come at my behest.

*

Charles was great to work with. The days were full, so were the evenings. Larry's work hard, play hard ethic was well-engrained. The hardest thing was keeping up with him. I drove him to the airport late Thursday after doing enough business to earn him a bonus, make Larry happy, Barnaby worry, and give Henry the shits.

I spent the last two days interviewing four hopefuls, making an almost immediate determination. Marvin was the fourth man. He was fifty-two and spoke with a slightly affected speech meant to show he was well-read. He'd been laid off a year earlier from a manufacturer of industrial tools and had spent that year working at a local golf club in a variety of capacities.

He wasn't a likely candidate. He was the only possible candidate, which was surprising because the remuneration was extremely generous. The second interview would be with Barnaby in three weeks and I told Marvin to come prepared. I'd be talking with him about methodology, technical aspects, and his knowledge of the Ontario marketplace.

By the time I got to the office the following Tuesday Marvin's letter thanking me for my time and consideration had already arrived. Nice touch. Not so the message from Kelvin.

If he was my favourite Newfie, I certainly wasn't his favourite mainlander and the tirade of popular Newfie expletives and invectives went on for an hour. We screwed up big-time. Now the problem was that Yoakum wasn't accustomed to customers with that kind of potential and they took the situation rather lightly with the exception of Césaire who worked hard to resolve the problem. Deliveries were six weeks late and Sea & Double U was in the unenviable position that we and Shenandoah had put them in. From one office I heard: "What should we do?" That was Barnaby. From the other office I heard: "We told you so." That came from everyone who could fit into Félix's office.

The major setback was corrected by Césaire, Marty and Larry, not to mention drop shipments from Virginia by air that eliminated profit margin on the first shipment. The next week I was in Newfoundland doing damage control before the boxes were even unloaded. That's when I got the call from Manitoba, complaining about their late delivery and another from the High Tide fishery plant in Sydney that I'd given to Bubba because I just didn't have the time. They were wondering why the new guy hadn't been by to see them. There were belts to inspect together and they couldn't put off ordering much longer. Was he coming, or wasn't he?

It wasn't a good start and Barnaby's "you take care of it" attitude wasn't reassuring. It was easy to tell when Barnaby got really upset because he'd use words like "bad" or "horrible" and every so often he would come out with the big guns and say "damn." This situation needed more than that kind of minimalist reaction; this involved two accounts on their way to giving us a quarter-million USD, and a fishery plant that had several other plants throughout Nova Scotia with applications worth several tens of thousands each.

They were prepared to give Yoakum a chance because of my past relationship with them, but the new season was coming on fast and being ready was all they cared about. Once they started they would operate twenty-four-seven for six months or more, and they needed to know we'd be there for them.

It took a few more belts from Hawk before we could resolve the delivery problems for Manitoba, by which time Shenandoah's production problems were resolved. We were back on track.

*

No One to Tell

The Seafood Show in Boston was an international exhibition held every March, an occasion to do serious business, make several new contacts and exchange information with potential customers, OEMs, and even the competition. Three days of intense activity with very little time for casual exchanges. The show was Elmer's first.

He'd been given information that included a listing of exhibitors, booth locations and pertinent details about each company. I suggested the show was classier than most and that he should dress accordingly. Jackets would be appropriate. Come prepared with an ample supply of business cards and sufficient cash to pay for taxis and drinks. He was told what to look for and to remember exhibitors were there to sell, not to buy.

So what did Bubba do? Bubba came with no American money, he took a free shuttle to the hotel that got him there hours after Marty and I had arrived, his suitcase smaller than his briefcase that was held together with white household string and missing the brass tag. The thing cost two-fifty, was brand new and tied with string. He had no jacket, but did have a white cotton shirt, *one* white cotton shirt.

Marty had come to evaluate the benefits of sharing booth space with Yoakum the following year. I'd already convinced Barnaby of the importance of being there, but the show was one of the most expensive to exhibit at and having Shenandoah alongside to share cost and help man the booth would be a significant factor in his decision.

We did one of the three humongous floors each day. Marty and I spent half days together so I could introduce him to key people from the Atlantic Region and Québec. In the afternoons we separated so he could check out American potential and I could spend some time with Elmer whom we left alone in the mornings.

The first night Elmer and I went to Cheers for dinner

without Marty who'd arranged dinner with a potential US client. The food was okay, for those who don't mind eating in a souvenir shop, and the conversation revolved around the day. The second evening I joined Wayne and his wife for dinner at one of Boston's elegant rooftop restaurants, along with Vicki and Morena who'd come up from New Orleans. The evening was fabulous without shop talk, just good times and a toast to Linda who had been with us in Boston the year before.

Later at the hotel, I joined Marty who was just stepping out from the elevator on his way to the bar for a nightcap. The three days were worthwhile; Marty and I had already arranged for tentative floor space the following year. Marty developed new business potential on his side of the border, I made more headway with Newfoundland accounts on behalf of Sea & Double U and Elmer came away with show experience and a handful of new contacts he'd work into his upcoming trips to the Maritimes.

The final night our legs were throbbing, our throats were sore and our backs ached. We agreed to meet at the bar to decide on a restaurant for dinner. I'd told Elmer to open a tab on his room because I'd be joining him a little later. I wanted to check my voice-mail and change into something casual. Marty's idea of casual was taking off his tie. For Elmer it meant wearing the same shirt all week, so no one would realize he'd worn the same pants all week.

They were both on their second, Elmer with one foot on the floor, the other planted on his suitcase. News to Marty and me that he was catching a mid-evening flight to Montreal that would get him home at midnight, and he'd just seen the shuttle bus drive up.

He hadn't paid for anything but his room in the three days since his arrival. Either Marty or I covered the lunches, coffees, drinks, taxis, etc., including his admission. I took his seat, ordering a JW Black neat, asking him if he'd opened the tab. Yes, he said, he did, but on his card, not the room, and he left without a handshake for Marty, no see you tomorrow, just his back and the sound of a chair he knocked over.

Marty had one more, so did I, and we sat a while longer being mellow before hailing a cab to take us to a restaurant. We slinked off the stools, me telling the barman to close the tab and add twenty percent. And we walked away.

The barman cleared his throat, saying, "Gentlemen," waving the bill. "There is no tab."

"Are you sure he didn't open a tab? He said he did." I looked at Marty, who was already reaching for his wallet.

"No. He just ordered. When this gentleman came he ordered two more."

I grabbed the bill, apologizing for the confusion. Walking out we were smiling, shaking our heads at each other and not because anything was particularly amusing.

The following Monday I told Elmer to meet me in the office, not telling him that he required an urgent lesson in business etiquette, or plain good manners. Bubba got his ass kicked big-time, understanding not so much what I thought of him, but of his place in the world.

I believe that when I was finished he wanted his mommy. But she wasn't near to care for and suckle him, so he went to his daddy who did.

*

I met Barnaby in Toronto during mid-April to interview Marvin who seemingly had great potential, reinforced by what appeared to be familiarity with the customer base. He was also fully computer literate.

I called Marvin a few days later to tell him he was hired.

I began working with him in Toronto the next week, after which he'd spend a week in the shop, spend time with Césaire inside and with Elmer on the road. Then he would leave for a week in Virginia.

No One to Tell

Because Marvin would be responsible for only plastic sales he wasn't involved in any way with Félix who'd become increasingly morose over the previous several weeks. He seldom came in and when he did he would close himself in his office. I questioned Barnaby about this the day I called Marvin to welcome him to the company.

Félix had quit.

"When did he quit?"

"Last month."

"Say what?"

"Last month. He's been coming in to ease the separation process." He shrugged.

"When's his final last day?"

He didn't know. What's worse, he didn't care or think it important. Félix would leave when the time was right. Apparently, brokering information wasn't particular to Félix. They both played the "I know something you don't" game, which benefited no one. Intellectual inbreeding.

I had realized for some time that I was working on the fringes of Bizarro World. They'd been together too long, managing to suffocate each other over the years, letting their thinking become insular and stale. Barnaby was a company owner with no control over sales, apathetic and pouty regarding his VP of Sales. Félix was a Sales Manager with no concept of selling, no motivational ideas, no concept of new business development and no contacts. That he left, was leaving, or would leave, was good for the company. Possibly even for him, definitely for me. He'd been there too long, or Barnaby had.

The final date was May 12th; the end of Marvin's training, everyone meeting at a local restaurant to send Félix home. The function doing more to depress Félix than I ever could, which was no less gratifying. No one was consoling him, lamenting his departure, preoccupied with eating and drinking on Barnaby's tab. Apart from Clément who pulled his shirt from his pants to his chest during the main course to compare his bloated sphere with Diane's who was at full term, spending the evening telling offensive jokes and projecting bursts of stale, beer-flavoured gas across the table.

Monday would bring a new era. Barnaby had never wanted me working in Québec or the Maritimes. He wanted me to train, develop Ontario and manage plastic. Although now he only had two reps for all Québec and the Maritimes, not nearly enough, so I was asked to hire a third.

The timing was perfect for change, and I knew just the person, someone whom I'd worked with previously, who lived in Québec City and knew traditional belting inside out. He also knew nylon core transmission belting. When I met with Didier the following week to discuss his interest he agreed with one proviso: Félix's permanent disappearance. The next week he was in Virginia with Marvin.

Then I called Gordon to set up a lunch meeting with Barnaby who seemed to have forgotten about Clément the Peddler.

*

Gordon's current job was bringing no satisfaction, problems exceeding rewards, working for a boss who berated him for everything he did. The pluses for Gordon were many, not the least of which was doubling his income and car allowance.

All I said to Gordon was that he should be positive, not criticize his current boss, and forget I was at Yoakum. When he asked about Clément I said the time had come to make changes that would benefit the company. The job was his; all he had to say was "thank you for lunch" and "I accept."

Lunch was typical of interviews: Polite conversation before the job description, expectations, goals, reporting and time management. I had a written offer in my jacket pocket with blank spaces for the start date and signature, but he needed time to consider the offer. He wasn't sure the job was a good fit for him, causing me to wonder whether his brain was a good fit.

That he would even think of making such a comment surprised Barnaby and me. Gordon was long overdue for a reality check. He would consider the pros and cons over the coming week and get back to us. He was insane not to jump at the offer, but he went home undecided and I went to New Hampshire for an impromptu week of seaside R & R.

Straying slightly from my conviction about never working on vacation, I called Gordon the following Thursday not expecting to hear he was declining the offer. The day was beautiful and hot, I could hear the ocean from the deck outside my hotel suite. I'd been expecting a two-minute conversation during which he'd say "yes," confirming a start date. What happened was a two-hour conversation during which I spent much of the time in my car to keep the cell phone operational.

He had another offer from a belting company wanting to penetrate Québec. They needed someone with Gordon's experience and contacts, albeit with no increase to his current income. I told him he was crazy, but he'd been promised the possibility of becoming Regional Manager of the company at some later date. What that meant was Gordon would manage a second man. I asked him if he was nuts, or just fucking stupid.

Gordon had three weaknesses, one of which was never taking a chance; the second was an inability to analyze facts; the third was low self-esteem. He joined Simple Belting as their Québec Territory Manager, believing he was a manager, not a salesman.

Barnaby's disappointment was real over the phone. He knew Gordon would have done well, and now he was stuck with Clément the backdoor peddler, the one the entire industry recognized as useless as teats on a bull, the one Barnaby referred to as the Hawaiian beach bum, a ne'er-do-well buffoon in a printed shirt.

Not having Gordon to train gave me more time to spend with Marvin who needed the attention. Didier was self-sufficient, familiar with designing territory grids, reporting, the customer base, and was technically competent.

I called Marvin on the Wednesday following his return to see how things had gone in Virginia and to hear how his sixth week was shaping up. He was "cozy and comfy in my nicely set up office" and would take the next few days to peruse the product information so he wouldn't come off as the "new guy" when meeting with customers. When I asked whether he'd read my e-mails regarding key accounts and a certain number of pressing issues he should place at the front of his To Do list, he replied that he hadn't gotten around to retrieving his mail, that he'd never used e-mail.

I gave him a list of companies to call for appointments the following week, telling him I'd arrive Monday morning. He asked whether he should meet me at the airport, or was I renting a car? With that issue cleared up à la JT, the words "nicely" and "cozy" and "comfy" resounded in my mind until then.

I'd asked Marvin to meet me in the hotel lobby at 09:30. At 10:00 he hadn't arrived. Nor was he answering his phone. So I went for a coffee and there was Marvin, enjoying breakfast. He stood, shook my hand and sat. I remained standing, signalled for his bill and advised him not to expense the twenty-five dollars. Marvin was beginning to piss me off.

The appointment that morning was with the Maintenance Manager who came out as though we'd interrupted his day, which we probably had, or maybe he'd seen Marvin cutting across his front lawn.

No One to Tell

As we waited I told Marvin about a client who once explained to me why a sales rep who'd left his office ahead of me was from then on excluded from future business. He'd seen the man walking across his lawn, saving three or four metres to the main walkway. The man's actions were viewed in two lights: He was lazy, and showed no respect for the work or cost of manicuring the customer's lawn.

Our visit wasn't planned. When I asked Marvin what he'd intended to talk about with the gentlemen, curious, he answered. "Whatever he wanted to talk about, he's the customer. He knows what he needs better than me."

Marvin and I had a talk, the afternoon turning into an impromptu training session. He thought we might have as many as four or five appointments for the rest of the week, which he had yet to confirm. But I wasn't staying a full week for a possible four appointments, rebooking my flight for Wednesday PM, telling Marvin to use that timeframe for whatever we could do. Had any possible alternative existed, I would have tossed him on the spot.

The next day we arrived at the country's largest bakery, the one confirmed appointment. We arrived at eleven and waited. I'd asked Marvin during his interview "how long would you wait for an appointment, and how would you leave a plant where the appointment was late without acknowledging you?" The answer was thirty minutes, forty for a good customer before leaving a message indicating he would call to reschedule.

Eleven-thirty came and went, so did 12:00 as Marvin read The Sun, stood, sat and fidgeted his way towards twelve-thirty when we left with no appointment and nothing planned. Instead we went to a local trade show he knew nothing about.

Marvin blew through the show like he had a hole in his Depends, slowing when he noticed me stopping for information or a business card. We got to the end of some

150 booths with his hands empty. Somewhat the same condition as his head. I gave him my brochures with corresponding business cards, asking him to enter the information into his Customer Management programme and qualify them as soon as possible.

Wednesday morning we were back at the bakery hearing profuse apologies from the client who took the time to give us a full plant tour and show Marvin every possible piece of conveyor equipment. Though one specific area was giving him problems. The solution was simple: Cut the belt. He needed a narrower width. Whereas the competition was already preparing a new belt.

Curious, I phoned Césaire to ask for a price while I transferred to Barnaby who was quick to remind me he only wanted plastic business in Ontario, nothing else. I asked if he was sure about that. Couldn't certain exceptions apply? He didn't see how, it would create too much paperwork.

He was about to say something when Césaire went into his office with a figure of 75K annually, ten percent of the client's total annual belting requirement and a twenty percent saving.

"So, let's be clear about this, Barnaby. You do want the order, even though it's not plastic? You're certain?"

Marvin walked out with his first order, feeling good. I walked out wondering why he felt good.

Passing the guard at the gate to the parking lot, the man returned Marvin's wallet. He'd dropped it. He tripped me twice in the plant, almost tripped the Plant Manager, and dropped his wallet once more at the car. He asked me to pick it up. He had trouble bending. I had answered what any guy would, he retrieved it himself, and stood beet red. Then, before starting the car, he said he hadn't managed to note all the particulars of the meeting and could he borrow my notes?

I asked him if he was feeling alright. He said he was.

No One to Tell

Not that I cared, telling him to phone me the next day for the missing information. When he phoned I told him I'd be sending him a test sometime over the coming week that he was to complete and return. I had to determine what information he was missing in order for him to do the job properly.

The fifty-question test was open-book because I needed to know Marvin was aware of where to find information. He had an entire week, answering fewer than half the questions correctly.

I had a bad feeling about Marvin.

*

I'd been with Yoakum nine months, nine years in my mind. I was working in the office of our fourteenth floor penthouse, still without an office in Goonieville, not aware the clock was about to signal the sun was at its zenith.

Two non-descript cars pulled into the curb-side parking spaces on the main road intended for those who wanted to spend time by the river, a daily event, in no way unusual. The setting was tranquil and beautiful, a perfect camouflage for couples arriving from separate directions, from separate realities to enjoy the solitude.

Within the next few years the area would become a thriving complex of several dozen riverside luxury condominium homes, winding bicycle paths with park benches, picnic tables and a magnificent view of Montreal and the St. Lawrence Seaway. But then the natural parcel of land was idyllic with trees, a carpet of wild grass and a decaying cement jetty with a single weather-beaten picnic table.

Our second summer in our condo, still dazzled by the 270° panoramic view that changed by day, by night, and by season. The Seaway was twenty metres from our windows with its constant churning motion caused by the commercial, pleasure, and military vessels heading one way to the Atlantic or the other to the lakehead. One oversized picture window in my office faced north, framing the entire city of Montreal. The other faced southeast, capturing the mountains of Vermont and the Cantons.

I was finalizing my abridged version of the Customers Management Guide, gazing into space beyond the glass panes.

They were walking at a normal pace, holding hands. Nothing unusual. Except that his head was bobbing like a top, craning, twisting when the land surrounding them was flat. Something was going down! Her skirt was micro-short and tight, not summery. Her peasant blouse more like a halter top, her feet flipping and flopping in rubber sandals.

I stood from my desk. They were nearing the river's edge, stopping, searching. He pulled at the solitary table, kicking it when it didn't move. He jumped onto the weathered planks, tripping, banging his shins before finding his footing. His head swivelled 360° with his feet firmly planted, then again, talking to her as he leaped awkwardly to the ground, thinking to land on his feet, landing on his knees.

Oblivious to her surroundings she yanked her skirt past her bare waist in a blink, sitting on the bench before he straightened, her legs wide apart, her sandals kicked into the air, not waiting for him.

Customer Management would have to wait. My 60-power German scope turned those twenty metres into centimetres, excluding her knees from the frame, giving me everything but her name. My framing changed to abrupt darkness, forcing an easy adjustment. He was in front of her, on his knees, his head vibrating erratically as though he was having a seizure, his hands mauling where he could and where she let him. He wanted her breasts, but she was already there. She'd worked her flimsy top high over her breasts, squeezing them hard, expertly, not letting him near.

No One to Tell

They were perfectly proportioned to her body, well-maintained. She understandably didn't want them bruised by rough groping mitts. She arched backwards, jerking involuntarily, causing him to lose his balance and fall back. Her hero. She told him to stay.

I could see her wetness up close and very personal, the change of colour as though I was between her legs, which I was, deprived of olfactory intimacy.

She stood. He was prostrate, fumbling to free himself from his plumber-crack jeans, not doing very well, the girl in complete control of the programme. She deserved more, straddling him anyway with expert ease, her skirt holding itself high, her flimsy blouse gone, her hands pushing away his rude groping. Her way or no way. She wanted herself as much as she wanted him.

The unimpeded entry was smooth, bodies rocking, faces grimacing, time stopping, the girl in control of her breasts, him mauling and clutching and pulling at her widening ass, wanting to probe, failing.

She arched, jerking once, twice, grinding faster, harder, trying to push him in deeper, stopping. She came away from him lifting one knee from the ground, then the other, her skirt held in place, her breasts glistening, heaving, not missing a beat. Laying on the rough, grass-covered ground, her knees parting and closing to a rhythm, teasing him, teasing me, she rolled onto her side, her palms telling him to stay.

Easing onto her knees, facing away, her open legs close enough to touch, she began slowly, mischievously, the lacquered tips of her right hand working greedily towards a liquid crescendo of excitement and pleasure between her glistening, soft folds and pear-shaped buttocks; darting in and out, invading until she shuddered, her left arm folding, her forehead touching the grass.

He was done, ill-equipped, moving to the table, his arms

spread-out against the planked top. He wanted to go, leave. He'd finished. He'd done what he'd come to do. His expression showed worry, not enjoying the moment she was creating for him, his head scanning nervously, his eyes finally catching the sparkle from the disk in the window on the fourteenth floor.

I smiled and spoke to him. He didn't answer, bolting upright causing her to prop herself onto her elbows. She was enjoying. He stood like a clown, bending his knees, fumbling, struggling for modesty while she repositioned herself onto her knees and stood, her breasts bare, her skirt pulled high, her feet parted wide.

I had to admit, very nice, too nice for him. Though she did require a better sense of fashion.

She glanced around, seeing nothing, shrugging. Then skyward, smiling. She knew I couldn't do anything but watch. And if she hadn't wanted me to, she would have run from sight. Instead she sat on the bench, her hands gliding together from across rival thighs, tracing wetness to its source, her fingers strumming the delicate pleats as though playing at the strings of an erotic instrument, her lips and thighs sparkling in the midday sun.

She'd gotten what she came for. She was being naughty, reluctantly reaching for her blouse, concealing her breasts, standing to straighten her skirt as slowly as I would. She would have stayed longer, I know. She smiled again, coaxed away by whoever he was. I smiled, and went for a swim. My day was done.

I would see her twice more. Once disinclined towards romance, alone, preferring instead to strip with a high degree of patience and precision from her jeans and tee-shirt. Taking more time to fold them neatly, placing them just so in her shoulder bag. I gave her early to mid-thirties. She wasn't at all hurried, bathing herself with dry or moist hands, nonchalantly placing a skirt and sweater on the table,

No One to Tell

leaning soft flesh into the dried wood, slipping one foot then the other into the flighty material, tugging, adjusting, patting.

Reaching for her sweater, one arm in then the other, cupping seductively, smoothing dreamily. She tousled her hair, glancing skyward, perhaps a glimmer of a smile, slinging her bag over her shoulder, sauntering from sight. A deep breath: Mine. Somebody somewhere would certainly be the beneficiary of the day's gentle breeze.

The third time we were into early autumn, by which time she'd done better for herself. The guy was driving a foreign import with the top down, with her beside him. Good girl.

Unlike the quickie with Mr. Weenie, when she could easily have done without him, and the delightful striptease still fresh in my mind, they'd come for a private picnic lunch. She was also much better dressed for the day or for him, her deep yellow cami top perfectly complementing her bright red wrap-around, ankle-length skirt and low-heeled leather sandals. No flip-flops for this guy.

They were strolling, holding hands, smiling; her cheek against his shoulder. Lovers. My lover wasn't home yet. So I strolled alone to the bar for a vodka thinking to sit on my desk to relax a few moments while appreciating the new fall colours. My 60-power scope in the corner, until I realized their dilemma: No requisite blanket. Accidental omission or purposeful foresight? The latter, of course. And she was wearing bright yellow panties which I supposed were brand new for the occasion. Silk, cut high, detailed with lace. Nothing cheap and definitely purposeful.

The guy was actually taken aback, her skirt without warning fluttering in the warm air like a matador's cape, cloaking the grass, her sitting nonchalantly, waiting, smiling while patting her skirt for him to sit. She was the perfect accompaniment to his Bordeaux or Bourgogne, French bread and cheese.

He smiled, and so did I as occasional cyclists toured by, waving, undoubtedly savouring the lady sitting side-saddle or laying on her front, propped on her elbows for him, me, and them to enjoy. Lucky guy!

At some point I went back to work, but I can't exactly say when. What I do know is that, with him or without him, she remains inherently naughty and nice.

*

I completed some preliminary marketing campaigns for Newfoundland's seafood industry, sending my design work to a printer for a more professional touch. I'd also completed the final version of the Customer Management programme Barnaby didn't bother to read. Francis studied the document, later explaining her abridged version of my abridged version. By which time she'd told her husband Jacques, who was the Production Manager, who told Henry, who told Césaire, who told Elmer, who called Clément to cry on the phone.

They were in the conference room. Anthony and Barnaby, school chums from the 1800s. Anthony was as tall, grey and gaunt as the average telephone pole and sat with a permanent slouch. I doubt I was in the room a minute before Barnaby asked me to describe what I'd accomplished for the company. Barnaby always wanted to appear erudite, smooth and unruffled. He was putting on a show. The thing is, tie or no tie, one advantage a city boy has over a country boy is that he can smell bullshit before he steps in it.

"For what purpose, Barnaby?" His jaw dropped, his eyes blinked. "Why haven't you told him if he needs to know?"

"Anthony's interested in your progress. I've been telling him about you."

"That's my point. He should already know." I glanced from Barnaby to his lanky friend.

"Barnaby simply asked me to stop by to have a discussion with you; nothing formal."

"That's about fucking right, nothing formal. Barnaby, you know me. You know I don't like sneaky shit. You know I don't come to meetings unprepared. I'll see you both tomorrow, 10:30."

I drove home, pissed.

Ten-thirty the next morning I was in Barnaby's office with printed copies enumerating my accomplishments by date. Barnaby commented that I was being defensive. I answered that his perceiving me as defensive meant me perceiving him as offensive, which certainly wasn't the case. Right, Barnaby?

Anthony was too politically correct, his effusive compliments blatantly exaggerated. I knew what I had accomplished would soon lead to needed reforms and a professional approach requiring a professional team. Anthony's time might have been better spent reviewing Barnaby's accomplishments. I was beginning to believe that his first and last was opening the company.

I had lunch at home.

*

My time spent with Didier was for specific reasons, at his request. He was very conversant with flat belt applications, which accounted for most of the business in his territory, the plastic applications either very simplistic or very complicated, which is when I got involved.

However most of my time was spent with Marvin, addressing specifics he wasn't grasping. He was still more fascinated with the equipment in various plants than with solving the particular problem or need a customer was experiencing. He was seeing three, possibly four customers each week, thus far selling nothing other than the single-ply polyurethane belt we'd come across at the bakery. He restricted himself to very small companies, avoiding those with greater potential requiring extensive application and product knowledge and interaction with engineering staff or management.

Then came the golf tournament.

He was invited, of course, driving in on Friday, arriving at his hotel just after noon. He spent the day touring the wine region before phoning Barnaby to invite him to dinner on his expense account. If that wasn't a comfort zone, I don't know what was.

Then came Saturday.

We all played according to our skill or interest, ate and drank with a purpose after the eighteenth, got our prizes and went home, Linda commenting that they seemed friendly enough, down to earth. Or from under it, reminding her about Christmas.

I saw Marvin again nine days later, with a different mindset. That first day he was wearing exactly the same clothes he'd worn at the tournament: tan dock shoes, beige pants that had the front 120° hidden by his monstrous gut covered by a shapeless golf shirt with a missing button.

When I questioned him, he said, "That's what the guys wear."

I said, "Bullshit," entering into a very brief conversation that led to him wearing a suit and tie that afternoon. In a suit Marvin looked the part, in his 'golf outfit' he looked like a tired, beat-up old man with no stamina.

I was always an easy person to travel with, but Marvin was pushing the envelope. Travelling with him was extremely stressful. I'd planned two days, he'd planned two appointments. He'd been with the company three months, still introducing himself as the "new guy" and completely baffled by most applications.

He didn't hold his own in meetings, his grasp of customer need was simplistic, the data required to properly prepare the few proposals he was ever asked for predictably incomplete. On the second day I told him I would add a segment to the technical session of the upcoming meeting that would help him understand many of the applications. When I got back to Montreal I phoned Barnaby to suggest that he schedule time with Marvin in Toronto. He asked with what in mind; I answered, getting rid of him, and Barnaby agreed.

Marvin made an initial mistake: Playing hard doesn't mean playing all the time. I'd invited him to dinner the night of his second interview, essentially to gauge his table manners. During his first week at the office he'd stayed at the same lodge I'd reserved for the Shenandoah meeting, their menu surpassing many of the finest restaurants in Montreal. He was very well cared for during his time in Virginia, a little spoiled. Then came the company golf tournament.

All this apart from lunches with Barnaby or me who thought nothing of having a glass of wine with lunch. That was part of our Québec culture, not a work habit. He was living the good life, believing he could simply go home and curl up with a good whodunit technical manual.

What he failed to realize was that all the perks came from one source: The bottom line. Something he hadn't contributed to in three months.

*

The week before the meeting I had a one-on-one with Barnaby to discuss content, Marvin, Didier and the West. The meeting was off-campus. Not the first such meeting. Barnaby had a proclivity for secrecy bordering on obsession, if not paranoia. Every discussion to-date was closed-door, eating lunch often the secondary purpose, part of the "I know something you don't" mentality left over from the Félix era.

I had two topics to present. I would spend five minutes on Newfoundland because no one cared, requiring two hours to present my abridged version of the Customer Management programme. Barnaby had one hour, which he thought was enough to broach the issue of a company dress code and professionalism. He'd intended to address the subject of sloppy attire in April, continuously delaying that meeting, and now he was giving me a heads-up on his other subject. He was taking over the sales management position, responsible for Clément, Elmer, Césaire and Marcel. Didier and Marvin were mine.

I thought to drill a hole in his head, to see what might squirt out.

He knew full-well I was measurably more qualified. How did he expect to manage even a small sales team when he had no competencies, no skills? Hadn't he learned his lesson with Félix, splitting loyalties, creating division? Only one year earlier he'd told me the company was up for sale to the right buyer, that he wanted nothing more than to bounce his grandchildren on his knees. Marvin acting like an old lady was bad enough, now we had a grandfather pretending he hadn't passed his prime.

He had no idea what he was doing, letting unskilled peddlers determine his future.

I wrote him a letter in April, perhaps serving to shoot myself in the foot. Barnaby always listened to what I said, but didn't always hear me. In the letter I explained the time had come for me to take over sales management responsibilities for both flat and plastic product lines and that he had to stop confusing everyone with the duplicity of management and management styles.

What he hoped to accomplish by bringing me into the company had backfired on him big-time and immediately. His fault. He should have possessed a better sense of how his people would react. He had to remedy the situation, bite the bullet one more time. Better to bite the bullet than feel it, Barnaby. My product and application knowledge in both product lines were equally balanced and his staff still had much to learn.

His application knowledge had become virtually non-existent.

Then came the one-on-one, in a restaurant of course. Francis had ears like parabolic antennae.

Taking over sales management to placate junior salesmen and a couple of inside people wasn't good reasoning. If he did, he would ruin everything he'd hoped to achieve. This wasn't Barnaby's idea. We both knew. He didn't function that way. He and Anthony thought that by dividing the sales team the animosity would be eliminated. They were wrong, but decided.

Anthony, although not physically at the table, was as much in front of me as Barnaby.

Working with a dreamer was one thing; working with someone who had no sense of the real world was something else. I had my own interpretation of what should be. If Barnaby wanted grief so badly, he was welcomed to a full measure. He would also take on Marvin and Didier. Two managers for such a small company was ludicrous.

From that point I would be available for information or guidance in matters relating to plastic, the Western provinces and Newfoundland. I would do Ontario on a temporary basis, fully expecting Marvin would be sent home by month's end. Temporary meaning three months.

I would also limit my time at the office. I would work independently and not attend any meetings unrelated to Shenandoah.

Barnaby was a gentleman, not comfortable with confrontation or ultimatums, but I wasn't threatening. Not my style. I was presenting my agenda for however long I would remain. He'd given me a job to do without understanding the consequences, fearing what from the worst sales reps in the business? That they'd quit?

He hadn't once stood behind my programmes and what appeared to be a stand at the first sales meeting was soon forgotten by everyone including him.

He was flustered.

I didn't understand, he said.

Didn't I?

He was taking over as a temporary measure until things stabilized, he assured me. At which point I could manage the team as I saw fit. All he wanted was an adjustment period so he could get used to everything that was happening.

I could smell the bullshit. When Hokum said "temporary," I knew he was lying. And he knew. His credibility evaporating, made worse when he said something that amazed me. I actually coughed a hoarse laugh. He said: "I don't even know how you've managed to come in here these past months…with those people."

I sipped my wine, standing to leave. "It's who I am. Certainly not because you're the master of your house, Barnaby. And, Barnaby, those are your people."

*

August 14th was a Monday. Marvin arrived the night before, Didier left Québec City early to arrive at the hotel for nine. I opened the meeting, Barnaby spoke for a few moments and the four reps did their presentations. Didier's was technical and informative, Marvin spoke about "his" 75 K order, Clément lamented how MacLeary was beating him, and Elmer spoke about specific flat belt orders. None of them spoke about plastic.

I took the full two hours to elaborate on every possible facet they would need to know about the Customer Management programme in order to make the most of the new system, telling them to stop me any time for questions. I was going through it once only, and if they could open their computers they could do this. If not, they should call

Barnaby, which is when they opened their individual copies and picked up their pencils. When I finished, Barnaby stood and walked to the front.

Effective immediately he would be the new Sales Manager for both product lines. I would have independent responsibilities, he explained. I always had the utmost respect for Barnaby as a person and businessman, but he was making a grave error guided by illogic and the fear of whatever fallout might have occurred if he'd followed my recommendation. His reps were completely unprepared for the new complexities of sales, and didn't care. Nor had Barnaby done anything to reverse that trend.

With the exception of Didier, their experience was narrow, their thinking restricted to the influence Félix left as his legacy. Barnaby was ill-equipped to take them anywhere but to the lowest common denominator, far from the higher level he'd originally mandated. He lacked the qualifications, particularly the technical qualifications, because he'd let himself become redundant.

He had undermined everything I attempted to do for him, in blunt fashion, most of the ten people present gloating.

Following the meeting, I absolved myself of any goodwill or interest in saving the company from what I considered was Hokum's self-destruct mode. What I would do from then on would be for my gain, my sense of achievement.

From that point I seldom went to the office. I had no capacity for working with underachievers, never before seeing so many standing still so willingly.

You can lead a horse to water, but you can't make it drink. That's the expression, which makes no sense at all. Unless you need the horse to carry you somewhere, what's the difference whether it drinks or not?

*

At the meeting Barnaby simultaneously took over management of the sales department, and lost control. He spoke to peddlers of the need for professionalism without saying how to go about it, and from then on Pre-Call Planning, Action Business Plans and Time Management did not exist.

Subsequent meetings were randomly planned, the consistent and common theme being "we have to do better." But no one knew how.

I wasn't invited, and didn't enquire. Barnaby didn't do one joint call, excepting the one time with Marvin, nor did he do performance reviews. He never provided more solid technical training and never questioned their ability or skill. They were on easy street, though for the next two years Barnaby, dreaming of his retirement by then, was unable to go on vacation or a long weekend.

Barnaby hadn't made a sales call in fourteen years. I can only imagine how he felt spending most of his second week as Sales Manager doing joint calls with Marvin. Marvin must have thought he was having a great time. He was travelling with the boss, having nice dinners and would no longer have to submit his reports on time because he was told by the others that Barnaby never read them, which was true. Best of all, he was guaranteed freedom from me, according to the others. And they were partly right. Partly.

I have no idea why Barnaby called me to review what he'd done with Marvin. Perhaps he wanted confirmation, but Marvin was into his fourth month, was no better, and still saying "new guy." So, what's the question? Barnaby went back the next week and fired him.

One option was to hire someone else; the other was to work through a secondary distributor, though no one wanted to take on the line. I suggested Bob and Pat who'd left Swiss to start up their own company and those negotiations went on from September to January 2001 when they finally failed due to an impasse on what was a reasonable profit margin.

During that time I had three main objectives to complete before year's end. One was to set-up a distribution network between Manitoba and Alberta; another was to keep Sea & Double U happy while controlling their growing tendency to hold ICS over my head. The third was to replace direct representation with a distributor in Ontario, an almost impossible task.

More importantly, snow was falling horrifically the evening of the company Christmas party.

*

January 2002 Barnaby met with and hired Yoakum's second direct rep for Ontario, telling me after the fact. He was an old acquaintance Barnaby hadn't seen for years, someone who hadn't worked for over a year.

They'd met for dinner one night when Barnaby was in Ontario visiting family, Barnaby calling me to ask that I put a plastics seminar together for Adam who'd arrive at the office the following Monday. He had several years of experience in flat belt distributor sales, a good man for the job, probably only nerves that made him drunk during the interview. Good move, Barnaby: a drunk.

He was sixty-two. He lived 150 kilometres north of Toronto in the woods. Barnaby hired someone who should have been thinking about retirement, not appointments, shutdowns and methodology. He had no résumé, no history of achievements, nothing.

When I met Adam February 05th the first thing I saw were his winter boots laced to his knees, his pant legs tucked in. He was wearing a thick cable sweater, from which protruded a red and grizzled head that was pot-marked, rough-shaven and studded with a bulbous and purple-veined nose.

Barnaby had hired a backwoodsman; all that was

missing were a dogsled, snowshoes and a jug of moonshine.

The meeting was concise. I didn't like him.

When I saw Barnaby before leaving I asked how much time he planned to spend with Adam on the road. None; Adam was experienced. He knew everyone in the industry and had several Key Accounts he could call his own. Yeah, right. After a year of searching Want-ads.

I, however, should spend a week with him to guide him through plastic per our previous agreement. Fine. I'd meet him in Toronto on the nineteenth and, when Adam asked what he should do in the meantime, I suggested that he go shopping.

His car was fifteen years old and filthy. When he asked if I could rent one for the week I said no. But when I opened the passenger side door, I changed my mind. I wouldn't, but he would while I waited at the hotel. Again, his pants were stuck into his boots, he wore the same heavy sweater and a white parka. Against the redness of his face and purple nose he looked like a paint-splashed igloo. We made one call.

The second day we made two. On the third we made one in the morning and I rebooked my flight from Thursday to that afternoon. No one we saw knew him, the appointments lasting fifteen to twenty minutes.

When I'd called him the week before to remind him to send me his Pre-Calls, he'd asked what that was, promising he would have something for me when I got there. He didn't. What he did have were pills for his heart and blood pressure. He actually found driving the car difficult. He wheezed words from his mouth, often coughing, had trouble keeping up during our plant tours, remaining behind during one occasion because he couldn't manage the ten-metre ladder to the catwalk.

After my second set of joint calls with him in early March, as unsuccessful as the first, I told Barnaby he'd hired someone worse than Marvin and that he should spend time as Sales Manager in Toronto to see what was going on.

He never did.

Instead he waited six weeks to fire the washout, during which time Adam brought in zero business, Yoakum losing important ground in a key marketplace. As well as in Québec following Didier's resignation before the end of his first year.

Didier was never given a chance, excluded from many of the better accounts on the periphery of his territory which he could easily have captured. Nor was progress made at Blanchette, a catch-22 situation. Didier never grasping the rudiments of plastic due to the disproportionately small number of accounts to whom he could sell.

Two junior reps were now maintaining Québec and the Maritimes, Césaire filling in when a local need arose.

*

The Packaging Exhibition in Chicago was an escape I attended throughout the third week of April to assist Shenandoah. The show was successful with new business potential for both companies. I limited my input to plastic, leaving steel to them. Nor did I promote flat belt. Not after Barnaby made the bakery in Toronto a house account to avoid paying me the two K commission on the second order that was days away. From which point he was on his own to maintain contact. I was done, and he never did. He simply waited.

Shows normally take the better part of a morning to gain momentum, the evenings all but dead during the last ninety minutes. The last afternoon is always forgotten by visitors, exhibitors left to do knee bends, twiddle fingers and tell each other how good or how bad the week was. Even short days at trade shows are long, most of us ordering up to our rooms after a couple of drinks at the bar.

Linda was with me, making the evenings our own

throughout the week, going to any place for dinner not crammed with sales people.

The Friday night was everyone's last. The show closed late afternoon. By early evening everyone was either returning home, sitting at the bar or crowded into someone's HS.

Being in century-old hotels always made me wonder how women at the turn of the last century managed to stand in those tiny rooms, let alone undress and store hoops, bustles, muffs and chapeaux.

We were going to dinner where quiet was on the menu, after a cocktail in the hotel lounge. I was seated in an armchair wedged into the corner between the bed, which was my ottoman, and the radiator, which was the coaster for the vodka I was nursing in the two-fifty-a-night room. I was set to go. Linda was in the bathroom putting the finishing touches to her make-up before coming out sans towel.

Everything was laid out on the bed: Black laced demi-bra, matching silk thong, stick-up nylons and a red dress with a discreet tailored slit that could be daring or not. But was.

Sitting on the turned-down bed she reached for the panties, aligning the three openings, leaning back, raising one foot to the target, then the other, standing with her thumbs tucked under the waistband, tugging and wiggling in concert until what little I saw disappeared. The nylons were next, the first foot coming up to perch on the bed as she pulled the stretchy silk to her ankle. Again she stood, sideways, pulling, unrolling to her mid-thigh when a final pull and snap left the black lace securely in place. She sat. A repeat performance dressed her other leg, leaning forward, smoothing out imaginary wrinkles. With a half-turn, reaching for the bra, one arm went in, then the other, adept hands joining at the centre of her back performing the blind manoeuvre most men can't reverse with both eyes

No One to Tell

open.

She bent forward, reaching for her shoes. The left foot wiggled in, then the right. She seemed satisfied, standing, doing the standard approval-rating three-sixty, leaning across the bed, reaching for her short and sexy red dress. One foot into the open waist, then the other.

The show was over, but I didn't stand for an ovation, I stood because the zipper was my job; something most women don't manage well, despite the bra thing.

First resting my drink on the radiator under the window, my peripheral vision took a snapshot of the crowded window across the narrow courtyard one floor up.

"Think you'll have to change your dress."

She didn't like that. "Why? What's wrong with it?"

"Nothing, but a room full of guys just watched you dressing."

She didn't look back, raising one foot to the bed, pulling back her hem, adjusting the black lace top of the nylon, turning her knee to the left and right, smoothing her dress before smiling into the open window.

She went to the TV table, waiting for me to gather my money clip and keys. She told me they looked old enough and that her dress was staying on, pausing at the door, "until we get back."

She knew not to ruin the experience with a flurry of panicking hands and flailing arms in a clumsy attempt to undo what's been done, turning erotica into ribald humour. Just as the young woman I came across while at Swiss who was standing at a corner waiting for the light to change with both hands gripping the handles of full shopping bags.

Her dress was summery light, the wind sent by my guardian angel sweeping her hem shoulder high, maintaining altitude, her panties doing their best to hide from the sudden exposure. She turned, seeing my smile. She smiled, which I don't believe would have been any different had her hands been empty. They weren't beige, not six-to-a box, and the bra strap across her back was a tan line. She was also a complete picture: Expensive shoes, purse, hat, and a body she took pride in.

She was in the right place at the right time. So was I. Win-win.

*

Not many weeks after, Larry invited me to Virginia for the annual four-day Shenandoah sales meeting. I arrived the Sunday evening for dinner with Larry, the president of Shenandoah, a VP who was Larry's boss, Frank from South Africa and Brent from New Zealand.

I'd been invited to explain our progress, difficulties, western Canada and where we anticipated being at specific future dates. Frank and Brent would do likewise, my second presentation on the Tuesday comprised of application reports. Wednesday, as a courtesy, we foreigners were invited to sit in on non-confidential segments of the Shenandoah meeting. We declined, renting a car.

After ninety minutes on and off I-66, wrong exits and wrong turns, we arrived in Washington by 1:30. Every time I took a curve, gave the right-of-way, or turned right on red, the Commonwealth-lefties were ducking in their seats, grabbing door handles or cursing a variety of their local favourites.

We were starving, searching for food and drink, finally choosing a classy eatery with some guy in formal wear telling us the wait would be two hours, the two hours between two and four. When did these people work? And how long were the people behind us going to wait? Or were they in line for dinner?

With no bar to pass the time in, the people behind us seemed fine with standing for hours, doing nothing. Or perhaps they'd eaten a better breakfast. Or perhaps we were less diplomatic. In any event Frank, who was built like a brick shithouse, moved in a laser-beam line toward a man sitting alone in a booth for four and oblivious to our plight. The silver-haired, burly South African leaned into the booth, reappearing moments later to signal us over.

"He's just finishing; won't be but a moment."

The three of us stood over the table as the man finished his coffee, his cake, gulped the rest of his beer and put cash in the leather envelope that accompanied the meal. It was the first time I'd seen a man dress himself in street wear while sitting, first wrapping his scarf around his neck, which wasn't needed, adjusting his hat to the perfect angle before wriggling into the lightweight all-weather coat I thought Frank would stuff down his throat until at last, "Sir, I would gladly pay your bill if you'd please just stand and get the fuck away."

Brent jerked one way; I glanced the other. Perhaps Frank's offer simply sounded as though screeched through a PA system, the gentleman quickly forgotten as he stood and walked off. What mattered was eating.

The first beer was good, the second was better. They had a third, I abstained. The food was alright, each of us comparing the fare with restaurants the others didn't know. Then we left, sticking Frank with the bill. Brent paid for the parking and gas. I paid for the car.

The Smithsonian was too vast, the Hill was too congested with tourists. So we walked around to wear off lunch before heading to the car and the valley.

He was rough-looking, because he was. Not a candidate for any girl to take home to Mom. He needed some quick cash to turn his life around, "not just a couple of quarters, man, but maybe, like, twenty, thirty bucks. I know you got it, man. I could really use it, man."

He'd hit on Brent who was walking on the inside, holding out one hand while taking a drag on someone else's discarded butt.

Brent explained that he was a tourist. He didn't have that much to spare, but his new friend wasn't giving up. He knew a philanthropist when he saw one. Frank and I walked ahead when Brent made the huge mistake of slowing, though we went back when we saw he wasn't getting away. Not only was he not getting away, he was getting into a conversation about the guy's future, where he'd gone wrong and what he could do.

Frank could not "fuckin" believe it," when we heard: "In prison? Is that right, then? What for, mate?"

"For murder, man. I killed a guy on the street. Knifed him. But that was a while back. Can't say I remember much. Know what I mean, man?"

We pulled Brent away, despite the new information that we were assholes. I already knew I was from the goonies in Goonieville. We laughed non-stop, not at him, at everything, twice pulling off the highway to clear our eyes.

That night we exchanged farewells at the hotel. Frank would retire before the next meeting, Brent coming from too far away to make the annual event a tradition and we knew that "let's keep in touch" didn't apply.

Thursday was breakfast with Larry and Marty, Marty asking whether I expected to join them in Atlanta in October. I told him my agenda was booked through to December, though I was open to a week of joint calls in Alberta in June.

*

When Barnaby first opened Yoakum twenty years earlier his few products were an easy sell, not overly technical, mostly a matter of replacing existing belts by copying or supplying equivalents according to spec. Competition at the time wasn't severe, the flow of business constant and predictable. Although as Barnaby stood still, his competition did not. As their product lines expanded, his did not. Only in the mid-nineties did he get into plastic with

No One to Tell

Hawk.

I'd told him a hundred times he needed nylon core belting for transmission applications to compete, but he was reluctant because Félix had disputed the need, the sales guys near paralysis at the thought of more calculations and charts.

Gordon had been with Simple Belting for six months, getting by. He had a mandate for the entire province of Québec, restricting himself to Montreal and the western environs leading into eastern Ontario. In fact he had very little knowledge of Québec, the possibility of achieving any significant outcome minute to all but him.

The answer was to have a company like Yoakum working with him as a distributor, thereby covering the entire province and much of the East. All he had to do was set up a meeting for me with the owner of Simple so I could give his staff a seminar on the plastic they would distribute in Ontario, Gordon adding plastic to his product line as well as his revenue.

A win-win to everyone but Gordon who now had no choice in the matter.

The day Gordon did his presentation at Yoakum, I gave mine to Simple in Toronto. Barnaby attended neither, comfy in his office.

Before I left Simple I had an agreement with the owner, phoning Gordon the next day to tell him Yoakum would now represent him in Québec and the East. I asked him to meet me at the office on the Friday for a one-on-one plastics seminar, which he did, making my day. Not really. Gordon was always a challenge to the central nervous system.

The following week I did my preliminary joint calls with Simple in Ontario equipped with names, addresses, histories and potential sales figures ranging between ten and fifty K per customer per the agreement. They would take over completely, with the exception of the bakery which

Barnaby saw as an automatic revenue, demonstrating his unique grasp of the sales process.

*

A well-known clairvoyant of the 60s once stopped a man about to pass him on the street, telling the man he should go home immediately to see his family. When the stranger questioned the clairvoyant as to why, the psychic replied that he would die that afternoon. That he should go home to say goodbye. Well, the man went home, and he died. Not unlike what I saw each time I went into the office. I went in so infrequently that changes unapparent to others were plainly visible to me.

Barnaby was changing as the months passed him by, becoming lethargic and indifferent. Ten months after the August meeting, not only did everyone continue wearing jeans and sweat shirts, Barnaby had transitioned from wearing jackets and ties to the lowest common denominator of golf shirts better suited to the back porch or working around the house.

He relied increasingly upon Anthony to play an active role in the company without explaining to anyone what that role was, spending much less time in his office. He'd spent a considerable sum renovating the interior of the building, but hadn't thought to spend a few hundred dollars for bilingual keyboards. We were in Québec, after all.

All quotes, follow-ups, and correspondence to Francophone customers lacked accents, a virtual pidgin. When I asked Césaire what he thought of the recent improvements to the building he shrugged. So did Marcel; the changes not enough to keep Henry from quitting his job. He'd reached his breaking point, the stress of taking up the slack for Barnaby, Elmer wasting no time commandeering his daddy's empty office, making the concept of home offices a thing of the past, as was the concept of Barnaby being in control.

No One to Tell

*
Alberta was progressing according to plan.

Marty and I had planned a weeklong trip of in-depth technical seminars for the fifteen reps and managers at NorthWestCom and joint calls to their key accounts.

Departing Sunday, returning Saturday in coach was four grand, the approximate cost of a pacemaker to revive Barnaby, although I had a solution he really couldn't refuse. Nor did he have a choice. I would fly on my points, which he thought was great. In exchange for which he would assume Linda's full expenses for the week. He was getting off cheap.

Monday and Tuesday went like clockwork in Calgary with the NWC staff ready and waiting, appointments pre-planned, the purpose of each and the intended outcome provided to us. The seminar consumed Monday morning and I didn't see Marty again until Tuesday night, when we drove to Banff for dinner. That's how things were supposed to work: smoothly, like clockwork. Not like mindless chipmunks in a rotary cage.

Wednesday we drove to Edmonton, stopping in Red Deer for a fast lunch and an appointment set up for us by the staff in the Edmonton office. Marty and I came out from the account patting each other's back, the Edmonton office receiving the sixty K order before we arrived.

The routine was the same as Calgary, coming away with equally good results. I'd also met separately with the VP of Sales, advising him that Saskatchewan was his if he wanted it. He did, replacing a company that had done nothing in six months. A big difference between growing the problem and getting rid of it. That's what Barnaby wasn't understanding, allowing his problems to fester.

Marty flew out late Friday afternoon from Edmonton. We drove to Calgary to enjoy the weekend before flying home late Sunday.

No One to Tell

*

Despite my promise to self that Barnaby was on his own, I was constantly urging him to do something or other. He was like a widower who couldn't find his underwear. He took my marketing ideas for Alberta, Newfoundland and Ontario and applied them to Québec, yet I wasn't allowed to work in the East.

From my home office window I could literally see hundreds of companies Yoakum was ignoring, potential sales that might have had a significant financial impact, particularly since his frequent absences from the office were for meetings with perspective buyers.

Simple said things were slow due to summer vacations and a poor economy, predicting business would pick up by September or October, while the Yoakum reps had done absolutely nothing with nylon core. Whenever Gordon felt the urge to broach the subject, I told him to talk with Barnaby. I also reminded him that he'd done nothing with plastic.

I wasn't surprised when nothing happened by September, writing Simple Belt to give notice they would no longer have access to Shenandoah product effective immediately, other than as a regular customer on a per order basis. The marriage annulled by mutual disinterest.

They were as intimidated by plastic as Gordon, Yoakum no better with Simple's nylon core. At which point I should have walked out and stayed out, my proclivity for giving the benefit of the doubt taking over from reason.

I was travelling forty percent of the time, my closest customer 600 km away, the furthest 3600. St-Anthony, NF came in second at 2900. If I didn't fly, I didn't go.

Barnaby thought Anthony might have the solution to the problem of representation in Ontario, which continued as Barnaby's priority. His solution was that I travel there every other week; this in addition to Alberta, Manitoba,

No One to Tell

Newfoundland, Virginia and various tradeshows. When I asked him what the second part of his proposal was, he asked what I meant. I asked how much he thought that would cost. He shrugged. He had no idea. He didn't know. He just thought the idea was a good one. I told him to go fuck himself and walked out.

I met with Barnaby in November with the intention of showing him the need for a revitalization programme, before he screwed up big-time. I told him I didn't need Anthony pissing on my pant leg and the most I would travel to Ontario was ten times a year, as a temporary measure, which equated to forty man-days each year compared to the competition's combined 1900 man-days. Despite which, he refused to see the writing on the wall, ignoring failed attempts at direct selling and one involving Simple. He was making no sense at all, which I put in writing so the point wouldn't be lost on him, unless intentionally.

*

I couldn't disregard that my interest in Yoakum was disproportionately high to their interest in me, not that I was reneging on my philosophy of putting myself first and the company third. More likely was that Barnaby didn't understand that he too could be first if he took the time to plan long-term strategies and not short-term wish lists.

I prepared a detailed graph depicting the avalanching sales in plastic and steel in Québec and the Maritimes. Alberta was self-sufficient, so was Newfoundland as long as Hokum didn't raise prices after promising he wouldn't, but he was having one of his hissy fits, forgetting that Sea & Double U had gone out on a limb for us two years earlier.

I all but implored him to let me sell in Montreal and the key plastic accounts in the rest of Québec. He refused, despite the others avoiding key accounts because they would have to deal with upper management and engineering staff. The potential from only a few A and B accounts easily exceeded a million dollars, the most conservative estimate translating into a third for him, including Blanchette where no one had gone in almost two years. It was not too late for serious damage control, but he had to do something immediately.

His staff had dropped to nineteen due to Henry and a few production drop-outs, projected year-end sales twenty percent under the previous year. Not good. If he ignored the trend, Shenandoah would break off relations and either deal through someone else or go direct. Larry and Marty weren't impressed with the current activity in Québec or Ontario. Nor was Larry one to sit and wait.

Referring to a minor snag in the initial meetings with Shenandoah, Barnaby had once said that he didn't know whether to "shit or wind his watch." At the time I suggested he wind his watch. Perhaps I'd suggested wrongly.

He refused, believing Elmer and Clément would quit. So what? He'd always wanted Clément to quit and losing Elmer was tantamount to losing a gangrenous leg. He was useless, destined to remain a peddler. In fact getting rid of Elmer was the healthy option. The whole industry knew Félix had a pipeline to Yoakum. Guess who? Merely a matter of time before he'd leave Barnaby and join with his much-missed and adored hero at Yoakum's newest competition.

My ultimate goal had become Barnaby's ultimate failure, a matter of time before he said as much, or I did.

*

I promised NorthWestCom I'd be in Alberta every quarter. Their enthusiasm was refreshing, boding well for the coming year, Calgary's call timely because I'd just completed the preliminary layout of a proposed joint marketing programme.

January 21, 2002 wasn't unusual: extremely cold, blustery and dark moments before the 6:30 flight. I would have flown on the Sunday but the flights were more expensive, equal to 100 dollars for each work hour I'd lose on the Monday and Friday. Not my accounting strategy.

Flying direct from Montreal to Calgary in four hours on the Sunday wasn't an issue; the cost was. That was a red flag, for me, as was taking the entire day to get there. My lost weekends in order to accomplish a corporate objective and accommodate those who placed no value on my time were at an abrupt end.

I left Monday, hop-scotching my way across the country on a series of connecting short-haul flights to save Yoakum a few hundred dollars. Peanuts compared to the business I would have gained the Monday and Friday morning

The itinerary took me to Toronto, Winnipeg, Brandon and Regina, before landing in Calgary near four o'clock local time, doing the land portion by taxi because NWC would drive me to our joint calls on Tuesday and Wednesday morning. Wednesday afternoon I flew to Edmonton where I was met early Thursday morning to begin a day and a half of calls. I was back at the airport for a one PM flight, local time Friday, leaving NWC with the impression that Barnaby had more money than brains when, in fact, he was losing both.

The return trip took me from Edmonton to Calgary, Regina, Brandon, Winnipeg, Toronto and Montreal by two AM, exclusive of the two-hour time difference.

I was on the same twin-engine plane from Calgary to Toronto, which could well have displayed crossed fingers as an insignia. The aircraft accommodated thirty passengers, though through to Brandon each leg was half-full. The pilot, co-pilot and attendant wore ski jackets and after each touchdown we went with them into the airports while the plane was refuelled.

We were at my psychological halfway point, boarding with the newest passengers, on time, most of the seats empty, waiting for the heavy drone to rupture our eardrums, the vibrations to pulverize the contents of our cranial cavities. The pilots waited as well, looking at dials, looking at each other, tapping this one, tapping that one, exchanging glances.

Then we started exchanging glances, our hands too cold to tap anything. The outside minus 30° C was starting quickly to equalize with the cabin temperature.

They had a problem. We had to disembark. The problem wasn't serious, but would take a while to fix, perhaps thirty minutes. We could leave our briefcases and carry-ons. The area was secure, but if any of us believed the "nothing serious", we didn't believe the "secure."

The seven or eight of us went our separate ways, pulling out cell phones, searching for coffee or a washroom. We'd gone into the terminal through the Departures doors, redirected through a few more openings onto the main concourse, which meant we'd have to return through Departures, which meant going through security with only boarding pass stubs. Oh, joy!

Security was on high alert, walkie-talkies pulled out, hands in the STOP position, supervisors called in, ticket agents summoned to testify on our behalf. And we were the only ones in the airport, thirty minutes grinding into ninety. Part of those ninety minutes were used to warm the plane, so no one complained.

The problem was insufficient oil in the landing flaps. Apparently we would have been able to take off, but landing in Toronto would have been less than ideal, taking me back to the woman who once crushed my hand to purple during take-off, after asking if she could hold it for reassurance; the guy sitting beside me who began yelling "fire" as we taxied to the runway, thinking the vapour from the air conditioning system was sending him to his death; the aborted "missed runway" in Toronto, and the plane

No One to Tell

stacked for so long over Atlanta that the pilot had to reroute to Charleston because he was running low on fuel.

One of the gems was landing in Buffalo in the late 70s onboard a now defunct airline, watching the flight attendant, a.k.a. stewardess, bounce her way along the aisle because she'd waited too long to take her seat. She was taken away by ambulance. Or landing in the Dominican Republic with a jammed landing gear, which was only half as much fun as wondering what was going through Linda's mind when flying from Les Îles-de-la-Madeleine over the Gulf of St. Lawrence, the tail end of a hurricane buffeting the nineteen-seater like tissue paper that we all could have used. When I'd looked across the aisle with a smile and thumbs-up, I got the finger. She wasn't always a lady. Or the time Wayne and I were connecting to a commuter flight in Atlanta, and the pilot asked him to change seat assignments with a petite woman for better weight distribution. That got me another finger.

Still in Brandon, the cabin acceptably not cold, passengers seated, the door closed ready for take-off, we heard loud thumping coming from the portside. Thumping noises on a plane aren't good, those who could craning to see what the matter was. The pilots were on the outside, freezing. They'd left their coats in the cockpit, the zealous attendant a tad sheepish.

I survived the twelve flights in five days, arriving in Montreal to clear a week's worth of snow from my car, arriving home at three, thinking I'd reached the saturation point for travel. I hadn't. That would come a few years later.

*

Travelling wasn't the problem, per se, more the type of travel, the frequency, and knowing that Barnaby was taking very little interest in current events. I was away as much as I was at home, putting in twelve-hour days while Hokum was increasingly unreachable, coming in late, leaving early, not doing much when he was there. His mood had transmuted from lethargic to solitary, grimness etched into his face for everyone to recognize or question.

Potential buyers were turning him down, as he rejected those who didn't fit his profile of the perfect guardian of his legacy. He would only sell to someone who promised to protect the jobs of the current employees. The most serious buyer blamed the foreseeable downturn in the economy for his decision to terminate discussions. Barnaby believed him which, to me, meant he believed in the Tooth Fairy. He was trying desperately to sell his company, but he wasn't a salesman. He wasn't convincing.

I spent February in my home office or Ontario. The marketing programme was accepted with tremendous enthusiasm by NWC, which would pretty much be my primary project from March to June, be industry specific and include 250 of NWC's best accounts or best potential accounts. Despite Barnaby putting his wife Anthony in charge of coordinating, we seldom spoke. He brought nothing to the table. I ignored him, as did NWC whose branches had contacted all the selected companies by the end of March. The preliminary feedback very encouraging, though Barnaby wasn't finished fucking up.

The man most familiar with the assembly of plastic left for a better job. Barnaby, in his clouded wisdom, giving over the job to the guy who was also the shipper and receiver. From which point the number of belts going out didn't greatly exceed the combined number of complaints coming in. Or belts being returned. Worse, most of the complaints were coming from Newfoundland. The only light in the tunnel was Manitoba, running smoothly

Answering the phone had become a crap shoot.

I was restricting my activities in Ontario, highlighting, Marty asking to join me during my March trip, confiding

No One to Tell

that he had concerns, confused as to whether he was working for Shenandoah or Yoakum. What I said to Marty was: "Do what you have to do."

Marty had reason to be nervous, but he was talking to the wrong person. Every move taken by Yoakum was being recorded and analyzed in Virginia. Larry had left them for unexplained reasons in January and Marty had a lot to lose. If Larry somehow reappeared in The Swamp, everyone would pretty much be up Shit Creek.

*

When I got to my room that night I kicked back, timed the planes coming into Pearson and watched TV. The day was full and changing the flight I'd missed to the next day made more sense. That way I was reserved, not on standby.

At some point my foot hit an object barely hidden by the overhang of the bedcovers, protruding enough for me to tug at it without seeing under a hotel bed. A folder. On the front cover was the name of a company and individual I was in the process of developing business with. The proposal was replete with technical data and prices, making for good reading over the next hour after which I trashed the document as an anonymous gift to a competitor.

The document was a comprehensive proposal prepared by a German manufacturer, outlining an extensive annual contract comprising a variety of flat belt applications. The proposal was well-prepared and any serious contender could have used the information to their advantage. Unfortunately, I had no mandate to sell flat belt in Ontario or anywhere else.

Friday. I was once again going home. The 10:00 AM flight was on time, three-quarters full. I've always marvelled at those who pull out their computers, annoying the rest of us with incessant tapping. They should realize we know it's all for show, or that they've waited too long. Or perhaps that we know who they are when they don't know us.

    Diagonally across the aisle, one row back, were businessmen talking business above the drone of the plane. They were speaking Spanish, musical compared to most idioms.

    They were discussing the possibility of establishing ties with a second distributor not far from Montreal. Their current distributor was below anticipated levels, losing market share. They needed and wanted to respect the existing distributor, but the newcomer seemed more aggressive and should be given a chance to prove themselves. Yoakum would have to understand.

    I had to pinch myself to stop from laughing. Much like watching the couple doing the dirty in the field or the nude resort, no one would believe me. The conversation lasted a good half-hour as they elaborated on promises given by Félix and their suspicions surrounding the effectiveness of Yoakum in promoting and selling their belts. Every word of their conversation would have helped Barnaby, if I'd told him. However, upon arriving home I listened to his message on my home office voice-mail, asking if we could get together on Tuesday, April 16th.

*

Going into the office that last day, I remembered once saying that going to Yoakum was like beaming onto the deck of the Mayflower from the USS Enterprise. The first few weeks were like that, becoming more like an F-18 pilot fighting a winning war, changing to a single-engine Cessna and fighting the same war without a joystick.

    Leaving Yoakum wasn't an unhappy occasion in my life. On the one hand, I left somewhat numbed by the knowledge I had so much to offer and for the better part of three years I was ignored. I left with no idea why he'd hired me in the first place without knowing anything about me. He'd never seen my résumé, had no idea I was fluent in a third language or that I'd owned an art gallery. He had no idea what I'd accomplished in the past or how. Other than I'd been with Swiss, Euro and ICS, he had no idea of where I'd spent my career or who I was.

On the other hand, leaving was like leaving the car I'd discarded prior to joining W&W: The doors didn't work, the roof lining always caved in when the windows were down, the battery was in a beer case, the front fenders were held in place with coat hangers and the rear bumper had fallen off. But the determining factor in getting rid of it was the steering wheel coming away in my hands as I was doing 110 km suddenly without steerage, no control. Not a good feeling.

That's exactly what happened at Yoakum. I'd been trapped in a moving hazard with no direction and no control. And the time was indeed right to get out and find something brand new.

I didn't harbour ill-feelings against Barnaby, but I did harbour disappointment until he became unworthy of my time spent thinking of him. My dream and Hokum's evaporated because success is either limited or propelled by the scope of the corporation's vision.

Hokum wanting a presence across Canada wasn't a vision, rather wishful thinking, a dream, and dreams are for those who sleep. He would have seen a vision through, the development and realization. He would have shown more pride in himself and his people. Instead he slept.

Not only had he never seen the limitless potential in the West for himself, he never once phoned the management of NWC to express his determination to succeed. Thereby creating a more meaningful relationship.

His knowledge of them was limited to Account Receivables and quotes. Nor did he ever actively support his sales team, such as they were. In a sense, my ultimate goal had become Barnaby's ultimate failure because he'd transferred ownership of that responsibility to himself.

All that might have been was ruined by lack of vision, which speaks to putting oneself first. Hokum disappointed both of us. What's worse, for him, he could have retired a much richer man. Instead giving into the fear of what his underlings would do, say or think. Peddlers without a future dictating his.

When I joined Yoakum his sales team had a combined experience of forty-three years. When I left they had a total of nine, reduced to barely five within a month, the competition they'd spawned boasting eighteen years.

He gave consideration to those who would disappoint him, stab him from behind. Such was the way in Goonieville. He was too blinded by sentiment to see the worst coming, too deaf to outsider presentiments to hear. I sat in front of Barnaby incapable of words to express how exhausted I was, how entirely pathetic I found his attempt to buy me off. We shook hands as a reflex reaction from so many years in business.

Walking through the front office and my gateway to another phase long overdue, Césaire was the one person to acknowledge me as though I'd be back after lunch. The others busied themselves, which I thought was spooky and unnatural.

Stepping into the fresh air I felt invigorated, even the spring breeze wafting over the farmers' fields smelled sweet. I'd climbed from the grave and wasn't walking across a parking lot, but across a threshold that would lead to yet another segment of my life filled with experiences and events I could never have imagined.

For a time I would share a world of mixed cultures, mixed views and opinions, a world of intellect, observation and determination, an experience amongst people from the four corners of the world, different religions and different ideas. I would witness the transition from reality into eternity of one of the co-authors of my life. Being with Linda to hold my mother's hands as she journeyed across her own threshold would be the most important of those experiences adding to my life's mosaic, my time at Yoakum a flickering candle lost in the universe.

They were the least satisfying chapter of my career, and soon forgotten. A few years later Césaire bumped into me at a café-terrasse. I'd forgotten his name.

No One to Tell

R.I.P.

Barnaby retired to stroke the dog. Césaire now runs the company that's worth a fraction of what its value might have been. Félix continues competing with Yoakum, most likely coding and decoding to protect himself against the likes of Elmer who I'm certain still leaves for work with cow shit on his boots. Never did like Bubba.
    Clément was irrelevant. He will be until his expiration date. Marvin, I imagine, is sitting on the porch with a cozy cushion and scotch if he hasn't himself expired by reaching for his wallet.
    Didier left before the end of his first year, unable to adapt to an infected corporate subculture. Adam went somewhere that makes no difference to anyone.
    Larry had issues, as did Shenandoah. The last time I spoke with Marty, Larry was a gentleman of leisure, thinner, happier, and still very much Larry whom I remember very fondly.
    Marty was always a Shenandoah man. He lived for them, was married to them. He had said on many occasions that he longed for retirement, spending quality time with his wife. But men like that don't retire, their hearts do.
    Pat left Shenandoah weeks before I left Yoakum. Charles left after Larry. His travelling had taken a personal and domestic toll, choosing balance over stress.
    Gordon remains stuck in mediocrity. I know. Because I

know Gordon. Or I did. He blamed everyone but himself for his stagnation, for standing still, never listening to good advice. This is where I leave him, despite having known him a few years longer.

As for me, as before, nothing existed behind me.

No One to Tell

Chapter Eleven
February 28th, 2006

Three minutes. Now you see it, now you don't: The amber skyline of Montreal. Everyone onboard contemplating individual epilogues to the journey: This was when shit happened. To my dismay Legs wasn't a nervous teenager.

"Flight attendants take your seats."

No shit. They already had, several minutes earlier. Nice of him to stop what he was doing.

Murphy was snug against his pillow, dreaming of his own pillow made puffy and warm by his mommy, his face a little grimaced, possibly wondering whether the pilot had read Ten Steps to Arriving.

Two minutes. I leaned slightly forward to see Legs. She was calm, her hands clasped in her lap. I smiled. She smiled, faintly nodding. For my money, Legs was going home to a high-rise condo, something classy, not ostentatious, perhaps a place with a doorman. No ring. Perhaps to a boyfriend, or another girl, or no one.

One minute. Strong winds were blowing from the north, south, east and west, and points in-between, from the top down and from underneath. Tailwind my ass. Then we were on the tarmac, then we weren't. Then we were, first on one landing gear, both, swinging to the right, swinging to the left. Do-se-do.

Applause. Though not from me, nor from her. Not from Murphy either. He was in the wrong row.

Then eternity, temptation. The greatest distance between two points: Touchdown to gate. Harsh reminders. Flashing orange lights. Jerking. Bright lights. Bells pinging. Permission granted. Release. A mindless horde. A jumbled mess. Bodies clashing, rubbing, reaching, straining, bending. Man and womankind reduced to their basest and most common elements, which is to say "get the fuck out of my way. Please."

The lady seated across from me was up first. Burger Boy might have been tethered to her as a conjoined tumor, all but launching the guy seated in front of him. Murphy was trapped. No way out. Feet tapping. Temptation. Twitching. He wanted to bend, reach for something. I believed at that moment he felt stupid. An easy and natural assumption.

Then a lull, blockage, an airline bottleneck. Some cretin's oversized carry-on, jammed, creating murmurs. Murphy saw his one chance to save vital seconds. He was gone, without a nod, ignoring the loveliest girl on the plane. And our mystery loser is…Murphy Law!

I didn't bother standing to let him by. Instead I leaned into his seat to avoid cranial damage and intimate contact with foreign body parts housed too long in festering conditions.

I looked at his seat, to Legs. She shrugged, grinning. One might say almost pleased.

Murphy Law, the very one pushing his way into the corralled herd because Burger Boy was probably plugging the exit, had forgotten his French-cuffed guru. What would he do? What would become of him?

Legs was right up there with Zelda, the once-was Emma-Mae, Desirée, Christine, and Wendy in the Bahamas…and Linda. She wasn't impressed. Nor was she in a hurry. Why? We had yet to face Customs, the carousel of jumbled luggage, and a ferocious snowstorm.

We were the last to disembark.

I had no carry-on. She had a single designer shoulder bag for her coat and boots that I reached for, thoroughly despising my sense of chivalry when I might have remained seated, letting her believe I had degenerated into a modern man. I've always been inconsiderate of myself that way.

I held her coat. Her name was Jennifer. One arm, then the other. We disembarked, the Code of Silence broken. She thanked me for the reassuring smile, from which point walking several hundred metres to Customs so far behind the others without talking would have been silly. No need to run, speed-walk or otherwise appear frazzled. We strolled.

She was an Account Executive. She lived in the downtown core, close to work. She wasn't driving home. No way. Safer to take a room for the night. Good girl. She asked what I thought of Murphy's book. I told her the fable about The Oracle's Bible and the Spider. She giggled. She understood, waving goodbye when signalled by the Customs guy whose day just got a whole lot better.

I got stuck with the midlife crisis delight who blamed me for every period she'd ever had before sending me to Gestapo Headquarters for interrogation and close inspection of my week's laundry. Again.

How disappointed they were to discover I had none. Baggage that is. Nothing unusual. Twenty-two times in twenty-four months, the Lost Baggage Claim filled out the night before in my hotel room. Another humourless Customs Agent's question not so much anticipated as heard before, ad nauseam.

"Did you pack your own bag?"

"What's your point, after fifteen hours in Miami, wherever else today, and Philly tomorrow without a lock? Your rules. Not mine. Salut."

No One to Tell

11:30 PM. The snow wasn't abating, the shuttle delayed.

At my car ninety minutes after arriving, the thing was covered with a half-metre of thick snow, another half-metre ploughed and compacted against the sides and rear bumper. With the heater on full, one window partly lowered as a precaution, my suit jacket tossed onto the rear seat, my sleeves rolled, I was en route by 00:30. The thirty-km drive lasted ninety minutes.

For the metric-deficient, that's twelve m/ph. Not exactly a race to get home, where I arrived at three AM a tad damp. A double vodka waiting for medicinal purposes. My luggage got home the next afternoon, decorated with the airline's Frequent Flyer Priority Service tag and yellow strips of Customs tape.

Friday I monitored a call from Mr. New Salesmanager. He wanted to meet me Monday morning. He wanted to strategize, assist me with customer-time expenditure ratios. Eight-thirty was good for him.

Strategize? That other thing? I told the phone to go fuck itself.

Before Monday came Saturday and Sunday. Linda convinced my previous week was influencing a rash decision, that I would change my mind. Wrong. Maybe.

Monday I called Mr. New Salesmanager at nine. I would meet with him Tuesday at 11:00. He questioned why. I responded that I didn't have a 6:00 AM flight. Then, coincidently, I had a call waiting.

I went outside to shovel snow, leaving him to shovel whatever.

*

Leaving Yoakum was a good thing. I needed downtime, a trip to the sunny Caribbean, a winter of 'me-first', the spring 2003 beginning on another sandy beach.

Throughout the previous fall, into yet another winter, I spent much of my time interacting with newly arrived émigrés from Europe and North Africa, many of them Muslim, one in particular becoming a good friend, not all of them strangers to fine cognac and wine. None of them defined by chadors and burkas, but simple outfits and simple customs, relieved to see that we're not all infidels. Certainly a validation to both that what we're too often led to believe by narrow minds, slanted news reports and resultant factoids is false, xenophobia revealing more about ourselves than any foreign culture we choose to misinterpret.

Then came my mother's departure into the unknown, for which I feel no great impatience to personally discover, making for a busy winter.

In the spring, descending from fourteenth-floor sophistication and anonymity to single-dwelling suburbia, suntanned, relaxed, wondering how to avoid talking over the proverbial fence with neighbours who were strangers, Linda suggested I write a book.

"About what?"

"Your life."

"What life? I don't have a life. All I've done is fly, drive, work, and fly."

"What about Gutter Slut, the SEAL, or losing your weight belt at 175 feet in the Thousand Islands? Or piloting our first thirty-footer to the marina in the dark with a fire in the bilge? Or the time you walked into a bank robbery? And Janys. Let's not forget Janys."

No. Let's not.

So I did. I wrote *No One to Tell*, taking a year, thinking I would forevermore enjoy my life. Didn't exactly work out that way. As though the goonies of Goonieville weren't a lifetime of Halloween nights crammed into three years I had to meet Audelle Sirac. Although not physically unattractive in the eyes of any desperate seafarer, I soon understood she was the meanest, most hateful little android

No One to Tell

I'd ever met.

She had a jar of jawbreaker candies on her desk, which I'm sure, in her mind, were the nuts of every man she'd ever met. With one exception: Me. Love at first sight. So much so that she wanted me to meet her daddy. Even daddy liked me in his own caustic, coarse way, which is surprising because he didn't like anyone else and no one liked him. They were afraid of daddy.

He had a humungous desk in his office that was a stale, a fire hazard of strewn papers. In front of the desk was a worn chair whose cushion once must have accommodated something or someone quite beefy, the concaved leather never fully recovering.

He waved me to sit, which I did in due course. We were playing a game despite our combined ages of 500 something. I sat on the edge of the discoloured arm, eye-to-eye with daddy, my briefcase lost in the bowl-shaped seat. We understood each other, arguing semantics for the next hour. A thoroughly unlikeable fellow.

When we were through challenging each other, Audelle asked me what I thought of daddy.

"Your father's an arrogant ass."

"Did he hire you?"

"Yes."

"Then you must be one also."

"Good point."

A week later I was flying to Virginia with Clod, the Sales Manager. Actually Claude, but you get the idea. More importantly, we understood each other as well.

I met Clod the day after meeting the she-devil and daddy, in her office. We had an instant dislike for each other, somewhat aggravated when he opened a McNally map book and thought to teach me how to plan a trip. I closed the book and walked out, telling him to fuck off.

Audelle phoned me later in the day to tell me I was rude,

which is when she understood you can't be rude to rude people.

To my surprise a third guy came with us. Saying the tag-a-long was inexperienced would be an understatement. Up close he smelled of mother's milk.

The first appointment was 200 kilometres from the airport. Two hours. I stayed in the car. Three reps walking into a company for an initial appointment was fatal anytime, an onslaught, overkill. Five minutes later they came out. Why? They weren't wearing ties with their polo shirts. The client was, with his French cuffs. He clearly didn't like peddlers.

Continuing on, another 200 km, we pulled into a liquor store parking lot across from a Marriott, my assumptions obvious. Not so. Seems Clod never made hotel reservations, each of them studying the pages of booklets they'd gotten from yellow and green dispensers the way a teenager would salivate over a girlie magazine. They were searching for discount coupons to local motels. I called the 800 number for the Marriott without them noticing, they were so engrossed. Take your home with you. That's the rule. My motel-nights pretty much ended with Lake Turd.

Then came the highlight of the week after telling Clod to pop the trunk. Numbnuts, the newbie, had left the portable demo equipment at their five-minute appointment. Thing was, how could I break the news at 2:55? Chuckling, of course, pointing to the Marriott where they could meet me the next morning.

That wasn't company policy, Clod said. He'd never spent over 49.95 on a room. Or on a suit, I suggested. We are what we are, and I was going to the Marriott. Ciao.

Five hours later Clod called, wanting to meet me for dinner. Sure. Why not? He knew a place that sold pizza by the slice and soda refills were free. No kidding. Wow. Listen, you enjoy that.

No One to Tell

I went to the Olive Garden, then to a bed without fear of being perforated by a spring or waking the next morning smelling like a mouldy facecloth.

And so the week went. I never again spoke to or travelled with Clod who Audelle fired a few months later. As for the newbie, one of so many past, present and future, I never saw him again.

*

The second manager came a few weeks later. Some sort of office type with no sales experience. He had a lot of ideas that he wanted to run past me and Jean, the one other rep with serious sales and life experience.

We listened. He listened. Then I went to Jacksonville for a tour of the world's largest ship transporting rolled paper and lunch with the captain and Michelle. Jean went to Chicago.

Michelle, in a word, was hot: Blue jeans, bobby socks and button-down starched shirt hot. Her long, blonde ponytail accented her pinkish-white complexion. Her teeth, when she smiled, which was often, were bright like chiselled icebergs. She was cheerleader sweet, the girl next door. Though she had one firm rule: If you can't answer my question, get out of my office. And, if she ever caught you with your back to her door, that's as far as you got.

Siracband, an ego name immortalizing daddy, specialized in industrial strapping, primarily for lumber. A narrow vision at best. I wasn't ending my career selling to lumber yards, neither was Jean. Unbeknownst to each other we'd determined high-demand niche markets in our respective states. His was Railway, mine were the US Port Authorities in the Carolinas, Georgia, Florida and Alabama. Lumber I left to distributors.

The manager lasted six months, fired with tears in his eyes, during which time the blonde bitch was hired to assist Audelle in generally making people unhappy. I'd already

No One to Tell

heard of a dozen reps coming and going, most not lasting a month. Heard, because despite living only thirty km from the office I very seldom went in.

A week or so later we discovered the bitch would become Sales Manager, which didn't last very long since we'd decided, Jean and I, not to travel with her, not to return her calls and generally disregard her. Simply put, she didn't know shit from sugar, though she *was* adept at tugging her skirt to new heights each time she thought to adjust her stockings, which was generally when a male of the specie was nearby.

We had to be more polite, Audelle told us. We were hurting Bitch's feelings. Aw. We had a better solution: Get rid of her. Jean soon after assuming the management role, giving Bitch more time to make goo-goo eyes with the Plant Manager.

Jean and I had a synergy: Ask no questions, hear no lies. Let's not waste each other's time with joint calls, the only Call Report being the continuous stream of business.

His first management decision was to no longer hire peddlers. In fact, he and I were the only hires passed by the old man. Audelle, for some reason, was hiring the worst of the worst, peddlers, hawkers, once thinking to hire the kid who pumped her gas at a nearby garage.

By this time I'd completed *The Viewing Room*, Linda travelling with me to Savannah, Jacksonville and Miami where South Beach consumed more time than ports. One particular trip to Florida, already into a year with Audelle, was no different, business and pleasure, beach and shopping as well as our first and last experience with Alligator Alley dissecting the Everglades en route to Naples and Tampa from Miami. Memorable. Running over an eight or nine metre Anaconda any time is memorable. The thump has a particular and lasting resonance.

Not long after Audelle asked me to drop by for a visit.

No One to Tell

She hadn't seen me for several weeks. She was curious. About what? Who knew? Audelle, despite her tendency towards distemper, was shy with certain people.

She closed her door, sitting on her leather loveseat, patting the empty cushion.

"Sit beside me. We almost never talk."

"I'm not sitting beside you, Audelle. That's how rumours start."

"I'm married."

I knew she was married, to a castrated cardiologist, for which reason, Jean and I agreed, her kids were probably leased for appearance sake.

I leaned into her desk, facing her. Not looking up her dress wasn't difficult. Her legs were short and her dress was long, sort of matronly. Somewhat surprisingly her shoes didn't have laces.

She wanted me to work with two newbies and a peddler, as a favour. Jean was on vacation. I agreed. Two days each. No more. Only because two of the three had clients directly related to my best distributors and I didn't want them screwing up. The third was Johnson, better suited to a tin cup on a street corner. He redefined loser, staying in motels with microwaves, buying hotdogs and frozen pizzas for dinner while submitting higher receipts that he'd collect from other shoppers at the checkout. Classy. Johnson was on his own.

She asked when I thought I'd be in the office again. I didn't know. How would that make either of us money? That, she understood.

*

The following Monday I flew to Indianapolis to meet Dale. I thought he'd flown in on the Sunday. He didn't. He'd missed his flight on Monday, arriving too late in the day to work. So I wrote. For lack of a better word, Dale was an imbecile.

No One to Tell

Tuesday at his account, we signed an annual contract without Dale saying a word. To show our appreciation I invited a half-dozen of *his* clients for dinner and drinks at the casino that evening. When the check came I passed it to Dale, he passed it to me. He'd left his wallet at the hotel for safekeeping, afraid of being mugged…in a casino. I didn't see him for breakfast. In fact I never saw him again. I called room service before flying to Charleston.

Like Dale, I hadn't previously met Brenda, or Brandon, though somehow Brenda was more appropriate. He joined me for breakfast Thursday morning before a planned tour of the Port Authority, and before meeting my South Carolina distributor who was big on lumber with several high-profile accounts in Brenda's territory.

Getting into a Port Authority is a big deal, worse than airports, security always on high alert.

And Brenda didn't have his wallet either. He was also afraid of a mugging. The obvious question was: Did he trust underpaid hotel maids more than he did armed guards? So Brenda stayed put for three hours basking in the sun, learning squat.

Just past noon I suggested lunch. But Brenda wasn't hungry, he'd already eaten, sharing a sympathetic guard's sandwiches. Brenda was a charmer, long straight hair draping his shoulders, tight black pants defining his slim figure, his belt better suited to a little frivolity at a gay bar, his white blouse silky and billowy. Worse yet, the only vehicle available to me the previous afternoon was a bright orange Mustang convertible and we were heading to Myrtle Beach.

Brenda wanted the top down. He wanted to feel the warm and gentle breeze against his skin. How wonderful would the wind feel flowing through his hair? I didn't know. I had other issues. The top stayed up.

Friday PM, at the airport, dropping off the car, Brenda

stopped a lady passing us on her way to the concourse. He wanted a photo souvenir of the trip. He thought a photo of us leaning against the Mustang's hood would be so lovely. I thought going home would be lovelier and I walked away.

The next time I saw Brenda was the last time.

*

The eighteen months blew by, along with twenty reps who couldn't or wouldn't stand up to the she-devil and Bitch. Jean knew better than to ask me to do joint calls, Audelle pouting whenever I refused her. I only saw the woman smile once, the time I whistled at her from behind with an "oh, baby" when she was wearing something vaguely resembling au courant fashion. Everyone else held their breath, even her favorite inside guy, her lackey really, whose well-trimmed goatee had once belonged to Audelle.

Easy money says she closed her door and giggled, twirling in front of her mirror before crunching on a candy.

I had intended to spend the week in Mobile and Gulfport, both the city and the town casual and receptive in the way they lived and worked. New Orleans was an easy drive to the west, a day of R&R with Linda for lunch with a few of the ICS ladies not sufficient to cast Audelle into destitution. Then into Florida for a long weekend stretched out on white sand. That was the plan.

Instead I went to Georgia alone, a last-minute change, to Atlanta and Savannah whose Port Authority had an urgent need. That was the last week of August 2005, the week Katrina devastated not only New Orleans but Gulfport and Mobile.

The client Port Authority in Gulfport no longer existed. The entire facility swept out to sea. Nor did much of the town exist, the head office in Mobile transformed into a veritable aquarium, the atrium and first floor submerged.

Atlanta was boring because distributors are boring. The first thing they plan is lunch; the exception was Belmont

No One to Tell

Beaurivage in Montgomery, Alabama.

The Atlanta guy couldn't get through lunch without a few Grey Goose...before the meal. Needless to say I never invited him to dinner. Nor did I drive with him, always meeting him. Behind the wheel he was a danger, equal to the drivers of Nova Scotia where staying alive on the highways remains a skillset.

I left him late Monday PM, taking with me Atlanta's torrential rains. Midway between Atlanta a Macon on the I-75, an anomaly was happening. Rush-hour, and all drivers in the passing lane were squeezing to the inside, giving space. I was the only car passing everyone else. I signalled, waiting, the guy behind me flashing me in. The weather wasn't freaking me out, the drivers were. The sky was a mass of rolling black clouds, the kind of black that billows from a raging rubber fire, pierced with titanium-white streaks. The thunder was an ominous symphony, deafening; the radio was useless. The windshield wipers and hectic water between me and the storm adding to the drama in no small way.

Then cars were exiting, no one ahead of me. The car behind flashed. I went with them. That many people couldn't live nowhere and that's about where we were, cars beginning to pull onto the soft shoulder. The guy behind me pulling in front of me, the one whose taillights led me now behind me.

The air around me became so dark I could barely see the other cars. But the sound accompanying the blackness is what I remember, the ground trembling. Blind without being blind. Seeing without seeing.

What we don't see not hurting us is a questionable wisdom, certainly that day.

When I was a kid, a preteen, invincible, a few of us got our kicks by crouching on the steel crossbeams of a train trestle used mostly for commuter trains of maybe fifteen or

No One to Tell

twenty coaches. Steel wheels on steel rails reverberating a metre above our heads, which for the most part were empty. That was the sound, amplified, a commuter train gone wild inside my car.

I learned later that a rogue tornado had swept across the region, heard, felt, and unseen. If that doesn't shrink the boys, nothing does.

The rain never let up, the sky never brightened, the intimidating rumbling lasting five, maybe six minutes. Cars one by one U-turning onto the road.

Driving into Macon I was staying the night, weather warnings increasingly in effect, Katrina's side effects worsening. Desirée's hometown was eerie, streets abandoned, drenched, streetlights blinking intermittently, stores and restaurants closed, every Cold War air raid siren screeching.

I pulled into the Crowne Plaza. The restaurant and bar were closed, those spaces and the lobby partially lighted. I was told "when the phone rings, don't answer. Just come to the lobby by the stairs. Quickly."

The woman knew of one store that was open, five minutes farther on, questioning my sanity. Got to love the locals. The place was ten minutes away, like driving in a river, the sirens worse than dental drills. Dinner was a roasted chicken, potato salad and Coke in a dark hotel room with no TV, no fork and no knife. After which nothing happened.

Tuesday I saw the Port of Savannah, solved a problem and took the first flight out through Philly. Katrina wasn't finished, 1000 km to the west much too close.

*

Belmont Beaurivage was a different story. The first time I met him he was in cowboy boots, designer jeans, a tailored shirt, two massive sterling rings, a sterling neck chain, and a stainless steel dive watch he never wore when diving because he didn't dive. He was a mid-thirties, redneck good ole boy and I was with him for a day.

Belmont worked five-day weeks in and around Montgomery, reporting to Birmingham a safe distance away. The larger question was, how many hours each day? Not many, but he got things done.

His day began with a fresh six-pack under his seat. Much of the litter on Alabama highways came from Belmont's car. Lunch generally consisted of another beer or two, depending on timeframe, maybe a stew or some other Southern speciality served in a heat-resistant bowl. That day, and not for the last time, in a diner whose owner made absolutely clear by a sign hanging over the bar that FARTING WILL NOT BE TOLERATED.

Then on to a corner store for another six-pack to last the afternoon, no empties left in the car by the time we got to his favourite watering hole at day's end for a beer or three before he dropped me off at the hotel and went home to a solitary dinner.

I forget her name, though I was introduced at the time. Southern folk do that.

She wasn't typical barmaid quality. She wore nice shoes with heels, a short black skirt and a red décolleté raglan sweater off both shoulders sans bra. Nothing cheap. Nothing gaudy. Simple jewelry adorned her neck and wrists, her fingers devoid of rings or tan marks. And she knew about make-up.

She had clear skin, mahogany lips and green eyes. We shook hands. Then she passed Belmont his beer. I ordered a double Skyy, neat, more appropriate to a redneck bar. Wine, not so much, passing her a twenty, telling her to keep the change. She slid it back. Belmont had a monthly tab.

On our seconds, Belmont signalled her. She sauntered over, smiling, a sweet smile, sincere.

"JT wants to feel your tits. Spectacular, JT. None better

nowhere."

Five bucks of booze surged through my nose. Say what! I guess so. I also want to live a while longer.

"Thanks, I'm good. Maybe another time."

"Seriously, go ahead. Feel her tits."

Her expression hadn't changed, Belmont's face still on his head.

The girl, late twenties, pushed her sweater over her breasts. They were, from the perspective of a casual observer, perfect. She was waiting.

"She likes guys feeling her tits." He demonstrated, leaning over the bar to cup one, inhaling a deep breath before fondling the other.

She said, "I don't mind. Truly I don't. Sort of a custom, suppose. C'mon, a little feel won't hurt none. They're just tits, won't bite."

Shit. Shades of Emma-Mae. Maybe on a beach somewhere, or if she'd needed medical attention, or was dying, or I was. Not in a dimly-lit bar with a dozen rednecks just beginning their evening.

"Really, they belong in a magazine." I told her. And they did. "Perfect." And they were. "Let's say the next time Belmont brings me in."

Belmont apologized for me. The first time he'd heard tell of a Frenchie who didn't like tits, he told her. She let her sweater fall, telling me she wouldn't let me forget. Next time. I promised.

Belmont ordered another round, disgusted.

*

Christmas was a week away. Everyone was last-minute shopping, me included, in Atlanta, at the new Atlantic Station, the place where Samantha Peachtree lives in *Bordello Nights*.

The store was high-end, Christmas coming but once a year. So why not?

No One to Tell

Midway through the first decade of the new millennia and women dressing neutrally, asexually had reached new heights. They weren't simply dressing down for casual Fridays, they were plain sloppy. And, with it, the loss of good manners was well-entrenched. The primary requisites to being a lady is first being a woman, and dressing like one. Essentially: Dress like a man, be treated like a man. These three women obviously had their fill of manliness. Not curiously, not unexpectedly, these three young women off to the side of an in-store demo were learning how to dress like a woman, to be feminine. Sad, really. They were learning how to fit and wear stockings and stay-ups, when to wear either one with shoes, and when not to, when to wear thongs and when to wear backless. Clearly I'd missed my true calling.

The educator was wearing a classic evening slip dress to a hand above her knees and spaghetti straps with a silk shawl. Her shoes were closed, low-heeled patent-leather pumps which did require nylons. In this case, clear stay-ups.

Unfortunate, that we have arrived at an era where so few women dress to enhance their femininity, that when we see one, those of us who appreciate a well-dressed, good-looking woman, we are obliged to stop and stare. Pay homage, if you will. Men are a separate issue, not my concern.

Thing is, happily so, the young lady couldn't demonstrate how to properly dress a leg without one, and she had two very fine legs. First one leg, creamy white, as I recall, between the bands of her stay-ups that shouldn't be any higher or lower…than whatever she said and the hem of her dress. As with the garter, on her other silky leg, not so much leg left exposed between the panty and the stocking as to cause embarrassment or scandal. At which point I realized I'd walked too quickly. Despite knowing that "a

No One to Tell

lady should never dress into her panties first. We never know, do we, ladies?" Apparently the fascinated threesome didn't. The solution, of course, being black silk laced undies with detachable silk ribbons and clasps which she demonstrated with a flourish and alluring twirl. Backless, of course "which we have on special this evening."

Not one of my teachers or professors ever looked that good. Class was over.

I don't empathize with men whose women don't dress that way as often as possible, or when possible. They're likely no better. And so goes the world. The cart and the horse.

*

Christmas came and went. So did Jean. He had enough of the she-devil and Bitch.

Over the previous twenty-two months I hadn't gone into the office a dozen time. Why? Who had the time? My purpose in life wasn't to validate nine-to-fivers who went home every night.

The first two weeks were mine. Psychologically, after spending December eating and drinking to excess, spending excessively to make certain their wives, husbands, and children will love them for another year, even those with hefty corporate budgets hesitate to spend money.

Instead I travelled during the last two weeks of January to Georgia and Florida, because I could. The weather was more agreeable, and I, amongst others, was able in December to arrange that timing for a seminar with Michelle's crew at the Jacksonville Port Authority.

We were four, in Jacksonville for a week. The other three, well-known to me, representing rail, sea, and land transport. I represented containment, addressing, teaching and training forty of Michelle's crew Tuesday AM through to Thursday PM.

I left home Monday, January 16th, through Philly,

landing at eight PM...without my luggage, arriving at the closest shopping mall near nine o'clock, something like 8:58.

The next morning, and all day, my three co-presenters were dressed in suits, shirts, and ties. Professional. Michelle, normally dressed in blue jeans, girl-next-door accessories and a hardhat, came in wearing what? A frigging dress, a hot frigging dress. I was in crumpled cords and a last-minute-grab black and blue argyle sweater a size too small straight from frigging Happy Days or some geek academy.

But Michelle was good, a lady. She didn't fall onto the floor laughing. She left that to the others.

Wednesday was a repeat of Tuesday, just better dressed. With Thursday came sighs of relief and a 3000-dollar dinner for the forty attendees split four ways. Unfortunately not enough to cause Audelle sudden heart failure. Before leaving, Michelle asked if I could meet her the next morning at another terminal to resolve an issue. No problem.

I saw no gatehouse where I thought one might be, so I drove further. Until two jeeps cut me off, until eight uniformed soldiers with M-16s leaped out and wanted to know "what's your business, sir?"

Michelle had neglected to tell me I was meeting her at a military base: a slight oversight.

They weren't interested in my driver's permit, the usual port requirement. No driver's permit, no entry. Apparently they couldn't read French, including the numerals. They wanted a passport, creating more questions. They didn't know any Michelle. They didn't know of any issues. Entry denied.

Michelle thought that was pretty funny, probably a female thing, suggesting that I meet her at her office. Twenty minutes later we drove into the same port through

No One to Tell

the 'backdoor', Michelle's government-issued port credentials and my driver's permit adequate. Not long after the issue was resolved and we went for lunch in Michelle's car, though I couldn't resist waving to my eight army friends from earlier in the morning as she slowed.

She also had two favours to ask while driving me to where my car was parked. One was that I see her again throughout the first week of March. She wanted me to give her crew a follow-up session, classroom and practical. I told her I would.

We were waved through the gate. They knew her, she was a fixture, and I hadn't officially signed out. Michelle, a kilometre later, uttering a quiet "shit."

We counted twelve of them. Big mothers with FBI-type blue bomber jackets and big yellow ATF and XYZ, whatever, embossed on their backs. Like we cared. Like we couldn't see the machine guns and ten millimetre handguns. Just maybe, a little over kill.

The main guy, I supposed he was, all pumped-up from time at the gym, his shirt a size too small, wanted to know what port I arrived into. Really? A pretty stupid question.

I answered, "The airport." I thought Michelle would pee her panties.

Of course he had to do something. The driver's permit came out, which he didn't understand; my passport so filled with stamps it was more like a colouring book.

"Go," was all he said. Though what he really meant was "fuck off."

Which I did, arriving home near midnight.
*

Monday I went to the office, early. In and out. I filled a box with a dozen sweatshirts, as many golf shirts, hats, a few dozen pens and pencils, loose-leaf binders, paper, notebooks and a dozen mugs.

Once sealed, addressed to Michelle, I gave the box to

shipping. The home of one of the guys I'd trained the previous week had burnt to the ground. Nothing was left.

A few days later Michelle called to thank me. Then Audelle's accountant called near four o'clock, curious about my 750-dollar dinner. I asked her what she didn't understand about Michelle's annual contract. Still curious, she asked what the noise was. I said, "The Atlantic Ocean," promising to email her a photo of South Beach. She hung up. Apparently Montreal was experiencing a blizzard.

Two weeks later I was in South Carolina. Two weeks after that I departed Montreal on the Monday for a week in Tampa and St. Petersburg, one you already know about, decidedly the bitch of all bitches, my worst in thirty-one years. The only good thing was that my client who died did so at home, not while having breakfast with me. The week went south from there, precisely seventy-two hours of hell.

Friday I woke late. That happens when you get to bed at five AM. Lunch was thick pea soup, a chunk of bread and a glass of wine. I was half a chapter from completing *The Fourth Man*. His nibs could wait. Thinking I would meet him at 8:30 on a Monday after driving across a snow-packed city cursed with out-dated bridges pretty much told me what I needed to know about him.

*

Monday he sounded a little pissed on the phone. I'd ruined his day, which made me feel bad. I asked him when the last time was that he crawled from bed at 3:00 AM to fly 3000 kilometres feeling like a zombie, or when he crawled *into* bed at three AM feeling like one. Or when he last regularly worked sixty to eighty-hour weeks.

He didn't see the relevance.

He didn't have to. I did. I disconnected after suggesting eleven o'clock Tuesday.

*

No One to Tell

Tuesday the air was crisp, the new snow already grey with big-city pollution.

Bitch was standing at the reception's desk, at the top of nine or ten very steep steps. She was frowning, pouty, wanting to convey that she was upset with me. Or possibly with herself for not having thought to drop something she could retrieve so that I might determine whether or not she was wearing panties. My best guess: Not.

I ignored her, walking into his nib's office without knocking. Rude? Yes, but intentional.

"So, you got in late Friday."

"No. I got in early Friday. The week was a total bitch. Four bad flights, a dead client, a near miss with another car exploding, a Black Moccasin under my car and lost baggage twice."

He laughed. "We all have bad weeks once in a while."

"Yeah? When was yours?"

He laughed again.

He was wearing a short-sleeved shirt in February, a tie he probably hung a doorknob at night, and a tweed jacket with Dockers. We were not going to get along.

"So yesterday...I was expecting you."

"I was writing a novel."

This time a snort. He checked his watch. I could see Audelle crunching this guy's nuts one day very soon.

"I spoke with Audelle. She agrees with me regarding your travel schedule in relation to your potential year-end."

"Forty percent more each year isn't enough?"

"Last year you travelled twenty-nine weeks. I believe with an additional ten weeks of travel you would exceed fifty, very possibly much more."

"Thirty-nine weeks each year? Is that about right?"

He nodded. "Leaving a week open each month for planning appointments, travel. That sort of thing."

"What's your name again? Lorie?"

No One to Tell

He nodded, smiling as though pleased he had a girl's name. "Yes."

"Well, Lorie, why don't you go fuck yourself?"

I walked out, passing Bitch on the way to Audelle's office.

You're the only one who doesn't knock. Please stop doing that."

"No longer an issue. I quit. Just wanted to say goodbye. I give the guy a month, tops. Ciao."

R.I.P.

A few months later I heard from the grapevine that Lorie's nuts were added to the candy jar. He was gone.

Not long after, Audelle, having forgotten something, returned to the office after everyone had gone home, not expecting to see Bitch and the Plant Manager buck-ass naked on her desk doing the dirty. Knowing Audelle, she didn't close the door and faint. More likely she screeched at them for the mess they'd made of her desk. The scene defies imagination.

Not long after that daddy Sirac died of heart failure while in the backseat of Audelle's car that her cardiologist husband was driving at the time. Talk about stress.

Michelle called the office the first Monday in March when I didn't show for the seminar. Hearing that I'd quit she cancelled her annual contract.

As for Legs, I'm certain she got home just fine, has done just fine, probably as VP or head of something. Murphy Law? He's wearing the same clothes, reading the same books, and learning nothing. He's standing still. His thoughts, everything he was or is, plagiarized.

As for me, I broke a promise. I never did return to Montgomery to see Belmont's favourite bargirl.

No One to Tell

Seven Years Later

The first thing I did was shred my résumé. I was done. Time to relax, breathe, live a little and complete The 4th Man before adding Audelle to this book and writing four more novels over the next three years before moving to the coast: The Madam, Family Lies, Mother of Pearl and From Inside Her Bedroom.

Since then I've written: The Feast of Tombola, Deferred Prejudice, The Hunt for Gilligan Rose, The Fatal Diners' Club and Silent Conviction. With, I suspect, more to come while still awake at three, four, five and six, preoccupied with characters as much as I ever was with clients. Some things never change.

That's my preoccupation, writing a story that's never been told. Linda's everlasting preoccupation: Janys.

No One to Tell

Other Mystery – Suspense - Thriller Novels By Doug Booth:

Split Verdict

The 4th Man

The Madam

Family Lies

Mother of Pearl

From Inside Her Bedroom

The Feast of Tombola

Deferred Prejudice

The Hunt for Gilligan Rose

The Fatal Diners' Club

Silent Conviction

A Christmas Killer, Comfort and Joy

Pariah In the Mirror

***

No One to Tell (Creative Non-fiction)

www.ingramcontent.com/pod-product-compliance
Lightning Source LLC
Chambersburg PA
CBHW020826160426
43192CB00007B/536